UNSTRUNG LIVES

By

Gaby A.M.

INDEX

Prologue

Humans have been secrets of lives simplified with the harmony of each life connected with other lives.

Imagine a tennis racket with no strings; it will be hollow and Dead.

Imagine if a magical force comes from above the clouds and simply reforms such a racket with strings and magical modifications to such a frame.

What would be the new enhanced performance of such a magical racket in such a case?

The real magic will rise above any imagination.

Our lives are Unstrung Lives, just waiting for a magical human being to string and connect them all in heavenly harmony, leading them to a mystical journey above the clouds and bringing them all to life.

Once upon a time, I envisioned letting myself float above the clouds.

High in the sky, far from an eye, I realized that to do so, I needed to learn how to fly.

My thoughts and dreams have always been in the dark, deep inside me.

I have tried to find the courage to open up and let them see the light. As ME, creating a knowledge book throughout a life's journey is honorable. My life has sailed to unknown oceans of so many private shores that, in some mysterious ways, the keys were permanently lost.

The keys for each coast were hidden beneath the deep, obscure, dark ocean. My life's journey was somehow unwritten, yet I found the shore of my missing treasure box throughout the years and the rough high seas. The joy of fulfillment relieved my heart and mind, as such a box had my magical pen and its secret ink. To speak freely in this life could turn into a frightening nightmare.

I must be careful and hesitant about what I say, to whom, or where.

On the other hand, writing a life story in literature can be much more straightforward, safer, and delightful. You feel safe and free to express your heart or mind in stories.

Far and close to my aching beating heart, the tragedy and the laughter of these private doors will not only lead me to just some locked gates but, moreover, too much more complicated eternal alleys of life's dramatic changes. The journey of such a story may have a beginning, yet oddly and mysteriously, the tale may not find an END.

Sailing in an ocean was never as smooth as I thought when I set sail to the unknown.

A long time ago, I experienced so many changes, problems, situations, complications, imaginations, inspirations, dreams, fantasies, illusions, lies, faces, lips, love, laughs, tears and fears, victories and defeats, countries, cultures, music, art, lives, and after all, Death.

Private doors are my thoughts, and after so many scary considerations, I've decided to let them get out freely to the world to be acknowledged, to be taught, and maybe to be repeated, but to be cherished and to be part of this life, regardless of how my final unwritten chapter would be.

All human beings are not alone nor distant in our universe.

We are all tangled through the hands of times with strings of lives that connect us.

No matter how hard it is to deny, all human beings are not as One. Reality proves them wrong, as we are all ONE.

The Unstrung Lives of Humanity can be linked strangely and mysteriously. It is a true dream. Just one dream can find the shore, which could be the only dream I have dreamed of throughout my life.

Again ....What is life?

Life has value, but only when it has something valuable as its objects. Life is a concise journey. It is a flashing moment; if you don't understand its purpose, it will pass you by, and you would've wished you'd never been born.

My private doors will take you and me on a journey never been told before. The magic behind this journey lies secretly in between two parallel worlds. The Fantasy world is where I want to be, and the objective cruel Reality I live in. I am on board and set to sail, so join me. It will be the most magical journey of our Unstrung Lives.

CHAPTER I

SHATTERED FACE 2005

The faces were pale, the eyes were tearing, and scary silence was all the deadly ingredients of something tragic that was about to happen. I had no choice but to listen to the tragic, devastating, loud announcement over the central PA at Malaga-Costa del Sol Airport-Spain.

Ladies and gentlemen, due to some technical reasons, the Captain of flight 1313 has advised that he will be making a precautionary emergency landing.

Once the ground and maintenance personnel have inspected the aircraft, we will notify you of our next departure and arrival time. Thank you for understanding.

Suddenly, the airport became a replica of the chaos in the old movie" Airplane."

People are trying to run everywhere, panicking about the plane's impact on the ground.

Boys and girls were hysterically screaming and crying, not because of their complete understanding of the chaos that their stupid parents caused, but because of their fears of the crazy people running everywhere like chickens without heads.

In some corners, nuns and priests gathered people for their final prayers and confesses before landing at hell's gate. Other men and women dressed for an opera, pretending they were so important that the airport authority had to comply with their arrogant demands before anybody else. The most interesting people were the ones by the bar lounge.

They have no concept of anything other than the colored glasses of liquor.

A strange woman was standing by herself, smoking a cigarette.

Yet, every time she dragged a puff, she looked around her, observing people running all over the place, then glanced at the smoke of her cigarette and then went hysterically laughing, pointing at them. I was so damn anxious to get out of the Airport, but in the meantime, I was so much eager to get closer to her and ask her about her hysterical laughs.

I was close enough, then I started to laugh, only because I detected from the scent that she was smoking a marijuana joint(cigarette)...... Unbelievable.

Loud noises of the ARRF(Aircraft Rescue Firefighters Apparatus) outside on the dark runway were causing more panic than ever. I was one of the hundreds trying to find a way out of this before it got out of control. The loud noise of the heavy rain pounding on the metal structure of the Airport roof made the horror more intense than the real thunder above the dark sky of Malaga. I found a way through the passengers to the outside gate, yet the heavy rain made it almost impossible to see the streets. Sometimes good fortune may come my way, as I heard a woman calling me in Spanish: Taxi, Taxi.

She was my savior as I rushed inside the Taxi with all my suitcases, not waiting for her to open the trunk of her Taxi. The driver was dripping water all over her face, yet her smile was the first encouragement statement since my arrival. She turned her head and said in English: Where to, my dear?

I was so clumsy, rational, and impatient, yet with the airport shit, I lost my cool.

I was digging in my damn knapsack trying to find my hotel reservation, and of course, it had to be in a small pocket out of a hundred, as this Swiss Knapsack is the best and the worst at the same time. It was the perfect one to fit everything necessary but was the worst as it had so many pockets and zippers. " Here it is."

I said: La puerta del Paraíso.

La Puerta del Paraíso, si si.

Even though I couldn't see shit from my window as the falling rain was coming down so hard, I felt the speed of her driving. She was almost like a race driver, a real professional on a road with poor visibility. I had to close my eyes to find my confidence again until she said: You're a lucky charmer; you brought the rain with you, my dear. It hadn't been raining for almost a month, and we needed this rain.

I was trying to zone myself out from everything, exhausted. My head nearly hit the seat's headrest ahead of me as she stopped with a sudden brake, followed by a short statement: We're here, my dear.

Apparently, the rain didn't slow down, so I had to pay her while in the Taxi to avoid getting wet. She turned around and said to me: Gracias, oh wait, wait...That is too much, my dear.

I had no time to get small bills; I only had hundreds of Euros, so I gave her two €️ bills or two hundred Euros. The meter read €32, so I overpaid her, but at that moment, I didn't care about the money as she was my savior and was fast to bring me here.

I said: Keep it; you deserve it.

Her unexpected response shocked me as she opened the door, carrying all my suitcases to the lobby. In the rain, she smiled at me and said: You're so generous and pretty in the light. May god bless your family and fulfill your purposes with joy.

The poor woman had no idea why I was here in Spain, but it wasn't for pleasure.

I was dripping water all over the dry red carpet, standing before a young, beautiful front desk girl with a wonderful smile saying; Welcome to La Puerta del Paraíso.

I slid my passport to verify my reservation and got my key to my room as fast as possible.

I was somehow prepared for something similar to the weather and all the shitty rain, so I had my raincoat and my NY hat, so my face wasn't clear to that young receptionist, and she didn't recognize me at all.

I was so exhausted that I took all my clothes in less than a minute and was under the cover with just my underwear and a shirt for a long sleep.

The golden sun rays were spreading across the horizon of the Mediterranean Sea, altering the arrangements of colors that somehow manipulated the scene with a warm, colorful feed, as the warm blood flooded through the veins, feeding the entire organ of a human being to maintain the circle of life. The sun's rays announced the beginning of a new day; meanwhile, a single beam of light decided to split from the pack and take another course. Such a magical ray traveled with its warmth to a faraway place with a purpose and only one goal.

Finally, the ray had reached the destination of the balcony glass door on the 3rd floor of La Puerta del Paraíso in Malaga, Spain. The light was secretly merging, traveling through the curtains, pushing and moving all obstacles away, until it landed so gently on her lovely, beautiful rose cheeks, dazzling with her long eyelashes, trying to leave them up for the great awaking. The humming soft noise and the twinkle of her eyes ensure the mission has been accomplished, and the princess returns to life.

Far away above the sky, the great Queen Sun was smiling proudly at her youngest daughter and her accomplishment, yet the princess's mind was somehow mysteriously playing games on her back on Earth. However, a dream still hung between her fantasy and Reality in her awakening. Lying in bed so ruthlessly, I thought about making a wish that may come true somehow.

I wished for a nice, simple day with no surprises and no bloody rain, so I closed my eyes briefly, trying to meditate on a faraway place. It has been raining for the last few days, and I wished for a dry, sunny day to enjoy my stay in Spain. I had to pretend I was blind so as not to burn my wishing surprise for myself. I pulled myself out from under the Royal blue laced satin bed cover sheet, which had a magical scent and comfort that put me to sleep when I blended my bare naked skin with the fabric. I started stretching my long arms, but my fingertip caught up with a long blue satin bed throw that ended with golden fringes under my Royal blue satin pillow.

I couldn't resist the temptation of covering my eyes with such a magical bed throw to complete the preparation for my wish. I had to blindfold my eyes with such a long blue bed to ensure I couldn't see a thing until I reached the balcony.

I start walking towards the curtains of the balcony. I had both arms stretched out as a blind person, sauntering until I felt the drapes on my fingertips.

So I opened the terrace door with my eyes closed, but I couldn't resist the light breeze, the scent of the sea, and the sun rays warming up my cheeks and tingling my eyelids with their warmth. The moment I dropped the cover off my eyes, I was Alice in Wonderland.

The view was so magical. The true blue of the Mediterranean Sea was something that I had never seen before in my entire life.

The hazed horizon and the deep blue water look so far. Yet, the light blue gradually merges in as you come closer to the shore, riding some light white horses that break in across some parts of the open view of the tremendous magical Mediterranean sea.

I took a few steps ahead, leaning on the edge of the terrace painted white with red brick stones, designed and built elegantly in a beautiful way. The view of the sea and the sun's rays that spread out the gold across the water have fulfilled my wish for a lovely day.

I spread my arms so widely and let everything go through me and Breeze.

Standing like that, I felt like I was Superman getting energized by the sun.

I was somehow glad that I booked the room in this hotel because La Puerta del Paraíso hotel is not such a big one or even a famous hotel, but I do like it for the convenience of my status and also because of the main reason why I am here in Spain. My true bloodline is from España; even though I wasn't born here in this magnificent country, I am here in Spain for a week to honor the memory of the most remarkable man I've ever met.

My loving father. I must keep reminding myself of such a fact at all times. I have to be vital for nothing to prevent me from honoring his memory correctly. A father that I wish I could've known better, longer, and most of all, be able to express my emotions freely with the real chance to tell him face to face the excellent magic word that every little girl dreams of saying, "I love you, Dada."

I promised myself not to shed a tear, but I can't control my weak emotions, as my sorrowing heart will not comforted, my eyes are bursting, and the tears must fall. The tears between my half-shut eyelids flow, bother and burning hot, and flow again. I am ashamed.

I am ashamed that in this wise, I weep and weep. So strange my sorrow is, so strangely deep. The tears between my half-shut eyelids roll for a mortal sorrow of a human soul.

The echo of an author's poem I read so many years ago that I can't even remember his name slipped into my mind, representing how I felt in such a moment. Reading so many books at a very young age opened my eyes to many possibilities, ideas, and points of view.

More deeply, it helped me gain indirect experience about life through the minds of authors, poets, and even songwriters. I never understood my gift, as I used to force myself to understand strange, unfamiliar languages. So often, I closed my eyes and picked a random book from the library, regardless of the subject or content. I started to enjoy the shapes of words, the deep volume of the sentences, and the hidden deep meaning behind each phrase as they used to be reorganized and re-arranged in front of my eyes. I was always an odd kid with the wrong books for my age; even my mother couldn't understand my gift, yet she always supported me and encouraged me to explore all the universes hidden and known.

I recall one time that she mentioned my father in such a conversation regarding the similarity of my gift of knowledge through books. She mentioned that he used to read strange books(Russian, Japanese, Cantonese, and so many more). Sometimes, he even read Arabic books, which was always odd to me as it is considered one of the most complicated languages, yet he used to read any written languages as long as they were in books.

The slow motion of my weak knees commenced the great collapsing as I fell on my knees, spreading my arm to the sky and asking God for a why.

He answered me with a sign of the great sun being blocked by a passing cloud that darkened the sky for a few moments, and then he permitted the sun's power to rule again, announcing a new look with a new hope.

I closed my arms and hugged myself tightly as if genuinely hugging someone so dearly, but it was only me and always me with my pain and sorrow alone.

I ran away from the terrace as my burning emotions were overwhelming, and I needed to cool off my body, but more likely my brain.

I rushed to the bathroom, turned the water, and slipped under the shower with just my red Nike T-shirt and Nike black shorts, trying to cool off, but that did not work, as I felt hotter, and the steam filled up the bathroom so quickly.

One of the main things I've always had trouble comprehending while traveling worldwide is the shower faucet handles. They never give you an instructions manual at the front desk on how to use them when you first check-in, and they are never common fucking standard ones.

Every God damn fucking shower faucet's handle on this planet is entirely different.

I do recall being in a room at a hotel, and I don't remember the name and don't even remember which country, but I do remember talking to a shower faucet as if I'm about to open the magical secret door to somewhere, but sure shit that required a password to enter.

I was talking to the goddamn faucet to tell me how to turn the bloody water ON.

I may sound fucking stupid for thinking that way, but again, for god sake, I'm not asking for a miracle, but a simple, easy FUCKING faucet.

ON and OFF...turn to the right or fucking simply to the left....makes no difference.... It's just a simple thing to wish for. I forgot to turn the cold water in and was boiling myself alive. God damn it. "I said."

My best decision was to save the day, but my poor skin was jumping out of the shower so fast.

Be calm, and let's get out of here, as I was talking to myself again.

My dear mother was like that and still is as well. She always talks to herself as if there's another person with her. I've adopted such a terrible habit from her.

However, I was sure that my mother mentioned to me once that my dear father was far worse than her status. He used to talk to others, yet he was the only one who could see them. Sometimes, my mother used to tell me that in his sleep, he could talk to other people in so many different languages simultaneously.

Sometimes, he speaks Spanish, yet he answers himself (or the other person) in Russian, German, Mandarin, and many different languages, which used to go on while asleep. Again, as my mother told me so many stories about him, I felt he was not just a typical man.

The word "Special" is not even close to describing him correctly, but he was one of a kind as if the mighty God was tired of thinking about how he would create him, and in the end, he decided to put everything in him to be that special.

I am getting so irritable and frustrated that I must leave this room. The quicker I leave this room, the better I will be. I start laying down all the stuff I will take on the big oval table in the middle of the room. I got my camera, notebook, phone, and tablet.

Oh, wait, No, no, and fuckin No, I told myself.

Drop all this technology crap and take the camera, and maybe the phone, and that is it. Meanwhile, another question was spinning: What shall I wear, casual or formal?

Somehow, I sounded like every stupid girl, or even a woman, saying it out loud: I have no clothes. I was still soaking wet, dripping water from my hair all over the room, so I had to go back to the bathroom to dry my damp hair; on the other hand, I had to give the shower faucet a dirty look, saying, "Puta-Bitch.

I grabbed a towel and started drying up my long hair and face. In the meantime, the rest of my body was still wet, and the t-shirt was stuck on my bare skin, showing my well-constructed athletic body as I saw myself in the mirror across the other side of the room.

That was not all of me because I had to take everything off and dry myself up completely. The significant part of being completely naked, alone in a room, and above all in Spain was an incredible feeling of liberty, independence, maturity, and self-confidence.

I have yet to open up all my suitcases and don't remember where the casual clothes are from the formal ones, but I remember my mother stuffing my favorite dresses in the red ones.

I placed it on the bed, and there they were, my Levi's jeans that I managed to re-adjust to how I liked. There were no back pockets as I ripped them off, but I was too much of a lousy damn fashion designer, as I made a nice big hole that will show my great firmed butt.

The truth was it did; as I was checking myself in the mirror, I saw how exotic my half-naked butt was exposed; however, it did not bother me.

My eyes were like a radar, searching for the right top, and definitely, it was folded nicely, as it was my blue T-shirt with a significant symbol (?) On it.

I was more of a fanatic about simple types of clothes, and sometimes my mother told me that I reminded her of an old actress who used to find the cheapest and simplest fashion to match everything about her. Occasionally, she would choose something to match her eyes and other times, she would wear a simple blouse to match her.

She had a petite body, permanently slim yet fit like an athlete.

She also mentioned my father during her conversation about such an actress.

My mother used to describe their relationship as an odd one.

However, she also told me that he was a strange person. Blue has been my favorite color since I was a little girl, but through my life and the mystery around it, I discovered why it has always been my favorite color, as it was my father's color, too.

Woof, I took a deep breath to avoid my tears from coming out every time he jumped into my head. I spun around the room with my eyes, checking if I had everything I needed before I went.

All good. Oh, please wait, the cap that I bought at the free shop at the airport and it was very uncharacteristic of me to pick that specific one, as it has the logo of an old rusted dagger stabbing the bleeding sun, but I did find it meaningful, and unique in some different crazy ways. My sunglasses-checked. Somehow, these sunglasses weren't really mine, but they are mine now, and the story behind that goes way back when I was 12 years old.

My hair was in a sloppy ponytail, yet still wet from the steamy damn shower (Puta); I said that with a smirk. One more thing that I always miss as a girl is makeup.

I never wear makeup as I always sweat, so I have to do something good for my face.

Hair down or up, I asked myself, and the answer was down and loose.

The mystery behind the hair being up in a ponytail always puts me in a terrible comparison situation. It is my signature with the hair up in a ponytail, and to add more excitement, I can wear a baseball cap. However, I'm not too fond of baseball; I'm only fond of the cap style.

That mysterious look is always a question mark, including my mother.

Why do you have to do that with your hair and look? Are you a lesbian? Mom asked.

Mom can be very old-fashioned when it comes to sexuality, but we are the new generation, and we don't care about all the rules and principles from the old era.

I never had any problems with any of such bull shit, as it is not my call to differentiate between what's right and what's wrong. It's a new world, and new ideas are Freedom.

After some minor blush, I was finally ready to go out. I had to take a quick, fast look at myself in the mirror just before I closed the door behind me. As I stared at myself in the mirror, my inner voice was just a TV commentator describing how I looked.

She was like a Goddess with features and beauty that can't be missed.

Her face is oblong, her eyes deep in the socket, and she has a small mobile hazel green lid with a deeper green on and just above the socket line, blending up and out. Her forehead is narrow; the cheekbones are hidden beneath the rose cheeks.

The nose is turned up at the end in a magnificent way.

The lips are full, luscious, and lopsided; however, the lower lip is large with a perfect cupid bow and a fascinating mix of colors, glossy red and pink. Her skin is like freckled peaches; the chin is rounded with a slight dimple beauty mark.

The ears are small, covered with her long golden Balayage with light brown hair. Her neck is long and gracefully symmetric, blessed with smooth, soft skin.

Gaby's look has no explanation; it is as if God had to take a week off after her creation, as it was complicated to repeat her undisputed beauty.

As I stepped out of La Puerta del Paraiso hotel, I felt a great deal of life in the streets.

The people and the entire Spanish culture made me realize how much I needed all that.

I was standing there in front of the hotel, thinking about how I could be different without any help from my mother. Today, there is no running nor practice, just me, España, and the memories of my father.

I walked until my feet got tired, so I took the first bus anywhere, as I didn't care.

I wanted to get lost and not be found. Some of the good and bad memories about sitting back on the bus made me realize there are no bullies on this bus anymore.

The school and some bad memories about being bullied by some girls made me realize that it was always a safe place to sit at the end of the bus close to the window, almost invisible to all of them. The bus movements let me lean my head by the window and look at the infinite Costa del Sol. The vibration, the direction of the bus, and the sun tingling my face as I leaned by the window dragged me to a peaceful place known as the land of fantasy for a little nap.

The idea was planned well enough to give me enough rest for the coming unknown of such a beautiful day, yet my little plan and the nap didn't last as long as I had anticipated. In real life, I realized that not everything you wish or plan works your way, especially if you have a maniac bus driver as the one driving this bus.

The bus's driver somehow jumped on the brake so hard and fast for a running loose stray dog across the street. I got up from my little nap with all the commotions and stood up to see why.

I couldn't believe my eyes when I turned my head to my left to see such a little dog waving to me, and I was pretty sure he was saying he would be fine.

I removed my sunglasses and started to clear the "sleep" or crust of my eyes, trying to acknowledge what I had witnessed. "A dog that can talk and waves to me." What the hell was that? " I said to myself."

THE DOG WAS GONE when I opened my eyes, and my eyebrows rose from shock.

I moved fast to the opposite side of the bus, to the left, as I was trying to see if the dog crossed the street safely to the other side, yet there were some big trucks, buses, and speedy cars flowing one after another blocking the view of the sidewalk. I was so impatient for such a rush manic traffic jam, hoping to clear the way so I could peak and see the mysterious talking dog.

My great disappointment came right after all the moving vehicles cleared the way, as the view began to show no sign of the mysterious talking dog. Such a disappointment didn't last long as its replacement came to me in such a great view. The scene of an incredible combination of rocks and the sun added more color to its nature as if an isolated beach suddenly appeared out of nowhere. The bus started picking up speed. Meanwhile, I was sitting on my knees like a little kid, looking back, trying to get another glimpse of such a beach or even the mystery dog. That spot was calling me, and I couldn't miss it.

I got up fast, moved quickly to the middle of the bus, and rang the driver to let me out. He did have that scary look through his gigantic mirror when I rang the bell, yet he completely ignored me and continued his route.

I started to jump up and down, waving my hands like a maniac for him to stop the damn bus. Only a few people were on the bus as it was still early in the day, and most were still at work, school, or college. Some people were riding the bus for a destination they believed was evident and written through their life path. Their faces were almost dead, as that place was known as Work. Another example of different kinds of people that were forced to get on that bus was the lady sitting by the door. I understand that this middle-aged woman, roughly 35 years old, is crying because she was trying to think of an excellent possible excuse to cover up her affair with the milkman from her husband. She has a beautiful wedding ring on her finger, yet the stamp of the exotic vampire kiss on the left side of her neck can't be easily ignored or not be noticed, even with some magical makeup. The main thing for her is to use the power of vagueness, a solid concrete lie, and deception for a good excuse that can buy her a pass one more time.

I just moved my face away from her sin, yet on the other hand, I felt a strange connection towards this stranger. I had to get off the bus, but I felt obligated to tap her shoulder and say: Be strong, and you'll be fine; men are stupid and gullible. I walked away, leaving her in total confusion, and started to focus on a different strategy to convince the bus driver that I was desperate to get off his bus. I had no choice but to stand there so politely, looking at the bus driver with a fake smile, for him to acknowledge my damn existence, as I felt that I did not delay anyone from some important stuff.

I saw his reflection through the big mirror, with his eyebrows sticking up to the sky in anger, yet I also managed to catch his left hand creeping towards the push button for the door.

The door finally opened, and the sooner I stepped out of the bus, the faster the driver took off as if he was pretty damn happy to get rid of me.

Everything in our unstrung lives has many symbols and signs that appear and disappear in unusual, mysterious ways. Sometimes, those signs can confuse us, and other times, they can be instrumental in guiding us to such an unknown path.

The unwritten path made me wonder about coincidence and signs.

I was standing on the long sidewalk and dead ahead of me across the road, that magical spot.

I had no clue what just happened to me at such a moment. I wonder.

One of the many things I have learned from my mother is to know and follow the path with whatever symbols and signs may occur in my life. Also, she said that I must walk the unknown and the unwritten without fear or hesitation. I was still looking desperately for the dog, but there was no sign. The dog was somehow implanted in this moment of my life with no explanation or reason. I had to look up to the sky and travel to the infinite imaginative world of mine and whisper asking God.

Hey..." Are you playing games with me again? What is that all about, and why now?

Mysteriously, he always answers me, or I feel he does most of the time.

A gentle sea breeze has blown on directly at my face as if he is attempting to interact with my soul. I had to close my eyes and move back a few steps on the sidewalk.

I realized God had just saved my life with such a breeze. The truth is that I've acted like an idiot, not living the moment of Reality and just remaining wondering in my fantasy, ridiculous, stupid world. I was eager yet impatient to get off the bus so fast.

However, I never saw where I was standing on the sidewalk. I was almost on the edge of the sidewalk, cursing the hell of the bus driver, and that simple, gentle light Breeze was nothing but a hint to push me back a few steps as I was about to kill myself.

The prick bus driver took off so fast that I never noticed what was coming off his tail.

A big, extended car carrier trailer was tailgating the bus as if they were chasing each other at the Daytona 500. The damn truck just went by, passing in front of my nose, and that crazy gentle Breeze was just the after-effect of its speed. Wow, What the fuck was that?

I was breezing so heavily as I was scared stiff of the whole damn situation, but again, I knew how to control my nerves and breeze and let it all out of my head and chest. After I gathered my shattered mind, I slid my glasses a tiny bit, tilted my head slightly to the sky, and said to God: "Thanks a lot for that."

But you did not have to push; I get it now.

A few moments later, I was walking back and forth on the sidewalk, practicing a short hawk-eye observation of all the cars from a mile away to ensure that no more crazy drivers would do the same shit to me again. When the cost was precise, I crossed the street running to the other side, where the shore of the magnificent Mediterranean Sea was stretched out to infinity.

I walked towards that spot I had seen on the bus, but for some reason, and of course, because I was a rational girl, I found myself in the wrong area as they all looked magnificently alike.

I had to look back and forth, hoping to recognize the spot again, but I couldn't tell the difference. I was amazed by the sand's color and the rocks scattered around the shoreside.

I had to take my camera out and start taking shot after shot. I stood there momentarily, breezing the air and letting it all penetrate me.

Taking a long, deep breath helped me decide to cross over the beach sidewalk to feel better about the longest seaside as it was breathless. When I started walking on the sand, I felt the warmth inside my sneakers, so I decided to feel much more loose and let everything blend with my body. I must take off my sneakers to get such a natural feeling. I made a knot at the end of the sneaker's lace, wrapped them around my neck, then walked. I needed that so badly, feeling the sand between my toes and enjoying everything naturally. Walking on the sand can make you feel like a drunk person.

I was unbalanced as my weight sank through the soft sands with every step I made; yet again, the color of the scattering of the broken rocks was pretty fascinating, as if they were gold with some mixed diamonds.

The place and the feeling of all my surroundings made me feel as if I was back again as Alice in Wonderland with my wild imagination. That was simply the effects of the sun's rays, and that was why they called it "Costa del Sol."

I walked and walked until my tinny, burnt-out feet got tired and hot as well.

I was planning to take a break and just lay back on the sand, yet there was another sign from somewhere that somehow made me change my mind.

This time, it was something completely different.

A bloody damn seagull was diving in a Kamikaze way directly so close to my head that I had to duck to the sand, not because I was afraid of it, but not knowing why it was so close.

He took off after that crazy dove towards my head, but again, I felt it was flying to a destination, yet it turned its head to me as if it wanted me to follow.

I had my hand on my forehead, blocking the sun off my vision to see where that lonely, crazy seagull was heading.

The sun was intense and almost abeam around one o'clock, but again, as the seagull vanished away, I said, "The hell with that crazy bird." Saying that was simply an invitation to something new, unique, and yet wacko this time; as I turned my head to the left to continue seeing the rest of the shore, I had to freeze my body as a statue because of what was flapping right in front of my nose. A butterfly was just about to touch the tip of my tiny nose, and that was how close it was. I have never seen any butterfly that close to me; moreover, that was not just a typical butterfly.

The right-wing was almost like layers of colors. The outside layer was black, then red, curved to the inside with purple dots, while the left wing was ultimately the opposite, as the external layer was deep purple, then red, and again curved to the inside with black dots.

I had to take a few steps back to keep a distance between myself and that magical butterfly.

Yet, I was somehow fast and again unbalanced with my feet, specifically on such a hot, soft sand platform, and without any further due, I was falling backward. The fall was prolonged, as it felt like I was falling from the sky, hitting the sand. I know that when you lose your balance, you think about the fall in two different ways, and it all depends on you and how you want to accept the fall. If, in some ways, you subconsciously refuse, deny, and are afraid to fall, the high percentage possibilities will cause your body to drop so fast, hitting the ground so hard no matter how much you're trying not to fall and possibly hurt yourself badly.

The other way was when you were in my status as you've entirely undeniably surrendered yourself to the laws of gravity, accepting the unknown as if you do, welcoming whatever impact that follows the fall. The last one subconsciously lasts longer, and you feel like you are floating on thin air before hitting the ground.

The way I hit the sand, I felt my whole body sinking in through the sand, and a massive amount of sand was scattered all over and around me.

I was covered with sand, and also, because of the heat, my body was somehow wet from sweating, which led the sand to stick to my body and face. That reminds me of the famous Italian Zeppole. They are very soft, small, round doughnuts submerged in honey.

When you drop them in a bowl of powdered sugar, they stick to them and become even deliciously sweeter; if you want more perfection, sprinkle some powdered cinnamon.

That was not my case with all these unfortunate events that keep happening and appearing to me. I was unhappy with all these creatures cutting in my path left and right as if they were annoying obstacles to the peace of mind I sought. They said that it is a common thing that many people tend to tell when they have no explanations or clues as to what the fuck is happening to them in such a state. The strange quote was: Happiness is like a butterfly; The more challenging you chase it, the faster it will fly away, yet if you ignore it—there is an excellent possibility it will rest upon your shoulder.

Well, that was a simple explanation of why I don't fucking believe a damn word from these fortune cookies that my mother will kill for after having a Chinese dinner.

She always asks me to read them in English and Chinese, even though she doesn't understand a single damn Mandarin word. I wasn't even an expert in Mandarin, but they cut the words into small pieces in English, so you can pronounce them as if you are fluent in such a language. Fools. I was still on my back, observing the butterfly flapping its wings so close to me, and I almost felt a strange connection between us. I was profoundly staring into its great big eyes, yet when I attempted to reach out gently with my hand to touch it, The theory of the crazy people who came up with quotes and wisdom crap of the Chinese turned out to be close to being accurate. The butterfly flew away from me, but not far enough.

I wondered why it did not go away, so I had to pull myself up and stroll, following it to wherever it would lead me.

Further ahead, the shore was blocked by a massive rocky round corner where you couldn't see the rest of the coast. I stood before that rocky hill and wondered if I had to turn around to where I came from or climb the mountain to get to the other side of the shore.

My answer was straightforward and clear, not because of me or my choice, but only because of that pretty little butterfly. It was flying up and up in the air, guiding me to climb that hill, and so I did. It took work as the rocks were unstable, and the surface was slippery and sharp.

Step by step, I made my way up to the top of the hill, and as I was just about to touch the upper part of that rock, shaped like a cone head, the view on the other side was so magical and fascinating. I was so overwhelmed, yet hypnotized by what my hazel green eyes had discovered, and I was about to lose my footage and slide down, but I managed to get a firm grip and pull myself up to the top again.

I stood on the top, looking at an isolated spot from the shore and the sea.

It was like a vast U-shaped remote beach, surrounded by hills of golden, fire-red rocks as if they were standing tall, guarding this Heavenly spot against any intruders.

I said with my mouth wide open to my astonishment at these hills. "Oh, my dear God ."

They said, "If the mind is paralyzed, the body will follow. "

My mind was frozen, paralyzed from the scene. My legs collapsed, and I was on the rocks.

I was frozen but had no clue what to do with myself this time. My guiding angel came to my rescue one more time.

The little butterfly starts dancing again before me and showing me the way down.

The beach was full of scattered, edgy, sharp rocks, but you could see the golden sand in between. I was tip-towing in the beginning, then started hopping on and off the rocks, and suddenly, all the sharp stones were my training agility rope ladder, so I was bouncing like a rabbit off the rocks until I finally found a clear sandy area without any stones.

Standing there on such a hidden beach made me look around the vast beach, trying to see the end of it, yet I realized that it was much simpler if I enjoyed being here in such a place and not act as if I was from the National Geographic explorers crew.

The scary part was the height of such a rocky hill, and I realized that I was so damn lucky not to fall or even get scratched by the sharp edges coming down such a hill.

The truth was that I couldn't believe my eyes, and no matter how hard I tried to accept that only a few hours ago, I was still in my hotel room, dreaming of a nice day, made me disbelieve the Reality in front of me. I couldn't resist the temptation to see how I'd managed to land on such a magical beach. The surprise was the scary height of that hill or rock.

I was more surprised at my daring ability to bounce like a rabbit, avoiding all the sharp cutting. Knives and stones; I was even more astonished that I had no single cuts nor scratches, and just looking at such elevation height with the scattered sharp rocks made me wonder how the fuck I'll get out of here alive and in one piece.

I wonder.....

In such a moment, I was not thinking nor caring about how nor when I would leave this place, but again, I'm always stubborn and rational, so maybe later I will use technology and call for help, and that was the least of my concern in such a magical moment.

My great surprise was that my phone had no signals as if I had landed on a different part of this planet or maybe another world.

I lay my nap sack down further back on top of a rock, opened my arms so wide, and screamed so loudly of happiness and joy for finding a majestic spot like this. It was a long session of pleasure and disbelief simultaneously. I was running wild on the vast, long golden like an idiot on such a magical sandy shore, jumping up in the air, doing cartwheels on the soft sands, summersault flips. My scream of happiness somehow scared the hell of my dear angel butterfly as it was gone. The rocky hill was not just grey and red copper rocks but also bushes of green tinny short trees, similar to the bonsai, but different. They gradually filled in the gaps between the broken, sharp stones, creating a masterpiece of art painting.

The tide was low, so the sandy beach was vast, which allowed me to walk on the shoreside and go to sea, and step by step, I was getting in deeper and deeper.

The crazy thing about the water was the clarity. No one except me has ever discovered this spot, and I will put my marks and claim this beach for myself alone.

There were shades of colored water that represented the depth of the sea.

Deep blue was far from my spot, then navy blue, deep green, light green, and turquoise, as if you were sailing from the deep sea to the shore. The light green turquoise was so transparent that you could see everything under the water. I stepped into the water and dragged my feet, feeling the combination of the seawater and sand on the bottom tingling my tinny feet, and it felt great. I stood in the water, barely a foot above my ankle, looking down as the fishes were all around me, dancing with unique colors and shapes. Some were big, and others were just babies following their mothers, but again, they were all part of the masterpiece I discovered.

I head back to that golden sandy spot, take my camera out, and take pictures of my new property. The sound of my fast snapshots attracted the fish underneath my feet as if they were trying to get in the moment and be acknowledged as part of this place.

Indeed, the sea always welcomes you in, but somehow, it cannot be warm-hearted and never let you return quickly. You can struggle to find your way back to the shore, and with that, you can get mixed feelings of hunger. I had some fruit on the bottom of the knapsack, but again, I had to take everything out just to get to them; what an idiot.

I stretched my long towel on the sand and laid all my stuff on it.

I had to turn around and wash my hands from the sand and wipe my face, and actually, I had to test the salt water around my rose lips.

The heat started to get to my head, and I did the most stupid thing a girl can do.

I looked around me and all over to see if anyone could see me. Still, again, when I did realize that I was all alone here in paradise, I felt silly to think that way, but only because I was about to reveal part of my beauty to the sea, yet I did not want anyone else to share that.

I took my T-shirt off and laid back topless, looking at the vast blue sky. That secret hissing voice in my head returned to me as a commentator once more.

This time, it was unbelievable to describe my body with details: She has a wide, muscular shoulder and gradually goes down step by step to her perfectly rounded, Balconette style breast that shows off her perky shape. It is very tiring describing them, and so I have to move down to her waist, which also, somehow, was softly curved in an athletic shape, yet her hips are very proportional to the rest of her torso. The rear is gently curved and firm, and her legs are.

The thighs are toned and shaped, the knees are knobby, and the clays are shaped, indicating steady delay exercise with such attractive ankles with the defined shape of an athlete; hmmm, this girl could be a model or a movie star. The Wacko commentator in my head said: what a waste of body, running and sweating with a stupid tennis racket.

Finally, such a voice was gone, and I was observing everything and enjoying being in such a magical place. The sky was clear, not a single cloud, so it was scorching, but the cool sea breeze was my particular fan. I was very much at peace from this world to an extreme limit to fall asleep. I closed my eyes and completely forgot about everything.

I believe the magic of this place made me forget about the time, as I realized the golden rays of the sunset were my alarm clock to wake me up from my long nap.

I had no idea how long I was sleeping, but I was somehow tired, and I wasted the whole day sleeping right here on the sand, not knowing where exactly this place was or even how I would get back to the hotel. I put my T-shirt on and turned around to gather my stuff, but I changed my mind and said," What's the rush ?"

I've decided to stay and watch the indescribable sunset all the way.

That scene of the sun setting took me so far away to a place I did not want to be.

The symbolism behind the sun dying reminded me of the end and the last breath of life, but not the sun's energy, as it will rise again for a new tomorrow.

I remembered the last breath of my beloved father. He dreamed of mountains, majestic and high, but he was waiting for flatness beneath the sky. He reached for something he couldn't explain when standing alone in the rain.

He had hopes, wishes, and dreams. He asked and tried, yet when he was alone, he cried.

These were some of his words and thoughts that he shared with me once, and so here I am alone, dreaming of a mountain that I couldn't climb; I needed to see him one more time, but he had to go, leaving me all alone in this cruel world.

I had a photograph to preserve your memories, which are all left of you.

The sun went below the horizon, and I fell on my knees, crying and crying.

I dogged my fist into the sand, grabbed a handful, and held it in my hand.

I stretched my arm towards the dying sun, then I opened up my fist, letting the sand slip out of my hand, atom by atom, until the last one that I kept in my palm, and said to my silent audience, the sea, the sun and the mighty God himself.

I said: Consider this small dust here in my palm. It was once a piece of the one I loved the most. Yes, in Death, as if life is unblessed to take my best, even ashes of lovers find no rest.

A very pressure drop of my tears slowly dropped on that single atom of sand that I have kept in my palm for the longest time, and when they had blended, they both slipped off my palm and rested on the shore, leaving a mark, but not for a long time.

The sea demanded a payment to relax the spirit of my father's soul, and that was when the wave came and dragged both of them to the heart of the sea. I thought leaving the hotel room would help me, but I was sad and lonely. The majestic golden-red sunset was the best thing of my day, or should I say whatever was left of it. I waited in silence until the last piece of the sun submerged entirely under the horizon, and with the final look at that incredible scene, I saw something unreal yet challenging to describe, and I couldn't explain it even to myself.

The question was why and what it meant.

As the Eastern wind was blowing, a moving cloud that somehow mysteriously shaped like a dagger stabbed the sun, as that incredible redness of the sun was almost like blood.

The remarkable scene turned to blood, and I had to close my eyes to make it disappear.

I was freaking out to leave this place, not just because I was frightened or disliked it, but because I had to return to the hotel and regather myself all over again.

My only friend of comfort was my shadow in the dark. The sun was down, and so was my spirit as well. I managed to collect my things and head to where I came from, but I couldn't tell if it was the same spot to go up again, yet I was running out of time as it started to get a little dark. I was trying to use everything for my dare trip, climbing up such a rocky hill, and so one hand with the phone for the light, the other hand to rise step by step.

Accidentally, I dropped my sunglasses in between the rocks, so I had to stick my hand to reach in and get them out. My hand was almost about to get stuck, but I was so fortunate to get it out; however, my surprise was not the small cut I had on my hand from the sharp rock but from what my eyes discovered. There were two letters on a rock that were almost identical. M and M. Two letters reveal that two people were here before me and had the same initial ...Amazing.

Also, it wasn't a symbol written by a piece of chalk, as I realized it was blood when I looked deeper. Someone's blood wrote the writing symbols of the M and M, or maybe two people.

I couldn't ignore something like this without recording it using my camera.

I had to take more than one shot to ensure I documented that. I had to touch the letters with my finger, yet I realized that some of my blood was spelled on the second M, and I tried to wipe it off, but I made it worth it as I smothered my blood on both letters like an idiot.

I was standing in front of that and did not know what to do or say, but I apologized to them, the real explorer of this paradise, and so I said: I know I don't belong in this Heavenly place, but I could be wrong as my blood is part of both of you (M and M).

Meanwhile, I never imagined being in such a place, but destiny is on my side.

Thank you for having me here, but I have to go now, and maybe one day we will meet, whether in this life or the afterlife.

I was hysterically talking to the two M, yet I had no idea if they were still alive or dead.

The blood connection, the place, and my sad status of losing my father made me desperate to find any reference to his past life. The strange thing about this place made me wonder again and ask myself a question: "Why me? "

I left the spot and found my way out of this beach and to the streets again with the first Taxi to the rescue, as I headed straight back to the hotel.

CHAPTER II

VOGUE

I did not realize that the front desk receptionist was calling me and even waived to catch my attention, but I was so fogged up and not in any mood to talk to anyone at all.

I know she was trying to do her job and probably had some important messages for me, but I kept going and ignored what she was saying like an idiot. Soon, I was up in my room and again attempting to take another shower, and when I was done, I felt so hungry and restless.

So I opened up the mini-fridge next to the bed and zoomed in to see if there was any exciting food to eat, but there was no food, all samples of different kinds of wine and liquor.

I was very tempted, but I slammed the fridge door and headed to the phone to call for room service; again, I was weak and broken, which was an uncharacteristic thing about me, as I was always pretty solid and rigid. I had to put the phone down, as I did not care about food then.

So I returned to the mini fridge and poured all the bottles into a big mug with the hotel logo. Then, I started drinking and drinking. Not for a long time, the effect of liquor started to impact me significantly, but somehow, I felt better, lighter, happier, and, after all, forgettable.

The main problem with drinking mixed liquor on an empty stomach is that it speeds up the absorption of alcohol into the blood, which will cause a fast reaction to instability and the loss of any common sense. I was that idiot. I started dancing with my underwear, swirling and spinning around, and I felt like flying. The loud music from the street made me very curious to see how the Spaniards live their nights. I was heading straight to the terrace, hopping and dancing around, but just before I was about to touch the sliding door's knob to the balcony, I saw the reflection of my shadow. I was barely naked, so I froze and cramped my hand as a fist, not really to punch anyone but not touch the knob. I looked at myself, and with a body of mine, I was pretty sure I would drive half of Malaga so damn Loco(crazy).

I took after my beautiful mother's body, as I used to call her a goddess.

I had long legs and a great athletic body, but the truth was that, for once, I wanted to be loose and not worry about who I was. Despite all the contradictions between what I was thinking about and what I wanted to do, there were two opposite things.

The hesitations did not make any difference to me, as I ended up being, again and again, the same wise girl who always did the right things and followed the plan and never broke, so I started walking in slow motion, backward steps away from the balcony.

I sat on the bed's edge, looking around me, checking the wall and the entire room, and soon, I started sliding down slowly to the floor, with most of my body on the green carpet, but my head was still hanging and leaning back on the bed, staring at the ceiling.

The silence in the room was broken by me saying, "I am getting out of here right now." So I decided to go out and have fun in this beautiful country.

The most challenging part of my present condition was choosing the right clothes for the night.

I want to know what the right clothes are and what I like to be or even look like.

Do I like to be Serious, elegant, crazy, and wild?

Do I want to feel like a woman and not just a young girl anymore?

I need help, so where are you hiding, you crazy one, as I was calling that big mug of mixed-up liquor? I rolled over on the floor away from the bed and crawled on the soft green rug like a soldier seeking shelter to stay alive from the constant plane bombing. Still, in my case, it was only to reach out for that mug until I was in the middle of the room, and there he was, that big gigantic mug sitting on top of the mini-fridge, waving to me with a smirk on his face.

I was on my knee halfway drunk and started walking like a dog on my knees to the mug until I grabbed him with both of my hands and said to him," Well, well, my evil friend...where are the rest of your gang hiding? "

"What did you say ?" The evil mug answered me back as if it were a natural person.

While we were arguing about who said what, something extraordinary did occur.

I felt the mini fridge was shaking as if it were an earthquake! It wasn't, yet it appeared that someone trapped inside wanted to come out.

Gaby: Hey, evil mug, did you see that?

I had to put the mug back on the table until I saw these crazy phenomena.

I leaned down to the level of the mini fridge and opened the door very slowly, and they were all inside, dancing as if it were a fiesta.

All the tinny mini bottles of liquor were causing this sick thing.

The significant effect of liquor on me made me see things differently, as if everything around me was coming alive and kicking animatedly. The cute one in the back was Goose vodka, and he was giving me that look as if he was the hot shot of the whole pack.

The great evil mug trembled, and the splash of liquid inside was overflowing.

He glanced at me and said: "Let's join the fiesta with all of them."

So, I put the mug down on the floor, reached out with my two arms inside the mini fridge, grabbed all of them, and started filling up Nicholas to the top again with more and more liquors. You are Nicholas Vladimir, my evil 4th-grade teacher I hated so much.

I lined up all the empty mini bottles on the floor, looked at them, and imagined each one as a real character. The grey goose vodka was that skinny French dude with a Salvador Dali mustache and the blue French beret, with horizontal blue stripes as a seaman and a red scarf tied around his neck. The Russian vodka was that gorgeous young girl wearing the traditional fire red, satin, silky Russian dress with hand-stitched shapes and designs.

The arms' sleeves were made of transparent white silk with more hand-stitched red flowers made of glitter and Rhinestone studs in golden and red colors. The lower skirt was decorated beautifully with golden lines, and the bottom was all ruffles, and on her head was the famous golden red Kokoshnik Headdress.

As for the German Kor bottle, she was a brunette wearing the traditional famous German dress that consists of a mini blue skirt and the bottom with a line of red and pink tinny roses, then another layer of tinny million blue stars, moreover the last line is all red tinny boxes.

The side of her skirt is wide open in a very exotic way, showing her great thighs, and the dress is attached to a blue vest with a red apron and laces.

The upper part of her clothes is a white blouse that shows her exotic popping-up breasts, and her brown hair is all loose and wild. Her lips are like a fire waiting to burn the hell of anyone trying to touch them so that I will call her Kora instead of Kor.

My favorite bottle is the Spanish Sangria, and she is wearing a fire-red Flamenco dress with golden ruffles on the bottom of the dress. The exotic dress is wide open in the middle, showing her magnificent thighs and long legs. The upper part of the dress is sleeveless, as it shows her beautiful blossom breast. Her dark black hair is all up, glowing in the dim light of my room as if she had poured the bloody bottle of olive oil on her head.

Hello, my hot guys. I said to the other mini bottles—Mister tequila-man. I love you. You are so cute, with your big Mexican hat, white shirt with a red scarf, tight light brown pans, and a big buckle in the middle of your belt. That cute belly of yours is so crazy funny.

I can't forget the great cowboy brown boots with the shiny spurs. Arribas

Hey, maan ..Me Jamaica maan..

The rum bottle is alive and kicking, and he is all colored with long dreads as Bob Marley-No relations. The dreads were coming down on his big shoulder and Big body, with all muscles puffing out from everywhere. He is wearing the Jamaican flag in a sleeveless shirt made of wool, yet they are all shiny colors. The top is green mixed with orange; the bottom is red in three horizontal lines, and an army khaki baggy long shorts with red sneakers.

His smile glows in the dark with his great white teeth and a white scarf with the same three flag colors dangling from his neck—Rummy maan.

The last bottle is the hottest one of all. The tall, handsome, Scottish, young, seductive guy with his ruffed-up hair and scruffy bear. He wore a white ruffled shirt with a black bow tie, a black vest, and that short-cut Scottish blazer with silver buttons.

The Kilt has always been my favorite part of Scottish men.

It's an old say, and with my condition, I can't fucking remember how old or who the fuck said it, but it said that they wear the Kilt because of the confusion of being either or.

I meant that men can be women and the other way around as well.

Legs and Balls, which one it will be, yet the British will answer that by saying: To be or not to be, that is the bloody question, to be a man or a woman with such a skirt, or maybe a fucking Kilt. A long, non-bifurcated skirt type, garments with pleats at the rear with blue, green, white, and gray colors.

The front apron has the kilt pin hanging with all the fuzzy, weird hair from his pony that he had chopped off for dinner. The long white socks are folded just below his knees, and his shoelaces are wrapped around the long socks.

I am looking at all of them, and they are ready to rock out with me as we go on the adventure of a lifetime. Please wait a minute, my fiesta gang. I have the right song for that, and It's my favorite one of all time.

Where is my iPod?

I jumped on the bed, and there it was, under my sweet pillow. I scrolled down from the menu and was about to play the song for the adventure of a lifetime.

I told them I was not ready yet; I had a magical device called mini speakers that I would connect to get it loud. Hahaha, mini speaker, mini bottles, mini people. Haha.

Welcome to my crazy fucking revolution party. They didn't like that much, and they all turned their back on me until the music was on.

The high note of the keyboard started to ease in, and then the Conga drum joined in slowly, making them snap their finger with the beat. The extended version of the Vogue remix drove them crazy, as they started shaking gradually with the rhythm. On the other hand, I was lips singing with Madonna, singing to them, "Don't you stand there, ladies with their attitude, fellows that we're in the mood..strike a pose.. there's nothing to it...Vogue"

The magic of my lips singing the words made them come alive to become real people and not animated mini bottles anymore. We were all dancing in circles, so wild and so crazy.

I grabbed my tennis racket and jumped on the bed, bouncing up and down the mattress, pretending that I was part of the band playing the guitar, lips singing the song with them.

We were all dancing the steps as if we had seen the video before, posing Vogue.

I know all the steps by heart, as I was practicing a lot with Vogue and having fun, but this now is more crazy, wild fun. During the dance, something else was going on behind my back, and of course, I never guessed that it would happen, but the whole thing was so fucking wild and out of this world. The iPod was somehow shaking on the dock stand, not because of the beat but because Madonna was trying to come alive and dance with us.

She struggled, kicking the screen, until she finally broke it and came alive, too.

The significant part is when the song slows down for Madonna to sing "Greta Garbo and Monroe." A spotlight goes to the room's far end, and Madonna shows up in the lights, wearing her exotic black leather outfit as if she were in a video for Vogue, with a golden microphone in her hand. She started singing and dancing live with all of us.

The best part that turns the party into a real loco fiesta is when she is talking, singing the names of all the stars, then suddenly she adds a new line singing: "Bette Davis, we love you, Gabby, Gabby tennis star, kicking ass, that what you are.

Ladies with an attitude, fellows in the mood, don't just stand there; let's get to it; strike a pose; there's nothing to it. Vogue Vogue"

As she sang these new lines to her song, she winkled her shiny blue eyes at me and bounced in the middle of the room. We were all dancing, following her moves and steps as a backup chorus line with her. We were so wild, and I was so fucking drunk that my sick imagination went far and beyond when I added the spinning disco crystal ball with all the laser lights in the room, and the party went fucking wild. Finally, when the song was over, it was just me and some empty mini bottles scattered all over the room's floor. The fact that I needed to feel alive again only existed in my mind and with the aid of all those wonderful imaginary friends of mine. The fiesta was all over, and I was looking around the room, but there was nothing except me and the evil Nicholas mug in my hand with a few drops of liquor left, yet I had to trip on one of the bottles and spill such a portion all over my T-shirt. I am on the floor, lying on my back with my arms wide open, looking at the ceiling, laughing, and on my left hand, the empty evil Nicholas mug, so dead and so empty. I think I had enough booze, so I stood up and said. "Now, I believe at this moment I know what exactly I'm fucking going to wear ... A bit of all that together. So I put on whatever was in front of me, trying everything I had in my suitcase, and not for a long time; I had to stop and look around me to acknowledge the tremendous damn mess that I'd created with all my clothes on the floor and all over the room.

I wanted to scream out of frustration, but finally, I put things together and said: "Well, these are the things that I am gonna wear, the hell with this world."

The top was a dark black fancy blouse. Dark as the night with thin straps and satin fabric, quite open, that will indeed expose my breasts. Bras or no bras.." Do I give a damn?" I said.

NO bras, viva La Libertad (Long live Freedom).

When I put it on my bare skin, I felt the soft fabric brushing and caressing my breast.

I looked at the mirror, and it was revealing my blossoming breast, but again, the hell with everyone. I liked it.

The bottom is a red floral lace skirt opened from both sides. It was very loose and comfortable, fitting into my body. I never realized how it looked as if this was the first time I had worn it.

The red is like a fire that burns anyone near me. At last, I put them on, looking like the famous Spanish Flamenco female dancers, but more fucking exotic.

I've always wondered about that and why they are always so fucking serious with their hair so glued to their heads. The hell with them; it is all about me right now.

Now, what shoes? Hmmm.

High heels. No, I am not in the mood to slip and fall. I remember that I brought with me those unique shoes that were made just for me. A red Converse sneaker with black and gold laces, WOW.

I never guessed that I would wear that one day as it will always remain in my closet, but this is the one, and it is the night. I grabbed my purse and phone and, again, I couldn't leave without my friend," my aviator Ray Ban sunglasses, the outdoor man type." Many things in my life slipped in my path accidentally, including those Ray-Ban glasses.

When I found them accidentally in my mother's hidden treasure box, I was so happy.

I never asked her about the owner, but I knew they were very special to her heart, and now they are the most special ones to me. They were my father's, and fear has no place in my heart whenever I wear them. There were so many stories about them, but I'm not going back in time with my mother's old stories. One of her old stories about my father's glasses is they were made only for him, yet again with no details. It was nighttime, and I didn't want to be noticed by people pretending I was an undercover agent. The fact is that when you are drunk the way I was, things appear very satisfying and very believable. I am all set to get the hell out for a real fucking adventure. Again, it was somehow very new to me as I don't drink, and I don't swear or curse, but the liquor effect is my new thing to learn and control. Oh my God, I almost forgot the most essential thing all girls and women do: Perfume.

My favorite perfume, Anais, Anais..I sprayed it in the air and ran under the falling drizzle to get them on me.

What the hell Am I doing?

I'm so stupid acting like those rich girls, Lohan, Hilton, and Britney Spears.

I always wonder why women and girls make those stupid habits all the time, and even in movies, they do the same shit, and for god sake, the way they exaggerate doing stuff like that.

I knew the fact that you do want to smell nice and attractive, but why do they do all those fake and phony crap, just simply to pour the fucking bottle on you and get it over with instead of acting stupid like that. I am more down to Earth in so many ways, but I couldn't help but notice all the crazy stuff that women and girls do these days. I believe if you like the damn fucking perfume very much, then pour the hell of it all over you, and that was what I did.

I even sprayed it on my sneakers as a statement. Anais, you are my best friend; let's get out of here. As I was heading to the door, I had to turn my head and take a quick look behind me to see if I had forgotten anything. The horrifying scene of the mess I made in this lovely room was a disaster, but again, "What the hell?".I said.

The last thing to complete the great fashion outdoor was my black Nike cap, as it would cover my identity completely, and that was the mind of a drunk girl thinking out loud.

I noticed my tone had changed, and I've become a wild girl in many ways.

The first thing was my attitude and language, as I was cursing a lot, but again, I blamed it all on Nicholas. Also, I've noticed that because I'm drunk, there is some wisdom in me as I am free. I can do anything and be careless, not just because I am drunk, but because I am the one and the only...Gaby.

I open the door slowly and quietly stick my head halfway out to see if it is all clear.

The hallway seemed too long, but no one was out there. I started to act very strangely as I imitated Tom's tip-toe moves, sneaking on Jerry and looking around me with my tongue out and dangling to my chin. I realized it was time to grow up and stop watching Tom and Jerry.

The fact is that sometimes, without realizing what you're doing, you act like someone else with the same moves. My mother does things with her hands, and I have learned that through the years, I began to imitate her indirectly without meaning such a duplicate imitation, yet I couldn't help it and still make the same hand gesture or move almost as the way she used to do them.

On a cold December night, just before Christmas, I was cuddling with Mom on our tiny sofa, watching TV. Accidentally, I sat on the remote control, which switched the channel to Tom and Jerry, the famous American cartoon. I jumped off the sofa and started jumping in the air as it was my favorite cartoon. My mother was smiling, then suddenly, her facial expression changed to sad. I ran back to her and said: Why is Mommy sad? It's Tom and Jerry; you should laugh as they are always funny.

Mom: What did you say?

Gaby: It's Tom and Jerry; you should laugh as they are always funny.

It wasn't just the repetition of my words but my actions that made her cry even more.

I was tiptoe as Tom tried to sneak on Jerry before he hid back in his tiny home.

Mom: I can't believe my eyes, as your father used to say, and do the same thing you did to make me laugh.

Gaby: Was Dad funny?

Mom crying, saying: You have no idea!

Such an old memory made me miss Mom, yet the one I truly missed the most was my Dad.

For God's sake, no one is out here; sprint to the elevator and press the key.

I pushed the elevator's button a thousand times, rushing for it to appear—another vital observation about pressing the elevator button thousands of times.

I believe only stupid people do that, and I'm on the list. It's a switch button to call the elevator, like the light switch; one is more than enough to turn the lights on.

Otherwise, it will be on and off flickering until you burn the switch or the damn light bulb.

It was the same thing with the elevator button; once is enough, but yet again, I'm the drunk one for sure. The melody of the song "The Girl from Ipanema" was playing while I was waiting for the damn elevator to show up. It made me swag in the hallway, pretending this great song was about me. I have waited and stayed forever, but it was only just my drunk imagination that seemed forever waiting.

At last, I heard a noise (Ding) as if the mighty elevator was announcing his arrival.

The door opened, and there was an exquisite woman in her mid-forties with a better elegant dress than mine. She had a beautiful red and black scarf around her neck with golden birds spreading all over it. Gold and diamonds were the main attractions to any human's eyes.

I still looked at her and said, "Wow, this stupid woman will get fucking mugged sooner or later."

The fact that it took me longer to make my first move to the elevator somehow intimidated her so severely, but it was only just the beginning.

I was putting one step in and one step out. In and Out.

I was playing a small game with the elevator door. The door elevator sensor was about to give up, so finally I got in and moved quickly to the left side, far away from her, yet she gave me that smile and said Hola(Hello), so I was so relaxed and drunk at the same time, so I just waved my right hand and said "Hola....Linda(hi pretty lady) "back to her...

I was checking her out as she was doing the same thing to me, yet I said to myself: "Why don't I have that scarf? I want that scarf, I love that scarf, and I will have that fucking damn scarf; I will stab and cut this lady with my Barbie nail filler for that scarf. In the elevator, the atmosphere was very inexplicable, curios and unknown.

Two minds are wondering about the identity and the appearance.

Hers was all about my identity and how I dressed for the night. However, mine was only about the goddamn scarf and nothing else. The door opened up, but it was not the lobby; it was her floor. She eased out so quietly, then she turned around and stood there staring at me, from head to toe, trying to understand what the hell I was wearing or who the crazy damn fashion designer who did that to me. The strange impression on her face, looking down at my Converse sneakers, was an invitation for an unexpected reaction. She raised her head so slowly as if she was in a slow motion phase, looked straight at me, and said: "Nina Loca....(crazy girl)

I did not care what she said to me, but I knew for damn sure that the bitch called me crazy.

My eyes were so fixed on the scarf and nothing else. As the elevator door started closing, yet again in that slow-motion shit that I could only see, I felt the need for speed, wishing for just a glorious second, imagining myself as a character from the Matrix, plugged the fuck in with the same power and speed they had.

I dropped my head to the left as the break dancers moved, looking at the scarf.

My green eyes were halfway exposed from underneath my sunglasses, yet in a flash, I had one step outside the elevator, blocking the door from closing.

Yet, the other was still inside, stretching my arm as fast as if I were Mister Fantastic, snatching the scarf off her neck, and flying back inside the elevator in a split second before the door closed. I felt the cold metal of the elevator door brushing the tip of my nose. Wow.

I can't believe it. I fucking did it. The last thing I do remember was that thin space line before the door closed, seeing her standing there frozen, with her mouth wide open, speechless, from just what had happened. I wrapped up my prize, the beautiful scarf around my neck, as I looked at the big elevator's mirror and said: "Wow...Now I look fucking stunning ."

I knew very well that I was drunk, yet I didn't care and started dancing in the elevator for my great victory. I couldn't enjoy my dance victory as they were playing the stupid elevator's music, and it was a song from the past by the father Iglesias, not the fabulous son. Enrique.

What the hell was his first name? What else would be Julio singing one of my mother's favorite songs: "El Amor." Alcohol makes us so different: happy, dizzy, enthusiastic, gregarious, loud, and stupid. The poison can make us invincible, with no fear of the future, and of course, as Jean-Jaques Rousseau famously quoted: "Drunk mind speaks a sober heart. "

There was something wrong with this elevator as another song after "El Amor" started playing. However, it was encouraging to my status. Iglesias was gone, and another familiar melody began to blend in.

They were playing a dance version of the famous" Asturias."

Such a piece of Spanish guitar music goes back to my grandmother, who used to know so much about music and was very attached to that one in particular, Asturias.

The elevator version was excellent. However, it was the first time I got attached to such a fantastic piece of music, as it represents Spain in so many ways, including me.

I was spinning around dancing to the music as a flamenco dancer, and because I had no space to move around, I hit the freeze button accidentally, so I was there for a long time. The noise of the people screaming for the elevator made me realize what I'd done. Suddenly, the elevator's door opened, with an exceptionally pretty angry crowd waiting for the damn elevator. Still, I couldn't care less as I felt I owned the world.

Then, I strutted, singing Staying Alive, heading out to the fountain in the lobby, splashing the water all over, and just going to the front door.

Everyone was staring at me with my red dress and light brown hair all over the place; I even heard a few words in Spanish saying: "Quien es esa chica caliente.....(who's that hot girl?) ".

I turned around and acted so cool, smiled, and waved with a kiss. That was the hard part: leaving the hotel before I got caught.

CHAPTER III

THE KINGS

The streets were full of people, and no one would notice my condition or look. Unfortunately, I was wrong. This is the incredible Spain, and it is simply a country where you feel alive.

In Espana, you can forget who you are, where you come from, or even what you do.

You can blend in with the people as they are so friendly; they are all your brothers, sisters, and lovers. I was floating with my crazy, wild, magical night until that thought was interrupted by that voice saying: "Taxi Bonita(Taxi..pretty one)

I looked at the young hot taxi driver and said: "Si, si."

I jumped in without hesitation, wanting to be from La Puerta de Paraiso hotel as far as possible. "The driver kept asking me where, and I just said: "Drive away from here to a crowded place with people."

My head was spinning all over, I was pretty drunk, and the street lights were like a Starry Night over the Rhone Painting by Van Gogh, so magical, not clear, but amazingly mesmerizing. Hey, what is that square that is coming up called: "I said to the driver."

Right here, this is the Plaza de La Merced, yet before he finished talking, "Aqui es buena," I said,"

The moment I stepped out of the Taxi, I started to circle myself to scout the place, as it was pretty damn wild and full of people, and that was the nightlife at the Plaza de La Merced. The street sidewalk was long and full of restaurants and bars.

The best spot is outside, where all the restaurants have their tables and chairs out more than the inside. The street was like a carnival, as the lighting and the decorations were different, which made the strip very attractive for the tourists. I walked until my throat felt like a desert that needed the rain. I was pretty damn hesitant about where to get a drink as soon as possible. I saw that place, and there were a lot of tables outside, so it should be the place to be in such a moment. I headed straight to the nearest table, threw myself on the chair, and sat down.

I thought that my undercover look would drive people away from me, but I was a total mess with the combination of the wrong clothes at the same time.

My head was so oozy, but I was happy as hell.

Soon after I sat down, the waitress at the Restaurant La Gitana(the Gypsy) came to me, gave me the menu, and asked me in Spanish if I needed something to drink.

The fact that I wasn't good at languages made me smile and ask her if she could say that again in English. I couldn't tell if that waitress really hated me or hated the way I talked, or maybe the entire me did not agree with her at all, so she said: What's your poison?

I just asked you for something to drink, not poison. You know what? I will have the same drink as that lady next to me having".

She understood me very well, as she said," Si Mojito, muy bien."

She smiled, turned around, and walked to the bar to get my drink.

I knew she was calling me names as she headed inside the restaurant. It was not a usual walk, as if she was dancing, swaging. I also noticed that she turned her head in slow motion and stared at me again before heading inside the restaurant with a smile.

I am an idiot and drunk, too, and I hoped she would not recognize me for the crap I was wearing, but all that just disappeared as I leaned back on the comfy wicker chair and enjoyed the crowd. A few minutes later, she returned with the Mojito, smiled again, and said in English, "Enjoy...Mojito.

That drink was awesomely refreshing, and I was so thirsty, but unfortunately, the superb Mojito was not so great after a few fast sips. It was all in my stomach in one shot.

The moment I slammed my empty glass on the table, there was a sound that couldn't come out of a girl like me, but it came out so loud with such an attractive, erratic tone, saying: "AHHHH."

Such a sound attracted attention to my table as most of the tables were so close to each other, but again, I was still in my own LaLa world until she came back, standing in front of me again. I looked at that waitress and said, "Wow, she is so damn pretty and wild simultaneously." She was an exotic brunette with dark hair and a stunning body.

Her red and black top vest somehow revealed her body shape; meanwhile, her black pants were so tight, but again, I know that very well from being around so many girls and women from all over the world and during my life. When deeply drunk, and your head is very light, everything else seems heavy and slow.

The way I'd slammed the glass so hard made her turn around and head back towards me, saying: "Another Mojito."

I wanted to laugh, but I managed to cover my mouth. I looked at her beautiful exotic face and shook my head with a signal: "Yes, keep it coming, gorgeous." She had pretty light green eyes, the same as mine, and I also noticed a small tattoo on her arm, and the drawing was a dagger stabbing the red sun. Oh, my dear God, that is the same thing on the hat I bought from the airport, and it is the second time today that I've seen that, first at that magical beach, then now. I said, whispering in my mind. Again, I wonder about the mysterious links of everything I've been encountering when I opened my eyes today.

What other signs may come my way? I wonder.

She picked up the empty glass, placed it on the tray, smiled, turned her back to me, walked two steps forward and slowly, stopped, and then turned around again and came straight forward to me with a fast pace, leaned down with her face so close to mine as if her nose was about to touch mine. A slice of her hair dropped down in front of her green eyes, annoying her way from staring at me straight into my eyes.

So she had to blow it away with a side blow of her mouth, which was a fantastic move, but her eyes were not saying a word, yet her thick lips were the only thing that I was staring at, moving in slow motion with such a whispering voice saying: "If you need

Anything... Anything at all asks for me. Amaranta, that's my name. She paused, then said: "What is the name of your Royal Highness? "

I slid my glasses down to my nose just a bit and leaned closer to her face as she leaned down with her cheek towards me simultaneously to hear what I was about to say to her.

I whispered: "It is Gabriela...shhhh, don't tell anyone.

My whispering was like a magical smoky mist that floated over a dry field of dead roses that once were filled with life. The whispering traveled slowly, spreading over the field in waves like an echo to bring them back to life. The dead area was magically transforming, and roses pushed the soil to come back to life and bloom with the most mesmerizing scent a human can smell.

Gabriela finally reached her inner ear, boosting her heartbeat with a robust and shocking pulse as she breathed in my name like a ghost had touched her inner soul. Meanwhile, she took a long breath with her mouth halfway open, and at that moment, my eyes magnified her divine, desirable round lips. That frozen look in my eyes was witnessing an unusual phenomenon, as if she was dead and my name had brought her back to life. She closed her lips and breathed slowly from her nose, yet her lips shaped out again with a smile and said to me: Of course, you are Gabriela (paused). Then she said: "And who else would you be?

She stood straight, looked at my eye, and said, "Take your glasses off per favor....".

The second I removed my glasses, she leaned down with her body, looked straight into my eyes, said:" Anything at all, just for you...Gabriela", and walked away. In such a moment, I felt like an idiot revealing my identity to her, but again, I had doubts that she may not caught that.

I could not ignore noticing how she said my name, as if it was more like flirting. Ironically, I do not walk on that alley at all. I am a girl. Yet again, that waitress is such a unique, attractive young woman. Unfortunately, I'm just an old-fashioned girl who likes guys more.

As she faded, I put my glasses on again and wandered to a strange place called infatuation. There is something extraordinary about that girl that made me feel that we are linked, connected to something weird and very mysterious.

My wild imagination was somehow interrupted by the noise of the people next to me and the people in the street as they brought me back again to this world.

I have been to so many places worldwide and seen so many faces, but to describe the crowd, the lights, and the sounds were all in harmony as a moveable feast. Various types of art are everywhere around me, as if the place was designed, created, or even sketched in a certain way. Not far away from where I was sitting, I could see the statue of the magnificent Picasso standing still in motion, yet in a very mysterious way, he sat there as if he were alive, conversing with people from all over the world.

They go, sit, and take pictures of him, yet a lovely little girl causes a fascinating connection. She was whispering in his ears; then she started kissing him as if he was her forgotten grandfather, then suddenly she sat down next to him, holding his steel hand, and just looked around, monitoring the crowd of people, including me.

I can see from where I was sitting and from behind my glasses that the narrow streets filled with tables and seats were all colored and very well organized.

The lights were incredibly fascinating, as if the extraordinary Pablo Picasso was here to arrange all that, but again, he is and was a proud Malaga son and citizen.

Besides the fact that I was very drunk somehow, on the other hand, I was more sober with my imagination and vision describing the people around me, and for the first time in my life, I felt that I was Home. Young girls and boys running around, beautiful girls walking by, and the Spaniard men are gorgeous and somehow loose with their behavior, more like free and arrogant. Even the older generations of men and women were elegant and prepared for the night.

The moveable feast was like a symphony with the crowd's looks, faces, and souls as if they were almost strung together in a tremendous harmonic way. The smell of food was terrific, and even though I was not that hungry, I couldn't resist the smell of the excellent Spanish cuisine floating all over the place. The blood in their veins was coming down from the fountain of life.

The red wine fountain was filling up the streams, and a massive faucet filled up all the bottles of wine, coming alive to the tables and going back dead and dry with the restaurant's staff.

And here comes again, my friend Mojito. The superb Mojito was coming, dancing, swaging, and sweating from outside the glass. I looked at the glass and said: Buddy, you did miss the fiesta we had back in my room. You should've been there with the gang, but I am here for you and willing to support you all the way; just come to Mama.

I was so excited, drunk, and immature, imagining things as if they were real.

The place was bustling, and the servers, waiters, and waitresses were moving pretty fast to cover the great rush of all the customers, so she just left the drink on my table and bounced away to another table. That did not bother me, as I was excited about my new friend joining my company. Wow, that is good. I said to myself. I look at the girls, the waitresses busting their asses for just some crumbs called tips. The guys were even faster, cleaning up the tables to get more clients as if today was a memorable holiday. The line of people and tourists waiting for an empty table made these poor staff move like bees.

I was chasing a ghost, and that drink did not touch the table as it went straight to my stomach. I saw her serving another table from a distance, but I couldn't wait for her to come around to check on me, so I said to myself and probably sharing my thoughts loudly enough with the table next to me saying:" That drink (paused), Mojito(stayed), is excellent.

The big commotion of my big mouth had no red light, but it was green to me. I shouted the name loudly: "Amaranta."

She looked up, and so did many other people, but not really in a pleasant way because of the way I shouted her name in public. So, I gave her the sign for another, raising my empty glass with one hand and pointing with my finger to repeat it. She walked far away, ignoring me, and vanished momentarily inside the restaurant. I lay my glass on the table, wiped off the sweat and moisture still dripping on the cold drink, and then licked my finger. I was so drunk that I started to eat the mint and the ice.

The truth was that I became like a dishwasher with my tongue.

I was licking everything off that long glass, and at last, it was dry, so I had to flip over upside down and slam it on the table as I finished a tequila shot. I leaned back on my chair, looking up at the sky as the stars lined up unusually.

I am not a super girl, nor do I possess any hidden powers, but my ears were so alert and sharp that I had to put my head down and leave the undiscovered world of astrology because of the noise I heard. The fast footsteps clicking on the Stoney Marrow Street sidewalk were enough for me to tell that the wild, gorgeous waitress was heading my way, and I knew that the aftermath of my act would haunt me. She was coming so fast, charging at my table, and somehow angrily banged the Mojito on the table. Mr. Mojito was trembling from the sudden impact and somehow choked, spitting out some of its liquid as it splashed all over my hand.

Her fast turn away from my table wasn't fast enough for my quick reaction.

I rushed, bouncing myself forward off my chair, grabbing her wrist tightly, and said to her in a furious, drunk tone: "What the hell was that? "

You said a few minutes ago that if I need Anything at any time, you will be there for me, so keep it coming (paused), Amaranta (broken again) Inmediatamente.

My tone was like a dagger to her heart, as if I was ordering her to speed up with the drink.

She pushed my hand away and walked away. She was like a machine back and forth with drink after drink, one after another, until she told me, "Hey, you had five already, tranquilo."

So I told her in a bossy voice: I am relaxed and do whatever I want, so go there and get me one more and do your job. " She shook her head in total disagreement with my behavior and walked away. The number six was the one that put me up above the edge, yet I started enjoying the Spanish crowd walking by. Some were laughing, some were singing, some were in love, and some were trying to forget that they were once in love with the wrong person.

For the first time, I felt I belonged here in Spain with the culture, the language, the music, and the faces.

It was my first time experiencing the Spanish blood that ran in my veins and soul.

The people around me made me come alive. So strangely, in such a moment, I've realized how brutal and unfair it is to be mumbling in Spanish words, saying something about me, believing that I am just a stupid young foreign girl coming here for just the toxic enjoyment of the Spanish nightlife. I heard what she called me, and I was not so happy with what I heard.

She called me "Puta....Bitch"

My blood rushed to my skull, and I waited for her to return. It was a while as she ignored me, ultimately serving other tables. I was angry, but I wandered off again to that place where I talked to myself, trying to find answers to many things about my life. I was not angry at her. However, I was so angry about being denied from this world, whether by fate or not.

The truth about who I am made me angry and upset until I arrived in Spain.

If I am a Spaniard and it is in my blood, why the fucking mystery, the cover-up, and the lies, and why the fuck I was never informed about who I am?

I wonder.

I was still wearing my sunglasses as if they were my telescope and shielded at the same time, which helped me see things that were not meant to be seen until I noticed a little girl staring at me from a distance. She was the same girl who had kissed Picasso a few minutes before.

I took off my glasses slowly, took off my hat, too, and leaned with my head slightly forward, making my long, dirty blonde hair fall off, covering half of my face.

The little girl was doing precisely the same thing as me, imitating my exact moves, then suddenly, when that distance between her mind and mine became so close, she jumped up and down, pulled her older brother's hand, and started pointing at me.

At that moment, I felt I had returned to the Reality of who I am.

I was uncomfortable with all that, and it was pretty damn late to avoid what was coming at me. The little girl drags her big brother almost to the ground, then starts shouting: "Es Gaby, Es Gaby! ".... It's Gaby; It's Gaby. Everybody started, looking in my direction meanwhile, and from another angle, I saw Amaranta dropping the tray off her hand with whatever was on it. From another angle, some young men and girls stood up, pushing their chairs away, standing up, and looking in my direction. As the tray hit the ground, about five glasses were shattering all over, which diverted my attention for just a few seconds. Another delay was caused by another young girl, who, when she heard the commotion, lost control of her scooter, rammed into some table, and fell on the ground, but she was not hurt as the speed limit in the area is almost 5 km/h. The arrangement of the events was so rapidly fast and somehow synchronized in harmony and all in slow motion to my eyes. There was a race about to start, with many people involved, and the finish line was pointing to ME.

The shattering glass was the shotgun, and the fastest runner was that little girl.

She reached the finish line and threw herself in my arms, saying: "Gaby te quiero....Gaby, I love you." Her cute brother tried to grab her, but I told him to let her be.

She raised her face, and all I saw were her beautiful green eyes like mine. She said in her sweet voice: Would you please sign your photo for me?

My Spanish was not excellent, but somehow I understood that she wanted my picture autographed for her, so I asked her about her name, and she said: "Gabriela."

And so I smiled charmingly and said, Yes, it is me, of course, "Gabriela."

She said :" Mi nombre es Gabriela demasiado" .

The woman next to my table was my life savior, as she was my private translator when she told me in English: "She is saying that her name is Gabriela too."

I said: "Wow, (paused), that is so unbelievable what a small world.

At the same time, and from a distance, Amaranta was late to reach me.

Meanwhile, her biggest mistake was shouting out so loud: "Mi queried dios, Ella es la campeona Gabriela."

She shouted out my name so loudly, trying to warn me or avoid any of what may happen.

That was her announcing my true identity as the new 23-year-old Wimbledon Champion and the number one player in the world, saying: My dear God, she is the champion, Gabriela.

The wild thing was that I was very well-known globally, but I was surprised to find out that in a small place in Malaga, Spain, some people still recognized me as well.

The street was at my feet, and the crowd was heading towards me more and more from every angle. The cheers became louder and wild at the same time.

The flashing lights of their cameras were blinding me, and I was trying to block them with my hands, but accidentally, I knocked off my hat, and my hair just got loose, wild, and dropped down above my face, adding more flare to the fire of the moment. My beauty was taken after my gorgeous mother; some still call her a goddess. The loud noises echoed from all angles, including the terraces and balcony above me. The words were in the streets for someone famous at La Plaza de la Merced. The thing is about the narrow streets in Malaga, especially in my section, which was all connected from alleys to narrow streets to the main strip of Calle Larios leading to Soho and Puerto de Malaga. The place's owner started blocking the crowd from approaching me. Meanwhile, Amaranta was trying hard to make ways to get to me.

Finally, she was behind me but still angry at me. Then she said: Listen to me carefully, act fast, grab my hand, and follow me. She was pushing everyone away with her shoulder as my private bodyguard to clear our path to the inside of the Restaurant.

On the other hand, the owner and the other servers were trying to block the crowd from rushing inside the Restaurant and following us. It was like a rushing wave that hit the shore with a massive impact, and the damage was all over as the tables were down and everything was crashing. On the other hand, we started running to the kitchen and from there to the back door to a long dark alley; then we waited until it was all clear, then sprinted across to the other side of the Restaurant to an old building with a blue door.

She slipped her key from the chain around her neck into the door, pushed it with her foot, and slammed it behind me. We ran up the stairs that led to her room, then again slammed the door and started locking up ten thousand locks as a fortress.

I was living in a movie for a few minutes, chasing me, running, laughing, and being drunk, among other things, such as this girl or, I should say, Maravilloso. Amaranta.

She pushed me into the middle of the room and turned on a small night lamp. It was a blue light, quite fascinating and impressive as well. There was a frozen moment where everything was on pause. The silent sound of our heavy breathing lasts for a while.

Her heavy breathing sounded like a Parado or a wounded, bleeding bull that just had enough and was ready to charge for a kill the Matadora, Me. She angrily took off her red vest and apron and crumbled them like a ball, just about to throw them in my face. I had to duck down to avoid that. Still, she managed to control her anger and instead slammed them down to the floor and took a deep breath, with her hands covering her face to cool off. Suddenly and unexpectedly, she jumped up and landed before me, growling: "Usted esta loco y bebido demasiado. "You are crazy and drunk, too much," she said."

I knew I was drunk and crazy, but they were my fans, and I raised my hand to stop her from coming so fast at me and said, "Hey, you didn't have to do all that.

They are fans, and I have to go back and sign that autograph for the little girl. " You are going nowhere once you get a grip; come here.

She said as she grabbed my arm firmly, rushed me to the window of her room, and stated: "Mira loco." Look, you are crazy. The crowd was across the street, still waiting for me to come out from the Restaurant, cheering my name louder and louder. She moved away from the window and said: "You should've told me who you are?".

But I did, "I said to her with anger."

You didn't say you are the famous rising Tennis star Gabriela, and I was so blind not to see that. I had a feeling, but I was unsure about how you dressed and......I had to cut her off, saying:" Well, I came here for a specific reason, and I was not expecting all that; I tried to look different so no one would notice me." She laughed hysterically and said: "How much did you have to drink before you put on that dress, the scarf, the red sneakers, and the ravishing hairstyle?" You had a clear sign for Spain to acknowledge who you are, and that indirectly is wild but beautiful at the same time.

I have never met a famous person, but tonight you are here in my room, which is incredible and will change everything. So what do you have to say about all that, Loca?

Gaby: I don't know what to say, but maybe I am slightly drunk.

Well, you are more than just drunk, with all the Mojitos you've been pouring into your tinny stomach, and God knows how much more before you left your place.

Amaranta said with a serious face: "Listen to me and stay focused. I will help you get out of here, but I have to call my cousin to sneak you out from the back door away from the crowd; stay here and don't open the room's door until I return." She said.

I must change my clothes first, so feel free as if at your own home. She went to the bedroom and started taking off her clothes. Still, she didn't close the door behind her, and I had no choice but to accept my first theory about her incredible body from underneath her greasy working clothes.

She was about 1.7 meters, her waist was so firm as if she worked out every day, and her butt was so rounded and tight, or as they call them, "heart-shaped ass." There was another tattoo with a blue-robin bird on her waist, right above her butt.

As she turned around to put on her black fitted t-shirt, her reflection in the mirror showed the other beauty of her body, as her breasts were about 32c and her hips were terrific.

I had to turn around and move to a far corner of the other room, pretending I was not looking or checking her out. I was doing all that, but in the meantime, just watching her was all new to me than any other girl I had seen in the Locker room. Amaranta is not just an everyday girl you see and walk away from; she is different and extremely hot to be ignored.

She came out of the room, and God, she looked so different and gorgeous.

She looked at me and said in Spanish, "Por que me miras de esa manera? "I know you were checking me out while I was changing, and I am not that type, so wipe that smile off your face and be more mature. I was just about to answer her, but she did not give me any chance, and she said again: "Stay here and keep the door locked..do you understand me, loca...?"

So I said: "Si, mi angel de la guarda."

Amaranth: Did you call me your guardian angel? Wow, where did you learn Spanish? I'm sure in a fancy private school with mom and daddy's fortune. She wanted to laugh, not because of my funny Spanish accent but because of how I said it. She headed to the door, but she came back and gave me a fast kiss on my cheek and said: "Keep it locked and keep it safe," then she slammed the door behind her. I locked the door, stood in the middle of the room, and started looking around. The room was small, yet there was plenty of stuff everywhere to tell about that girl. The room was so much alive with strange radiation, magic, music, and amazingly different and incredible things around, and it was worth the search for the beautiful Amaranta. My mind, eyes, and all of me were floating with everything in this small room, yet when I was just about to feel that I belonged here, the rumbling sound of a volcano was more than enough to scare me. Her banging on the door like an animal interrupted me, so I strolled to the door, laid my ear on it, and said: "Who is there?

Amaranta : " It is me loca.. Open the door.

Gaby: I opened the door with a smile and hugged her, but she pushed me away seriously, saying:" Which part didn't you understand when I said not to open the door to anyone?"

I told her I knew it was you from your voice and was so happy to see you again soon.

Amara: Mira, I was testing you and want to warn you about my room, too.

DO NOT TOUCH ANYTHING IN THIS PLACE...

I am worried about you and willing to help you, but don't let me change my mind. As she returned to the door, she turned around and gave me that crazy sign with her hand, saying: "If you touch anything, I will cut your throat."

Her statement ends with a smile as she turns her head and vanishes behind the closed door.

She is exceptionally wild and beautiful, and I wonder if she has any blood from the Gypsies around Spain. On the wall was a giant poster of the famous Spanish group "the Gypsy Kings."

Please wait a minute; the picture on the dresser was also bizarre, as it includes Amaranta when she was a little girl, it seems, with two musicians, and one of them is actually in the Gypsy king's poster on the wall. Oh my God, she does know them. But when she said she would call her cousin. What cousin. I wonder. The dresser has plenty of scattered fake jewelry, but they were so damn pretty good, too.

Can I buy some of them from her? I wonder.

Something looked very familiar, and I couldn't ignore it, so I said: Here comes my friend again.

That bottle of Tequila is sitting there for me. I need a goddamn glass, I said.

I couldn't find a damn cup in her room, but my foot accidentally hit something interesting.

I had to put down Mr. Tequila and get on my knee, leaning down to see what I tumbled on from underneath the bed. I was reaching out to get that small wooden box, as it was very well crafted with some symbols, and one of them was the same as the Tattoo on Amaranta's arm.

I became more curious to see what was in the box.

The mystery about stuff like that, especially the old Spanish ones, is that you can't open them with a key. Those boxes are rare, and the old Spanish ones were interesting. Kings and Queens, even old pirates, used to have special boxes like this one, full of mysteries.

They were full of mazes trying to find the key.

I remember watching a documentary about these mysterious treasure boxes from the olden days. So I had to feel the box from all the angels to find a gate and discover the key to the bloody box. Shaking the box lightly, you can hear the key rolling between the wooden mazes inside the box.

I was frustrated by such a box, so I had to pour some Tequila into my mouth to feel invincible.

The great thing was that I accidentally moved off a small piece of wood that was loose from the bottom, and amazingly, it pushed off another piece. Another one moved away in a different direction, and suddenly, I heard something shifting and clicking.

Finally, a metal tongue emerged, and the key rolled on my palm. Hey, I found the key, I said.

I put the box on the dresser and turned the key. The moment the key clicked, the box opened up with an enchantment melody that sounded very familiar to my ears.

I stood in front of the box saying to myself: "What an idiot, It is the great Swan Lake by Tchaikovsky ." The box had some black and white photos of some people.

The hair and the fashion were so different but old. I had to take another sip, sat on the floor, leaning back on her bed, grabbed the box on my lap, and started flipping through the old pictures. I couldn't tell if it was a flash from one of the cameras down in the street or if being so drunk blinded me completely. The great flashing shock was a picture of my Grandmother, Maria, from my father's side, in such a box. I had the same one back at home, and I had it in a lovely frame, yet it still bewilders me to see her picture in this treasure box belonging to a stranger like Amaranta. Who is she?

The scary part was the writing on my Grandmother's picture, symbolizing the two MMs and the year. This is wild. The two MMs are the same as the one on the rock in such a hidden shore, but that wasn't all.

There was another picture of two beautiful girls; one of them was my grandmother standing next to a lovely girl, and again, in the back, it had the two MMs(Maria and Marbella) and the year. The scariest picture was of the two of them next to a beautiful kid, and in the back was the shocker as it had the symbols of MMM(Maria, Maribella, and Mondo) and the year. I dropped the box and everything off my hand.

I was shocked to see a picture of my father when he was a kid, which was unbelievably rare.

My head started to hurt, and the liquor mix made me stand up and look closely at everything around me, trying to find an explanation for this mystery.

I was digging in the box, attempting to find any clue, yet there were more photos of a lovely young woman who looked like Amaranta. Is this her mother or sister? I wonder.

I had to sit on the sofa and accidentally sat on the remote control.

The image on the screen made me feel like I was back in the streets again.

The station was local, and they were showing the crowd outside; I swear I heard my name more than once in Spanish, which means that the media was out there, too; oh Fuck.

Wow, forget about the damn glass. I said.

The taste of liquor on my lips tasted as if I was poisoned, and the magnitude of the shocking wind. Such a sudden wind blew my hair off my face as if it were a hurricane, but only the apartment door opened violently by her and a tall man behind her.

What the hell are you doing? "She said."

Her speed was so intense as she pushed the bottle from my hand that it flew straight to her mirror on the far side of the room. I had to cover my face as the shattered glass flew all over the room. I was afraid that the scattered glass would cut me somehow, but to my surprise, that man was faster than me and covered me with his body.

Amaranta, surprisingly, rushed toward me and pushed the man to the side, slapped my face not once but twice, and said in Spanish," Primero es para la bebida, y el segundo para tocar mis cosas personales." She said the first slap was for drinking, and the second was for touching my stuff. My tears were pouring down my red cheeks as she had heavy hands, and it did hurt, but somehow I did understand what she said and why she did that, as she said that I was drinking too much as if I was about to die and the second time slapping me, was for me touching her stuff. The radiations of the intense heat generated off my face made my weak tears dry out, and an evil force possessed my body and mine, taking control of my coming reaction towards Amaranta. The crazy thing about me was my hidden secret that only my mother knew about a long time ago, and at some particular moment in our lives, she used to tell me such a statement: "I wish that you'd met your father as you do have a lot in common.

The incredible power of our minds can manipulate the future and present but never the past.

My mind went so far away, or back in time. I was a little girl, and my mother was telling me not to cry, to close my eyes, to feel my true power, to let it guide me for the future, and to be able to see what might happen.

She also said: Now, open your eyes and change the future to something you desire.

I had the ability, as a gift, to see moments from the near future, and with such a gift, I was able to improve my skills and be a better tennis player. Also, I could see things in school before it happened, but I wasn't mature enough to understand such a gift. Catching a glimpse of a few seconds in the future helped with such a crazy gift.

This was different, and it will be my first attempt to use such a gift away from tennis.

My gift somehow was to be able to see a glimpse of a few seconds from the future, just a few seconds, but again, I never measure that as sometimes it could be more than 10 seconds, but I was never sure how it came to me or even when I was blessed with such a gift. I saw Amara rushing at me so fast for another attack, yet I managed to move slightly sideways, avoiding her rush. Meanwhile, I extended my right foot one step, clipping her legs for enough balance distraction for her to fly in the air and land hard on her face. In my mind, the following clip was me on her back, punching her face. Are you going to stand there crying like a baby? Say something, Campion. "She said with a star-casting voice."

To ignite such a gift of mine, I will need a trigger or a word that might be my flame to burst out. One of her words would soon trigger me, but I never knew which one or when. She never stopped yelling and screaming in my face until the word came out of her mouth, calling me, "PUTA." The future scene was all in my mind, but somehow it was duplicated.

She was on the ground, and neither her cry nor the pain of my fist stopped me from punching her harder and harder, smashing her face with my fist. I felt my power growing in me, but in a different, strange way, as if I was flying in the air, and I wondered if that was another new gift for me (Flying).

I close my eyes and whisper to my soul: I can fly.

The truth was the complete opposite of all that. There was neither power nor flying; it was just the big man separating us, and he had to lift me in the air like a baby to do that.

The moment he put me down on my feet, I pushed his hands off me, and before I said a word, he raised his hand to block my lips and said in broken English to both of us, "I am here to help, but not that way."

First, you, Campion, must calm down and act mature, so you must come with me.

He took my hand, dragged me to the bathroom, and turned the shower on.

He carried me like a cat and put me under the cold water with my clothes on and forced me to stay there, yet I was screaming, kicking, struggling to let me go, but he did not lose his grip on my head and forced me to stay under the shower. He was tall and strong as a bull, and I couldn't fight him anymore but stay under the cold shower. Amaranta, on the other hand, was laughing in the far corner of the bathroom until he finally let me go.

I was so angry and started slapping him, but somehow, I felt awake and a little bit sober; then he said a few words in Spanish to Amara.

Amara was her nickname, and he asked me to remove the wet clothes immediately.

He closed the bathroom door behind him, and a minute later, Amara came in with a beautiful gypsy black dress with red ruffled and gold lines and said: "Please wear this."

I looked at her with wide-open eyes, red as lava, and said, "I hate you, and I want to get out here right now." She did not speak a word, but she smiled, then stretched her arms, one with a dry towel and the second with the dress, for me to accept it.

The magic of her smile and her eyes were just like a key to my heart, yet the look on her face was more than enough for me to cool down and control my anger.

I looked into her eyes and said softly, almost whispering to cover the shame of my wild 'behavior. 'I am so sorry about everything; I do not act like that or drink at all.

My tears fall like a river over my cheeks from shame and desperation.

I looked at her again, saying; I can't wear this dress. It is so lovely, and I can't tell you why I'm here in this country; I wish I could, but I'm sorry for all the pain and the frustration I had to put you through, and I'm so sad that I touched your stuff, and I'm also sorry for being a Puta. Amara got emotional with my words, yet the magic of the word Puta made her crumble and laugh, then say: It will be my great honor if you accept it, as it represents my family in heritage, so please put it on, but before you do so, I have to ask you a big favor, and please do not be angry at me again.

At that moment, I felt a strange, warm affection, as if I had an older sister trying to protect and take care of me. I smiled at her and said," Anything for you, and I promise I will not be angry. "

She smiled at me, then said," Please look up above at the ceiling, as there is something so magical that I want you to see."

I was somehow disappointed in her strange request as I was expecting a hug or a kiss.

I was so naive, gullible, and blind to see what was coming my way, and even with such a gift that I have, I trusted her unthinkingly, so I did look up without any doubts; I trusted her at that moment. She waited until I was fully relaxed, staring at the ceiling trying to find that magical object, then out of nowhere she punched me in my stomach so hard that I'd to throw up so badly as if I had emptied my stomach from anything and everything since I'd landed in Spain. I was throwing my guts out from such a complex, powerful punch.

I was on the ground with all my shit on the bathroom floor. She was standing there so severely with a wet, warm towel in her hand, waiting for me to finish.

I raised my head, looking at her, and my green eyes were not green anymore but red as fire from anger, pain, and frustration. I told her in that demon-hush voice, and it sounded like Linda Blair from the Exorcist movie. Thank you, but tomorrow, when I am fully sober, you are a dead girl. She went down on her knees with the shit on the floor. Yet, she did not care and covered my face with the wet towel, wiping off my vomiting or whatever was left.

Yet, she was also hysterically laughing about my condition and said in a soft voice: "Well, you promised to forgive me, so I am going to ask you another favor, and this time, I want you to get under the shower one more time to get cleaned up the right and don't worry about all the vomiting and the other mess, I will take care of all that. I had no choice but to trust her this time and obey what she said, not because I was afraid of another punch, but because I felt the security around her and the things that she was trying to help me as a girl and not as Gaby, not the champion. The thing is, the amount of alcohol in someone's system, such as mine, can take time to get out, and the most common one is to stick your finger deep in your throat and cause vomiting. However, I wasn't planning on doing any of that, so the best way was to empty my stomach by force, and that was precisely what she did.....Indirectly.

The steam was building up in the bathroom from the hot shower, but in the meantime, she had to leave the bathroom carrying all the wet towels and the bucket full of nasty vomiting.

I was all naked in no time, yet she turned her head back and said, "Hey, you have a great body too, but I wasn't watching you the way you were watching me earlier.

She left the bathroom with a smile on her face. The warm water was helping me get back on my feet and transforming me into a standard and sober girl again.

I was laughing under the shower at what she said about my body, which reminded me of when she was stripping my clothes piece by piece earlier. The thought of her checking me out and getting me undressed felt to me as if it was not sexual, yet it was more of treating me as a little girl or maybe as a younger Sister. It felt so good knowing, or even believing, that some people could still see me and judge me as a person out of the lights and the flashing cameras.

This time, she knocked on the door and asked my permission to get in, and I appreciated her behavior and respect. I opened the door slightly with only my head sticking out, as I was fully naked, and said softly: What now?

I can help you dress up and have brand-new things for you. I let her in and walked to the middle of the bathroom, which was not that big at all, pretty narrow, but unique with some painting on the ceramic black and white tiles of seagulls and breaking waves on the shoreside and from a far distance a woman standing on the shore looking at the infinity of the distant horizon as if she is searching for answers. It did remind me of myself on that' beach.'

I have some new underwear and a new bra for you to wear until you get your stuff.

They may not be a famous name brand, but as I said, once you get your fancy stuff. She was correct about the name brand, but they were all new and had yet to be touched, with the price tag on them, and they were very cheap as well. My lips were tangled, and my words weren't clear enough to respond to all that, but when I looked at her, I felt the connection, yet as stupid and naive, I went to hug her; she said, Loca, not now. Please stay away from me; again, don't get any ideas. You are just all wet and naked, too."

So we laughed and started ripping the package open, yet I looked at her and said: I am glad you have them in black, gracias.

I dropped the towel on the floor, put the panties on, and handed her the bra, saying, "I don't need no bra."

She turned her face, looked in the mirror, and mumbled in Spanish in a low tone, "puta." Hey, I heard that, and we laughed again.

One more thing. May I call you Gaby? She said to me.

I looked at her with the water dripping on my face from my wet hair and said: Well, everyone in the world calls me Gaby, but if you wish, you can call me Gabriela.

Mara: I do like Gabriela very much, as it exposes the true you, and I thank you very much. Also, I am so sorry for slapping you and punching you. When I saw you carrying my sacred box and the tequila bottle, you made me so furious. I could not control myself and forgot who you were, so please forgive me (paused). I interrupted her sentence and said: Come here and hug me.

Mar: Oh, no, stay away from me. You're still wet.

I was upset that she rejected my constant hugs, yet she opened her arms and said: Come in, Loca. She laughed, and this time she hugged me so hard and of course she got all wet too, then she said: Come with me to my room so we can get you ready.

The room was another statement of her identity with everything on the wall: the colored drapes, the scent, and finally herself. She handed me another dry towel to dry up my hair, then said: Well, I will leave you alone to change the dry clothes. As she closed the door, I turned around and looked at myself in the mirror, saying, "Hey, I think I like that girl."

It didn't take me long to put on the dress, and I started seeing a new person for the first time.

A real Spanish girl that I had never imagined existed in me until this moment.

The dress, my wet, loose hair, and my glowing green eyes sparkle when I am happy or even when I am blue, and, after all, my name is Gabriela. I am a Spaniard by blood. Meanwhile, I have yet to ask my Polish mother the main reason for naming me a Spanish name.

The strange mystery behind my name, Gabriela, is still yet to be revealed, and for whatever reason, and with all the Polish names, she decided to name me Gabriela. All these thoughts swirling in my head made me realize my true Me.

I am Gabriela Mondo, the daughter of the most remarkable man I've ever known.

The father that was missing from my life, the ghost of my happiness, and above all, the dagger of my bleeding heart. The gentle knocking on the door saved me from drifting to my father's memories and his missed face, as Amara called me.

The moment I opened the door and walked out of the room wearing the dress, they covered their mouth from the shock as I looked astonishingly ravishing, with my hair all messed up, wet, and no makeup or Anything.

Amara's tears covered her face, and she pulled me hard into her warm body.

Her hug lasted longer than I had expected. When she let me go, she moved back a few steps, looked at me again, and said, "Es con gran honor y admitir por primera vez que decirte querida. Gaby, que son desde este momento una verdadera gitana Española."

I was just about to ask her to translate what she said, yet the big man translated everything in a deep voice, saying, Amara, it is with my great honor, admit and for the first time to tell you, my dear Gaby, that you are from this moment a real Spanish gypsy."

I was so overwhelmed by the sweet words that I threw myself back in her arms and said," Gracias a mi angel."

She walked me back to her room, grabbed a brush from her dresser, sat me down on the bed, and started coaming my hair and putting on all kinds of makeup; on top of all that, she gave me some of her favorite jewelry that I did admire from the moment I laid my eyes on them. She headed to a small cabinet, took an extraordinary bottle, blue as the sea with some gold design, and returned to me and started spraying the most seductive scent I've ever smelled around my neck. I had to turn around to see the bottle of perfume she used, but I couldn't recognize it as I'd never noticed it before.

So I told her, "My dear god, what is the name of this perfume? It is out of this world. "

She answered me, saying, It is called the Gypsy Water. My mother used to wear it, and so I interweave after her.

Gaby: I am so sorry for your loss; I am sure your mother was something special just wearing this magical perfume. Amara said, Well, it is yours if you wish.

I have more.

She pointed to the small cabinet. There was a great stack of bottles similar to the one in her hand. Wow, really. Of course, I will be so grateful to have one of them, and I thank you for that from the bottom of my heart. The last thing was the shoes: the famous Zapatos de baile flamenco and red as fire. The mirror was broken so that I couldn't see myself entirely, yet from how they looked at me, I saw my new me through their eyes.

I felt that I was flying on clouds. She glanced at the big man and said, "This is my cousin Tonino, and he is here to help us, so let's get you out of here.

Gaby: I almost forgot everything is happening, so please come with me and sit in bed.

I ran back to the bathroom, grabbed the small first aid box, and said: Now it's my turn to fix you up. I start cleaning the dry blood off her nose and face until her skin becomes natural color again. I started putting some coloring makeup to cover the shit that I did to her face, and when I was done, I said to her: I'm so sorry, but if I ever found that truck driver who hit you like that, believe me, I will cut his throat. No doubts.

She looked at me in silence until she started to understand my joke, then she jumped on me for another punching round, but the big man Tonino sounded that noise: Ahem, come on girls, stop fooling around as we have to go. On the other hand, Tonino had other plans we needed to be aware of. As we exited the back door, four men were waiting for us in the dark alley, but they were very familiar. I was about to scream as I recognized Cantos Reyes, the famous Gypsy king's leader, but they covered my mouth to stop me from screaming, exposing their identities. They all hugged me and said," If Amara asked for help, we will, and we are very honored to play music for you here right now.. let's go. "

The distance from Plaza de Merced to Plaza de Constitución was not even 10 minutes apart, yet they got in and out from dark alleys until we arrived at Plaza de Constitución.

The main street, Marqués de Larios, is considered one of the busiest streets in Malaga Centro, yet there were more people than usual. What a scene! The band was on my side from left and right, and Amara was next to me, holding my hand, yet I felt a secret sweat off her palm from the excitement. She had that baby face, and her eyes were glowing in the dark.

She was holding my hand so tight as if she'd finally found what she'd been looking for her entire life, yet she was a solid girl, and her emotions were somehow very well controlled, but again, I'd noticed all that. We walked together as a gang to a massive crowd, and the sheers were historically crazy as we came out to the light. A small stage was put together in no time, yet their guitars came out from nowhere as if they were planning and preparing for something like that. It appeared that someone from the band had leaked their presence, so the owners of some of the restaurants set up the stage with lights and cool stuff for the great band's performance. The crowd created a big circle around the stage; then, the Kings started playing SOY.

I did not know what to do with myself at that moment. I was standing there, not believing what my eyes were telling my mind, yet my heart was pounding so loud that the beat went on with them singing SOY.

I was not the main attraction anymore as everybody was just dazzled with The Kings and their music, yet a young man took my hand and led me to dance with him, and the moment the music started tingling my toes, I couldn't hold myself anymore.

That young man reminded the crowd of my existence again, and I was dancing as a Flamenco dancer while my dress was completing the magic and the sheers of my name became louder and louder; even the Kings were adding some crazy lines with my name in the song, and it was magical. I felt that the entire Spain was at my feet, dancing with me.

I cried and cried, but I laughed simultaneously. My feelings at that moment were indescribable, as I felt as if the ground was shaking from underneath my feet.

It was a moment of glory, madness, magic, and unforgettable, even more historical to my heart than the Wimbledon Final moments. Their music and songs were like medicine to my aching heart, the joy I needed since landing in Malaga. The song Bamboleo was the spark of my fire. These first notes of my favorite song, Bamboleo, struck my soul; the rest was my fiesta's madness. I was somehow sober, yet I got drunk again with their music, and I lost my stability as I was dancing on air. The music, the dress, the gypsy water, and the red shoes transformed me into a flamenco dancer. I had so many moves that I'd learned from my mother, and the dance classes I'd attended when I was young all came alive.

I was an unstoppable dancer or a maniac on the floor, locking rhythms to the beat of my heart. I was shocked when they reached for my hand to get me on the stage and sing with them.

The sheers went wild as to Malaga; that could've been one of the best nights they've ever had for such a long time. My eyes were like a Radar looking for Amara in such a magical moment, but she was lost in the massive, crowded fans.

The moment I stepped on the stage, Malaga went crazy, sheering up my name, and it was powerful yet loud enough for her to see me. She was far back, jumping like a wild animal, when I started calling her Amara Amara.

The fan's response was phenomena. They lifted her above their shoulder, and she was crowd surfing to the stage over the bodies of hundreds of fans.

That sudden move from the fans sparked the hell out of the Kings, and the moment she came next to me, her tears burst out of her eyes like a running river. She was thrilled, even though they were her family in a way, but the fact that she was on stage with the great Gypsy Kings and the Wimbledon Champion while singing the song was the world to her.

The Kings were delighted but surprised by our synchronized dancing as if we had been practicing the moves together for a long time—they were prominent.

And concerned fears were about the stage and how solid it could be, as we were tapping the floor so hard; yet to add more fire, they put some of their microphones on the stage floor so the sound of our tapping could be heard as if it was part of a new remix of the song.

Volare was another song, yet with such a great song, the Kings made it up as if it was written for me, even though my eyes were green, not blue, as the lyrics state.

Tonino started to dedicate the song to me, and he said that it was their great honor to have me on stage with them on such a magical night, but what struck me was his strange announcement.

He said: From this day on, this lady, girl, campeona, Gabriella, is our new family member, and she's more than welcome to live with us any time, but at last, we are proud to call her Gitana Gaby.

Amara translated all that so fast. However, I never got the chance to respond, as the fans did that for me, and it went wild again. The fans were going wild during the song, not for the music, but they asked us to come off the stage and dance among them.

The crowd surfing brought us back to the ground, and we were dancing our hearts out to the unstoppable beat and music of the Kings. I couldn't tell if I was still drunk or if it was just a strange, hidden sort of energy that possessed my body. I danced with everyone, boys and girls. Young and old, without any doubts, dance with Amara.

The music was so loud, yet all I was able to remember was Amara telling me in Spanish (Ralentiza Gaby, Slow down Gaby)

I was so happy with every moment and every musical note of the Gypsy Kings, and with all that, I managed to forget the crying tears of my heart over the memory of my dear father. A few hours later, the Kings were ready to wrap it up, yet they all came to me, hugged me, kissed me, and said: "Somos familia ahora....we are family...Now.

They were a hilarious group, as one young member got his Spanish guitar and started the melody of We Are Family. It was an acoustic version, his way, then slowly, the rest of the band joined him, and we were all singing the Sister Sledge song " We Are Family." And it was a fantastic finale for the night.

It was getting late or early in the morning. The streets were empty as most of the crowd were gone. Daylight broke in, and I was exhausted, but Amara was always by my side and asked me to stay overnight. I insisted on returning to my Hotel to rest and promised to replace all the stuff she gave me, including the dress, but she said, "No, my dear Gabriela, they are all some small gifts for you to keep."

I was so tired that I could not even control my emotions, and I felt the rain coming down on me, wetting my precious dress, yet there were only my tears of happiness.

I was touched by her gifts and everything she did to save me. She made that night the best living night of my life. Soon, my surprise Taxi arrived; she hugged me and said, "You are my sister now, and I will see you later after you get some sleep and NO more drinking." Por Favor. "

My tears did not get a rest as I saw her fading away with the street lights; as soon as the car turned on the corner, she was gone. I was smiling from the deepest part of my heart, and my eyes were somehow smiling as well, as I was thinking of the night, but that dream stopped when I heard the Taxi driver's voice asking me to autograph a scarf. Dear god, another one.

I said that in my mind, yet I couldn't say no to him, and I did.

When I arrived at the Hotel, I wanted to pay him, but again he refused to take my money and said: "Goodnight Campeona." I smiled at him and headed to the Hotel's lobby.

I had to stop for a second and rewind my entire day, and I smiled at how it turned out to be one of the best days of my life.

CHAPTER IV

THE GIRL WHO GOT AWAY

I was so happy yet exhausted at the same time. However, that did not mean anything.

When I entered the lobby, I saw plenty of people waiting for me, with the police everywhere.

I was so scared of the scene, and I wanted to avoid them and head straight to my room. However, a tall man with a sharp look on his face and a big mustache, a scary one with such a severe look, was heading my way.

Hola señorita, por favor un minuto!

He was the police chief with two other, much younger officers.

He came to me and asked me to follow him to the dining room hall; then, he invited me to sit down and be calm and quiet.

I wouldn't say I liked the tone of his voice, as he was addressing me as a suspect, and that was also because of my Gypsy fashion. A few minutes later, that crazy rich woman from the elevator entered the hall where they had this interrogation. The moment she laid her eyes on me, she started screaming: La ladrona, la ladrona(The thief, the thief). She was screaming at my face and was rushing towards me, yet the police stopped her from coming any closer and forced her to sit down and be calm as well. The entire staff looked at me, whispering and pointing at me, saying my name, "Oh, Dios mio, esto es Gaby."

The whispering turned louder, and the manager came rushing and said: "What is going on here in this early hour of the morning, and why are the police here?". He arrived to me and said: "My dear Miss Ludwik, is there something wrong?".

The crazy rich woman and the police realized that I was not a thief, and things were so confusing until the Lady started to open up her big mouth and tell the whole story and what I did to her. The chief inspector looked at the Lady, then at me, and asked me if I still had her scarf and if it was wrapped around my waist.

I handed the scarf over to the chief inspector and then apologized to the Spanish Lady, but she couldn't shut up and kept on saying that they should throw me in jail or hang me, or burn me like a witch, cause that is where I belong then she pointed at me and said in Spanish :(Mirala ,se vestia como una gitana). Look at her dressed like a Gypsy, she said. The night staff was laughing, except the hotel manager, who shouted in her face and said in Spanish: "Suficients, usted realmente sabe quien es esta gran dama joven que sigues insultando" or, enough, do you know who is this great Girl that you keep on insulting. He rushed back to his office and came back with very rapid steps with an old newspaper in his hand, that had me on the front page holding the Wimbledon trophy and on the bottom saying: "The new young Wimbledon Champion Gabriela Ludwik" and just put it in her face.

The Lady turned red from her embarrassment as she was reading the article.

She lowered the newspaper off her face and looked at me, then again at the paper, trying to compare what she was reading and the reality of her standing face-to-face with a genuinely famous girl. Suddenly, when she found out about my true identity, she waved the paper in the air, grabbed me, hugged me, and then apologized for her ignorance.

Still, I was somehow ashamed of my foolish act, and I had to kiss her and give her back the scarf from the police officer's hand.

She said in broken English: "I can't take it back; it is my great honor to give it to you as a gift." She was unstoppable with her fast, broken English, expressing her sorrow for what she had put me through with the police; meanwhile, out of nowhere, she invited me to visit her in her place to show her apology in much more appropriate ways.

The police had me sign some papers and waived all the charges.

The chief went to the Lady and said in Spanish: { Next time you call the police, don't say that your life is in danger unless it is true; you've caused a great public disturbance by saying a lie like that, so please think before you rush to a wrong accusation.}

I thanked everyone for their consideration and asked them to let me go to my room as I was exhausted.

The Lady "Isabella," her name returned to me, opened her purse and took out her handkerchief with her initials. And it was pure white silk with hand stitches all over it.

She asked me if I would kindly sign it for her daughter as an autograph.

I couldn't say no to that, and after all the hell I put her through with my foolish act.

So, I signed it, and the moment I reached out to give her back the handkerchief, she pulled me back in her arms and hugged me so dearly. I had the scarf wrapped around my neck again. Also, with her card in my hand, I started heading to the elevator, waving to everyone and thanking the police for the misunderstanding. I apologized to the hotel manager for waking everyone and promised to leave when I got my luggage ready.

I will pay for all the damage that I caused to the hotel. His blue eyes were wide open, and he said: "No way." You can stay as long as you want, and there is no damage.

It is our great honor to have you here in our small hotel, and if you need anything, ask for me. This is the first time we've ever had someone famous, yet with our luck,

we have the most renowned Girl on the planet. I had to stop him and say: It's my honor to be at your place, but I must return to my room. I thanked him again for his kindness and hospitality and apologized again, then waved to everyone as they clapped their hands while I was heading to the elevator. The door opened up, and I had to rush in. My feet were giving up on me, yet I looked at myself in the mirror to acknowledge my beauty and the way Amara made me look.

That was nothing compared to Julio Iglesias's voice singing that song again. El Amor.

The moment the door opened to my floor, I rushed out and straight to my room.

As I closed the door, I went down on the floor, laughing about the entire night and what had happened until now.

I was so tired that I possibly fell asleep on the floor for a long time, as it was night again when I opened my eyes. I've lost track of time but lost the entire day sleeping on the floor.

The room was so dark, and the only light was coming from the street with just enough to see my way. I got off the floor, turned the lamp next to my bed, sat down, and drifted away to yesterday.

I fell back on the bed and stared at the ceiling, watching the reflection of the lights from outside the balcony and wondering about everything happening before yesterday.

Something came to me as a voice from a faraway place, but of course, I didn't think anything of it, so I felt I needed another hot shower to clear my mind from everything.

The fact that I still had traces of alcohol in my system made me strip everything I was wearing piece by piece, leaving a trail of clothes behind me until I was fully naked under the shower.

Another factor of not being fully sober was the shower as I was about to cook myself again with the hot water. Still, this time, I managed to adjust the temperature of the water so quickly and stood under the shower for quite a while, washing everything away.

The bathroom was foggy and steamy, so I couldn't see anything except my way out.

While drying up my hair, the same voice returned to me again, but it was like a voice whispering to look at the mirror. I had to open the bathroom door to air the steam out, yet such a hissing voice drove me crazy, saying: "Follow me, and find me." I had to turn around again to the bathroom, head directly to the mirror, and, to my shocking surprise, something there scared me. There was a faint writing on the mirror.

I couldn't see the words, but quickly, I noticed the crazy idea of creating some extra steam as if I were Indiana Jones trying to read the secret terms that were hidden behind the evil mirror. The only difference between Indy and me was that he burned everything to get the words, yet it was a different method for me. I turn the hot boiling water off the sink and let the water run for a few seconds, and miraculously, the writing appears again like magic.

M.O.N.D. O. ...these were the letters on the mirror.

My feet were shaking, and I was about to lose my balance moving backward away from the mirror, but I managed to hold on to the bathroom's door knob.

My throat was dry, choking, yet my mouth was wide open, and my eyes were also. I felt my heart was about to explode, my eyes were burning, and the tears must fall.

That was my father's real name, oh my dear god...Am I still drunk?

I said in a frightened voice. This is a haunted hotel and a haunted country.

Since I arrived here, there have been so many symbols, voices, signs, and people that made me believe for so many reasons that I should do something about all the unfortunate things that have been happening and appearing to me since my arrival in Spain and Malaga.

My life has always been connected in mysterious ways with my roots in Spain, yet what has been happening to me recently made me believe that the only way to know who I am is to dig deep into the history of my father.

The first thing that jumped into my head was to record everything that happened in his past life.

So, I've decided to write a memoir or simply the story of my father's life.

I shook my head as such an idea would take time, and I'm a girl with no time to spare, but again, it would be a shame not to find out who was actually my father and why he was still hunting me in so many mysterious ways.

I don't believe in witchcraft, nor dark black magic, but that phenomenon was natural, and it's not what they call" the after-effect of the liquor' in my system.

I wonder about crazy things, like that great movie(Ghost). Is his spirit stuck between now and the afterlife? Is it possible to feel his existence even as a ghost in this modern life of mine?

It could be a very slim possibility that his spirit is reaching out to me somehow. I'm going crazy thinking that way, but I can't deny what my eyes saw a few minutes ago. I wanted to prove that I wasn't going crazy, so I jumped on the bed, reaching out for my bag to get the phone to snap a quick picture. I repeated the same thing: I ran the hot water to get some steam out, but unfortunately, nothing happened; there was no writing on the mirror, as it was clean as crystal. I went far back to see if anything would appear, but it was just a desperate failure attempt on my behalf. I was acting like a maniac, blowing steam out of my mouth for desperate results, but I was choking myself to death, and I started coughing like crazy.

The idea was wild, unbelievable, daring, and, most of all, incredibly historical.

I never knew my father very well, yet I'm almost positive I never knew him at all.

I am here and can feel him everywhere as if he is with me in every step.

I wanted to know him closer as if I had been here from the very beginning.

I would love to go back and shadow every step of his life.

I needed more and more. My heart was aching so severely that I felt I had a name, a father, and an identity for the first time.

My sir's name is fake; my last Polish(Ludwik) name is not connected to my stepfather, as he was never a father to me from the very start. My mother's marriage was only for my security; she never loved that man. The fact that he was beating her for money made me afraid and angry at him, yet I was only five years old when he was killed in a car accident, drunk.

I am Gabriela Mondo, and I have all the right to be a pure-blood Spaniard.

I swear on his soul that I will dedicate my life to finding the truth about my birth father, MONDO.

I will be as strong as possible to live his life through my blank pages; I will never say die until the World knows his truth. No matter how ugly or terrifying the truth will be, I will not stop searching the whole wide World to find the missing pages of my life with and without him.

I am beginning a new road, a journey to the unknown.

I must string his life correctly, as I'm sure that my life, without a doubt, is connected to so many unstrung lives, including his life. Malaga is the beginning, and it should be.

His life started here, and where else would it be to find my deep roots in this life except here in Malaga?

I need to get my shit together and find a way to start my research for the absolute truth about who my father was and who I am. So many lies in my life denied exposing the truth about my authentic Self. All I know is that my mother and I are from Poland, and my father passed away before I was even born. How convenient?

There is no history or memory of him from my mother's side, not even a lullaby.

The fact that she wanted me to be able to find my way in life made her sacrifice her memories with my father.

How do I live knowing I had a father who gave his life to me indirectly?

A father who had that look in his eyes to tell me the truth, but yet fate and destiny stripped him away from me. I was torn between two times, the time with and without him.

I've seen you on so many nights and through so many dreams.

Along with so many sunrises, yet with so many missing sunsets.

I love the rain, yet every drop breaks my heart as I've cried over you for so many years and missed you. There were so many candles in my life, with so many missing cakes, and with that, I've hated you. I had so many laughs and yet so many tears; then again, I've forgiven you.

If I live so many years and among millions of tears, my aching heart will always love you. Your scent is in my blood, and your memories are accurate enough to follow you wherever you are. I am a girl who has lost her daddy, so you see, with or without you, I will always be the little Gaby. The silence and tears were the rhythms of the moment until the goddamn phone rang. I was drifting away with my thoughts, and the rest of the World was extremely silent until that bloody phone rang. Hello, WHO IS THIS? I said.

The voice of the hotel manager on the other side sounded very concerned yet hesitant, judging from how I answered the phone.

He said: I'm Fernando, the hotel manager, and I was worried and wondered if I was all right as no one had seen me coming out of my room since last night.

Moreover, he said that the cleaning girl knocked on your door, but you didn't respond, so she'd reported that to me, and I was very curiously worried about you.

I smiled and said, "Thanks for the concern, but I am fine and need rest.

Please send me some food if you want to help me, as I am starving. "

He laughed and said: How hungry are you?

Gaby: I don't eat much but can now eat a whale.

He laughed and said: Well, I will surprise you with our excellent menu, so be ready and thank you again for being here in our hotel. I hung up and started picking up the mess I had all over the room. I never looked closely at the room's condition, as I was sleeping on the floor, and I forgot the terrible shape of my room when I left at night, so I had to fix this room quickly.

It was an image from the past as it reminded me of my old room back home.

They couldn't come to my room with food and see me like that with a towel, so I put on my Adidas black shorts and the red sleeveless T-shirt, saying, "M.E.?".

I have loved that T-shirt since I saw it in Paris a year ago during the French Open tournament, where I lost in the semi-final. I looked around, and I was proud of myself as the room started to look like an actual room for a regular, organized human being. Soon, I heard the knocking on my door, and it was the room service with my food .." Great timing," I said.

When I opened the door, two young guys and three girls pushed tray carts one after another until they filled the room. I was in shock, but again, I never said what kind of food I wanted, so the sweet manager sent me the best of the best from the hotel menu. Wow, you are all great, gracias, gracias a todos ustedes.

I spoke to them as they were leaving, but I went after the young girl, held her hand, and said, "Is there any coffee in this fiesta?

She smiled at me, pointed to the middle part, and said: "The tray has all kinds of drinks and, of course, coffee, too. I let go of her hand and thanked her again. The gang was about to leave my room, yet that nice coffee girl turned around, held the door, and said, "We love you, Campeon..Vamos".

A hidden smile was just a cover of my invisible tear, and I couldn't let her go without a dear hug. She was delighted, shocked by my unexpected reaction, and again she said: You're the best Campeon. I stood before all the trays, and something hit me; oh, my god, what a fool!

I said to myself. I ran to my bag, took a handful of money, ran after them, and stuck my foot inside the elevator door.

And at last, they were there with all surprised, smiling faces. I told them I know my Spanish is terrible, but I would like to accept this money as an appreciation for all your excellent work.

The fact that I had no concept of money, especially at such a moment, made me give them over 300 Euros in scattered bills.

The second I took my foot out of the elevator door, I ran back to my room without even waiting for their response to what I'd just done. I swear that they were screaming with happiness as the elevator was heading down to the lobby.

The people here in Malaga somehow misunderstand me, yet when they realized my identity, they changed utterly towards me. It felt pretty damn good to be acknowledged and belong here, and in such a moment, I didn't care if it was because I was famous or not.

With a closed door, I stood there in silence; then I said with a laugh: "My God, it is so fucking great to be famous."

I started to uncover all the plates, to the last one. I took a few steps back and looked at the plates, each with a golden card tag and the food's name.

Breakfast stuff :(All types of eggs, Spanish omelet as I've never seen before, with sliced tomato, pepper, onion, paprika, and dill. Another plate of grilled burritos with eggs and tomatoes is stuffed with potato and melted cheese. Another plate with deviled eggs with smoked paprika, my favorite, sliced fresh tomato on a bed of lettuce, shredded carrots, and cheese sprinkles. Scramble eggs with mushroom, onion, parsley, tomato, and melted cheese.

Here comes my favorite. Spanish mushroom quiche with excellent stuff in it that I couldn't identify until it ended up in my mouth—another great dish of Scottish eggs.

Oh my God. The next tray was even better. The dinner one. All grilled steak, salmon, shrimp, and monster lobsters that I've never seen. So many different types of shrimp are cooked differently. The main thing I've noticed is the shrimp's size, which makes me wonder and ask myself," Do they feed and raise the Spanish shrimp differently than the rest of the World."

The shrimp were huge but unbelievably wonderful and tasty. The rice was also terrific, yet I had to read the golden cards to learn the names of each type of rice.

Back home, we were more of a potato people, but through my travels, I came to appreciate the test of rice even more. This one said potatoes, Arroz Amarillo, and that one is Caloso with Cod, con gondolas, con bogavante, al caldero, al colds, negro, meloso, banda, and the famous Paella that I've never seen before. The veggie was everything from the field of green.

The desserts were really out of this World. There are so many slices of different types of cakes. Black Forest, Opera, various types of cheesecakes, Tiramisu, The Tarta de Santiago, Crema Catalana, and my favorite of all was the famous Spanish Churros with a cup of hot melted chocolate and more that I've never seen before in my life. Finally, the drinks, and there it is, my coffee. I poured a cup of coffee and sat down, looking at all this food just for me.

I don't even eat that much, as I have to watch my diet and health all the time, but this is a feast, No, a Fiesta, and I can't resist all that anymore. I must take pictures of all that and send them to Mom. I started eating a bit of everything, and finally, I fell on the ground and lay on my back, as I couldn't breeze from the excessive amount of food in my stomach.

Meanwhile, I laughed hysterically and wished my mom could see all that. At last, I was so full to the limit of exploding, yet there was a missing part or an empty tinny spot that needed feeding. When I got off the floor, I remembered that I had bought the top sangria wine (Tres Picos- Garnacha) from the free zone at the airport on my arrival in Malaga.

I went to the closet, which was still in the same bag, wrapped up nicely and ready for me.

My great dilemma was to crack open this baby, as I was not prepared and never ready for any drinks. I was like a virgin when it came to liqueurs.

Last night was my bachelorette party to break free from all the rules and restrictions to stay healthy and fit. I searched the room and my suitcases, but there was no sign of the corkscrew. Here is the part that baffled me much. Why must it have a cork? Why is it not a twist and open? No, it has to be complicated, like shower faucets.

The thing is, I've never been a setback person, taking defeat as an answer or giving up easily on anything in life, so this will not be the end of this dilemma.

I was trying to remember a moment like that, which may be something I've seen in a movie, yet the unknown actress opened up a wine bottle without a corkscrew.

The significant side effect of being stuffed from the food and the frustration of not remembering the name of the movie or even the name of such an actress made me angrier and pissed off.

I froze up for a moment and let my eyes circle the room from all angles, searching for a clue until I found the key to the puzzle.

Where the hell have you been hiding all that time? I said to the stake knife.

I placed the bottle on the dining table and pushed some of the food dishes away to have the space I needed for my mission impossible. I inverted the knife from the top right above the center of the wine cork, and I was thinking of using the screwing method as a wine opener, but even that, I screwed it up so badly that the soft cork started to deteriorate and fall apart in my hand. I pushed my soft palm hard on the knife, and the whole damn pin went entirely inside the bottle, causing the wine to splash all over my face and some on my precious T-shirt, too.

Shit, fuck, puta-bitch. Those were a few of the opening lines of my new song from the hell album that I am about to record in Spain.

I can't believe this shit; what a freaking idiot. I should've called the room service or done things people usually do. But of course, I have to be different, unique, and stupidly stubborn. I said to myself.

Mission Impossible went to a bloody Sangria disaster. This situation bothers me, Tom Cruise. Where are you now when I needed you the most, Prick bastard? Maverick: I said all that with anger.

He is still my favorite actor of all time, and I don't care about what other people say blablablabla. Who can make movies like him? No one.

I'm also a big fan of 007.

It would've been a great factor if he came into my room saying: Hi, Gaby, it's Tom Cruise at your service.

I had to dump the blame on someone, which is typically what we do as tennis players.

We never admit that it was our fault, even though it is always in our hands and control, but when things go wrong, and we lose a point, a set, or even a match, we have to look for someone else to blame but ourselves. So many players, men and girls, do stupid things, making me wonder about them. Some toss their rackets, yelling at their coaches; others smash the shit out of the poor racket, then they point to their team, yelling at them, waving their hands with all kinds of gestures that it was their fault for losing the point of the match.

I'm not like that on the court, but right now, I am acting like those idiots.

The bottle is opened, and that's all I've wanted, regardless of the shit I had to endure.

I grabbed an empty glass, the Sangria bottle, and then my laptop to start the journey of the unknown.

The story of MONDO.... my father's story.

I asked myself what it would be; it couldn't be just MONDO.

It must have a connection with his life, and everybody was involved.

The name of my story, or his story, must be connected with the string of other lives.

Unstrung Lives is the name of my future book.

My father is the stringer of their unstrung lives, and he's got to be the one with the answers and the mysteries. I head out to the terrace, and after all that chaos, I put everything on the tiny white glass table nicely and pour a glass of my precious wine.

Wow, this wine tastes great and is worth every penny; however, with such a relaxing mode, I noticed the edge of the balcony and how it was designed, and that for sure caught my attention to get up again and enjoy the view.

I have to express my great admiration to the architect who designed this magnificent corner, as it is structurally white, shaped as half a circle or a Crescent, then it cuts going up with the shape of a seat, then curved up again as a leaning lounge.

That shape is designed for anyone to sit there, lean back, look deeply to the horizon with the magical view of the Mediterranean Sea, and forget about the rest of the World and die in peace. A significant part was also designed with protective rod iron black fence bars shaped with growing vine leaves. It is all made of iron but is wonderfully done as a piece of art.

I lay down carefully, positioning my body on such a comfy curve with the wine glass in my hand; then, I gently placed it above my stomach and floated away with the view.

The thing with me is that I've always been on edge, fidgety, snappy, irritable, rational sometimes, and impatient, as I wanted tomorrow before the present.

My movements from such a comfortable spot were the cause of all that, as if I wanted to have the whole damn World in my possession in such a tight spot.

I was up and down, getting the bottle and back and forth with the laptop, then again changed my mind to just the bottle without the fancy glass. Oh my dear god, what a freakin nightmare. At last, I am back in such a corner with the entire wine bottle on my stomach and nothing else.

The three of us were like floating shadows that blended into one.

The moon had never tested a wine until now.

The great seduction of the moonlight, the bottle of wine on my chest, and the cold, fresh breeze relaxed me. The three of us were flirting with each other sip after sip until the fancy bottle of wine found a home in my stomach. The moon's reflection above the sea was a gate about to be open to something magical.

The wine and the view began dazzling my eyes and head, and I couldn't resist the weight on my eyelid as they closed my mind. I went somewhere far, back in time, and started drifting away. The moonlight was fading away from my mind and quietly taking me away to a faraway place. I needed my father's company so severely in such a magical moment.

I had to get off that curve and head back to the chaise lounge, and I just leaned back, staring at an infinity of stars that gathered for something incredible to happen.

To complete the journey to the unknown, I had to run inside and change my wet T-shirt, yet I was so crazy looking for another one to replace it.

The voice came back and started pounding in my ears, whispering, helping me choose as I was uncertain what to wear. Standing in the middle of the room, topless, looking everywhere for a clue, I remembered the small green bag.

I opened it, and it had some old stuff from my father yesterday—the only T-shirt.

It is my mom's favorite T-shirt, and it was in my green bag. The truth and absolute truth is that it wasn't my mom's T-shirt but my father's.

She never stated the story behind that shirt, but I remember her wearing it occasionally whenever she was lonely and sad. The shirt is old, yet my mother kept it in a very decent condition. The unique part was that it still had his scent and an old Adidas blue T-shirt.

The first time I saw her wearing it, I asked her about the meaning of that symbol and why she was wearing an old T-shirt.

She said it is the brand with the three stripes, and it's German, and they call it Adidas.

I was a young girl, so I never bothered to ask so many questions about such a matter because the more I asked, the more she got sad. My naked body finally found the right cover to fulfill my emptiness. I returned to my chaise lounge, stretched my long legs, lay back, and pulled the T-shirt up to cover my nose and merge with his scent.

Again, I finished another bottle of wine so fast, and I had to break my promise to Amara and everyone else to stay away from liquor.

I wanted more, as at such a moment, I felt the need for a drug or anything that would allow me to float or fly. That fiesta had a small mini bar with more liquors, and without any more complications, I looked for my evil Vladimir mug and started drinking every bottle on that tray. I breathed in and out, letting his scent penetrate my nose, lungs, heart, and soul.

I wanted to be the wind beneath his wings to take me away to his World.

Everything was extraordinarily set and ready for me to begin the unknown journey.

From a far corner of the room was a whispering voice with the tone of an angel singing a familiar song. I was blending to a different dimension, and I couldn't remember if I played any songs on my iPod or, I should say, one of my father's gifts to me while back in New York.

That iPod is my life, as it has some of his favorite Music and songs.

I remember very well the day he got me this iPod, as it was a gift from him after I won my second-round match in the U.S. Open. I was somehow surprised by such an expensive gift from such a stranger.

The iPod had few songs; my favorite one was "Don't You Forget About Me by Simple Mind"...I do love that song very much, but again then, the song was just a good song with no connection nor attachments to my soul, but now in his absence, I feel as if he wanted to tell me something through that song.

Somehow, the connection between his soul and mine could be linked with symbols and signs, but above all, Music. If I had to tell his story to the world, I would have our common secret language to fill the gap between the lines, and such a language is music.

I will use music as my background throughout the lines of his story.

As I imagine it, writing his story will be my biggest challenge.

Meanwhile, I will need a miracle to find the hidden secrets of his actual life story.

The song was almost like an echo from a faraway place.

"The Girl Who Got Away, by one of my favorite artists...Dido started to play by itself as if some magical forces controlled my fate and everything around it.

I was so damn bloody convinced that she'd written this particular song just for me and only for me to cope with my status and terrible condition of such loneliness.

The words started to penetrate my soul, and I felt as if I was floating with the words to that faraway place.

I want to move with the seasons, go with the flow, take it easy, and let stuff go.

I like to sleep like a baby, rise with the sun, kick it all back, and get nothing done.

I want to make this day the longest with a warmth that delivers happiness.

If only for today, I want to be the Girl who got away.

The lover who loved, the dancer who danced to the last song.

I don't want to take sides; I don't want to make sense.

I want to be alone; I don't want to hide.

The heart is more significant than the head.

My tears were coming down when she sang the last lines as they were the images of my reflections on how I wanted this so badly to be real.

I want to follow you but not be led, if only for today.

I want to be the Girl who got away.

A force from such a world attracted me to the clouds, as if I had been lifted closer and closer to the gate between my World and that mysterious World from the past.

The light of a bright star from the sky was tingling my eyes, yet I couldn't look away as if such a mysterious star was hypnotizing me. The whisper of a shadow traveled to my ears with magical words: "Your wish will be granted.

The speed of all the movement around me made me feel like I was being pushed, dragged, or lifted to something magical.

My father's scent and soul blend with mine as one, so strangely, so deep.

A light, cold breeze air blew my hair, yet it felt like a soft kiss on my cheeks.

I closed my eyes, hoping for something magical to happen as that breeze gained power and speed. The lighting struck the far horizon of the Mediterranean Sea, and the first drop of water landed above my nose as a sign of the coming rain.

The gusting wind was pushing me backward toward the room, yet with the second striking lightning above the water's surface, the ghost's shadow was so evident in front of my eyes, and the myth became a reality, glowing in the dark of the night.

I was reaching out to the ghost's hand to pull me to the opposite way of the gusting wind.

I felt him closer to me, holding my hand and leading the way to the past.

My eyes were closed as if I was saying so long about this cruel world until we both faded away entirely as one to an unknown, mysterious world.

The last lighting was so powerful that the night's darkening turned into a phenomenal flash that brightened the horizon. I vanished into a new unknown world, leaving behind just an empty chase lounge with the memory of the Girl who got away.

CHAPTER V

EL NINO MAGICO 1970

The sun blended in with the first sign of daylight for a new magical day.

Waves were breaking down and rushing, accelerating to the shore and providing the cool breeze air; yet in the far deep water, there were still traces of silver grey light caused by the reflection of the dying moon. The far side of the Mediterranean Sea had a magnificent view as the clouds were clearing off the sky with degrees of the sun shades, which manipulated the scene with a magical sight of the Malaga shore.

The cool air blew gently towards that small part of the world as if Neptune was blessing the sea to breeze for a lovely and possibly magical day.

The small fishing boats swung with the light swell spreading over the water's surface as if dancing alone in great harmony.

In that part of the world, the journey of a great story is about to begin.

Once upon a time, a very young boy was full of life and hope and was blessed with a great gift. His light green eyes were only the world that expressed the present and the future of a beautiful, passionate human being.

The young boy had a unique gift of adaptation, which was unusual and indescribable.

He was able to adapt and gain knowledge at a swift pace within a very short time.

Day by day, his gift and talent were blossoming in a very unique way.

He absorbed everything around him, and through the years, he became confident to turn it around and master his signature invention.

On such a magical day, he was walking back home to his mother's place after a long school day, whistling and hopping on and off the long sidewalk.

His heart was an infinity of life and electricity. On such a day, he felt that something magical would cross his path, with the possibility of merging into his fantasy world of being the ghostly boy who brings life, laughter, and, after all, love to everyone who crosses his path.

He was confident it would be the most incredible day of his life.

His heartbeats increased rapidly, yet his feet were stumbling, dragging as if unsure how to begin his journey to the unknown. He created a phobia of such a place in his troubled mind, so he had to stop and stare deeply with fear and hesitation at the long, Long sidewalk.

It was the same daily thing he had to do when reaching that long, wide sidewalk. Such fear and the complexity of his strange phobia made him change his mind about taking that road heading back home.

He felt that such a long road was typical in his mind, yet it covered a mystery he couldn't resist. He had to convince himself to be more positive and brave, exploring and conquering his fear.

He must challenge and overcome his demons and desperation.

The fact that he was also known for his dairy ability to invade the world of doubts and fear made him start moving his feet, step by step, slowly along the sidewalk, until he'd arrived at his favorite and scary part simultaneously, a sidewalk spot. He stopped and let his ears listen to the music. The truth behind the music in his ears was only a matter of his mind's imagination.

It was a special kind of music that made him wonder about the composer behind it.

He closed his eyes and continued, following the rhythm behind the green and white fences covered with vines of all colors. The flowers blossomed between the vines, filling the gap to complete the most remarkable natural piece of art his eyes had ever seen.

The light breeze of the cool air was like the grand Picasso rising from the dead, touching the canvas with a magical brush for a new masterpiece.

The light, cool breeze was slightly blowing, simply brushing and shaking the weak stem leaves, allowing them to fall one by one to the ground, creating a magnificent carpet of colorful leaves on the wide sidewalk. The private sports club he passes by every day after school is just a few feet from his sight. The same daily thing he had to do when he reached that part of the sidewalk was to stop, be very silent, and listen to the music to his ears, which was somehow known as the kids' laughter of having fun playing.

Listening to the boys and girls from behind that fence, laughing while they were playing different games and sports, was the actual music that he heard, and many, many times, he wished to sing or play along with them and feel the same way they do. He always wanted to get closer and closer and peek through the thick fence, but the dense green shield matts and the green vines were adding more impossible gates to his eyes and wish.

The long, high gates resembled the impossible line between his fantasy and reality, which can never merge and be one. Because he was a speedy learner, he could read adult books, not for his age, yet again without the knowledge of his mother.

Reading so many words made him capable of feeling the time, the moments, and the locations that authors implanted through their pages. He became very well aware of different types of philosophies and made his philosophical theory about life and many other things.

A fantasy is an imaginary dream that can never exist, yet he felt that if he could force his mind to slice those fantasy dreams into tiny, small plans. He believed that fantasy is a parallel world that moves with everyone's life, and with a miracle, hope that may be, the two worlds may collide in someone's destiny. Time and only with time, with a strong will and inspiration, did he know that one day he might bring these dreams to life.

His ability to believe made him stronger and stronger through the hand of time.

The cruel reality killed his sense of imagination but did not kill the other implications of hearing the fun that different species were still experiencing behind the green gates.

As he was accepting his fate of being the kid from the other world, the one behind the gates, the one with no right to dream, the kid from the low-income family that can only get what life may toss at him in crumbs, moreover and somehow a strange force from above the clouds, dragged him to a new world to deny and reject all that. In such a doubtful and indecisive moment, he wonders about the existence of God.

He was always looking for answers that no one could ever provide, but again, in his heart, he'd felt that if God wanted him to know, he could've given him some signs or maybe talked to him at least. His doubts about God were odd, as he comes from a traditional catholic gypsy bloodline. He used to skip going to church with his mother with so many different excuses.....sick, tired, or unwilling to be part of something that he couldn't understand at a young age. It was a mystery to his mother, yet she was always linear and straightforward with him regarding what to believe. With all that in mind, he was so upset passing by this road every day because of the unanswered questions and doubts. Somehow, he knew it was the only common link for his questions, but he needed to know when or how.

The only common shattered thoughts and his reality are if he can honestly believe in God's existence, as his mother always said to him occasionally. Suddenly, the wind started to pick up, lifting the leaves off the sidewalk as if it were the sign he'd been waiting for.

He observed the leaves taking off, forming a spinning circle as a tornado, flying up to the sky in a group. He wished that whatever this phenomenon was, with some miracles, lift him to the clouds as well, but he was standing there alone on the sidewalk, following with his eyes the departure of the leaves to such an unknown place.

A red leaf attracts his eyes' attention more than the other flying ones.

He was profoundly focusing on that one alone as if it were a special leave on a mission to the unknown. The red leaf kept flying higher and higher, trying to follow or catch up with the others until he couldn't see it anymore. Meanwhile, the sun's rays were clearing up the sky from all the doubts and clouds, and in a second, as the sun became more vital than ever, he was utterly blinded as it was blocking his vision and broke his trail for the red precious leaf.

He put his hand above his eyebrows to block the sun, but something unexpected happened.

The sign from above was finally coming down to answer all his mysterious questions.

A strange object was coming down at him from above, but with the sun teasing his little green eyes, he couldn't tell or recognize the identity of such an object.

The flying object hit a tree branch and bounced back, then landed in front of his tiny feet.

He took a few steps from such an object, yet he wasn't afraid to examine the unfamiliar yellow fuzzy ball. He went down on his knee and started touching the ball with his fingertips, and when he became confident, he picked it up and placed it on his palm.

The ball was so strange to him with all the yellow fuzzy hair and soft texture.

He kept flipping it, turning it over and over, then placing it on his cheeks and closing his eyes. The pale yellow hair tingled his face warmly as if he were holding a bird.

He stretched his palm wide open with the ball lying flat there.

Meanwhile, the golden sun's rays blended in, changing the yellow into gold.

He closed his eyes and drifted to an unknown world he couldn't describe.

His wild imagination took him so far away to a strange place with many people cheering his name in a loud, uncontrolled way. The only sad part was when the cheers started to fade away, another soft voice traveled from his fantasy world, silencing the cheers, saying: "Will you throw the ball back, please? "

He couldn't understand either what that voice was or where it came from, and despite all the languages that he'd learned at school, that one was very unusual to his ears.

He shook his head to return to reality, but he was happy that he still had the golden ball in his palm and that it wasn't just one of his fantasies or dreams.

Again, and this time, the voice was much louder, which put fear and doubt in his little heart as he couldn't move and froze like a statue. The voice said in Spanish: Por favor tire la pelota hacia atras......Will you please toss the ball back?

This time, he understood that the golden ball belonged to someone else, and the voice wanted it back, yet he thought it was the sign that came to him from the sky, but again, he was very wrong. He strolled, dragging his feet, cutting through the scattered falling leaves, and going to his path like the long-missing prince who had just found his way home.

The boy stood before the gate, but the mysterious gate was almost invisible to his eyes as the leaves, vines, and branches covered the door's structure.

He put his hand on the vines covering the fence, trying to make a gap to enable him to see through, but he couldn't see anything. The third time he heard the voice, he got scared and started stepping back slowly away from the fence and preparing himself to run.

A magical small door opened up, and he couldn't guess that there was a hidden door from the dense vines covering the fence. When that door opened, he heard that voice saying in Spanish, "Don't be afraid, young boy, please come closer."

He looked at her with his wild green eyes, and for a second, he hesitated to make a big decision. His mother's words came to his ears:" Don't trust strangers, especially women.

Mondo: Am I still dreaming, and is all this just in my mind? If it is a dream, why do I still have this thing in my hand, and what should I do?

His final decision is to run fast away from this place, yet on the contrary, another moment of hesitation makes him freeze like a statue. Her open hand was that sign that made him change his mind, and step by step, he was inside and behind the magical gate.

He stopped, frozen, and turned his head back to acknowledge that he did cross the line between fantasy and reality. He smiled in his mind, accepting that God does exist after all, and he listens to his wishes and dreams. The door was just the beginning of an arched tunnel of green vines with some flowers that bloomed in between, and the scent of the tunnel was mesmerizing to his nose. The path was all green, with some grass mowed perfectly. Such a path led to stepping stones that were also covered with grass, and on the side, there were big stones well organized in a very symmetric way, and in between the rocks some magnificent flowers.

Some of them were red and yellow, but the ones that attracted his attention the most were the miniature, deep purple roses that his eyes had never seen before until such a moment.

The arrangements of the flowers were as if he was heading to paradise.

He was following her and was deeply hypnotized by his surroundings.

The truth behind his disbelief was her white clothes and the shape of her body as well.

He followed her until she turned to the right, then she stopped and said: We're almost there; keep going.

Mondo said to himself: I must be dreaming!!!!

She opened a mystical gate that led to a vast, long green garden, and in the middle, there was a long shallow pool or a fountain with water sprinklers on both sides.

The design was like the famous Alcazar gardens in Cordoba.

In this part of the world, it is well known as Andalusia. The architectural designs and the imprints of the Islamic culture are everywhere in Andalusia.

This is the last unexpected place for me to see such beauty from such a defined artistic design from such a culture. The golden redfish were swimming in such a long pool, and I was mesmerized by the entire garden until she said: Now you can enter.

Mondo: I must be dreaming, but I will go along with such a dream before my mother spoils my dream for the last call to prepare for school.

She opened another gate that led to a strange and unique place I'd never seen before.

It was the first time in his life to witness a tennis court.

He stood there frozen, yet his eyes looked around, observing the new world of lines, net, and red clay. In his mind, he was wondering: What is this place?

Is this the place of my new life in Paradise?

The woman that led him to this place pointed to a corner with a group of people wearing all white, and then she said to him: Well, all you have to do is to raise your hand with that ball in your hand to indicate that you have a ball for them to use and someone will come to claim it. She patted his hair nicely and then left.

He raised his hand with the ball as a sign for someone to come and claim the ball.

In reality and only in his mind, he lifted his hand to announce his presence and, with such a magical fuzzy yellow ball, told the world that, at last, he'd just arrived.

By fate and determination, his destiny will be blended with the red clay as one, yet the first alphabet of his unwritten magical journey will be right here in this place.

At such a moment, he knew that this was the location and place that would turn his life upside down. A hazy shadow of a young girl was heading his way, yet the sun blocked his vision, and he couldn't see her face. He raised his right hand to block the sun again; meanwhile, his heartbeats were racing each other, and his breathing was not enough for the oxygen to fill up his lungs to accept that it was not a dream but a pure reality.

Mondo had to open his mouth to increase the amount of oxygen to help his heart control its beats. The anxiety of all that was caused by the appearance of the shadow of the mystery girl. She was not just a girl but an angel in a white dress.

A girl with the face of an angel is just standing in front of him with a smile that mesmerizes his little green eyes. The most beautiful face he'd ever seen was standing in front of him, with her red hair waving like fire, yet her blue eyes reminded him that she was the one from paradise who visited him in his wild dreams. She fell on her knees, looked into his green eyes, and said softly with a smile, "Hola."

He smiled at her and said: "Hola."

She wrapped her arms around me, and I felt at home.

I never knew that she would be the one to hold my heart. She walked with me, sat me down on a green bench, opened my hand to release the ball, and said in poor Spanish: "Just relax and let go of the ball.

I was blind to everything around us until I opened my eyes to see her face and, more deeply, her eyes. My staring and concentration at her blue eyes helped me find a few words, so I said in Spanish: "What is this place and (pause) who are you"?

She said: I am Anna and this is called a clay tennis court.

People come here to play and have great fun. However, sometimes, you get to see and meet someone extraordinary in a special glowing moment that is not planned or expected.

Mondo whispered to himself: When I opened my eyes this morning and felt the scent of the Mediterranean Sea blowing up my hair to the sky, I thought something special would come my way in mysterious ways.

Anna: "Now, it is your turn. "What is your name, and how old are you?

I was still stuck with my dreams and imagination and never answered her.

She looked at me and said with a beautiful smile: Do you understand me? As I stated, my name is Anna, but what is yours?

I felt as if someone had smacked me on my head, and suddenly, I was back, yet still staring at her blue eyes. The silence was killing her, yet she was patient until I moved my lips, saying: "My name is Mondo, and I am(pause) 10 years old."

She gently took the ball off my hand, then walked backward a few steps, staring at me, and said: "Mondo, hmmm...Why do I have a feeling that your unique name will be carved in my head for a long time?

Moreover, you will enjoy being here. Also, deep in my heart, I believe you will have the world in your hands someday... Wow...What a name.

She repeated my name, "Mondo. "... Meanwhile, the way she said it was very strange to my ears, as if she was enchanting them. She smiled at me, tilting her head to the left and right with the ball in her hand as if she were tailoring me a suit.

Then she made that funny noise...HMMMM.

She turned around and walked away slowly, so elegantly as a dancer.

She went to a small box behind the baseline, yet I did notice that she turned her head to peek at me again. She had long, attractive legs, and the fact that I was well aware of the anatomy of a girl made me judge that she was very special to my young eyes.

She returned with a cold bottle of Coca-Cola, and with the heat in the air, the moisture was dripping off the bottle, wetting her hand and dripping down slowly on the red clay, dripping like weeping tears.

She handed it to me and said: "Here you go. Mondo, enjoy the coke and let your eyes see the magic of this sport."

She asked me to follow her to a green bench, and she ran back to her bag, got me a cool towel, spread it on the hot bench, and said, "Now, sit down and watch the magic."

She was right about the magic of this place and the sport as well.

I felt this moment was just a dream, but if I could continue living this dream, my life would never be the same again. Mondo's eyes were moving fast all around the place, observing everything. His gift of adaptation was highly active in every detail around him, even the direction of the wind and how fast it blew.

The clay, the net, the green posts, the white lines, the players with white clothes and sneakers, and Anna. The magic of such a place fascinated him, as the players were having a great time, and all their movements were something very new to him to experience. His gift did not need an invitation to adapt and learn what he saw.

The sun was flirting with his long eyelashes, forcing him to obey the power of dreaming and exploring an unknown territory. It was clear that I had been here before, yet my mind trembled from the confusion and the disbelief. He had to close his eyes once more and start dreaming, yet this time, he was sure it wouldn't be just a dream, as if he could know what he wanted for his life. In such a hazy dream, he sees himself conquering the world of tennis with his talent and new invention.

He sees the magic of his accomplishments in his life and after death.

He sees people's faces; some smile and others are in tears.

He sees laughter, tears, angels, and demons of life and death.

The dream commenced with her saying: "Well, Mondo, do you want to play?

That was the voice of young Anna inviting me to feel the magic, and nothing was brighter than my white teeth smiling back at her from such excitement of being part of this world.

He was too young to comprehend the significant impact on him, listening to her voice, language, hair, scent, and beauty. Reaching her magic as if she were from a different yet forbidden world was beyond his limits.

CHAPTER VI

THE REINE OF LIGHTS

In such a magical moment, the sun blinded my sight, and I had to close my eyes but not my ears. There was a hissing secret poem that traveled from a different universe to my ears, enchanting words of a poem that I couldn't either understand or know where the words were coming from. I couldn't resist the wish of listening and listening to such a voice, the words that came to me from a different time and world that I could not describe, yet it was so clear to me as if I had been there before. All I had in mind was one thing...listening to the poem and her words and imagining the words sailing on a floating ship to this unknown fantasy place.

I closed my eyes and opened my ears, and at last, the words of such a poem were moving in front of me as a mist.

High in the sky, far from an eye.

A world of lightness, a world of mysteries.

A hidden star with its flare bright through the nights.

It never sets and never dies.

I saw her light in my sleep, and with one look, I was ready for a flight.

A strange attraction comes from her world of affections.

The bright and light were signed from her world of lights.

I opened my eyes from within my dream, on a voice to command me to open the gates of choice and climb the mountain of love and glory.

High on that mountain, laying a Reine, selling dreams, and drying tears.

Life shines from her eyes, with hair that flares passion and desire.

Her dreams were treasures to those who lost their faith and pleasure.

She came to me and smiled at me.

She touched my lips with her magical fingertips and kissed me softly and slowly and slowly.

I felt her kiss as the heaven I missed, and in a secret sound, she whispered the words.

Love is all you need.

My world is bright and made of light, while yours is dark and full of fears and doubts.

"So listen to me while you're kneeling before me."

The space is so calm and quiet when my star is bright at night.

On a night when the moon's magic hypnotizes all your sights, look up and wish for a flight to where your love and dreams were always hidden.

There you will find my world of light, and there I will be, deep in your mind, I can only be found. You will hear my deep and loud sound when your heartbeat pounds. So far from here, it is better for you and me until my nights melt away all your fears and doubts.

Far away, until your gate of darkness will crash on my gate of light.

I will gift you magical abilities that you may not understand, yet with patience, you will understand everything in time, so don't be scared to use them, as they will become your secret and hidden new identity.

Remember, my gifts are only for you, and they are secrets, so again, with time, you'll learn how to bend them to your wish and command.

Mondo, you must never forget that if you ever need me, you must be true to your heart and believe in me; then I will be there for you.

I was so transparent and almost hung up between two parallel Universes.

I wanted to stay, but she ordered me to leave, and I couldn't see her face or hear her voice as she faded away from my mind. The last thing I recall was her magical rays of light as if they were merging from her body to mine, and somehow, in a very sudden and unexpected move, a stream of light struck my forehead like lightning, and then I was blind. I was down on the red clay as I'd collapsed, not knowing how nor when.

I was shaking, but I was still hung between two different universes.

Mondo, Mondo... Are you here with me...Open up your eyes.

The echo was traveling from far away, yet it felt so close to me that I felt my body shaking by her hands.

Mondo, my dear God, please come back, come back.

My long eyelashes were trembling and flapping like butterfly wings, struggling with a certain kind of gravity, fighting to find the power to fly again. My eyes were gradually opening up, and the light was still in my eyelid, trying to clear my sight, so I had to wipe off the sleep and feel the moment again.

Finally, I had my eyes wide open, and all I could see was the true blue of her eyes, as if the sea was blending in her soul. I couldn't take my eyes off hers, so I kept looking at her blue eyes and nothing else. A strange driving force merged into my body and soul.

I knew I was dreaming at such a moment, yet something was different about me; something struck me so hard. It felt so natural and not just a dream.

My face was generating a special kind of glow as if that fantasy world of mine touched my inner soul, blending deeply from within my blood, and it felt as if I was reformed yet recreated into a new person. My mind spun at the speed of light, trying impossibly hard to understand the phenomena that struck me. I wonder if I was just a daydreamer and the vast mind of imagination had captured my mind. I wonder if my entire day is just a dream, and I am still in bed, and all this was just a beautiful fantasy in my dream mind.

The only truth about all this can be quickly revealed if I open my eyes again to know that I am living the Fantasy, and if it is true, the Fantasy will be reality.

The moment I opened my eyes, I felt that if I was somehow, mysteriously, transformed into a new, different person, much more mature than my age, much more knowledgeable and aware of things that I didn't even know existed.

The blood that runs through my veins has a new formula that generates an extraordinary power that I will yet discover. I felt a unique glow on my face, as if that mystical vision of mine had something to do with all the changes I was going through right now. I knew who I was but did not know who I had become.

There were doubts, confusion, and a real magic out of me.

I felt a sort of sharp pain on my front head as If a real lightning had stuck me.

She let go of my shoulder, stepped a few steps back, and said tremblingly, "Are you... all right, Mondo?".

I started to breeze in and out, trying to energize my blood with fresh oxygen to help me feel normal again before I came to this place. My white smile was somehow a definite answer to Anna's fear, and then I said: "Si estoy bien," I am sorry; I meant to say I am fine.

She was on her knees as the red clay was soft as a baby's face, but when I smiled at her and said that in English, she stood up and stated: "Drink your coke, maybe that will cool you off, as you look hot from the heat."

Anna talking to herself: I am 16 years old, almost double this kid's age. Yet, there is something incredibly fascinating about his face and entire look, as if he glows some magic or a strange spell attraction I have never felt before. I can't describe why I was sweating inside as I talked and whispered to myself, expressing my strange anxiety towards this kid.

Mondo. The peculiar thing is that he understood my words in English and replied in English, too. I am overheated from the sun as well.

Anna: "May I have some of your Coke, please... I grabbed the bottle off his hand, but it wasn't enough to cool me off, and I had to run back to the ice box and get two more, then run back and sat down next to him, drinking the sweet sparkling syrup of energy called Coca-Cola.

I was racing him to finish my bottle, but the scariest thing was noticing him wiping the last drop of Coke off his lips with his tongue. His lips, for a kid, were highly erotic, as they were shaped differently, and so I had to close my eyes and clear my sick mind from this insane infatuation. I was denied and shut down as my other me encouraged the continuation of dreaming of his lips and wished that my lips would catch that last sweet drop of Coke and bring it back to his lips for him to judge and compare the better sweet of either the Coke.

Or Me.

STOP IT...God damn it......" Anna ordered her mind to do so."

Anna: I've wanted to ask you, but wait, it seems that you were about to say something, and I was rushing to say something to you, but you can say what you want to say first.

No, You asked me what you were about to ask, and I will wait for my turn." Mondo replied, but this time in English.

Anna: Well, I wanted to ask you, and I mean it in a heartfelt way, as you worried me in the last few minutes. My most profound concern was the shaking and trembling of your body, as if something terrible was happening inside your little body.

You were somewhere else, not here in this world, and then you came back, and then you were shaking, trembling as if you were possessed.

I swear that it was evident that your body was right here sitting on this bench, but on the other hand, I felt that you were gone too far away, and somehow, I couldn't get you back to me.

I mean to this world, so I was shaking your body, trying to bring you back to me.

I am so sorry again.

My dear God, why do I keep referring to and repeating? To Me.

I must get a grip on my sick emotions and act appropriately.

Was it some seizure you get occasionally? Are you all right?

Mondo was watching her lips moving up and down in silence, and with all of her confused questions, he wasn't paying any attention to a word she said but only enjoying the movements of her lips. He also adapted the reshaping of her words with her lips and how they move, and with that, he became a speedy learner of her English words.

Mondo talked to himself, saying: It was something new to me, something I had never experienced or even understood. I'm just a 10-year-old, almost 11, poor boy from Malaga; my life only evolved with boys from the school or boys from my football team.

The only females that I've known were my mother and my aunt.

I never had a girlfriend or even understood all the stuff on TV about all those things, so-called love and intimacy.

I had excellent tutoring from my aunt about the things between boys and girls, but never with the extremity of the real stuff. This is something new, and I wonder if such a scary change in me could've also had a different effect on my mind. I had no choice but to answer her for many reasons and, most of all, to be cautious so she would not notice my constant staring infatuation with her moist, erotic lips.

Mondo: I am fine, and actually, I feel way better than when I first arrived at this place; however, to answer your strange question about the seizure and the shaking of my body, it was only because of you.

Anna: "What do you mean ...because of me?

Mondo: "Well, you were shaking my entire body so roughly hard, and I was just trying to breeze the air and inhale the scent of this place and feel the little flying molecules of the red clay touching my face.

I was dreaming, and that was all ."

Anna: "Dreaming, and also how did you ...I mean ... Where and when did you learn to speak English like that ?."

Anna: "I am entirely shocked, but I would say more fascinated and incredibly astonished at your ability to speak English fluently.

First, you gave me the impression that you can't speak any language other than Spanish, but now, I don't believe it or understand it.

Mondo: I never said that I could not understand your words, but I also never said that I don't speak your language either, yet you've assumed so."

Mondo had an intense, sharp, serious look on his face.

The strange transformation allowed him to understand and speak different languages, and again, the new gift of adaptation was still a mystery to him to know how to use it.

His dark, thick eyebrows were lifted by some discomfort by Anna's remarks about speaking the language that made him say to her: I am maybe a young boy, Possibly, Yet for sure, and probably in your eyes, you might see a poor Spaniard student who's trying to understand life with whatever complex that surrounds it, but I am not that ignorant to comprehend your words in English or any other language for that matter.

I can explain it more scientifically if that would make sense to you, so please allow me to do so. It is growing inside of me, and it is a fact. I have no control over it, yet I have a simple scientific explanation. The Cochlea changes the vibrations from my middle ear into the nerve signals to my brain. However, those signals change to something significantly different as the vibrations alter the call to my brain with whatever language.

Finally, my brain changed everything so I could hear and speak the new wording.

Mondo: Wait for a second. What the hell did I say to her?

How did I know all that?

Who the hell Am I?

Anna looked at him, observing such a strange glow in his eyes. She had to look down at the clay while talking to him, avoiding looking directly into his eyes until he interrupted her confusion. Then she said more in Spanish this time: "Mirame, estoy bien. " I mean, look at me, I'm fine.

Anna: This kid is not for real, and there is something extremely mysterious about him, but I will go along with him for the moment. He is a Spaniard who is only ten, so how did he speak English like that?

The scientific explanations he could've learned from school, and that won't surprise me, but in fact, what surprised me the most was his accent; it was a fuking British accent.

I took a long, deep breath and said once more to Mondo in Spanish:" It appears that you are somehow shy with pride, and I do understand that entirely, but what just took place in the last few minutes is your secret or business, but I am just a little bit concern about your health, so if you are excellent and cooled off, maybe we can have some fun and learn how to play Tennis. "

Mondo: I want to clarify a straightforward thing that neither you nor I will ever understand. My ears are connected to my brain, yet something did happen to me, and I can't explain it for the two of us to comprehend in plain language.

The sound waves inside my ears transform into my brain, yet there is a strange thing as if it is a device that translates any language to my brain, and directly the brain sends a new corrected wave, and I can understand and speak another language.

Please don't push me for more details as I don't have any answers.

Anna: I'm impressed with the ability that you claim to possess.

However, I won't go deep and pretend that you're just a fast book reader, almost a genius, and that could explain the phenomena you possess.

Anna thought: My Spanish was very poor, but he was an extremely bright kid, and he understood every word as if he was reading my mind before I said the words."

Mondo smiled and said: You need to go back to school and learn to speak Spanish properly, but if I end up liking you(pause), Hmmm, I may teach a lesson or two.

He laid down his school bag, removed his school jacket, placed them on the bench, and started strolling in her shadow to the baseline. He began to roll up his shirt's long sleeves until it looked like a short-sleeved shirt. His skinny, long arms were exposed to her, yet she smiled and said, let's see how bright this kid can be on my tennis court. Anna was still trying to figure out how and where he learned to speak her language like that, but being in his shadow, she'd let her wondering go for the moment and maybe enjoy a good time with him on the red clay.

The fact that he was still shaking and afraid made her stop him to calm him down by rubbing his shoulders and, at last, handing him a tennis racket.

The wooden Wilson racket was terrific with the white stings.

However, she had the grip wrapped with a soft cloth layer like a cut-off towel. I start feeling every part of the racket: the frame, the long neck, and the grip handle. I was almost caressing the racket as if I had a girl wrapped around my arm, feeling her soft, long hair, brushing my fingertips gently through her hair until I reached her skull. My fingertips moved smoothly over the strings that looked to me momentarily as lines of lives that were put together in a remarkable harmony to create a path for each row.

Yet, they were all there in such a moment, just strung with a special kind of tension that can tell you they were all bonded uniquely to write a story about something that will happen to someone or some people.

My mind wasn't a child's but a genius or an older wise man. Some things were crossing my mind in a flash, and I still had no explanation of what the Queen of Lights did to me.

With this racket, I saw a secret wisdom behind the strings. I saw other people's lives as strings, yet they were unstrung. I caught a glimpse of the future that somehow, mysteriously, I would be the one to string those living in harmony as this racket; how or when I have no idea.

I held the racket so tight with both of my hands, but I didn't know what to do or how to do with it.

Mondo: "So what do I have to do exactly ?".

Anna answers, smiling: "Mondo, it is effortless; when you see the ball coming at you, swing the racket and hit it to the other side above the net....very simple. "Can you do that?

I shook my head up and down to say that I understood her instructions clearly. Meanwhile, I had no clue, but I said that to impress her.

I stood my ground, waiting for the ball to come to me as the man from the other side of the net said: "Here it comes."

The Fuzzy yellow ball was traveling, spinning around, going up above the net, traveling towards me. My eyes were so focused on the ball and nothing else.

The fact that mom was always working, and sometimes too late hours, made me an independent child, yet with that, we never had the luxury of real entertainment as the rich people in such a place. TV and the movie theatre were the only things that helped me see the other part of the world, whether it was trustworthy or just acting. Sometimes, they show strange sports on TV worldwide, one of which is an American sport called baseball.

I never understood that sport, yet in such a moment, with a racket in both my hands and the word swing, made me travel far and visualize that swing from such a far land.

Yet, the only person we saw playing that sport was in the movie theatre.

The movie Sabrina(with my favorite actress, Audrey Hepburn, was longer than we expected. There was an intermission, and they played a short film about an American athlete named Babe for just fifteen minutes.

He was somehow a legend in such a sport, Baseball. I remember that movie and his ability to hit the ball so fast and hard. How he used to hold that wooden stick with a firm grip and total concentration on the ball made me visualize the same look and the standing position and get ready to swing and blast the ball to the sky as Babe used to do.

My first swing at the ball was a total failure; as I swung the air, the ball just passed me by.

I was somehow a very emotional boy, maybe too sensitive, yet never accepted defeat.

I ran to the baseline and got the ball; then I kicked it with my foot above the net without using the racket, then I raised my hand in the air and said," Goal."

The players laughed at my act, as it wasn't Tennis but Football.

Anna: Wow, that was very good, but next time, try to use the racket instead of your foot because that is called Tennis and not Football. I wasn't happy about her star-casting comment about football, my favorite sport. However, she somehow corrected me as I must use the racket, not my foot. The moment the ball was in my reach, I swung the racket and hit the ball hard with all the power I endured from my tiny body.

The ball went up in the sky, higher and higher, until it vanished through the clouds.

The impact of my hit was a sign for me to grab my school bag and run fast out of this place. First, I dropped the racket so fast, yet as I was about to run out of the court, everyone started yelling," It's coming down again."

The sun was like a fireball in the sky, and it was so bright to spot the ball in the sky that I couldn't see it coming down. The moment I tried to block the sun off my vision, it was somehow too late to avoid the speed of the ball coming down directly at me, hitting my face so hard as a lethal bomb from an American jet pilot.

I couldn't tell if the weight of the ball knocked me down to the ground, a sudden impact on my face, or even both. My tears were mixed up with the red clay as if I was bleeding; my face was covered with patches of clay, yet the sad part was my white school shirt. This was a great mistake to be in this place.

I was highly filthy and knew my mother would kill me for that.

A fire in my soul was burning as hell because of my poor judgment and foolishness—the fire of embarrassment and shame. I was down on my knees, hitting the red clay with my fist so many times and so hard that my knuckles started bleeding.

The fact that I was transformed into something else made me act as Superman(Indirectly)

When I grabbed my jacket off the bench, I wrapped it around my neck and made a tight knot, and my school jacket became my cape. My position on my knees, hitting the red clay, was as if Superman used his fist to push the ground to the sky.

I pressed the ground, forcing it to fly, yet I could only run so fast out of the court.

I was so close to reaching the front gate, as I thought I was always the fastest kid in school and football team, as they described me...The Flash.

Such a reputation of my speed was not even close to her speed.

She did catch up with my pace, then threw herself flying in the air, and in a flash, she was on top of me before I reached the gate.

We were on the grass, and I was fighting her to let go of me, screaming in her face.

Let me go, LET ME GO. I HATE THIS PLACE.

She looked at me from above as she was sitting on my stomach, holding my shoulders down to the ground, and said: "Calmese."

Look at my eyes. Look at me, God damn it, and stop fighting.

Nothing happened over there to be ashamed of or even afraid of.

That was Tennis, and that happens all the time, especially in the beginning stages, so get yourself together and let's go back there to the court, and I will show you how to do things right; I will show you a new world, and I will bring you the world of light in your hand, She said."

The drop of tear was fighting its way out of my eye's lid, and the burn was intense, yet her words and her face helped me gain some comfort and confidence, and her strange last few words somehow echoed from that fascinating world in my vision.

I will bring you the world of light.

Can fantasy and visions be true? Is it even close?

Anna got off me to allow me to breeze; I had to remain on the grass, holding my knees and looking down to the grass in between my knees and whispering to myself, "I will bring you the world of light. "

My whisper became louder as I said: "The world of light. "

I was somehow angry on my feet, yet I started to raise my head, and that angry face turned to a wild, uncontrollable beast with firey eyes; then I said to Anna: "You said, the world of light." You said......You said(pause- while my emotional tears were racing to my red face): the world of light," and I repeated the sentence with a louder voice, looking into her blue eyes.

What world of light are you talking about? Why did you say that, and who are you?

I am Anna, and I meant indirectly a new world of Tennis that will be the light of your path if you ever choose to step into such a path.

I did not mean to upset you. Moreover, the language can confuse you as you are a Spaniard, and I am British. The miss translation can send the wrong message to you, and here I am again, apologizing if I said something to offend you or even dared to hurt your feelings.

Her words were my remedy to comfort my weak mind from drifting back to that place, and so I had to calm down and say: "I do also apologize for my anger and foolish behavior, and I also want to ask you to be my friend if it is not to much trouble to ask that of you. "

Her glowing white teeth were somehow the comfort and the answer I was hoping for, as she said with that smile on her lovely face: "Apology accepted, my Mondo.....I meant Mondo, and I would love to be your friend... Now.

She paused a little, then said in a softer, shaky tone, saying,.....   Now and forever.

So please get up and relax, but above all, try to trust me, even if it will be just a little.

Hands in hands, we walked back to the court, and the cheers, clapping, and laughs were getting louder and louder as the other players from other courts all came to me to cheer me up and welcome me back to the game.

She looked at them and somehow ordered them with a strange look to be quiet and stop all that. She had me under her arm and said to me:" Well, before we do anything, I want you to know that you're under my protection, so from this moment, we need to do something different about your look, so please come with me right now and don't ask any questions......do you agree...Mondo.

Mondo just shook his head up and down in acknowledgment and complete understanding.

She walked me to the bathroom, and being in such a place with a girl was awfully strange.

 We were in the ladies bathroom, and without any doubts, she locked the door behind us, and finally, it was just her and me all alone in the ladies toilet. Such a noise, click, click, made me jumpy as if we had altered our sexuality.

I became the girl who was locked in a bathroom with a charming boy, and the fear of the unexpected had reached my doubtful mind, saying: OH, NO.

Again, I'm with a beautiful girl in the ladies bathroom. I closed my eyes for a few seconds; when I opened them, I realized that it wasn't just a dream but a reality.

I'm in the ladies' bathroom; OH, NO.

I couldn't tell if she was a powerful girl or if it was me feeling like a featherweight.

She lifted me off the ground and sat me on the edge of a comprehensive, big sink as a baby.

I was shocked by what she did, but I was so happy to be the baby in her hands.

She started with the school tie, which was orange, red, and light blue with white stripes. She untied the giant knot of the school tie so quickly as if she knew exactly what she was doing with a small tie, not like me to shock myself to take it off at home. She dragged it gently from under the collar and placed it around her neck, then she reached out to the first top button, and I was almost positive that she was not herself until the last button.

I was hypnotized when she lifted me, and I fell in her hands hopelessly.

She slid her hands on my naked chest and smoothly ran behind my neck, reaching for my shoulders and dropping my shirt behind my back.

Then suddenly, I was half naked in front of a girl in the ladies 'bathroom for the first time. She took the shirt, dropped it in the next sink, and turned the hot water on until it was soaked. She knew her way in such a vast, long bathroom.

All around the walls were mirrors and some paintings of tennis players.

They were old with old tennis outfits, and they were in black and white photographs that resembled the old days. She opened a cabinet and then grabbed two clean white towels.

She placed The first one on the ceramic floor under my dangling feet; the second was wet from the lower edge. She went down on her knees on the towel and was precise to the level of my eyes. I had no objections when she started undressing me as if I was under her spell.

I was half naked, just topless. She started whipping the clay off my arms, neck, and face, and the unexpected dream started to happen, but this time it was all real. She looked into my eyes and said: "Now, this is the part of you staying still and not moving at all." She wet the towel again and gently cleaned my eyes and nose until she touched my lips.

Her movement slowed as she drew a line with the towel across my lips.

Suddenly, she let go of the towel, and I observed the towel falling to the ground in slow motion, yet she held the back of my head with one hand as her finger surfed through my hair and gently pulled me closer. Meanwhile, her other hand had a different, unexpected behavior as she licked her fingertips and started whipping off my lips so softly that I had to close my eyes and dream again. I was just a boy, but what took place outside on the bench with such a unique vision in my head changed something in me, and I couldn't justify the limitations of my capabilities about feeling things beyond my age as an ordinary boy. I started to feel the change in my mind as a fully developed man and not just a boy, in which case, somehow, it helped me understand the blend between a man and a woman, or a girl and a boy in our strange case.

The tingling sensation of her wet fingertips caressing my lips made me open my mouth, waiting for the unexpected. My eyes are slightly open, and I look straight at hers. I was confident in what I could do next.

The electricity in my body exceeded the limitations of a boy my age.

The rush of my new blood through my veins was more like a chemical reaction from within, and I couldn't understand all the strange movements inside my body or even my brain.

My next crazy, unexpectedly fast move is leaning closer to her lips.

I was aware of such a thin, forbidden line that was just about to be crossed, and the gate of innocence was about to be broken; yet another force held me from getting any closer. Rejections.

I was worried about my self-control and the beast that would be born in such a moment.

That thin line later vanished as the tip of her nose was about to touch mine, and then suddenly, the great gate of heaven was wide open to a place that only existed in my fantasy world.

The words of the Reine of light came back to me, and my darkness blended with her light, and we were both glowing as one.

On the other hand, Anna was traveling to an infinity of light that somehow glowed off my green eyes, blinding her vision to uncharted territory and hypnotizing, paralyzing her mind with such a glow as if it was the bridge to me. She couldn't resist the temptation of walking the long, forbidden road. She knew that crossing such an impossible bridge was something not to attempt nor dare. The doubts and misinterpretation couldn't correct her mind to do the right thing, yet he wasn't about to back off and retreat to the wise Anna.

The moment I closed my eyes, she melted away in my lips. The kiss may have lasted for only a few seconds, but the intensity of such a kiss seemed to be eternal.

On the other hand, Anna whispered, saying: "That kiss was never meant to happen, but I can't resist his spell, and I did not care about what may happen after that." The water was overflowing from the sink on the far side of the bathroom, but we couldn't hear or feel anything but our heartbeat as one.

Mondo's mind says: "Her lips were the Heaven I've missed, and the taste was not enough to let go... The longer our lips were as one, the more her sweet became sticky as honey, and her tongue was lost in a cave of mysteries.

Anna's mind telling her: "His lips were as soft as cotton candy, the more my tongue wandered inside his mouth, the sweater they tasted and the faster I melted...and I couldn't let go.

Mondo also wondered with his mind: "The eternal flame of the kiss of life burns my senses of knowing right from wrong. They say that when a soul can only find true peace, it will be in Heaven, so Am I in Heaven?

Why wait for the unknown? Simply put, Paradise can be here on Earth if we only feel and live it. I was living in Paradise at such a moment, and it was hard to let go of my Heaven.

I held on to her lips as the rose to a stem, as a hungry infant to a mother's nipple, as a dry land for a drop of rain, as a dying person to the last breath, as Mondo to Anna's lips.

Anna's mind: "The silence after that kiss drove me crazy as we were frozen, but somehow, not dead.

Mondo's mind: "My eyes were closed, and I couldn't resist the magic of such a moment blending with Anna in such a transparent way. She lifted me, put me down on the ceramic floor, and started to do things rationally and randomly, turning the water off and washing my dirty clothes. She turned around with her face to the ground, avoiding looking at my eyes, and handed me a white T-shirt with the club logo to put on.

She went to the far sink at the end of the bathroom and washed her face repeatedly.

She was standing alone, staring at me silently at the end of the long bathroom.

Suddenly, she rushed back towards me as a storm, with her wet face as the water was dripping on the ceramic floor, yet the sound of every drop was pounding so hard as if it was a drum with a constant beat in my ears. She stood with one hand on her heart and the other above her head, trying to find the right words to express what happened between us.

She said in a very soft, low tone, with sincere words, with her trembling tone of high anxiety, "I am so sorry for what I did."....She nodded(pause), her voice shaking again, and I couldn't tell which one was shaking more, her voice or her body... Her knees shook, making her red, shiny thighs shake in the way of asking for a warm hand to calm them down, but I couldn't touch that part of her body after my kiss.

She courageously resumed her sentence and said, " Please promise me not to tell...(paused) again... a word to anyone, please. I am begging you to keep this as our secret ....Forever.

It is true, as they say, that somehow, when you're static, erratic, enchanted, yet above all been ravished to a point where all your emotions and senses feel confused, and your mind is delusional for the truth of how your mind can react to accept the fact of been enjoying what you did or come back to reality and admit your sin with tears.

Her precious tears were the signs of such a status, but the color of her face and the glow of her blue eyes make you wonder if she was sorry or seeking more, yet not knowing how.

The top few buttons of her white blouse were open, exposing the rapid movements of her breasts. I wasn't sure about that part, but it felt perfect for a boy my age to have a peak of her breasts. The extremity of boys' and female breasts never cease to astonish me, as I was one of their victims. I started whipping her face with my bare hands, yet I couldn't tell the difference between the water and her tears as they all blended, dripping to the floor.

The crazy part was that some of those water molecules found a strange shelter as they were gently sipping into her wonderful blossom breast, and that was when my hands ended up frozen. That cave was guarded with her sharp eyes, observing my hand's development through her body step by step. The confused signal of eyelashes going up and down slowly sent me the wrong message, so I had to stop and pull my hand back towards my body.

Sometimes, girls or women can make a single move as a gesture of acceptance to be touched intimately. Anna suddenly felt my hand move away from her skin, yet she raised her head, looking at the ceiling, exposing her erratic, long neck as if it was the long road down to her breast. She approved me returning with my hand and reaching the impossible.

I moved even further from her as a perplexed, inexperienced young boy.

The crazy pose transformed into a much more dangerous condition, as Anna was biting on her lower lip, waiting patiently to understand her signal and crush her in my arms and suck her juicy eternal lips. I was standing by the sink looking at her, as I had never seen anything like that in my short life, and right then, in such a moment, I realized that I had made the wrong decision as I should've gotten in that cave, but again, I was still naive in such a wild world of boys and girls. Her eyes were red as the salt of her tears, were burning from the inside out, and her long eyelashes were constantly moving in a hysterical way, which led me to hold the sides of her face with my two hands and then say to her with a slight smile: "Nothing happened....... I promise".

In my mind, I was sure that something had happened between us, but why and why?

Was all that just meant to be... I wonder. I was debating with my following line yet and again, and for the second time, I said to her: "Trust me...Anna...nothing happened, and that moment will be locked in my heart forever with a lock that will never find a soul to use. "

I had to be the hero for this particular moment, not the villain.... Who saved the girl?

I have to be the prince who brought the princess to life with the magic kiss from the darkness of the everlasting evil spell, but I couldn't say that. Instead, I spoke to Anna: So will you trust me?

Anna: I trust you.

Mondo: Please close your eyes, trust me, and don't move.

Anna: Is there something wrong with my face?

Mondo: SHHHH.....Be quiet.

I had to reach out for her blouse so gently and button up her blouse the proper way.

Mondo: There you go.

Anna felt his tinny fingers button up her blouse, but with her closed eyes, she wished.... Yet, she dreamed with her sick mind that instead, he would've ripped off her blouse and kissed her pounding breast all over....but again she had no explanation for her sick mind until he said: "Will you please show me how to play Tennis now... Por favor..."

Anna: "I am now so positive that he is not for real and the mystery behind his words is not what is swirling in his seductive mind, yet I have to be the mature one to comply with his words and pretend that it was all part of a foggy experience for me and of course for him as well."

Anna: Yes, of course, my dear Mondo...she said with a calm voice, as her tears were still blending with the moisture of water dripping off her face, but she managed to gather herself quickly and whipped off her face with the towel and said: "Let's play some bloody damn tennis."

We laughed because of the way she said it with such a heavy British accent.

As she was heading to the door, I held her hand, looked into her eyes, and smiled: "Will you hug me as friends? ". Mondo said.

She rushed me into her soft blossom breast as the pillow to my sweet dreams.

I wanted to feel her heartbeat as they might have the answers to my questions.

The hug was more from her than me, as I started to feel she was willing to cross that line again, so I had to reply quickly to acknowledge my acceptance of her new invitation to the beautiful world. After a short period, I started to feel the pain of such an act as her hug turned into a squeeze. I was almost about to break my ribs off, but that hug was the beginning of a tremendously long friendship. The height between us helped me more than her, as my head was buried in her breast while she was hugging me, yet it was more of pulling to her inside as my lips felt the softness of her breast as if I was an Enfant searching for a mother's nipples.

She opened the door slightly and peeked out to see if anyone would see us coming out from the ladies 'bathroom together, and when she was sure that no soul was around, she waved to me to come out, and we ran straight to the court again.

When we were back at the court, her voice sounded different as she said:" Listen to me, Mondo, or shall I call you little devil... And listen very carefully".

Forget about everything, especially the last few minutes, and focus on me and what I do, understand.

Mondo: First, who else would I focus on? (Pause) You? The last thing I want you to understand is that it should be easy with me and my heart.

Anna: I can see that you're brilliant, but I'm warning you not to repeat my words after you twisted the meaning behind them, so for now, I want you to focus.

Tennis is a game of life; you can die on the court trying to win a match, but when you do, the whole world will change, and so will you. The first lesson is to learn how to hold the racket.

How you held the racket so tight and tense with both hands is different.

All Spaniards are good at football, but are you any good at such a famous sport?

Do you play Football?

Mondo smiled, looked at her, and said, "Football is in my blood.

However, some people in this part of Spain acknowledged my skills and chose me to be part of the Malaga junior national team. So yes, I play Football, but what is your question?

Anna: How do you feel when you're all alone with the ball?

Do you sometimes think that it is part of you?

Tell me how you feel about scoring a goal; how do you feel when your team wins? My question has part two as well.

Mondo: It is something you can't describe in words, as it is a feeling.

I feel like I'm on top of the world when that net shakes because of my Goal.

I think that I'm (pause)....Unstoppable, but there is another word in English that I can't recall...I feel as if I'm in.....

Invincible...Anna jumped off with the word.

Si, Si....Invincible... that's it.

I love the fans and the way people cheer when we play well, but I love them more when they go crazy when I score a goal.

Anna: I do understand now, and so does Tennis.

The more you feel the racket, understand the ball, and win the fans, the more Tennis will run in your vain. So, the first lesson is to learn how to embrace shaking hands.

I was not getting that part at all, but with the patience with which she demonstrated her method, it was easy, effective, and fun. She reached out with her soft hand to shake my hand and said: "Now shake my hand."

The truth was that.... I couldn't get over that past moment, and kissing and touching her again may lead to more things, so I froze again.

Anna: "Come on, Mondo...raise your hand and put it in mine.

Come on .... Shake my bloody hand." She said with a severe voice.

I started to get over that and shook her hand in a swift, gentle way, so she let go of my hand so fast as if she was furiously angry at me and said with an angry tone:" What the hell was that?"...Shake my hand the right way like a man.

So I shook her hand harder, then she said again, harder Mondo..be a man.

I squeezed her hand repeatedly until she was delighted with the progress, and finally, she said: "Well done...

I am glad that I brought the man outside of you... let's move on to the next step".

Every word she said had a volume and a deep, covered meaning to my ears, yet I must learn to overcome any distraction if I explore such a sport. I had to ignore the deep meaning behind her words when she said: I'm glad that I brought the man outside of you.

That man made her melt like a candle in a deep flame; that man melted her senses and emotions like hot chocolate ready to be poured on top of the famous Malaga Tejeringos or churros. That man's mind is still back there in the ladies 'bathroom.

She grabbed the racket and held it upside down from the head frame, then handed out the racket's grip to my hand and said: "Now, show me how you shake the racket's hand with a full grasp as we've practiced. "

I did and held a tennis racket correctly for the first time. She said again, as if she were reading my mind, "You must feel the racket as if it is an extension of your arm."

We did it repeatedly until I felt the racket was part of my arm.

Anna: "Mondo, my dear; look at me and pay extra attention to my moves....

I want you to shadow me exactly in everything I do."

Mondo: Everything. Are you optimistic about that?

She laughed, yet she replied, saying; Mondo, if you really wish to learn, you must stop that; I mean that thing; listen, I'm trying to say(pause).

Mondo: Relax, I was joking.

She had her racket down next to her right leg, then took one step forward toward the net with her left foot, and the right one shifted back one step toward the baseline, then started to move the racket up to the side slowly. She bent her elbow and moved the racket across in front of her chest, finishing with the noise above her left shoulder as a car windshield wiper.

The entire technique fascinated me, and I must make the same move precisely as she did it.

I was somehow confused with my footage, but she came to me and said: "Well, I am going to tell you another little secret to help you with your footage."

She was again on top of me from behind, holding my hands, moving my legs as if I were a marionette in her hands. First, you must have balance and use your non-dominate arm to guide you. So, stretch your left arm up in the air ahead of you...

Then suddenly, she stopped, looked at me, and said, "Wait, are you a righty or a lefty ?".

I looked at her and said, "I was born using my left hand, but I had an accident, and I broke my left arm, and so I had to learn how to utilize the right hand to do everything, including writing, but from time to time I go back to my left hand as I feel more natural using it, but my mom always advised me to use my right hand instead..so to answer your question.

I am both.

Again...Fascinating you are ...." She said. "

Anna: "Well, use whatever you feel natural and comfortable using, as tennis is a sport of experimentation and practice, yet if you want my true advice, use the left."

The highest percentage of tennis players in the world are righty, and somehow they don't like players using the left hand as it distracts them and confuses them simultaneously, making you even more special, dangerous, and unique.

Now, stretch your right arm forward and pretend that you are pointing to something ahead that is coming your way, such as the ball.

With that move, your right foot must comply with a step forward with your arm simultaneously, and take action back with your left foot and lower the racket close to the side of your left thigh with the exact grip we've learned. The rest is what I did with my technique.

I tried, but I was always mixing up my footage, so she had to stop me and say: "Let's try something fun."

She came to me from behind again and leaned with her head on my shoulder; meanwhile, her hair was dangling, brushing the side of my face, and with her being on top of me, I started to lose myself again, but when she whispered in my ears saying: "Focus, your little devil, don't let your mind go anywhere but the court and let your body loose as I will move you as a marionette ."

Suddenly, in a fast move, she was stuck to my back with her body as if we were one...again, then she held my two arms and started moving each one the way I should move them as she'd described before and at the same time she was also moving my feet with a push of her thighs until I got the move right.

She let go of me, turned around and faced me, and said: "You see, it is not that difficult after all, so let the fun begin. "

She tossed the ball and asked me to use her technique and swing gently to hit the ball.

The first trial could have been better, but with more practice, I started to understand the rhythm and the correct precision to be prepared for the coming balls. She was very pleased with my rapid improvement, yet she was still looking for more accuracy. She stood before me and said: "Mondo, please give me your racket. "

I thought I had done something wrong momentarily, but she was a bright, observant, magnificent girl. She caught my sad impression immediately; she leaned forward with her face, looked into my eyes, and said: "I need to show you something different without the racket, so don't worry.

I felt better and handed her the racket, yet she didn't take it too far and placed it beside me on the clay. I will toss the ball to you, and I want you to catch it with your non-dominant hand.

In your case, it will be the right hand, and you will follow the same technique we've learned with the racket. This technique will help you respond quickly and improve your reaction.

She tossed the ball, and I rapidly stretched my right arm, trying to catch it, yet it hit my fingertips and bounced off my hand. She did it repeatedly until my reflex became highly sharp and accurate, and I never dropped the ball again until she said: "Now close your eyes and try to listen to the sound of the ball moving through the air until it comes to your hand. " I did not object to anything she asked me to do, and the result was quite fascinating.

To be more challenging, she went to her bag and brought a white scarf with her initials on it, and actually, she covered my eyes entirely with the scarf and said: "Let's do it a, gain with your eyes completely, blindfolded."

I can't see anything, Anna, and I don't think this will ever work .. Mondo said with a frustrated tone."

Anna: "Listen to me, trust your instincts, close your mind, and open up a small window for the sound of the ball moving through the air." In the meantime, I had no idea that the other players from the close courts stopped and started to watch the unusual, unique technique Anna had invented to teach me.

Anna: "Just listen to the ball traveling in the air and nothing else, no minds, only one, and that is the ball and you ." I was unsure about her method, but when I traveled to that unknown place, something did happen to me, and I became somebody new with such an ability to adapt and improvise anything that came my way.

Life stopped for a few seconds, and everything was moving slowly, including the fuzzy yellow ball. Even though my eyes were blindfolded, I could see the movement of the ball spinning in the air and traveling towards me, and I was quick to take my position and stretch my right arm at the exact second to catch the ball.

The fuzzy yellow ball was spinning in a prolonged motion only in my mind, and I could even see the hairy yellow things coming off the ball fluffing through the air, and they were somehow the breaking point to feel the ball landing in my palm.

The ball's impact on my palm was the exact indicator to close my fist on the ball and secure it in my hand. The experiment fascinated me and everyone else on the courts, and when I felt the ball inside my palm, my heartbeats were over the limits of my excitement.

I was jumping up and down with extreme happiness and excitement.

Anna: Wow, that was great Mondo.

Anna: "Again, then she started with different variations of speed, tossing the ball faster and faster, ball after ball, and with the last 10th ball, the distortion of the loud noise around me made me feel uncomfortable, and I had to snatch the scarf off me eyes to come back to the real world. The players stood there, clapping their hands at what they had encountered.

The sight was strange to me, but the only thing that started to make sense was another big kiss on my cheeks from Anna's lips.

"You are ..Nino Magico," she said with a great smile.

There was also a glimpse of a tear on her face, but she wiped it off so fast, but I didn't miss that at all. The players were coming my way from everywhere, patting my head and shoulder, and a lady kissed me, too. And finally, a young man came and raised me in the air and started spinning me while he was carrying me from his happiness with what I did.

I was not quite sure of my emotions in response to all that, but I was excited, and after all, I commenced to acknowledge and believe in my gift for the first time in my life. For a while, all the players were coaching me in different ways, techniques, and tips, yet I couldn't stop learning from every one of them.

At last, Anna told them, "Thank you all, but this magnificent boy needs to go home ."

I couldn't believe I had been on the court for over two hours and that my face had turned so many colors as Anna said: "It is five o'clock. "

I was very distracted and couldn't tell what to do precisely, shall I run, get my bag, say goodbye...So many things all at once were swirling in my little head, yet the one thing for sure that I was optimistic about was the look on Mom's face, as I was very late.

Anna came to me and gave me another big hug and then handed me my school bag and said with a smile on her face, "Well, my dear Mondo ....today was the best day of my life, and I am so glad you came my way, but I don't want you to forget about me as I do and seriously want to see you again here on the tennis court, but I still need to know how do you feel about all this.

Mondo: I am speechless and grateful for all you have shown me today. I nodded for a few seconds, and I said, "Including yourself."

I can't promise I will come and play tennis here again. Still, I will promise you this...and (pause) trying to find the right words until I said: "I never thought that you would be the one to hold my heart, but you came around and knocked me off the ground from the start, you put your arms around me, and for the first time in my life I felt that I am home to where I belong.

I do thank you from the bottom of my heart.

This time, I felt her heartbeat, and her tears were dropping on my face as the hug lasted forever, as if she would not let me go.

CHAPTER VII

THE BEAUTY OF MAR

Now, I have to run home, and please don't try to stop me this time as I am in deep trouble. Anna's smile and tears were the last things I remember as I started running.

The flash cut through the crowd of people crossing the street, not paying any attention to the cars as there was only one thing on my mind: to be home before my mother arrived.

The only thing that made me wonder was that moment of traveling in time to another universe as if I was facing a woman, a singer, or a songwriter from another time mumbling or humming the words of a song she wrote. Her comments came to my mind, and I said them to Anna a few minutes ago.

How did those words come to me, and from where?

Who was that woman singing those words, and how and how?

How much have I changed with the Queen of Lights?

How many gifts she'd implanted in me, the thing with adaptation somehow can make some sense, but traveling in time and seeing and learning words from someone stranger to me was a mystery to my mind. I wish my Queen would come back and explain things that can make sense to all that. I desire that she could explain more details about....Why me?

The only thing that did make sense was her last words: Believe in yourself, and when you wish to see me truly, I will be there for you. I was flying off the steps leading to the second floor of my mother's apartment. Meanwhile, I was so terrified about the time that I stuck my hand to find the key, yet there was something different that my hand touched, and of course, it was not the key. I took that object out of my pocket, the fuzzy yellow ball again.

Anna managed to stuff the ball in my pocket, but It was not the ball that struck me, the words on the ball were a real thrill to my heart as she wrote:' Come back to me again" and also in the back of her initial A...

The smile on my face was a door to this moment with Anna until another door was opened, which was not good.

"Mondo, WHERE THE HELL HAVE YOU BEEN?

That voice was my mother; she was so angry and furious because I was late.

I entered the apartment slowly with my head down, trying to sneak into my room, but again, I was not that smooth or fast enough to make it. The door slamming did not indicate how I would explain myself to her.

The connection between my mother and I is one of the exceptional ones.

I never lied to her, no matter how bad I was in trouble, and in that moment, I had to tell her everything, no matter what the consequences would be.

Mom: Mondo, turn around and look at me and tell me why you were late, what you're wearing, where your school uniform is, why you are so sweaty, and why, why, and why?

Mondo: Mom, please stop and let me breeze. I will tell you everything, give me a chance.

I was trying to find an entrance or an introduction to my story; however, she was impatient and pushy, too. I strolled to the kitchen sink, grabbed an empty glass, and let the water run a little. Then, I slid the glass under the faucet and quickly drank the whole glass, then filled it up again and again almost four times.

Finally, I turned the water, carried the entire glass, and walked towards the table as she sat there with her hand on her right cheek, waiting for the great matador to enter the arena and start swirling his cape to hypnotize the bull and distract her attention.

Mom: Well, as a start, you have a full stomach with water as of now, but you will eat dinner, and that will be decided upon my discretion; however, you still owe me a full explanation with details about all the unstrung loose ends of your behavior.

Mondo: Mom, before I say anything, can I hug you, por favor...

Her arm was open with a magical smile that eliminated any questions or doubts about anything in my mind. I've thrown myself in her arm like a football in the arm of a goalkeeper. It was like he had an incredible shot from the other team, saving it from reaching his goal.

The truth was that the astonishing photo was like a cannonball. However, miraculously, it landed in his arm, and he couldn't let go, yet to acknowledge that he still had it, he kept squeezing it, pushing it closer to his chest and body so it would never slip away.

It was how I felt in her arms, and I had to close my eyes, enjoying her warm body.

Moreover, her heartbeat as well. I was in so much peace and comfort in her arm, as my tiny arms wrapped around her waist and my head buried in her caring and loving chest.

When I was fully content, I raised my lips close to her neck and kissed her cheek, then rubbed my head underneath her chin with my face breathing in her chest like a cat trying to get full sympathy and love.

She put her index finger under my chin, raised my head gently, looked down at my eyes, and said: "Yo tambien te amo....I love you, too.

She pushed me back away from her body and said softly: "Set down and tell me all about it.

Mondo: "As you know very well.... I take the same road coming home, but there is another road that I've discovered: a much longer way to go home.

I never told you about that road before as I was worried you might get upset or mad at me. That road has some attraction that always pleases me and depresses me at the same time, yet from time to time, I do take that road and always wonder if something different will change how I feel about so many questions that I always wonder in my mind. Today, I felt something strange from the moment I got up in the morning, something unusual that may change my life entirely. Maria was looking at her son, and as a mother or a single mother, she felt something different about him.

She felt a change in Mondo's eyes as if some force had touched his soul.

His green eyes were glowing in a very different way, and that was what she'd noticed the moment she raised his shin and looked at his eyes. I was trying to comprehend the cause, but I said it would be wiser to listen to his story....Maria thinking in her head.

Mondo: I had a good day at school. Mr. Cortez gave me a star for my history test result, and I also got another star "from Mrs. Annabelle for my effort in the art class.

I had a good day at school, as I scored three goals in the football match against Naturlauro school, and that earned me a big kiss from the young Blanca, a girl from my art class.

The main thrill was after school as things got better...I paused again as my throat was somehow struggling to swallow my saliva. So I had to take a sip of the glass of water and said: "Well, Mom, I had to accept that road I've mentioned to you before, and that was the beginning of all the mystery of why I was late and also it has many explanations about my clothes as well. My mom's green eyes were wide open with excitement and patience to know all about the rest of my story, especially that kiss from Blanca.

There was too much noise coming from the balcony door from the street, and I had to excuse my mom from closing the balcony door to be more peaceful and quiet. She was observing me and my moves, yet she knew that something beyond her imagination would emerge from my story.

I sat down, grabbed her hand, and pulled my chair closer to her as our faces were so close, as if I was trying to whisper my story in her ears. She kissed my hand and smiled, "Continue, matador. "

I described to her the road, the sidewalk, the change of nature, my brief contact with God, and, of course, the part of that little fuzzy ball.

At that moment, she looked at me and said: "God.. and what fuzzy ball?

I pulled the tennis ball out of my pocket and placed it on the kitchen tablecloth.

The tablecloth was light red with some blue birds flying on the corner, and right in the center of the tablecloth, another part of the painting elaborated on the magnificent sunset above the sea horizon with the waves washing the shore.

The tablecloths were handmade art pieces by my aunt Maribella, and I miss them so much. She was a very gifted young woman, unique, talented, highly exotic, and beautiful woman.

Her Death was heartbreaking to me; somehow, neither the light of new days nor the nights would erase her memories. I remember her laughs and jokes, but above all, her unconditional love. I can't say that she was a second mother to me but more of a girlfriend because the secret bond that we had together was more than just a mother-son bond.

I remember her coming to my room some nights while I was asleep and sitting for hours looking and staring intensely at my face. There were so many times that she used to fall asleep right next to me, but most of all, her sketches and paintings were fascinating, and the dearest one to my heart was a picture of both of us laughing as she transferred that photograph to a magical charcoal sketch.

The frame is still on my bedroom wall, yet it was also nailed and framed in my heart.

She loved my mother so dearly as she was the one who raised her after my grandparents dishonored them and erased both of them from the family tree.

Maria and Maribella were inseparable sisters, the most beautiful girls in Cabra, Spain.

The fact that they were the only two daughters of the great Armando Lopez, the leader of the Gitano community in Cabra, was the main reason they were also untouchables with their rare beauty. Life had no limitations to their wild dreams and imaginations.

Her memory was like a dream; part of me also died with her the day she died.

The age was massive between us, as I was eight when she passed away at 25.

She lived with us for only five years, as she was at a fast pace, traveling everywhere, meeting people all over Europe, promoting her art, and, after all, living her wildlife.

She was a great inspiration to me, and she was the one who made me understand the meaning of life within the mind of a female.

To understand how the mind of a female functions, you've got to hear it, yet learn it and know from the mind of a woman, not just a typical woman, but an angel like my aunt Maribella. I've discovered the anatomy of a woman's body from her, as she used to draw many educational sketches of different types of women with and without clothes. I was a curious child looking for knowledge, and she was the best teacher I've ever had. I used to love looking at her face as the sunset teased her long lashes, just lying on the sand like a goddess, looking at infinity.

I used to watch her dancing like a butterfly, swinging the long red dress she used to wear as an old Gypsy tradition when the grand festival was getting close to my little calendar on the wall in my bedroom. She had the magical features of Flamenco dancers, but even prettier and much more ravishing with her eyes that had some lava that would melt your heart out with just one look. She had no borders between us and no limits to her unconditional love for me.

Her love for me was unique and can only be fantasized about in a dream.

I never really knew her that well except for the last five years of her life, when she moved in with us and remained with us until she kissed me goodnight for the last time.

I've become more attached to her than my dear mother.

There was something magical and yet fascinating about her face, body, and soul. However, her beauty was somehow rare and incredibly indescribable.

Oh, and her stories about the places she'd visited and the people she'd met.

Day after day, I was getting to know her better as a friend, not as an aunt, and I used to tell her things that I couldn't tell my mother. We used to go to the shore and lie on the beach talking about dreams, visions, stars, and sunshine, but my favorite was her love words.

She had the most seductive body of a woman my poor, innocent eyes had ever seen.

So many times, I used to hear her magical voice singing in the shower with the door open, and so many times. I'd wanted to be close to her and listen to her voice straight from her chest, but daring to do so would be a sin, and I was too young to comprehend the magnitude of doing such a thing. One magical Sunday morning, she was washing her white blouse, cursing the hell of her bad luck as the blouse had some wine stain.

The wine she was drinking while she was working on her new painting.

Despite her excellent gift for drawing, I was eager to follow in her footsteps.

I was so good at sketching visions of my imaginative world, yet that day, I observed her as she stared at the painting, hoping to finish it. It was early morning, and the sun was warming the room with such a strange, magical ray of light.

Mom had gone to the hospital, and it was just Aunt Marbella and me in the apartment.

The sunlight was like a dazzling spotlight that rushed from the balcony, and suddenly, it paused on her. She was sitting on her vintage three-step wooden stool, bending her right leg on the upper step, which caused her exotic thigh to glow with the sunlight.

Meanwhile, her white blouse was extremely defective, showing much of her breasts.

She was staring at the painting with such a still pause on her face; meanwhile, I was hiding so she would not see me, yet I couldn't let go without imprinting such a magical pause on her.

My hand was preoccupied to an extreme extent with her pause setting on the stool in such a way. My small sketchbook was in one hand, and the other was roaming around in thin air as if I was trying to feel her body. The spirit of the grand Pablo Picasso inspired me to sketch her, just enough to express my imagination on a piece of paper. The warm sunlight was like a magnifying glass exposing her long eyelashes. Her long neck and her wild golden brown hair dropped off, covering half of her profile in such a magnificent way.

The smoke of her cigarette made a fantastic pattern with the sunlight, and the air was somehow reshaped to an old foggy room as all elements had disappeared except the existence of her and me. She had the glass of wine halfway full on her right-hand side, yet the dramatic warm effect of the sunlight had made the wine look like blood. She was a forgotten vampire queen, just waiting patiently for the right moment to swallow such wine or blood, then letting it spread in her vines with the hope of bringing her eternal life back again.

She was staring intensely through the painting for an answer, yet in a flash, or should I say instantly, she extended her long arm to strike the picture with her visionary mind. Instead of all that, she wasn't aware of the wine glass. She hit the glass with her elbow, which was an incredibly breathtaking reaction from her side.

The slow motion of her response to a miserable attempt to save the painting from the wine was somehow incredible. She dropped the cigarette on the floor and turned around with her right hand, successfully catching the glass and spinning away from the painting.

However, she wasn't planning to lose her balance or fall off the stool, but it did happen, and with such a move, she lost her footage and smashed her body to the ground, still holding the glass with both hands closer to her breast, and the rest was all blood...I meant wine.

The red wine splashed all over her blouse, and her beautiful eyes turned RED, as the vampire Queen was so furious for a vicious kill. She was so mad, cursing herself out so loudly, that I had to hide before she saw me, and so I ran back to my room, dove on the floor in front of the bed, shoved the sketchbook under the bed, and finally run out, pretending as if I was just wondering about the noise.

I was tip-toeing as Tom chased Jerry so she didn't feel my presence, watching her standing in front of the bathroom sink, scrubbing her blouse, trying to get the wine stain off it.

Her anger was somehow furious, yet knowing she was impatient, she took the blouse off and scrubbed it madly. Her madness was not a real issue to me, but her body shocked me to Death. I had never seen the naked body of a female in my life before, and her body was the exceptional body to visit for the first time.

The firmness of her breast was a fascinating phenomenon for my innocent eyes to encounter, and I wanted to run back to my room, to my shame, but her voice brought me back as she started singing my favorite song again. I had to go back and sit on my knees like a dog watching her, half-naked singing, and out of nowhere, she changed the song to a much more dangerous one. She tossed her blouse in the shower and started undressing herself piece by piece until she was completely naked. She turned the warm water, stepped in the shower, and began rubbing her thighs smoothly; meanwhile, the steam of the hot water started to fill the bathroom, and I couldn't see clearly, so I had to do the daring thing in my life at my age and crawl inside the bathroom. The singing stopped, and her soft voice said: "I know you are here, you little devil, and you don't have to hide anymore. I stood up and attempted to fly out of the bathroom, but her wet hand caught the back of my shoulder, and she forced me to turn around and look at her.

Maribella said: "So you're a big boy now, and it looks like your Fantasy started to be reshaped to cross the line ...she paused, then said: To be a man.

I had to cover my face, yet she said, "It is all right with me if you look; just talk to me while I am showering.

Maribella repeated: I said it's all right to look, so take your small hands off your face and don't be shy as from this moment you're not a boy anymore.....You are a man.

I slowly shifted my hands to the sides of my face to look at her, but I couldn't open my eyes until she touched them, saying," Mondo, open up your eyes for me."

I was standing in the middle of the bathroom, staring at her back, yet for a second, I felt that I had gone deaf until she said. So tell me, young ....Man, do you like my body?"

I was speechless, yet I shook my head at accepting her body as if the shape of her back hypnotized me. She was like an artist who had crossed the line traveling back from Paradise with her body, shape, face, and soul all put together on the tip of his brush to create a heavenly creature known as Maribella. The magnificent tan color of her skin and the shape of her back features, including her firm round behind(butt) and the continuation of her lower cheeks blending with her beautiful thighs dragging the water strips to her calves as if the water was another person feeling her body with an uninterrupted flow of passion caressing her body.

There was some strange tingling in my body that I couldn't understand at such an age, but I was not denying the great pleasure of what my eyes were experiencing for the first time.

Mondo, are you still? She never finished her sentence, and I'd turned around so slowly before she faced me again. Looking at her body, I couldn't stay any longer, so I ran to my room and hid under the cover sheet, shaking like a leave. Where did you go ....

Oh, Mondo, where are you hiding?

I felt her voice getting closer and closer with her wet steps in the room, yet I was still shaking even more with her voice being on top of me. She had a long towel wrapped around her naked body, and she started to uncover me slowly.

I was crumbling, holding my knees with my face between my legs and shaking even more as she put her hand on my head and said softly: "Mondo..are you afraid of me..."

She sat on the edge of the bed with her wet body, pulled me over closer to her body, and said with a severe tone: "Look at me and tell me. Are you scared of me? "

I started to loosen up and felt comfort, talking to her, saying: "I am not afraid of you; I just don't know how to describe anything at this moment, or even how I feel. I have no words, and it is as if my poor vocabulary can't find new words to match what I have seen. "

Mondo: "You are my lovely aunt, but you are in the bathroom, and at that moment, you were paused for just a few seconds and said: "Una Diosa. A Goddess .."

Maribella: "Una Diosa ... that's how you felt about me there.Mondo..my dear."

Maribella: "I wish you were older and not my....(paused for few seconds), then said, { Nephew}. I wish you could love me the way I adore you since birth.

I always want to break that barrier between us; as an aunt, I've wanted you to feel my heartbeat when you're away, sick, or even asleep. I want you to feel me, how I think of you, touching your soft skin, caressing your hair, and kissing you goodnight.

There were so many magical nights that I used to sit on that chair, looking at your face like an angel while you were asleep and wishing that things were different in our lives.

I hope that one day you will understand my burning tears when you leave my sight every day to go to school. I wish the day will come soon enough to release my desire to hold you inside me...

She was breaking into tears and sorrow that I had never seen before, and I also started crying. The shake of her body trembling with tears made me feel sad for her and hopelessly lost with her tears. She had me so tight to her body as if such a moment would be the last one in our lives. She buried my head in her chest, caressing my hair so gently with her tears dripping over my head. I felt her shin on my head, and then she pulled me closer to her body, so tight with such a fear of me slipping off her life. I felt her heartbeat as if it was mine.

The flowing river of her tears was dragging me somewhere, yet my fears and excitement of the moment and her words encouraged me to get closer and closer to her body and never let go.

The simultaneous fractions of our bodies made her towel slip off her body, and I was holding her naked body with my head buried in her magnificent breast, but I was not afraid or ashamed anymore; on the contrary, I had the desire to stay like that forever ....in... her arms.

That day and those moments so close to my aunt made me believe that there were so many secrets in her life, and I couldn't comprehend at my age how to reveal her secrets and get inside her magnificent heart and mind.

To let go of her body was not either my intention at such a moment...... Nor never.

I love my mother to Death, but my love for my aunt was more intense to an extended infinity of mysterious, confused ways of love. That moment was the turning point of our lives, and I couldn't imagine my life without her scent all around me. The more she tried to let go, the more I pulled her back to me until she whispered those words in my ears: "Mondo, you have to let go, to miss me enough to desire my return with the greatest passion of never letting go again.

I know that I am not supposed to be the one to explain to you the magic of the flesh of a woman, but sooner or later, the day will come for you to understand the great sense of tingling above your fingertips, touching the skin of a woman. She fears nothing in this life or maybe the next one. She held my hand and allowed me to feel her breast slowly, then her stomach, thighs, and entire body. My head was about to explode from such an electric sensation and excitement. At that moment, I let go of her, and then she jumped off the bed, stood up, looked down at me, and said: "Wait here, Mondo; I have something special for you.

My eyes followed her naked body as she ran on her wet toes outside my room. She left me for a few minutes, then came back dressed and looked at me, extending both hands and crumbling like a fist as if hiding something inside. Then, she said with a smile," Choose."

I chose her left, she smiled, then flipped it open. There was a beautiful golden chain resting over the palm of her hand.

She said," You chose well, Mondo."

She said: Well, it's my turn, but you must close your eyes."

I closed my eyes briefly until I heard her voice saying," Now, open up your eyes."

Her right hand had a golden heart with a lock, but when she opened it, I saw MM.

She linked the chain to the heart, put it around my neck, and said," Do you know what MM means."

I stood there looking at the heart dangling over my chest, then raised my head, looking straight into her eyes, and said," I think they belong to....(long pause) .... I was trying to put things together in my head, as one conclusion came to my mind: Maria Maribella.

They both start with M, but my second conclusion was Mom, Mondo, and finally, it came to me. Did the MM are symbols for Maribella and Mondo?... Mondo asked.

She pulled me closer to her chest so hard, playing with my hair, but her heartbeat was pounding so fast. Meanwhile, her flowing tears were dripping over my face, and I had to push her way to ask about her tears and sadness.

Maribella: My dearMondo, my only love, I'm not sad; on the contrary, I'm so happy that you start to feel about me that way and...

Mondo: Tía... will you please Stop with the crying?

I love you so dearly, and I don't like it when you cry like that, so please stop those precious tears. Thank you for the heart, and I promise I'll keep it with me forever.

Maribella: Well, let's make a promise: if you love me that much, never say No to me for anything. Do we have a deal?

Mondo: I promise I will never say NO to you until I die, and yes, you have a deal. Maribella's face was full of light, and with her bright smile, she looked at me and said: How about if you and I go out for some Ice Cream?

Mondo: But, I thought you said you have something for me.

Yes, you're right, but if you look closer, you'll see what could be more special than just (pause)...Me.

I laughed and hugged her, saying: So, what is your favorite ice cream flavor?

I will tell you later. She said.

That day, she was closer to me than ever, and for the first time in my life, I felt a unique, special bond between us. We went everywhere; we had so much fun dancing in the streets, and she was more straightforward in expressing her happiness just being with me.

She was incredibly wild and beautiful. Her body moves men's heads in the streets, but on such a day, I was her date and no one else. She took me to the photo booth, and we took pictures together, laughing and making faces, but the last shot was the best of all, as she imprinted her soft lips right on the upper part of my eyelid.

The pictures were the best thing that she ever left for me.

That day, she took me to an exceptional place that I couldn't imagine could exist.

The place was almost hidden from all eyes, and to reach the mysterious place, we had to climb a great hill, almost like a mountain. We walked on the shore until it was there as a gate protecting the secrets of the existence of the two worlds....our world and the Fantasy one.

We climbed the mountain, yet I got tired on the way up.

She helped and encouraged me to keep going and NEVER SAY DIE as long as I can breeze. These words were my inspiration to conquer the world without fear.

My excitement of keeping up with her pace made me more careless of checking my footage, and it was the first time in my life that I had encountered my first demon ... Death.

I was trying to reach the top. However, I lost my footage to some loose rocks, and for just a few seconds, my heart stopped beating, and I was floating between two worlds as they were well known.... by Life and Death.

I was falling, helpless, and almost dead from such a height.

They say some people can be very fortunate to feel the thin line between life and Death.

They also say that others can be blessed to return to life after experiencing such a moment.

In my case, I was both. Her hand grabbed my hand and started lifting me.

My tiny body was still dangling down, with all my weight barely hanging on the tip of her hand. My head was down, staring at the sharp rocks at the bottom of such a mountain.

The weight of Death and gravity were much more substantial than my will, as if it were calling my name, welcoming me, and pulling me down to the dark world.

Her screaming voice said: "Mondo.. Look up at me. Look in my eyes and nothing else.

In such a deadly moment, my favorite color was Green, the color of Maribella's eyes.

She had one of the most unique, attractive green eyes, almost like mine, yet hers had a certain kind of glow that could hypnotize the mind of a human being.

I couldn't tell which world I was heading to.

Could it be the dark side .... Death, or maybe the Paradise, the green one ...her eyes?

In such a critical moment, I'd choose the Green. She pulled me up so fast, and the rest was just a part of a nightmare. I was shaking like a leaf, yet she took me in her arms and rubbed my back until I felt safe. She raised my face from my shin and said confidently: "Do you know what that means?

Mondo: "No, and what do you mean about that?

I told her with a curious tone while tears ran down my face from the fear of such a demon.....Death.

Maribella: Well, I saved your life, and so your life is mine, and my life is yours for the rest of our lives as well."

Mondo: I still don't understand the meaning of all that.

It was difficult for me to understand her wisdom in such a moment, as I was so frightened, insecure, and afraid of Death in all aspects.

Maribella: There is an old saying or proverb, and it goes like this: "If you save someone's life, then that person is your responsibility till the end of time.

Maribella: So you see, I will be responsible for your life now.

I was looking at her and listening to her wisdom, and I couldn't help but bury my head in her chest for a long time.

Maribella: I would like you to close your eyes and promise me not to open them until I tell you so.

Mondo: I promise I wouldn't.

She took my hand and walked me slowly, so close to her, yet I did feel the ground beneath my feet. It felt as if it was broken, sharp rocks. Few more steps, Mondo....She said.

I was traveling to an imaginary place far away from Spain.

The fallen Ukon Sakura Cherry blossom leaves make it seem like I was in Japan.

I was in an endless field of exotic, magnificent, colorful falling Cherry leaves, with all the magic and beauty... A goddess appeared, running towards me with her arms wide open, welcoming me into her kingdom of immortality. I ran so fast towards her and blended with her body, raising my head to see the face of the Queen of Light, and it was Maribella.

I couldn't let go until I heard her say...Mondo, Mondo.

Now, you can open up your eyes.

They said: If your mind is paralyzed, your body will follow.

When I opened my eyes, my brain became paralyzed from finding the exact feeling to express what my eyes had come to see.

My legs were paralyzed, and I collapsed to the ground.

Maribella helped me and said: "Are you all right?

I was still shocked at this extraordinary place as the rocky shore was cut in a U shape.

The seawater was always invited to merge into a deep cave beneath the rocks. Such water was filtered to generate a magnificent beach, as straightforward as it was part of Heaven.

This place, or island or beach, was hidden entirely from the rest of the world.

The watercolor was not discernible in this world, as the shallow manipulation of the colors of the water layers. The closer to the shore, the Green was the color, and the further and more profound the layers of blue were merging layer after layer. It was an impossible reality to accept as we knew it was part of this planet, yet my mind refused to admit that.

Standing on a different planet, I wanted to see if I could touch the golden sand.

Maribella: "We must go to the shore together; give me your hand.

Step by step, we managed to reach the bottom, where the golden sands replaced the sharp rocky surface. The moment I touched the soft, golden sandy shore, I let go of my aunt's hand and felt as if this was where I belonged. I took my shoes off and felt the sand through my toes; I couldn't be patient. I start running everywhere like crazy.

I never thought that life could be so....beautiful and energetic, and it was like electricity that ran through my vines. She stood there watching me flying, spinning around, running, jumping, and finally, she said to me with a smile, "Vamos, Mondo, Vamos."

The fact that I was a child made me react naturally to this place: no fake feelings, no rules, just simply life. She joined my moment of happiness and took my hand, and we danced on the sand, splashing the water at each other until we dropped down on the sand.

The water was fascinating and hard to resist, but to roll over and over.

We were lying on our backs, looking at each other's faces, until she said, "Do you want to swim?

I couldn't wait for an invitation and started taking my clothes off, jumping and bouncing off the low baby waves with my underwear. The water was so calm and refreshing, and I was diving in the shallow part.

Soon after, I was content with all this. I looked everywhere for my aunt, but she was still far on the shore's edge, watching me from afar.

I waved to her to come and join me, but she gave me a sign of NO.

I was having great fun flipping over and over, diving in the water. Maribella stood far on the shore as the small waves crashed over her tiny feet, watching me with one hand above her heart and the other covering her smile of being happy for me having fun with the sea.

She sat down on the golden sand, staring at me in happiness and joy, but I wanted her to join me so severely. I ran to the shore and grabbed her hand to get in the water, and this time, she didn't hesitate to accept my invitation to the sea.

I was so excited, not paying attention to her. Meanwhile, she was removing her clothes piece by piece, leaving a trail of her clothes on the golden sand. She was running in her underwear topless and dove in the water.

The fact that I was so happy that she joined me, I couldn't recover from her sudden disappearance. I turned around from all angles, searching for her, yet she could not be found, as if the sea took her in and down. I was short as my body was covered up to my neck with water. Suddenly, I was growing fast, rising above the water with an unexpected force lifting me, and the gravity became obsolete as if I was floating on water. I found myself above her shoulder. She went in between my legs and left me up, and I was somehow in Paradise.

The scary part about being in a very secluded, deserted, yet private U-shaped beach is the bottom of such water. She was walking in the water with me above her shoulder, heading to sea, not to the shore. The water started getting darker, as she was getting shorter or more likely submerged with water until the water level was almost below her chin.

The incredible bright colors of the sea and the sky were so unique to my eyes that everything changed to darkness, and my Death demon returned once more to take me to the deep water.

I had no idea what happened, but my true nightmare started to be confirmed.

I couldn't breathe as I was swallowing water from my mouth and nose and lacked oxygen to return to life. I felt that life could be cruel, as in one moment you're in Paradise, yet the next you're at the gate of hell welcoming you with an open arm.

Such a magical shore had a different, unusual sea bed.

The geology behind that involved the successive waves that pound the shoreline, and with that, the sea bed in certain areas can have a massive drop as it is not a leveled beach.

My aunt was unaware of scientific facts about the sea, especially that hidden beach.

As she walked facing the sea, her body weight went down because of a drop(a deep hole), and we were both covered with water. She struggled to feel the sand beneath her feet, yet the harder she tried, the faster she went down to the deep bottom of the sea bed. It was a desperate attempt on her behalf, and when she realized the complete picture, she had to make a daring decision.

I wasn't letting her go anywhere without me, so I secured my position above her shoulder and wrapped my feet behind her back, yet my hand was almost choking her as I was trying to hold to her neck so dearly.

Suddenly, I had to look up, and I realized that sunlight was fading away and the water surface was changing to darkness. The oxygen level in her lungs was vanishing, yet I was still above her shoulder, and our combined weight was the main reason we were drowning fast.

Her unexpected decision was daring yet scary to me. She had to drop me off, rise above the water and breeze, and fill her lungs with fresh oxygen; then she dove deep to save me again.

In such a short period, my body was going down faster until I found myself in a place where I had to surrender my soul to the Sea Gods.

A voice came to my ears as an echo from a faraway place.

A place with a great gathering welcoming me with a smile and open arms.

It was something that only you can see and feel in your dreams.

I wasn't walking but floating, heading to that place. Dramatically, everything turned to ashes and darkness.

I was floating halfway dead until her fingertips touched me and grabbed me from the deep, kicking, paddling hard with her feet to rise above the water for oxygen.

We drifted far from the shore, but she was an excellent swimmer, and she had her arm under my chin, swimming fast with one hand to reach the beach.

Not only that, but she is a fast swimmer and a true lifesaver. She didn't wait for the shore, but she had my head resting on her thigh, and she started with rescue breaths through my mouth to get oxygen inside my lungs. She did that repeatedly until she saw my lungs moving up and down. The next thing she did was lift me, carrying me in her arms as a baby.

The way she was breaking the water with her legs was extraordinary.

Her speed cutting through the water got faster until she reached the beach's golden sands. She didn't waste any time as she laid me on my back and started CPR.

Gradually, I returned with the sign of spitting the water out of my lungs....lots of salty water.

She flipped me sideways so the remaining water wouldn't go back inside my lungs.

I was coughing repeatedly, spitting my guts out, and finally, I threw myself on the sand, looking at the sky. We were lying on our backs breathing quietly until she turned her face at me while still holding my hand, then said: Mondo, I'm so sorry...How do you feel right now?

I looked at her and asked: Do you want to return to the water?

Her face got serious when I said that, and then she said: Are you crazy?

We were just about to drown, and you want to return to the water?

Mondo: Well, I'm feeling good now, please let's swim again.

She couldn't argue with me, and soon, we were back in the water.

We were playing, diving, and having the best moments of our lives as if nothing ever happened, with the water only below our knees and no deep water for Mondo.

We walked towards the shore, and she asked me to lay down on the edge of the beach and let the water run through us as we lay on our back with our arms wide open, believing that the water would lift us above and carry us to the clouds to another place away from this world. Maribella was like a goddess with her dirty blonde hair, tan color, and green eyes, yet with the sunlight, they were like marbles, shining and lighting up my life. She was so peaceful, like an angel. The sun, the sea, and this magical place reflected on her face. It was the first time in my life that I started to understand the mystical beauty of a female, the mystery behind their faces, bodies, and, more deeply, their souls.

I was lying on the sand, leaning my head towards Maribella's face, admiring the details of every part of it, until I started to see something extraordinary that could only exist in my dreams. It was the first time in my life that I started seeing things much more profound and transparent than it was. Her side profile was almost like mine; her nose was the same, and we had the same eye color. She is my aunt, as far as I know. Meanwhile, it was almost as if I was looking at myself in a mirror, yet she was looking back at me from miles away.

The distance between us felt as if time was bending to bring back the past to the future on the same course as one. The incredible resemblance between us made me realize that my aunt could've been my mother, but that would be impossible even to imagine.

My mind only told me that; meanwhile, my heart denied such a fantasy as if there were more to discover...

The time was in standing still motion, and the longer we were together, the more my life started to have a meaning and a purpose. Her words were like a spell in my ears, enchanting with a poem that can only be true in my dreams. She turned her head and said to me: The most significant thing you will ever learn is to love...and to be loved in return. Then she kissed my eyes. Those words were the first steps to knowing who I am and what I will be.

The unknown was my second demon in this life, and to find the truth might be the real dagger in my heart. The blowing wind was such a dagger to my happiness as it made her realize it was time for us to leave.

When she put her dress back on, she extended her arm to me to get me off the sand, saying: "Mondo, get up. We have to leave and go back home before it gets dark.

I looked at her and said: "But I am home.

There was a secret soft tear in her eyelid, fighting up to stay hidden with my simple few words, but she couldn't conceal it any longer, and it was finally coming out gently dripping down, bouncing off her cheeks and to the sand.

My eyes watched the slow motion of such a tear hitting the sand, and at once, the sea came and swallowed it to its depths.

That is my only home, too..she said.

I haven't been here for a long time, and I never brought anyone here except you, as I feel that if this is my home, then it should be yours as well.

Mondo: "Maribella, I have to ask you something.

Maribella: "Yes, my love asks me anything.

Mondo: "If I say I do love you, will you love me back in return?

My words were like a dagger that went deep into her aching heart, and for that, I made her go down on her knees and open her arms for me to merge in with her body.

Her tears were genuine and dear; although I was just a kid, my words were the cure for all her pain and the key to her heart. That moment was more powerful than the first one we hugged on my bed, and it did even last longer. The dying sun was the only thing that could separate our bodies. We started our way back from where we came from, but she had to stop and lean towards a sharp rock.

The rock was shaped like a dagger, and she started scratching our initial on a big smooth rock; when she finished, she asked me to open up my palm and look deeply into her and only her eyes. I was almost floating in thin air looking at her eyes again, and I felt nothing.

She cut off my palm, and as the blood was about to drip off, she cut her palm as well, then quickly grabbed my bloody hand and placed it on top of hers, then pressed hard as our blood blended as one ....again.

She held my hand and slowly approached the rock, then scratched two letters, "MM," and placed my bleeding palm and hers and stamped the letters with our blood.

Then she looked at me and said: "I do love you in return, my Mondo, with her tears breaking like a broken dam that floods me with tears as well." In such a magical moment, so far away from the sky, a mysterious eye was watching us from a distance, and we were together as one.

The vision from another universe was smiling of comfort and acknowledgment of our unconditional true bond and love.

I was growing up to imagine things without logical explanations, and in such a moment, I felt we were being watched from above. I was just a kid, but my mind was growing up as if there was a special force that helped me understand things that may appear to my mind and mine alone. I turn to the sky, acknowledging my acceptance of whatever they see in me.

The last two years before she passed away, we were inseparable, as my mother was always working wild shifts at the hospital, trying to save money for all of us.

It was always Maribella and Mondo.

Such tablecloths took me to a faraway place, and my tears fell slowly down my cheeks.

And That ball setting on the tablecloth brought back her sweet memories.

Mom: Mondo.....are you all right? What is this ball, and from where did you get it?

Mondo, please look at me and tell the truth, but why are you crying before that?

I couldn't hide my past emotions, tears, and sorrow from my mother, but I had to pretend and return to the continuation of the story. I had to lie to her about my tears as some flying dust from the street struck my eyes.

I described to Mom how the ball came to me from nowhere as a sign and gave some details about the rest of the day, how exciting tennis was as a sport, and how it affected me.

I confessed to her my great admiration for such a sport and wished to continue learning and be a tennis superstar. I was so hypnotized by the beauty and the fun of such a sport, yet I could not tell her what had happened between Anna and me, as I promised her not to say a word about what had transpired in the bathroom.

Mom was so happy and all excited about my day and the Tennis, yet after I finished my story, she had to get up and pour a glass of wine and sat down holding my hand and said: "My dear Mondo, (paused) I am so happy that you had a good day, but the tennis thing is (paused) not for people like us. Her tone sounded like a wise woman offering wisdom to her dear son.

In the meantime, I am very pessimistic about the sport.

Mom: Tennis, my dear, is a sport for rich people, and you are old enough to understand how hard I am trying to bring that rare smile to your face all the time as much as I can.

I am working two jobs so we can afford a living and be able to meet all your needs.

I want to give you the world if I could, and you're my only world, my dear Mondo. (paused). So, tennis is a sport that constantly requires money, and I can't afford it, at least these days.

I am all alone, as you know, and your aunt Maribella is (paused).

I had to stop her, saying: "Don't bring her into our life and not now.

She did not care about you; she never cared about me. She left me without saying goodbye, and I don't want you to say anything about her to lean my heart or even to put the blame on her because of our present status. I had to leave the kitchen and go to my room and burst into tears as her memory couldn't just vanish off my mind, and my mother was wrong by bringing her into our conversation. If she were still alive, she would've done anything to make me happy, and she would've understood how this sport was getting into my head and would've helped me achieve my dreams. I was looking at her painting, squeezing her golden heart with my fist, and wishing she could come alive, hold me, and tell me it would be all right.

I was so angry at her simultaneously, as she was selfish, leaving me all alone.

I was staring at her picture and suddenly screamed at her as if she was standing before me saying, "You've promised to take care of me till the end of time.....My time and not yours....Mine.

I threw her pictures to the wall, and the glass was shattered all over the room.

The painting was on the floor, yet I jumped on the bed, covering myself, trying to hide as I used to do when I was a very young kid. The noise brought my mother in a hurry, and when she saw what I did, she acted very wisely and quietly as she approached the bed, uncovered me, sat down on the edge of the bed, glanced her hand through my hair, and pulled me closer to her with a warm hug. I was so fogged up with my tears, and my mind was somewhere else, and when I had my head buried in her chest, I closed my eyes and said to my mother with a calm voice full of tears, "I love you, Maribella ...stay with me and don't ever leave me."

My mother pushed me away from her chest, held my face with both hands, and said; Mira...Maribella is gone, and she will never come back. Look at me... I am right here with you and always with you (paused). She left us, and she will never come back, but we love her and can't treat her like that ...Come on, get up, and let's pick up this mess and do the right thing and light a candle in her memory. I started picking up the broken glass and accidentally cut my finger, and my blood was dripping on the wooden floor. My mother caught that with her eyes, rushed to her bedroom, got her first aid kit, and started cleaning my wound, then wrapped it up with a bandage and said,' It is a small cut, and you will be fine. Sit outside, and I will clean all that, she said.

When my blood started dripping, a few drops went on the painting, and my mother tried to cover that, but the blood stain spread on my aunt's and my face.

The belief in some superstitions can drive you crazy, and my mother is one of the people who believe in these things. Though she works in the field of blood and pain as a nurse, outside of her job, she can sometimes be terrifying and obnoxious.

She was in tears as she knew that having my blood on both of our pictures was not a good omen, and the part that my aunt's death involved blood was scarier to my mother.

She had our picture on her chest, crying like there was no tomorrow. All I heard was my mother's prayers in tears as she was holding the picture.

Maria: "I loved you, Maribella, and will always love you, but you broke your promise and left me all alone. You broke my heart, and now I am cursed with your blood forever, but Mondo had nothing to do with all that. Mondo is an angel, and you've passed your curse on him with your blood. Maribella (pause), My love, I could've saved you if you would've let me, yet you slit your rest and let your blood drain to the last drop until you died.

I wish I were there, and again, I hope I was there to close your eyes and say goodbye.

I was always there for you; I am here alone because of you: no family, love, or honor.

I stood by you, covered all your sins, protected you, and took care of you as a sister and a mother at the same time. You'd promised me that it would always be us against the world, but you've broken all the rules and, above all, your promises.

You've always told me we can be magical because of my strength and strong will, yet you ran away and left me with all your sins. I can't be strong anymore.

I can't. I can't.

I hope you're finally satisfied; his blood is on you now. Not me.

Whatever I did and how hard I tried to protect you, holding your secrets in my heart, you've always managed to hurt me. And your dagger is getting old and rusty, and its poison will run into my veins and kill me one day, too.

The best thing you have ever accomplished (long pause) was Mondo.

From the moment he came into our lives, you've always wanted to blend his blood with yours.... Again. I carried your sin all those years, I buried my heart a long time ago, and after all, I became a ghost of a mother to such a magical child as Mondo.

He doesn't know, but the last day I saw you before leaving for the hospital with tears on your face, I understood that bad news was traveling in the air.

I knew all along about you getting sick daily, getting up in the middle of the night, throwing up your guts quietly. Your blood couldn't hide the truth, nor your medical report, that I've managed to steal secretly. I could've helped you, saved you, but you were selfish, leaving me like that.

Maribella, my dear Mar....Why?

The light in the room was fainting, but only my tears blinded me.

Mondo: I listened to every word she said, and then my eyes burst into tears of fire that burned me from the inside out. The mystery in her words was a puzzle to my ears as each word had a deep meaning, covering up secrets after secrets and lies of my beloved aunt.

That part about the mixed blood was the greatest of all to comprehend, yet I do recall that we did mix our blood before on that shore, but it was the blend of love and immortality, not what my mother had described.

She meant something even more profound, way deeper, which my poor brain couldn't possibly imagine, and I couldn't understand that part at all. Blend her blood with mine.

Again.

That wasn't the first time I'd heard these words, as Maribella said the exact words to me when we were together on such a hidden shore. My mind was aching from the pain of the unknown, the mystery behind so many closed doors. I had to move on and find some comfort in my heart.

Meanwhile, the thought of my mother was overwhelming to be by her side at such a moment.

I had to return to the room, hold my mother's hand, kiss her forehead, and then say, Let's get out of here and go to the shore right now.

My mother was in worse shape than me, but I managed to save her from such a depressing time by taking her out. We walked by the shore, and the cool breeze of the sea was helping the two of us. We sat on a bench facing the sea and just sat there holding each other hand, looking at the sunset, the seagull, and the waves rushing to the shore as if all our sins and sorrows would vanish with the consecutive turning waves. That bench was so special to both of us.

Not long ago, the three of us sat on the same bench, looking deeply at the far horizon with shattered dreams.

It was my mother's birthday, and we were out all day celebrating her birthday.

There was so much fun that I can still see it as a mirage sitting next to Ma.

The significant part of such a day was her unexpected birthday present.

No one planned for it, but it was a good surprise. The far echo of the musical sound of a guitar playing a particular song attracts our ears to follow the source of such music.

There was a gathering, and people were dancing, enjoying the music from some unknown band singing Bem Bem Maria, by the famous cousins, the Gypsy Kings.

We may not be close related cousins, but we're all part of the great Gypsy tribe.

Three guitar players and a beautiful woman dressed in the famous Gypsy traditional Spanish dress played music in the street for some Pesetas.

We joined the crowd, and the music started to move. My Aunt Mar couldn't stand still, and her legs couldn't resist the beat and the melody.

She started dancing and attracted all attention to her and her alone.

She was a great dancer, but above all, she was simply fantastic in all aspects.

She grabbed my mother's hand and dragged her, and they were dancing like authentic professional Flamenco dancers. It was amazing to witness that, as I never knew that my mother could move like that. I learned that my aunt was a different person than Ma, but again, they were sisters. The crowd came from every angle, and the circle became bigger and bigger with the music and the way they danced. The band kept on playing the song over and over, not caring about their burning finger hammering the strings to continue with the music, as it was the only way for them to get rich and maybe find a way to make a record with all the money that kept on pouring in their guitar cases. The way Ma and Maribella danced, celebrating her birthday, was an incredible opportunity for me to memorize such a day.

The fun continued as they pulled me in and allowed me to dance with them.

The crowd was going wild, asking for more, and never stopped.

When the music stopped, the band approached us to share some of the Pesetas, but of course, they couldn't, yet we thanked them for their excellent performance and went our ways.

The moon was quite aggressive, pushing the sunlight away and starting rising, and the dramatic change of nature manipulated our minds with all our shattered dreams.

My mother felt the weight on her chest, not from the pain of her aching heart and the sad past, but because my head was leaning more and more, and I was falling asleep on her warm, loving chest. She had to help me get up, and we walked back home as I was so tired, yet the bright part of my day was that bulky thing in my pocket as I could feel the soft hair of the tennis ball as my lucky charm.

Walking the long way home in the shadow of the moonlight smiling on us made me realize there are some good things in this life. The warmth of my mother's hand gave me comfort as it inspired me to believe in a dream.

There was one thing in my mind: a promise, an oath I took on myself.

From this moment on, and no matter how much I will have to bleed, I will always believe that Tennis is for life and that I will live another day in our unstrung lives.

CHAPTER VIII

The Mystery of the M

Sunday is always my favorite day of the week, as I spend the whole day with Ma: no hospital, not even school, just the two of us and football.

I heard the far echo of Mom singing from my room, yet the sound of falling water from the shower somehow distorted her voice.

I said to myself: Today should be a great day, and I had to get up and help Ma with the usual chores around the apartment. I could hear my mother calling my name from the bathroom, yet I was making her morning tea, which she always gets from an old Gitana in the market.

It is a unique herbal tea, but Ma always adds plenty of honey and lime.

I never liked tea or coffee, but that was something that Ma had never discovered.

My Aunt Mar made me taste her coffee and wine several times, and I liked them very much, but I couldn't have them as Mom would kill me.

Mondo: " Yes, Ma ....I am coming.

I was standing by the door asking her if she was almost done with her shower, yet she said; I am drying my hair; you can come in now. My dear god, the reflection of Ma's face in the mirror made me freeze to death by the edge of the bathroom door.

The smile on her wet face with her loose, dirty blonde hair made me drift to a scary place as I thought for a moment that my aunt had returned from the dead.

The long towel around her body didn't cover her fabulous figure and body much.

The fact was that I'd never seen my mother coming out of the shower before, as she was always in a rush to the hospital, with her white hospital uniform, white shoes, hair all up neatly in place, covered by the nursing white cap, and her heavy blue coat.

I never knew they had almost the same look, yet Maribella was much younger and more exotic than my mother. She played with my hair and said with a kiss on my lips; The bathroom is all yours, my charming Prince.

We had that thing about the kiss since I was very young, and day by day, I started to understand my mother's point of view about the daily kiss on the mouth between us.

We had a conversation a while back, and she explained why: she always kissed my lips before we went our separate ways.

Her point of view was fascinating, buttered with superstitious beliefs.

"Since the day you were born, I'd promised myself to let you memorize the taste of me, and the only way to get inside the gate of my soul is my lips, and no matter how hard my life and yours will be, the remaining taste of our lips will always be the only light to bring us back, to each other no matter how far we will be separated.

Her belief in certain things greatly influenced me, as I had no choice but to believe in her theories.

Growing up with a mother like Maria made me agree with her ways, as I know very well how superstitious she can be if we miss that kiss. The day I broke my arm, the day I had that strange fever that almost took my life away, the day she was almost about to be crushed by a crazy drunk truck driver, the day she was separated from Maribella for the first time and for a long time and the worst of all.

The day Maribella took her life away.

I was not born yet when she lost Maribella in separation for the first time, as a sister and as a friend. My aunt took off to her wildlife, leaving my mother in shame and dishonor.

The strange connection between the kiss and my aunt led to a bad omen of something terrible in the air. They used to do that before I was born, so I've inherited the same tradition of Maria and Maribella. I woke up late and had to run out to school; I never got the chance to say goodbye to Ma or kiss her goodbye, and it was the same day that my aunt passed away or took her life. There were so many other days that I couldn't remember, yet each day I remember we had to be separated without such a kiss on the lips, strange bad things happened to the two or maybe the three of us. The bathroom was foggy, and I had to wipe the moisture off the mirror and leave the bathroom door open to vent the room. After she finished her shower, I had to do that to get some oxygen to breeze while I was in the bathroom.

My mother's fear and superstition about many things in life made her a fanatic about germs.

At the hospital, everything must be entirely sanitized, sterilized, and clean, and with hot water and soap, the germs will be blocked from getting to her body and skin.

The other impressive thing about my mother is her way of being the most spotless, organized human I have ever seen. Her yelling for me to hurry up for breakfast shattered my thoughts.

Maria: "Come on, Mondo, we have a long day ahead.

I had to finish with the bathroom quickly, then rush to the kitchen table for a fast, quick breakfast, according to Ma. She was the fastest person to make pancakes and the best as well. The layers were so rich in ingredients that she prepared them the night before we went to bed. She covered the dough with a linen canvas, "Couche," and placed it in the fridge to rise correctly. The three layers of Pancake were significant, and on top of the bottom layer, she brushed it with a liquid mix of brown sugar, cinnamon, coconuts, and dry pineapple, all crushed together and soaked with vanilla. That liquid mix is thick and sweet, so she brushes each layer separately on both sides and lets them dry until the combination penetrates through the dough. She spread the creme, which consisted of heavy milk cream whipped thoroughly with vanilla strip beans, then drained until it became very thick. Sprinkle raisin, wall nut, dry prunes, and the last thing is the orange skin that she shreds very fine on the side. She only spread a very tinny pint of that orange to add the scent and the flavor of the famous Valencia orange.

She covers that layer with the second one, and this one is always different as sometimes she spreads her special natural homemade jam of strawberry, blue, or blackberry, then the creme again and the same sprinkles as the bottom one, and finally the top one that only has real natural fruits. Sometimes, a slice of banana, pineapple, strawberry, or the Berry family.

Her syrup is from Heaven as she poured it all over the three layers and cut it into four pieces, and next to all that, a glass of squeezed Valencia orange juice. And that was my mom's fast breakfast. It is the most fascinating and complicated breakfast on this planet.

I always tried to convince her how to mix up things we used to eat, especially breakfast.

One day, I saw a commercial on TV about something very American called Kellogg's Corn Flakes, or as they called it in America.....Cereal.

I asked Ma to buy it. However, I couldn't tell where the storm came from.

My mother was always moving with the new world and technology, but she can be a nightmare regarding food and nutritious, healthy food. I see kids in school eating that, so I never had a chance to try it. I asked her if she could buy it, and her answer was the storm I wasn't prepared for. Those Americans have no taste of anything in life. They are on the run to make money every minute; with that, they eat anything fast to keep going and make more money. Their dream is money, and when it comes to food, they have yet to learn what good food is, so I'm telling you this once and for all.

Please don't follow the American dream as it is; it will lead you to your worst nightmare.

That Cereal is not a good food, and how can you compare something dry out of a box that you have no idea how they put it all together, and all the colors and crazy strange shapes of such a thing called Cereal with my great Pancake?

I will buy it today so you can understand the difference between real food and artificial food (paused). Hmmmmm. Rubbish.

I laughed so loud about how she said all that, but again, I was just a kid trying to explore new things outside the traditional Spanish Culture. Only my mother can be the one convincing person about the truth in life, and I do trust her...and undoubtedly love her.

Later, after all that, we'd left the apartment and headed to El Mercado Atarazanas. Reading so many books helped me see life differently than other kids my age.

I was much more interested in history books than others.

The Atarazanas wasn't a market as we see it these days, yet it was one of the largest shipyards during the Moorish era. The collapse of the structure was renovated and rebuilt to the way it stands today, near 1879, thanks to the great architect Joaquin Rocoba.

The market is considered one of the main attractions in our state of Malaga.

The market was bustling, and so many people were shopping for food, yet we were there only for the fish and some minor things.

Mom always prefers the older man, Pablo, who constantly reminds her of the grand Pablo Picasso. The famous Picasso was the most accomplished son of Malaga, and yet our close neighbor as well. We live across from his building at Plaza de La Merced as his spirit still wanders around the narrow alleys in that part of the old city.

The old fisherman, Pablo, was my mom's favorite place to buy fish and no one else.

The fish trays were in order of size, with ice all around them to keep them fresh.

The older man somehow was the only one my mother trusted about everything that had to come from the sea. On the other hand, I've always found ways to scare people in the market as I used to play with the Crap's legs while they were soaked in a deep barrel, and the fun part was when I managed to catch one with a stick and start waving the wooden bar up in the air to the passing shoppers. The fun part never ended in a good way as the shoppers, including my mother, were always angry and had no scene of humor. Just a slap on my head would kill all the fun, but the look on the people's faces was the main target of my attraction and adventures.

The old Pablo may not be a famous person or even an artist. However, how he'd arranged the fish and other seafood was always great to watch. The mixing colors of fish was always the artistic way to attract Mom's attention to which fish we'd get.

The budget is small, so we only get two fish. She picked one, and the other is mine.

The mission was successful, and we said goodbye to Pablo, but he always put two big Camarones free shrimps with the fish we bought. He wrapped them nicely with thick brown paper so they wouldn't leak in my shopping canvas bag.

I said: "So, what do you want to have next to the fish, Ma?

I didn't give my mom a chance to get the answer. I answered her rapidly: Let's get a potato, tomato, scallion, lemon, carrots, garlic, parsley, cilantro, coriander, lettuce, red pepper, and onion.

Maria: "Is there anything else you forgot to mention out of this market?

Mondo: "Yes, rice..of course."

So she said:" Well, in this case, let's get to the other side of El Mercado so that we can get all that."

The market was more crowded than usual, and we were trying to reach our destination.

I was waving my arms left and right, pushing people away to make a pass for us, yet the most incredible, unexpected thing did appear in front of my own eyes. The crowd was moving slowly through a thick fog, and the mist started to vanish and scatter away with the sun's rays.

I was the sun in such a moment, clearing the way for Mom to get through.

Suddenly, my eyes got caught by a sparking light from a distance, and I was frozen like a statue in such a moment. The air got so thick, yet the laws of gravity disappeared like I was floating on thin air. I was frozen in complete silence until a word was said in such an echo. Mondo, Mondo

My name was the break of such a silence, but it came from two opposite directions with two different tones of voice. The first was close to my ears; my mother called me because I was frozen in the middle of the market.

The second was not so far either, as Anna's voice called my name.

One voice looked down at me, wondering about my status, and that was my mother. Meanwhile, the other voice was just ahead of me, frozen. I tried to breeze, but my heart pounded like a Japanese Taiko staring at Anna's face. My name was called repeatedly more than once, attempting to find an answer to my status. I was like a lousy stage actor with no response, lines, or voice.

I was standing there, observing Mom and Anna's approach from two different angles in slow motion. The colliding was scary to me as I couldn't predict the next moves from all of us.

Anna: "We meet again ....Mondo. "

Anna broke the code of silence with a pretty smile on an angel's face.

A magical ray of sun found its way to her magnificent blue eyes, making them sparkle, radiating a great deal of magical warm charm. She stretched her arm towards me as an invitation to shake hands. The comfort of seeing Anna's face again made me hear the loud Taiko's beat again, but it was simply my fast-beating heart.

There was no scientific explanation for my current status, as my eyes started to glow again just by seeing her face again. Such an indescribable spell radiating off my eyes made Anna's face change to a certain kind of fear of my spell on her. She rushed at me, leaning closer to my face, saying: "I am so glad that destiny has brought us across our path again.

She stood straight, looked at my mother, and said politely with an extended handshake: "My name is Anna, and I am..."

Anna couldn't finish introducing herself to Ma, as the unexpected and unfortunate thing had happened. Mom looked at her with a smiling impression face with so many things in her mind that I couldn't read, as they changed dramatically and periodically according to what was on her mind and said to her: " Ahhhh, So you are "Anna," the one and the only.

Mondo: "Mom...what are you doing?

I pulled her dress down with anger to stop her strange behavior, as I was pretty damn angry because I knew Ma very well from the tone of her voice.

Her voice sounded very clear of star casting and a bit of anger.

I wasn't expecting that from her at all, but I couldn't help pulling her dress harder to stop her crazy behavior, and my reaction led to an opposite counterattack from Ma towards me, slapping my hand so hard to let go of her dress. I was so embarrassed that my face turned red like a tomato we hadn't bought yet as planned, but I was hoping that she could alter such a tone with some liking and respect. Meanwhile, I wasn't the only one who noticed my mother's casting behavior; there was another strange, beautiful Lady in white, with such a weird hat and dark glasses, but exquisite and chic.

Audrey Hepburn was always my favorite actress.

However, the Lady standing beside Anna looked better in all aspects and measurements.

She was about 1.8 meters, with a toned, firm body, yet her dark glasses didn't do her any good, as I saw her blue eyes fixed on mine in a way I hadn't felt before toward the other sex.

Her lips had a red stop sign announcing it was all green lights for me if I ever decided to cross that road, and she confirmed her wicked intention with twinkled eyes and an evil smile.

The great W. Shakespeare wrote the theatric coming dramatic scene, as the Lady starts reading her part, saying:" Do you know these people, my dear Anna?

With such a heavy British accent, yet in an elegant way, too.

The tone, the accent, and the star casting were much worse than my mother's, and I felt that if I didn't get involved and read my part in the play, it would turn out to be the Battle of the Armada. The entire moment was completely altered towards me, as I did not like the woman's tone when she said: "These people.

I took control of the entire situation, breaking all the ice and the confusion by saying in an earnest, respectable manner and in English, too.

The only thing that most likely amazed everyone, including me, was how I said it in such a heavy British accent.

"My name is Mondo...(paused), and I am delighted to meet you, my Lady.

On the other hand and above and more likely, regardless of your name, I would say in such a proud way that,(paused) then I slow down my speech with a soft, yet hush tone saying...., well, Anna is a friend of mine.

This lovely, fabulous Lady standing right next to me is considered the most beautiful, elegant, respectful, hard-working woman I've ever known in my short life, and that is not all. She is my wonderful mother, and we are so pleased to meet you.

Yet, we have to leave your court as soon as possible, as we do have some essential matters and places to be, so again and with all due respect and any further doubts and goddamn due Crap, it was my great honor to meet you and without any further due, please don't get offended with our simplicity, modesty, as we are some proud Spaniard who believe that human can be treated and respected by their accomplishment in life, not just their looks and fancy clotheslines, or even a Hat that made of the skin of {an... may be ...has been free} bird in the sky, yet some fat ugly bastard British hunter felt so lucky in his darkest drinking god damn hunting trip and possibly intended to get drunk after he recently found out that his young new wife was cheating on him with the daily milkman, so at last he felt somehow, invincible, to turn the peaceful life of such an innocent bird to an end. That fat bastard got his big gun loaded, ready, and ended such a bird's freedom to land above a stupid hat On top of your head...hmmm, my Lady.

My straight, robust, and deceitful answer in English left the three of them in total shock.

Faces, eyes, hands, and impressions were all that they had gone to say.

The first one to break the ice was my mother when she said to me: Mondo, when did you learn to speak English like that and{pause}, I had to interrupt my mother's words and say to her in Spanish: "I knew the language from my friend Anna and so many other things, too.

At that moment, I had to lie in front of everyone as I started to see the fast change in me of adapting things quickly, including the language, the crazy strange British accent, and lies, which was the transformation into a new person that I have turned to be.

Anna's face was glowing because of my compliment and the mysteries in between the words of what they did mean. On the other hand, the impact on the other two women was not entirely mutual, as one is still trying to understand {How}, while the other is trying to understand {When or Why?}

How was Ma trying to understand how I learned English like that?

The {When} was coming from the other side as the woman was still trying to figure out when I met her, Anna.

The last thing was significant {Why}, and again, the woman's mind was wondering with fear {Why} she was so damn attracted to this young lad, regardless of his indescribable disrespect to my clothes or even how I spoke.

There was a very dark cloud above us, and a storm was about to blow everything and ruin a beautiful day for all of us. For the second time, I had to get involved and clear all the dark clouds with a few words and a smile.

"Por favor, today is a great day as the Real Madrid match will start at 3 pm.

I am hungry, thirsty, and happy to be in the company of the most beautiful three Ladies in El Mercado, or possibly in Espana, so please let's get together without any borders of countries, names, languages, fashions or even(Pause) ....Hats.

I didn't want things to get more out of control. Suddenly, the loud explosion that sounded out of their giggles changed everything.

They were all laughing, and the actual introduction started to fill in appropriately.

The woman was Anna's aunt, and she was here to spend the rest of the summer with Anna at her fancy villa in Ronda. She opens up her hand to shake my mom's hand. IN PEACE, she introduced herself in Spanish very elegantly and said: "I am Victoria .... Anna's aunt, and I am so pleased to meet you; meanwhile, she did a fantastic thing to all of us, but above all.... to me personally. She took off her fancy hat and slammed it in the nearest trash bin, the nastiest in the entire market, as it was one for all the fish cleaning parts. She didn't stop just with that, but again, she removed her dark shades, then stretched her arm fully, tossing the sunglasses in the air, exposing her long eyelashes, the blue eyes, and the glimmering freckles above her rose cheeks.

The sunglasses were flying in the air, fighting all the laws of gravity, yet our eyes traveled with them until they landed in Pablo's Lobster tank. We laughed so loudly that the entire market looked at us, but again, there were so many other audience members who enjoyed the show, and they laughed as well, except for poor Pablo.

The main attraction was the sunglasses. However, she had to turn her head quickly, looked at me, and said; { Hmmm, and of course you are the famous mysterious Mondo.}

My mother was still in a state of shock. Yet, she responded very nicely to Victoria, shook her hand as well, and at last smiled, saying: "I am Maria, and the famous Mondo happened to be my humble poor son ...the one standing next to me, and I am so pleased to meet you Anna, and please forgive me for my bad behavior, and maybe one day when you become a mother, you'll understand how important for a mother to be overprotective for her son, so again please accept my apology. On the other hand, I'm very thankful for the tennis lessons you've provided for my son, which brought back some great pleasure to his heart. I can't describe to you how happy, {pause}. Another interruption, cutting my mother off, as Victoria jumped in the conversation 'saying," So' hmmm...It was the tennis, of course. Victoria said with a laugh."

The last unexpected thing was Ma, as she couldn't do any better than be friendly and show them tremendous Spanish hospitality by simply inviting the two of them to that cafe outside of the market at Tapas near Plaza de Merced.

They were very pleased with her gesture invitation, yet I had to remind her that we still needed to do our shopping. She gave me that wonderful fake smile that was immediately followed by a fast change of an evil staring look 'saying: Shut up in Spanish, then smiled back again."

I was slightly frightened, but I understood her quick looks and shut my mouth.

She asked them to accompany us while we were shopping.

Meanwhile, I was somehow not thrilled about my mother's plan, as she would thoroughly interrogate Anna to discover the whole story behind the tennis.

We walked together in the market as we got our list; meanwhile, as part of that extreme change in me, I've also developed another thing known as Observation.

I was fully aware of how Victoria and Anna were observing me as well and somehow amazed at how well I picked my vegetables as if I am a real mature chef, yet they had to ask me why I had to choose the third one all the time and not the first one.

Well, I've learned that from two people, and they are and were the best things that happened in my life, so I trusted them with all their wisdom, lessons, and judgments.

Victoria: I am sure your mom is one of the two, but who is the other one, and what is the wisdom behind choosing the third item, not the first one on top?

Mondo: My Aunt Maribella, God 'bless' her soul { pause} My eyes started tearing up, yet I had to control my emotions and complete the sentence saying,' and the wisdom behind that is straightforward. It is also somehow complicated, but the secret is that people always touch the first one on top. They wonder if it is the right choice, sometimes they take it, but some other times they put it back,' then' pick the second one, so the one they first touched will have their fingerprints and so many different things that may come with that, and there is no way in the world it will be my choice. However, the third one is always hidden, untouched, and unspoiled, as a virgin waiting for the right one to come along and choose it, so it is the right one for me unless it is(Pause). Unfortunately, Rotten..."

They laughed, but Ma rubbed my head as she was so proud of how I'd become a wise man, even though I was just a kid. The air started to have a different scent as we were about to leave El Mercado, with the people's scent in the streets.

It was like a colorful, painted carnival, a fiesta, and with all the tourists in such an area, some taking pictures, some other shopping, and among all of them, we were all mingling to blend in for a beautiful day or maybe as Ernest Hemingway described as the Moveable Feast.

At last, we arrived at one of the Tapas cafes, and my mother ordered some coasters of Spanish food and drinks for all of us.

The place was packed with people from all over the world, and no matter how busy the place was, my mind was only occupied with one thing: the look on Anna's face.

My mom had a long conversation with Victoria, and the conversation grew louder as she tried to explain her point of view about tennis, as we can't afford the expenses of such a sport.

Anna somehow had a different opinion about my mom's rejection of the sport, so she had to get involved with the conversation in Spanish so Mom could understand her point of view.

My mother was so anxious to hear her side of the story that she went above the edge and ordered a bottle of wine. Victoria was somehow pleased with my mother's choice as she loves Spanish wine, so she had a glass, too.

On the other hand, Anna started explaining to my mother that she sees great potential in me and feels I am gifted and natural for tennis. She is frank and committed to doing everything she can to help me thoroughly learn the sport. Also, she expressed her steadfast dedication to tennis and surprised my mother with a very generous proposition. She said she would pay for my entire training for a year, out of her pocket, in such a club{Athena}. Also, she will get me a job at the club, so the money can help me to cover whatever I may need in the future; also, during her stay in the summer, she will be there waiting for me for practice. She will make it her responsibility to pick me up from school, and when the training is over, she will accompany me to our place.

My mother, Victoria, and I, as well, were in disbelief at Anna's proposition.

The waiter was heading inside the cafe, yet my mother caught his arm and asked him for another bottle. I know our budget, yet Ma was getting semi-drunk and lost her wisdom in reading the price off the menu.

I tried to warn her, but I got another smack on my head.

The waiter came back so fast that my mother couldn't have a chance to begin her argument, but she was glad as the wine was the only way for her to lean her heart and accept Anna's offer.

I was unhappy with my mother's behavior with the wine as she was never a heavy drinker.

Yet, since Maribella left us, she had her long, lonely moments alone in the dim light, drinking and crying all alone in the dark; despite all that, there were so many nights that I had to help her to bed and sometimes cover her and leave her in peace on the sofa.

The present and this moment of confrontation were an entirely different case, and I couldn't understand why she was like that, yet I was somehow uncomfortable with her behavior.

On the other hand, Victoria wasn't helping at all, as the two were competing in a challenging competition over who would drink more wine. Victoria did something even worse than my mother's behavior and the drinking.

She leaned back on her seat, opened her fancy golden purse, and got a golden box.

The box was opened with a gentle thumb push. Then I realized it wasn't a magic box but full of goddamn cigarettes. She lit one, looked at my mother with her leaning head back on her seat, and said to mom: "You care for one(paused)... Maria?

I hoped my mother would be a strong woman and say: { NO}, but instead, she leaned forward, took the cigarette, and lit it up. She turned her head and looked at Anna, then at me, and with her blowing smoke in the air, she 'said,' I think I've heard enough, and so it is my time to speak.

The first thing I must ask you, my dear Anna, is your 'age.' How old are you?

Anna, I am 16 years old, and next month, on August 11, I will be 17 years old.

Mom: Hmmm, wonderful. You will be 17 next month.

Mom nodded, took a sip of her wine, then said to her: Do you know that Mondo's birthday was June 6, and he is now 11 years old, so you see where I am going with that ... and her serious face turns dramatically.

No, 'Madam'...I don't understand what you are trying to tell me.

Anna replied to 'Mom.

Suddenly, Victoria got involved in the conversation, saying: So, what is happening now?

I was not following the whole damn thing.

Still, my niece is trying to help this young boy with the tennis thing, yet you, on the other hand, are making the matter very complicated, and you should apologize to her about the age remark; she is almost half of his age, and she is from a very decent family, and she cares about that magnificent boy so much that somehow made me suspicious, about the truth, behind her sincerity for such a matter. My poor mother started to realize that the wine played a destructive role in her poor judgment of Anna's offer. It was true that she was so worried about me, and because of that, she asked questions in strange ways. She reached out for Anna's face and lay her hand gently, asking her to move closer to her face, and said as if she was trying to whisper the 'words'... Mondo is all I have, and he is my light, and if anything happens to him, I will turn blind and die, so please be gentle with my heart and consider everything I said to you and promise me to watch over him { pause, then she sipped her wine} as long as you live, por favor. Anna looked at my mother's face as her tears were in a race of coming out of her green eyes and said to mom: I promise you, Maria, that I will now and forever take care of him whenever he needs help, not only that, but I do swear to you that Mondo's life will be my responsibility until the day I die. I will do my best to show him the way to such an unstrung life.

That is a much better approach, my dear Maria, Victoria said with a satisfying smile.

Let's have another drink for that. The surprise that turned my head was not my mother or Anna but Victoria.

She was a beautiful woman, and Rich was as well. She was not that tall, but her body was shaped the right way as a woman, and her eyes were as blue as Anna's, yet she was funnier and more accessible with her statements and hands. Meanwhile, she liked me very much from the moment she laid her eyes on me at the market.

The fact that I was somehow the boy of her dreams changed how she looked at me, and she wanted to be part of such a great moment. With all that, she also wanted to express her happiness at my mother's acceptance of her niece's offer.

The other factor was my eyes. The glow that shone off my eyes made her race with herself. She drank her wine so fast she almost slammed the glass on the table, got up, and said, "Come here and hug me, my angel. I had to look at my mother and Anna simultaneously as if I was asking them their permission to do so, and only their smiles were enough as a sign of their approval.

I got up, then went to her and hugged her, but that was not enough for Victoria, and it was not entirely her clear intention.

She held my face with both hands, stared deeply into my eyes, imprinted a real kiss on my lips, and said: "Maravilloso.

My mother was quite drunk from the wine, and Anna was quite naive at that moment; yet again, that transformation in me made me so different, realizing things beyond my age. Victoria's kiss had so many hidden passions that I felt within the wetness of her lips.

She kissed me with such a passion for a man, not for an innocent child.

A creeping, falling single sweat was coming off the tip of her nose, and as they say, some women can show their infatuation with a male through a move of their eyes, lips, hands, and open legs. In Victoria's case, it was that crawling drop of sweat as if it were a sweat of her orgasm. I had to step back away from her, but only with a smile, and went back to my seat, drinking my orange juice in one shot and almost slamming the glass on the table angrily. The icy orange juice went straight to my veins, yet the blazing fire from my lips melted the icicles out of my brain with such a steaming hot Victoria's lips.

I had to raise my eyes and give her that quick look as if I was telling her yes, I felt it, too.

She looked back at me with her eyes wide open from the shock, as she quickly realized that I felt the same way with such a glow and passion in my eyes.

Her state was fidgety as my eyes were focused entirely on her face, straight at her chin, then her lips, climbing above her nose, to her eyes, and straight to her soul.

My way of looking at her as a woman was not a response from a child but from a mature man looking for a completion of a lusted woman like Victoria.

My looks were somehow killing her, burning her inside out, and her response to all that was frightening drops of cold sweat, freezing her mind and soul.

The more I stare, the more her body trembles and shakes.

Her imagination was combined with reality and me. She saw me coming back for her, but only with my eyes, and with that, she started to act differently.

Her legs began to open up as her great thighs spread enough for whatever may come.

She felt a strange, unusual desire of sensation just looking at my eyes.

The significant indescribable radiation from my eyes increased as I looked down at her thighs. She was uncomfortable, making her feel almost naked and vulnerable to my great seduction.

She had no control over her senses, eventually leading her to drop her glass of wine to the ground. The broken glass shattered on the fine small pebbles of the street; however, that was not the only punishment she got from me.

As I was staring at her face, then down to her thighs, she was losing control, and suddenly, I started backcombing my hair with a coy smile and open posture, then I started sliding slowly off my seat as an apparent gesture that I'm going down and vulnerable but open for you.

I used the faraway gesture, and I pretended as if I was blowing her off her chair.

But such a strange force came from nowhere, blowing her off the chair, and she was falling backward on the hard pebbles of the street.

Her body was on the ground, yet her legs were wide open for white fancy satin underwear to be exposed to the world. She was the center of the attraction with her act as everyone looked to see if she was all right.

Meanwhile, the waiter came rushing quickly, cleaned the spot, and got her another clean glass. She was laughing, trying to cover her deep sweat and the shaking of her inner body from my smiling eyes behind the dripping lines off my orange juice's glass and adding more ice to her brain; my long tongue liked the outer side of the cool glass as a devilish sign for her unexplained seduction. It was all gestures and signs of my admiration of her exotic body that she was the only one who was able to read it and feel it through her legs, mad more desperately in her insecure nipples. Her constant feeling of touching her body in different places assured me that my act was going far beyond an 11-year-old kid. I didn't know what had become of me, but I wasn't Mondo at such a moment. I was a different person, a Beast looking for lust.

Victoria saw what I did and couldn't stay in her seat anymore.

She bounced up so fast as if her chair was on fire. As soon as the massacre was over, Victoria said with a laughing, trembling, drunk tone{ I think it is enough, and it is time for us, my dear Anna, to go and let these two lovely people go to their normal lives.}

She rushed towards Mom and hugged her, then grabbed Anna's arm to get going, but Anna said severely, "Aunty, what is wrong with you? We still have to discuss so many things.

Please wait a little bit longer. What is the sudden rush, and why are you so shaky?

Victoria smiled and leaned to Anna's ears and said in a whispering, commanding tone: I said we have to leave right at this moment, now, Anna. Then she smiled at us as if nothing happened.

Anna: Can you give me a moment to also say goodbye to Mondo and Maria?

Victoria: "But, of course... Yes, why don't you do so, or if you wish, stay with them, but I must go now.

There was a strange, tense vibe, electrifying hot air, and the atmosphere was about to erupt with earthquakes and possible volcanos. The lava coming from Victoria's eyes was very noticeable and clear. Meanwhile, Anna approached my mother's side and said, "Mondo (Pause).

She stopped with whatever she was about to tell me, then looked at my mother and stated: "I would love to come tomorrow to your place and give you all the arrangements regarding Mondo's practice, and so I would like very much if you can write down your address and I will see you at 5 pm if that will be a good time for you and Mondo as well.

For the first time today, my mother, at last, acknowledged Anna's support and care.

With that, she admired her courage as if she were looking at Maribella standing before her, regardless of their enormous differences.

Still, she saw a caring person for Mondo, as Maribella used to care for him as well.

Mom wrote down our address, and they were discussing the time for her visit tomorrow, yet on the other hand, I was standing next to my mother with half of my body hidden behind hers, except my eyes as they were still looking hunting for Victoria and her state of desperation, confusion, passionate, and frustration of not being able of vanishing away from my eyes.

Anna hugged Mom, patted my head, and said in Spanish, Mañana.

My mother had me under her arm, and we were both looking, waving at them, until they were gradually about to vanish. I heard a strange inner voice saying to myself: Wait, Mondo, wait; she will look back, wait.

Then, I was right.

Victoria turned her head halfway and gave me that look with a smirk as if telling me: "I will see you again... Little devil.

I had to shake my head off and let that evil voice disappear from my mind at once.

Mom said to me: Let's get home. We must still cook the fish before the game; let's go, Vamos Mondo.

We headed to our place, and I flew off the stairs to the second floor, opened the door, put the plastic cover on the kitchen table, and started preparing everything for Mom to clean the fish while I washed the vegetables.

The food was ready, and so were we.

The game, Mom. I screamed at her to turn the TV on. I ran to my room, changed my top, and wore the Real Madrid club jersey. I also gave Mom hers to put on, too.

It is a costumery thing and 'moreover' being superstitious, so we must embrace our love and loyalty to the club by wearing the Real Madrid outfit every game they play as fans.

It is a unique custom to wear the shirt, as it allows you, as a fan, to blend in with your feelings as if you're a Substitution player sitting on the bench.

Our loyalty to Real Madrid as a club goes way back to when my mother and aunt were big fans of such a great club. One of our distant cousins used to play for the club.

Whenever he came home to visit my mother's little town, he used to tell them stories about the club, the training, the players, and the fantastic atmosphere at the great Santiago Bernabeu.

I like the local Malaga team, but my heart goes with Real Madrid.

There were so many times when I was younger that I used to dream of playing for such a great club, but again, it was just a typical dream of every Spanish kid.

I loved the football game because of Mom; as she used to tell me, if she was a boy instead of a girl, she would've played such a glorious sport and enjoyed the fun the sport brought around. She used to come to watch me play with the local team and cheer me like crazy every time I dribbled the ball or even scored a goal. We love football, as it is one of the everyday things we enjoy in our simple life.

Every Christmas, I wish to be at the Bernabeu and watch Real Madrid play, but Santa always tends to skip that wish. Sometimes, I used to think that Papa Noel needed to be fairer with all the kids; maybe he got paid to deliver the right wishes for only special kids, but never me. I believe he only listens to particular kinds of kids, Not my type, which never bothered me, as I was well aware of my status as a simple Spanish family no more, no less, ni mas ni menos. My mother knows the players' names, and with her superstitious beliefs, she used to pray a special one for the team to win. An exciting day like ours needed more joy, and with my team winning 3- 0, the day turned out to be one of the best days of my life.

Soon after, the night was blending in, and I had to help my mother to bed as we had a long day. I have to go to school, and she has to leave the house early for the hospital for the 0600 a.m. shift. I was about to leave her room, but she called me with a soft, tired voice as a whisper in my ears, asking me to lay beside her on the bed until she closed her eyes.

I did, but my mind wondered about the right words to help her fall asleep.

I sang to her: "Have a good night, and if there's trouble on your mind, there's always tomorrow, so for now, turn down the light and have a good night.

 I had no clue who wrote or sang that song, but it was one of those songs Aunt Mar used to sing to help me drift to the world of fantasy and dreams.

Maria closed her eyes in peace, and I had to kiss her good night, but this time I kissed her on her forehead. The distance to my room felt as long as a long road, and I was trying to understand the changes in my body and mind. The air in my room and the memories from behind the walls made me look for Marbella's album for one photo that was so dear to my heart. I went far and beyond, and finally, it was in my hand.

She was lying down on the sand with her face looking at her right-hand side, and in her eyes, there was so much love and peace, yet if I looked deeper, I might see her tearing blood instead of tears. She was so relaxed, looking at someone.

I remember very well that someone was just me lying beside her.

It was a moment when her face and eyes were glowing with a secret language of such beauty that wouldn't exist in this world.

 Her face cured all my past, present, and future pain.

On such a day, she allowed me to use her fancy Leica camera to capture whatever my eyes wished to see. I held the camera and started searching for the right shot, but there was no beauty anywhere but only within her face. My hand froze at her profile, with the golden sun dazzling her long eyelashes, blending the magical colors to her cheek, turning them to gold.

After I took her picture with her camera, she said to me: "So you will have me on a frame to maintain the memory of my face in your mind, but I need to know if you would be able, and maybe...., One day to set me free off such a frame."

My dear Mondo, my true love, will you be able to forgive me for not being close to you?

I won't ask you for anything except one thing and only one thing.

Her last statement was floating to my ears with an attachment of her broken golden tears.

The sunset was like the hand of the most significant painter's brush in history as it manipulated the color of each drop of her tears.

She called me and said: Mondo.

Mondo: Si, Mar.

I was waiting for the mysterious request to come out of her lips.

Maribella: "I want you to remember my name as Maribella, and if you say my name a million times, it will sound differently each time." Say it when you're alone, cold, hungry, happy, and sad. Say it in your mornings and nights. Say it when you need a friend, a sister, a brother, a lover, and even more (pause)—a mother.

Say it when you believe that two M, M can be one. Say it when your blood is finally mine.

Say it when you see a dagger stabbing the bleeding sun.

Only then will I be out of that frame to be there for you and back with me forever and ever? The day that sign appears in front of your eyes, I will be there to clear the mystery behind the M.

That photo was sitting next to my pillow as my goodnight and every night as there was no end to her goodbyes.

CHAPTER IX

The Black Sea 1970

The night was the gate to my dreams. I closed my eyes and started dreaming, yet drifting to the unknown. My mind was confused, yet my dreams led me to a new world.

An extraordinary world of lights. It was clear that I needed to find the road to the unknown, yet I didn't know the way. Ironically, in my dream, I had to close my eyes to dream within the dream as if it was "dream a little dream."

It was so strange to be able to see myself in the future. I was in a field of gold, an area of unreal flowers and roses that don't exist in our world. There was a gate that seemed close, and the more I walked, the further it appeared to my eyes.

At last, I managed to touch the gate. However, I was tired from such a long distance to get to this damn gate. It was brown, but again, I wasn't sure if it was brown or red.

My fingers felt the strange texture of the gate as if it were like dirt: red dirt or Red clay.

I pushed the gate hard with both hands, wanting to know my way in this wild dream.

When the gate opened, a very unexpected storm came from nowhere, and the entire gate was covered with a sandstorm. I couldn't see anything, but when the storm cleared away, my eyes witnessed the most fantastic place in this world.

The place was huge, and it was a red clay tennis court.

It wasn't any court, but amazingly, it was a well-known court by Philippe Chatrier in Paris, France. I was standing in the middle of that court all alone.

My dreams weren't normal anymore; my whole being was not average.

There is something different yet new about me.

Such a mysterious meeting, or colliding with the Queen of Lights, wasn't just magical. Moreover, it was just a dream. A dream that can only happen in a fantasy.

I was dreaming in the middle of the day, and I wondered if she was just a dream.

I was desperate, confused, and frustrated, trying so hard to understand what had happened to me since the first time we met.

Her words were actual, yet again, it felt like I was dreaming. It was not just my mind going crazy, but the complete misunderstanding and the loss of connection between my mind and my body. My body took a new phase, like a sponge.

My muscles felt different; they grew independently, without any exercise or workout.

I'm 11 years old, but in reality, such a transformation made everything completely different, as if I was living two lives in two other bodies than mine.

She implanted so many things that I'm still trying to discover day after day.

I've become stronger, wiser, and knowledgeable, but the most scary thing was the transformation of my eyes.

If I get angry, they glow, and I feel invincible and dangerous, yet capable of doing things that don't agree with my age or original personality. Such a glow can transform me into a person capable of manipulating minds, whether seductive or opinionated, with no dispute or challenge.

I was once a very sweet, naive, somehow weak, compassionate, and emotional child.

I used to be afraid and superstitious of everything in life, but not anymore.

Was it a gift or a curse?

I couldn't sleep as my mind was swirling in so many directions.

There is a new strange force in me as if I was possessed in a good way.

My energy level had reached a new level, where my heart could endure so much physicality.

I wanted to explode and let this new force out, yet I couldn't think of how or where.

I have read many comic books, yet they have never been confirmed.

They had ideas and points of view, but again, they were never confirmed.

I'm not a fictional comic book character, yet how I feel nowadays makes my mind react and think that way. My window was my gate to think. The smell of the sea breeze traveling so gently from the sea invaded my soul as an invitation to get to the shore.

It's late, very quiet and peaceful, but I have to get out of here as soon as possible.

Mom had to get up early, possibly in 5 hours, to get everything ready before going to the hospital. It was a long, hard day for her, so I had to sneak out of the house secretly as a ghost. I put on my football training suit but no shoes. The floors in the entire apartment were made of parquet, and the tinny gap between them could make a big noise.

I had to tiptoe to the door, carrying my sneakers around my neck. The moment I was out, I felt great relief, and the moment I wore my sneakers, I flew off the steps down until I was out of the building in an empty, silent street.

I wanted to start running, but my mind kept returning to how stupid and clumsy I was, jumping so fast off the steps, not realizing it was Thursday.

Every Wednesday night, all the tenant gets their trash out in front of their doors for Thursday pickup. Our building had different rules for sanitation, yet in other places, they leave their trash in the street.

The old man, Miguel, takes care of everything in our building, including maintenance and trash. All the tenants must leave the trash by their doors at night, and he clears them in the early hours. I was close to reaching the first floor, but I hit one of the garbage bags because I was jumping and skipping so many steps rapidly.

I kicked that bag so hard that it went flying, hitting the wall, then exploded and shattered all the trash over the steps. I was still in the street, indecisive about my options and choices, as I had two choices. One is to ignore what I've done and keep flying off the steps until I'm out of the building and be a bad boy, pretending that nothing ever happened.

My second choice is to feel guilty, responsible, and mature enough to start cleaning the mess I've made. The wisdom of my choice made me go up again, sacrificing the chance of getting caught, which might lead to big trouble with such a miserable tenant.

I decided to do the right thing and go up and start collecting everything off the broken bag, then tight it up in a good way so that no one would notice my crime.

My bad luck was, for sure, all related to apartment 55.

Mrs. Blanca.

She was an earnest working woman or a widow. She lived alone but wasn't entirely alone, as she had a cat. Hmmmm, again, it wasn't a typical cat, but I would describe it as a cat from hell. That cat was more vicious, mean, and evil than any cat I've seen.

Again, I was never a cat person.

The thing with cats is their persistence in wanting more. They look for more touch, more food, and more cleaning. They are very annoying animals; I don't care when people say they are brilliant; I don't think so.

The significant disadvantage of having a cat is that it can go on and on.

They can be very annoying with their meowing and weird noises.

Their fur and hair could be everywhere, and they require massive cleaning.

They bring Allergies to your place; if they get sick(flu), everyone gets it and forget about the damn fleas. Their pours are as sharp knives as they scratch everything, including the owner. They can be very tempered, disrupt sleep, and vomit their hairball everywhere. They are not easy to train, and above all, their litter box smells like shit; it is shit. If they sneak out, they bring stuff back—fleas, pregnant(female), and germs.

They are not loyal pets, as they are moody. They say that they are independent creatures, but they are more bossy creatures. They are always looking for more and more. More food, more cleanliness, more attention, and more sex.

Their food smells like rotten shit, and they are very picky.

They cause complications for travelers or even long-day working people, as they will destroy things in your places while you're away. The sad part will appear after your arrival, as you will find a hidden disaster they caused somewhere.

The last thing is their costly vet bills. I'm not too fond of cats as I do like dogs more, but we can't afford to have a dog as my mom was very strict about keeping the apartment clean or, in her case, spotless.

The cat's name was Puff, but again, I named the stupid cat as Puff.

I never knew the actual name of that evil cat, but to me, it was Puff.

Every time I pass by apartment 55, and if the door is slightly opened, Puff runs out of the door, blows itself like a blowfish, and starts hissing like a snake just because it saw me.

That fucking cat hated the hell out of me.

Mrs. Blanca, on the other hand, was a lovely lady, especially with me, but very cautious at the same time. She always smiles at me going to school, as we take the same bus daily.

I couldn't understand her affection towards me, but I knew deep in her heart that somehow, she cared for me as she used to have a little boy years ago.

I recall some stories about her and her family, as my mother used to gossip with my aunt while drinking wine secretly on the balcony. They used to talk about everybody in the neighborhood as they knew everyone, and everyone knew them as well.

One hot summer night, the air was very thick, and the heat was unbearable, so they wanted to get some cold breeze from the Sea to cool them off.

My aunt turned off the light and sat outside in the dark in her transparent nightgown, exposing her magnificent, firm body to no one. She sat on the chaise-long with a glass of wine in one hand and a cigarette in the other. Mom soon joined her, but my aunt always had a mind of her own. Mom tried to convince her to wear better clothes, but she denied her suggestions as she was more of an exotic young woman with no fear or shame. I had to sneak close to the balcony but keep my distance in the dark. They were talking about Mrs. Blanca's unfortunate, miserable, bad luck and how her life had changed terribly in a wrong way as a nightmare. She was happily married, and they were a delighted family. Blanca worked for the tax department at the Ministry of Treasure, and she's still there.

On the other hand, her husband was also working in the same place, but Mrs. Blanca was the one with the title of supervisor. Andreas was a straightforward, moderate, and, above all, a great father. He was just an accountant who preferred to stay humble and have no ego to climb the ladder as if life had turned its back on him.

My aunt somehow confessed to my mother that she used to like him, as he was an immaculate, handsome, good-looking young man who once had different dreams.

He was a footballer at FC Barcelona, but unfortunately, he had a terrible injury with his knee that disallowed him to continue with the club or even the sport in general.

After the accident, he got married and erased the dreams of football once and for all, and he preferred to be just a family man. The limp off his left foot prevented him from playing with their only son, Pedro. That accident was terrible and broke everybody's heart.

As the story continued, Maribella's tears fell over her cheeks, dripping over her nightgown.

My mother described how sadly Mrs. Blanca looked at the Mercado after the accident.

She was like a ghost waiting desperately to join them in Heaven.

She never cared about her looks, as she used to be elegant and pretty, yet Ma described Blanca as a woman without a future. Andreas and Pedro were on a memorable trip to Barcelona a while back. The father wanted to surprise his son Pedro on his seventh birthday.

He got two tickets, and they traveled early to Barcelona.

It was a Sunday, the day after Pedro's birthday. Barcelona's 3-0 victory over Seville was more like a spell on their minds. The thrill of being in the fantastic Camp Nou stadium leaves a mark on anyone, yet it was magical with Pedro. They had a wonderful time during and after the game. Andreas realized that they were about to miss the train, and with such a scary, hesitant thought, his mind wasn't clear. They were running in the street, hoping to beat the time to catch the returning train to Malaga.

Andreas's condition couldn't allow him to speed or to be fast, dragging young Pedro's hand to one of the most crowded cities on the planet, Barcelona.

His elegant Swiss watch was the beginning of the end. Suddenly, when he took his eyes off the road and looked at his watch, he realized that he had no choice but to lift Pedro off the ground and top him above his shoulder to be one body and eliminate the hustle and the street crowd. They said in the newspaper that the child saw it coming and tried to warn the father, but the response was extremely late. Andreas' long hair was falling off his face.

Meanwhile, he was trying to adjust Pedro's position over his shoulder in the right, safe way. The terrible, unfortunate chaos made the father semi-blind to his surroundings.

The motorcycle was dead ahead of the collision, but miraculously, and with the son's scream, the father managed to twist his body so fast to avoid getting hit by the motorcycle.

The people in the street were astonished at how the father managed to save their lives, but there was one woman that the news described as the authentic witness of the entire tragedy.

Standing so far in the open, she managed to observe everything. Suddenly, she was screaming out of her long, jumping up and down to warn them about the coming fate.

The unfortunate fate was not the motorcycle but the bus coming from the opposite direction so fast. They said in the paper that the impact of the bus shattered their bodies all over the streets of Barcelona. The devastation of such a tragedy left so many people heartbroken in our neighborhood, including Mom and my aunt, but the worst was on the poor Mrs. Blanca.

I wasn't born when the tragedy happened, but the story kept on hunting everyone, including me. So, leaving the trash all over the steps would've been my worst choice, as I couldn't have done that to Mrs. Blanca. The worst thing in life is to collect the scattered rubbish of a broken trash bag that belongs to a person who owned a fucking cat.

Puff wasn't a typical cat, but he was a filthy pig. He was so fat and mean, son of a bitch.

I was so positive he took advantage of the poor, broken-hearted widow.

It was ironic to discover later that Blanca never liked cats.

My aunt told the story about that cat. Back then, young Pedro felt so bad seeing such a cat starving in the street, so he begged his father to give the cat home so he could have a pet or a companion. They loved Pedro so much that they had to give him everything he wished for.

Also, I recall my mother telling Aunt Mar that Blanca had a loud fight with Andreas the day he brought the cat to her apartment without her permission.

Life passed, and she accepted that the cat made Pedro happy, so she had to swallow her pride and deal with the beast. I was so damn sure that poor Mrs.

Blanca might have spent the second half of her miserable life cleaning after what that cat did while she was at work. Sometimes, I heard her screaming: I can't take it anymore. One day, I will chop your head off and feed it to the starving dog in the park. I used to hear that quite often, passing by her door and coming home at night after practice. I did it off the kindness of my heart towards Mrs.Blanca.

My hands were full of shit, and the smell of the vomiting filling my mouth made me sick.

I had a wonderfully delicious dinner, like mine; Mom was the perfect chef, especially with her fantastic chicken Paella. I had to do this with no regrets, and I must be fast before anyone walked up and discovered what I'd done to Mrs. Blanca's trash.

Being in the street was a blessing, but washing my hands and face in the fountain by the park entrance didn't make me feel much better. Despite being clean, I still felt disgusted with the entire trash thing, yet the smell must have been washed with a different kind of water: seawater.

The scented breeze of the Mediterranean Sea, blowing and brushing my face, made me feel a different energy. I started sprinting slowly, but my main goal was to get to the water faster, which made me pick up my feet and start running.

The streets were empty, which helped me to pick up and run faster and faster.

The name related to my speed originated from the football club, as they call me. Flash.

The average time from our place to Playa Malagueta is roughly 30 minutes of walking.

I was there in 15 minutes.

My sneakers were hot off my speed over the street asphalt, and I was impatient to take them off or even my clothes.

My run continued when I was in the water. When I dove in the water, I felt great pleasure and relief under the sea surface. I felt or somehow believed that if I stayed longer under the water's surface, the result of the lousy scent might vanish from my clothes and body as well.

I wanted to be sure and more sure, so I started scrubbing my hand with the sand and salt water, then my face, then again dove one more time to wash all Puff shit for sure.

The scary part was when I stood up facing the horizon, looking at the deep Sea, I realized that there was no moon, not even such a dim light of the far fishing boats, yet the only thing for sure was the pitch black. In such a moment, the fear of darkness went under my skin.

I tried to look at my hands but couldn't see them. I wasn't drowning in the Sea. I was drowning in the sea of darkness.

The scary phobia of darkness made my chest so heavy, and I was sophisticated.

My legs were paralyzed, and I couldn't tell which direction I had to take to get out of this darkness. I realized that my feet were not feeling the bottom as the current pulled me to the deep. The oxygen in my lungs was slipping away, and I was choking helplessly.

Ayuda, ayuda....Help...help.

I was splashing the water so hard, for a dire to save my life, but the deep dark sea was determined to have me in the vast company of the dead bodies resting on the bottom of the sea. The strange hand that touched my shoulder was my string of life.

I wasn't sure what was happening to me, except that I felt floating above the sea's surface.

A shadow of a ghost came to my rescue, carried me to shore, and placed me peacefully on the sand. I couldn't see clearly as the lights by the beach were turned off; only the haze lights of the passing cars were enough to see legs standing in front of me. Those legs started coming down until they sat on the sand beside me.

My string of life was my soft, gentle hand tapping over my shoulder to calm me down.

The same hands gently cleaned the sand off my face until I saw her face.

A woman rescued me, and that made me even more terrified. Is she a witch or maybe an angel?

Am I in hell or Heaven?

I managed to get some courage; then I told her: Ola, who are you?

The voice: I'm surprised that you don't recognize me. Is it the darkness or possibly the fear of the Sea?

Mondo: I'm sorry, but I can't see your face clearly.

The voice: Let me help you, stand up and walk with me towards the lights.

The strange light's reflection from other objects by the shore was my guiding light to see her face bizarrely. It appears to my eyes as if the light passes through a prism; it slows and bends, but different wavelengths bend at various angles, forming a rainbow of colors. Mondo, you still can't recognize me. The voice said.

I was even more terrified when she lifted her hair off her face.

I jumped backward over the sand, yet with my fear, I tripped and fell on my butt.

I was scared, but indirectly, I wasn't.

I was scared in a psychological way of being guilty after what I had done to her trash, but again, indirectly, I wasn't afraid of that woman at all.

Why would I?

Mondo: Mrs. Blanca, what are you doing here at this late hour?

Are you following me...? Please believe me when I say I'm sorry for the mess and the trouble I caused in front of your door. I swear I didn't mean that, and I beg you to forgive me, please, please.

Despite the darkness and my terrible, frightening experience, her wonderful smile was simply the smile of an angel. I never noticed that she was charming; I only remember her sad face covered with a scarf. She was always in dark colors, including her conservative black clothes.

This was the first time I had witnessed her simplicity and beauty. She went down with her knees on the sand and reached for my hand to pull me up.

Blanca: Mondo, please relax, sit beside me on the sand, and forget everything you ever knew about me. But moreover, I want you to calm down, as I'm not going to hurt you but to help you. Listen to me as I'm about to tell you a small story.

I was lying down reading my novel, listening to Isaac Albania (Asturias). Suddenly, I heard a thunderous noise outside by my door(pause); Mondo started covering his face with shame.

Blanca, don't do that, don't cover your beautiful face, and above all, listen to the story.

I must admit that you were extremely fast, as when I opened the door, you were gone.

I ran back to my apartment and the balcony, desperate to glimpse the intruder.

I saw you flying as a flash of light running in the street, following you with my tired eyes, and then you were gone again by Antonio's bakery by the corner.

I went back inside and looked around in my apartment, and all I could see was the dark shadow of ghosts. I couldn't sleep and was so lonely, and I felt that a quiet place on the shore could help me, so I went to the beach to feel the sea breeze on my face.

As I was heading to the beach, I remembered having more than one bottle of wine, which also didn't help my loneliness.

Blanca: My dear Mondo, I have known you very well since you were a little boy, and I used to watch you return home from school alone. I used to stand by the dark curtains of my bedroom, watching you getting on the bus to school, and believe me when I say to you that I always carry a soft spot for you in my heart. I used to admire your courage for such a very young age, facing life as a mature young man, no father to spoil you and no mother to take your hand to school, always on your own, so confident and brave. Every time I see your smile, it reminds me of my beloved Pedro. The similarity of your smile was the candlelight of my hope for a better new tomorrow. I felt more responsible for you indirectly as Maria, your mom, always working long hours at the hospital. I knew getting involved wasn't appropriate, so I kept my distance and stayed in the shadows. When your shadow vanished from the street, my heart felt strange fear and worries. I was uncomfortable not following you at such late hours as I couldn't understand why you were out at such a very late hour.

I rushed and put on my clothes, and I was running, fussing with my steps in the dark street like a lunatic looking for you. Fortunately, I saw you heading towards the Sea, but I was still not thrilled about how you were running. Suddenly, my heart was about to stop, and again, try to believe me if I said that you were my rescuer, not the other way around.

The fear that you put in me made me feel happy that possibly, with all my high anxiety and fear, my heart might stop, and I would fulfill my wish and die.

I will finally leave this life and be united again with Pedro and my beloved Andreas.

On the other hand, part of me felt something new, something that you and only you made me think about. I felt responsible and connected emotionally with you.

I can't be selfish and welcome Death with open arms; I must fight, let go of my yesterdays, and wake up to save the present; I must keep you safe and alive. My heart sensed the great danger that was about to come your way, and when you screamed for help, your voice of desperation was my awakening call. I ran and jumped into the Sea, yet it was dark, and I couldn't see as you went down under the sea surface so fast. I was hysterically screaming, calling your name, Mondo, Mondo. I was hitting the waves, splashing the water, but there was no Mondo.

You were gone.

Live or die, die or live...I was in the middle of a dark road, a labyrinth I couldn't find my way out of.

Why, oh why, do I have to live in the shadow of Death?

Dear god, take my life once and for all, or show me the light, AHHHHHHH, please.

The ironic part was that I did see the light, but in an extraordinary form.

Such a light was in the form of your scent, Mondo.

It wasn't a pleasant scent; it was awful, disgusting; it was the scent of Puff's shit. Ha, ha, hah.

The way she said Puff shit made me explode laughing, and so did she.

She laughed at how I laughed, but her question was more of a joke.

Blanca: Mondo, what are we laughing about?

Mondo: Puff shit....ha ha ha.

The hysterical laughs made the fear barrier between us......Vanished.

Mondo: Do I still smell like Puff shit?

Blanca: I'm so glad that you're safe, and no, you don't smell like Puff shit at all, as that shit was floating above your submerged head.

Mondo: I think I misunderstood you, and I'm sorry for that. You look like you are not the way you seem to be.

Blanca: What do you mean?

Mondo: You're so sweet (pause); hmm. You are as beautiful from the inside as you are from the outside.

Blanca: Mondo, can I ask you a question?

Mondo: Si.

Blanca: How old are you?

Mondo: I'm 11 years old.

Blanca: Are you sure you are not 20 years old?

Mondo took a few moments in silence; then he said: Do you wish me to be 20 years old?

In such a moment, Mondo's eyes transform and glow again in the dark for no reason.

He gave her a scary look with those dangerous eyes that made her shiver, not being scared, yet being hypnotized in an extraordinary, seductive way.

Her black blouse top button was gone, and the light from nowhere exposed her halfway naked breast. She touched her breast to cover it and tried to feel her rapid heartbeat.

Her main confusion about the sudden change of her status made her go down slowly, then lay down on the sand, extraordinarily restless and peaceful with her arms wide open, as if inviting me to get closer, then enter her dark secret world.

Blanca: Mondo, please lie down next to me and relax.

I was going very slowly to the sand, not because I was scared, but because I couldn't take my eyes off her body. This is not the first time that I started to feel different regarding the seductive body of a female, regardless of their age. Anna, Victoria, and other girls at school as well.

That didn't stop me from increasing the intensity of such a thing with my eyes as I felt it so many times with my mother grocery shopping, especially if she was shopping for her stuff Female stuff(lingerie and makeup).

There it was, the jungle of the never-ending glowing eyes; even my mother noticed the strange looks on women's faces, turning their heads and staring at me from between the hanging clothes in the stores. The mystery of my strange transformation made me realize or begin to understand the change in my body chemistry. The movement of her legs side by side exposed parts of her thighs; meanwhile, her breasts rose up and down, and her fast breathing made me feel intense within my mind and body as well.

I was in a state of confusion or inexperience in reacting to a similar condition of being alone by a female. I couldn't understand why my hands went straight to her breast, rubbing them softly, thinking that such a rub might help her to feel better.

It is typical for someone to rub their chest when they can't breathe, which I did very naively.

I said to her, almost whispering close to her ears: Please calm down and relax; everything will be all right. Blanca felt my hands reaching in through her blouse, and with that, she was more surprised in the first few seconds, yet she was more relaxed and more aroused, making her legs curl and shift towards me. Everything was in motion so fast until she was on top of me, drowning me with her kisses. The evil minds were developing so fast, and we thought the same thing simultaneously. Her body was moving spontaneously all over my body, and I felt so aroused with her tongue in my mouth, sucking everything I had.

I wasn't sure what to do, as my mind and knowledge weren't helping me.

I've seen so many movies, but this was not a movie; this was as real as it gets.

Blanca is a mature, beautiful woman, and I was in a very unusual condition for any response except surrender to her entirely. She was under a strange, wicked spell that had lost all concepts of my age or even our location. Such an incredible tingling feeling spread through my entire body until I heard a strange sound. The sound of a zipper falling to open up the wonder of my magic box made me realize one thing: Her hand.

I felt something strange but wonderful as if my heart had been left in paradise.

Her soft, gentle hand was inside the Batman cave, as she broke all the rules by touching the Excalibur.

I did not invent such a name, but my Aunt Mar gave it that name.

She said to me that every man's dream is one day to be able to pull the Excalibur out of the rock and then start waving it up freely as a radar seeking the heart and body of a girl or a woman. My aunt was trying to make things very simple for the mind of a 7-year-old boy at that time, but it didn't work that way as there was no Excalibur; it was just a manhood organ penis. I felt the strange pleasure of excitement when she touched my Excalibur.

However, my mind was somewhere else, and it was clear to me that what was happening and what might happen was not expected nor proper.

Blanca is a beautiful, mature woman who has been alone for a long time.

I don't know anything about her family or how she was raised, but I could swear that she had reached the point of no return or regrets.

She lost everything, and she has no one, so for her, I'm the one disregarding the age or the consequences that may appear later in the future.

She did not care, except for one thing, and that was sex.

They say it will take a lifetime for a boy to become a man, yet they also say it will take another lifetime for a man to be mature and do the right things.

Our teacher or the outside teacher was very professional and helpful in such a complicated matter...Sex.

She came from the educational department as an exceptional teacher for such a study...Sex. Her name was something that I couldn't forget, neither the way she looked and talked.

Mrs. Emilia had a unique way of explaining the growth and development of the human sexual anatomy. She also had some images of how a woman would get when she reached the limit of being aroused. The rapid heartbeat will increase the blood flow to some regions of the female body. The fast breathing and the rise of the body temperature will increase the rush of blood and will target certain sensitive areas, such as the hand and the lips, and then the dangerous parts, such as the nipples, thighs, and vagina. On the other hand, the male will be more direct as far as sensuality, as they drive with a direct impact of the other sex.

In less than an hour, I was that boy, but at that moment, I matured so fast and realized that this was not it and was incorrect.

The tingling sensation was much more overwhelming than morality and wisdom.

I was getting stiff, but again, I couldn't resist the great feeling of her hands and what she was doing to me. The harder she strikes it, the more I close my eyes, bite my lips and moan like a woman. The last thing I remembered was her grabbing my hand and placing it inside her secret cave. Only then did I feel something I had never thought of until that moment?

There was a texture of wetness and stickiness inside such a cave.

She was more of the composer of the entire symphony, as one hand held my Excalibur, and the other was helping my hand to dive deeper and deeper inside her. To be or not to be, that was my question. My mind was shutting down until a voice with a whisper came to me from nowhere saying: Mondo, remember who you are and what is your purpose in life, yet most of all, recognize that the absolute pleasure in life is to be the savior of the vulnerable.

You're a savior, not an animal.

The supreme sound of wisdom came to me, and I knew what to do.

Stop it; end this quickly, Mondo, as Blanca is worth your savings.

In such a moment, I've chosen to be Mondo, not the beast, but the savior.

I grabbed her hand out, raised it to face her, then in a somber tone, I said: STOP.

She was overexcited and in the mood for a deep orgasm, as she wasn't listening to my call or the word Stop at all.

She was sure enough to feel that my Excalibur was stiff as a tree, and before I could do anything, she had it in her mouth as a lolly pop, swallowing it all the way faster and faster, and my heart was about to stop.

Still, the pleasure and feeling were all new and good to me, and I was almost about to surrender entirely to her. The magic of such a gift came to me; again, it was new for me to control my beast emotions and return to reality.

I was capable of controlling such an orgasm and managed to stop it.

I rolled her over my body and pushed her away to the sand, zip up my pants, crawling out from her entirely, squatting on the sand, holding my knee so tight, and just staring at her silently.

Blanca, on the other hand, was about to pass out, as she was scared of what she had done as she managed to return to the ugly reality of her sin.

She covered her face, yet her hands were stained with the sand that turned her into a sand face. She was moaning and crying so badly that I didn't know what to do, but again, I ordered my mind to stay away from her and to maintain a far distance.

She stood up so fast, as if a crab gang was biting her ass. She started fixing her top, skirt, and face as well.

Meanwhile, she was moving backward away from me. She stood like a statue, looking at me in silence. Meanwhile, her red eyes were like fire from falling, burning tears. Some women can be beautiful when they are not in a sober state of mind, and Blanca won that role.

The combination of so many elements made her look stunningly ravishing.

The ripped-out blouse showed her beautiful, fully developed breasts, regardless of her desperate effort to cover them of her shame.

Her failure to fulfill such a task exposed her blouse more than before, as it was ruined, and she couldn't hide anything.

I thought she wasn't beautiful based on the many signs I used to observe her extreme conservatory, such as how she dressed going to work or even passing by her accidentally in the streets or the Mercado. The dark sunglasses all the time, their hair up, and sometimes covering her face with a scarf made me believe she was someone else, as if she was a nun who claimed forbidden facts about any beauty in her soul.

This woman in front of me is not Mrs. Blanca at all. Her long, dark hair was still dripping sea water with some seaweeds dangling mixed up from within her hair, creating a visual painting of a sea mermaid. The red face, stained with the night-sticky sand, appeals more to the Lady by the Sea portrait. The formation of her body was something I had never experienced before about Mrs. Blanca.

Her black skirt... Is it a skirt or something else?

Something ripped off the center of her skirt; it could've been from her hard effort saving my life in such a pitch-black sea; her movement could've caused that extended skirt cut.

The thing is, life can be so cruel or unfair. Widows sometimes turn out to be a loss case.

The devastation of losing someone very close, especially a husband and a son, can turn a woman to be either lazy or lunatic.

She needs to be more active about caring for herself, her looks, and her body.

Weight gain is always a sign of loneliness, losing faith, or even interest in life.

The lower part of a woman's body will expose the extra weight in the formation of cellulite fat that always leads to the deformation of the tight skin, but again, that can vary from one woman's case to another.

Mrs. Blanca was not any of those cases; on the other hand, her skirt's extended cut exposed her tight thighs as if they were screaming for acknowledgment.

Everything was fully colored and ready for any man to take her down and make love to her over and over until the sunrise.

I wasn't that man, absolutely not, as I was ashamed of myself as well.

This thing, with my eyes, must be stopped or controlled; I can't be that monster; it is me, Mondo.

Mondo: I'm so sorry, Mrs. Blanca, so sad; please forgive me.

Her face changed again the second she heard me calling her Mrs. Blanca. Her tears were coming down like a running river until she did that thing. She covered her face with her hands and took a deep, long breath, then exhaled the oxygen out of her lungs, making a loud, noticeable sound. Ahhhhh.

Enough is enough, she said.

Blanca: Listen, Mondo, stop apologizing to me, as I'm the mature one.

I'm the one with experience, and I'm the one that must apologize to you.

I am a horrible woman, abusing you in such a way, but please don't remember me the way I look in this moment, don't hate me, and please forgive me.....(pause) she was chocking in her tears, but her last words were;

Blanca: Mondo, you are an angel, a gift to everyone, yet a curse for me, but I'm genuinely (pause). Love you, so please remember that and FORGIVE ME....

She ran fast to the dark Sea and threw herself in the water. I was standing by the shore, frozen by what happened, with no response. My mind was in shock, refusing to accept that she was gone, vanished in the damn dark Sea. It took me a few minutes trying to understand what took place. She had been talking to me in the past few minutes, and unexpectedly, she was no longer in our world.

Mondo, grow up, think and faster....You must go after her and save her....Now.

I ran to the Sea to save her but was again in the same old situation.

I couldn't see my hands, and I couldn't see Mrs. Blanca as the Sea took her away.

It was a Deja vu, but in this case, it was me.

I was trying to save Mrs. Blanca, hitting the wave so hard, hoping to feel her body in the hope of saving her. Blanca, Blanca, Blanca, please come back.

It's nothing but silent dark water. I had to swim back to the shore, then the moment I touched the sand, I threw myself and exploded crying as I'd never cried before.

I looked at the dark sky and asked for a WHY?

I spoke the words of rejection and provoked the wisdom of the life injustice. Why her, and why are you taking every love off my life?

I loved Blanca; She was another dear person to me.

Why do I have to believe anymore?

Why do I give a damn about faith and you?

 You will get your time, Lucifer will not laugh at me, mad evil is the cause of all that, I curse you till I die, and you will never have my soul.

I imagined the two faces looking down on me from above: God and Lucifer.

They look as if they have a poker game, and the winner will get Mrs. Blanca's soul.

The mighty God had a winning hand, yet the devil played his trick, and he slipped another Ace beneath his cloak.

I could hear him saying to God, This one is mine.

I couldn't see their faces in full detail, but the moment God's face vanished, I only looked at Lucifer with him, smiling at his victory over God and me.

He told me: Mondo, you can't win all the time, and you can't be the savior of every soul, and I will be watching you.

People always blame God, but in my case, it wasn't a God.

It was the devil in disguise, and I will never surrender to his wish or evil.

My frustration with God made me angry, as I couldn't understand his wisdom.

Like many others, I wasn't a religious kid because I was rebellious.

I must be entirely convinced to believe. No church, temple, mosque, or holy place can convince me about the wisdom and balance within our Unstrung Lives.

I asked why, yet I couldn't find the person to answer me, so I must read and educate myself to be a.... God.

If I can be a God, I can be fair and offer the links between our Unstrung Lives and connect them to the path of Paradise. My mind was wondering what to do, and the first thing was to find a great story different from what happened. I started running so fast back home.

Standing before her door, I couldn't tell if I was dripping water from my wet clothes or teary eyes.

I was so sad and helpless about her loss, and my mind was going wild about what had happened.

CHAPTER X

THE INVESTIGATION

I opened the door quietly and went straight to my mom's bedroom.

I silently stood by her bed, dripping water, hoping she would feel my existence.

I wasn't sure how long I stood there on her head in silence until water dripped over her eyes. My nightmare started when she jumped off her bed, looking at me with scary eyes.

She turned on her nightstand light, looked at me, and said: Mondo, what happened to you? for god's sake, why are you all wet like that?

Mondo...talk to me.

I couldn't say a word, as the story was still unwritten in my head.

She shook my body so hard, screaming: What have you done? Talk to me, god damn it, Mondo.

She dragged me to the bathroom, undressed me completely naked, ran the water, and pushed me under the cold shower. She returned to my room with clean, dry clothes, dressed me up, dried my hair, then grabbed my hand to her room and said: Now, I want you to sit on the bed right next to me and tell me everything and no lies.

Her frightened look of worry made me feel bad for her.

I couldn't help but throw myself in her arms and cry.

Maria: This is good; let it all out, and when you're ready, I'll be right here next to you.

I told her everything from cover to cover, as my story was all written, edited, and underlined with lies that had no limits. She dressed fast, then said: We are going to the Guardia Civil.

Mondo: What, but why are we going to the police?

I was still shaking, but my mother's hand comforted me and increased my confidence.

Maria: Mondo, listen to me carefully.

You need to understand that it is not your fault... It's not your fault at all; as a matter of fact, you're the victim. Her rushing and fast steps lead us to the police station in no time.

It was late, and there were few police officers at the station for the late night shift.

The officer on duty had a familiar face; she was a distant relative of my mother.

I used to call her Aunt Valeria. She was in her mid-40s, and she had two kids. Mario and Isabella. They were both my friends, and we went to the same school.

Mario was older than me ...13 years old. He was somehow shy, but he loved books.

On the other hand, Isabella was a year older than me, sweet, friendly, and dreaming of being a doctor. Aunt Valeria was a single mother who divorced for a long time because of her ex-husband's affair with Mrs. Laurels, my history teacher when I was 6.

She left the school after the scandal, yet some people said she hanged herself in a strange, cheap motel later. Valeria was an outstanding police officer, and everyone in the town respected her and came to ask for her help and guidance. When we appeared, she rushed towards us, hugged my mother, kissed me, and invited us to sit down.

She was a brilliant woman who sensed the danger and fear in my mom's face.

She got me a warm glass of milk and tea for her and Mom.

The moment Mom started sipping her tea, her tears came out, which was the end of the beginning. Valeria grabbed her pen and notepad and said: Please relax and tell me what about all your troubles.

Maria: Mondo, please tell Aunt Valeria what you told me back home.

Valeria: Mondo, before you say anything, I wanted you to know that no matter what happens, you're part of our family, so don't be afraid, as I will protect you no matter what.

Now, drink your milk and tell me what had happened.

If the word Protection or you're safe comes out in the tongue of a law officer, there's always a tail behind it. The thing is what your mouth says and what you get in return, and nothing will be a good thing for your Protection. I wasn't afraid, but I had to completely alter and change my entire story to protect Blanca's honor and reputation and mine.

Mondo: well, it all started when I was trying to sleep, but I was thirsty; however, heading back to my room, I heard a loud noise outside the hallway or the staircase.

I wanted to wake Mom, but I was also aware that she had to get some rest before her early shift at the hospital, so I decided to ignore the noise and try to find sleep.

Later, I saw something strange through my window(pause). Valeria: Something strange; what did you see, Mondo? Tell me.

Mondo: I saw (pause) a shadow of a woman wearing all black rushing out of our building in the middle of the night. In the mystery of my wondering and curiosity, I felt a strange force to uncover the mystery woman's identity in black.

The street lights exposed her side profile, and soon, her face was unrevealed to my eyes and(stop).

Valeria: Mondo, why did you stop? Who was that woman?

Mondo: Will you promise not to hurt her, no matter what the story will be?

Valeria: I promise, so who was she?

Mondo: She was a lovely woman and......Valeria interrupted him and said with a serious face: Mondo, stop worrying and focus on my question: who was that woman?

Valeria: My dear, why aren't you talking? As I said before, who was that woman in black? Come on, tell me.

Mondo: I'm not saying another word to you; I want to go home.

Valeria: Mondo, please don't be afraid; I swear nothing will happen to you, and as I said in the beginning, you're safe.

So, for the last time, I'm asking you who was that woman.

Mondo: You see, I was about to tell you everything, but when you say specific words, you frighten me not to say anything......(you're safe),(for the last time) and(I will protect you), all those words and sentences lead to something not good at all, so forget my statement, come on Mom, take me home.

Valeria's patience was running short, and she got up from her chair and said with a severe and angry tone: Mondo, sit down, and you're not going home until you tell me everything, so sit down; then suddenly, she switched her facial impression and smiled and said: Por Favor.

Mondo: She was our neighbor.

Valeria: Your neighbor, come on, Mondo; which neighbor?

Mondo: She was, she was...... I looked at Ma, and when she shook her head and nodded, I said: Mrs. Blanca.

Valeria: Blanca Torres?

Mondo: Si..si

Valeria : Hmmm, Go on.

Mondo: Again, I wasn't sure what to do, as she was about to turn or run.

 I wasn't sure of her intentions at such a moment. However, I felt she was in danger, so I had to prepare quickly and help her.

Valeria: Wait a moment; why did you want to help her, especially in the middle of the night for a 10-year-old boy who is supposed to be in bed?

I was not too fond of her leading question, but even though she was an intelligent police officer, I felt that I was the author of this fiction story and I didn't need her twisting interrogation to play games with my mind to get words out of my mouth that I don't need to say.

I smiled and said: I'll be 11 soon. However, it is not my age that concerns you.

 It is my story, so please, Aunty, let me tell you everything without constant confusion or interruptions. Such a bold reply on my behalf made the two of them simultaneously look at me and say, HMMM.

The secret of telling a fictional story to the police must simultaneously be tight, twisted, long, and confusing. Any police officer would not doubt the mouth of 11 years of a well-known boy who appeared to be frightened of such an experience.

 That was one of my advantages.

Such confusion will take the police in different directions, trying to reveal the tinny pieces of the puzzle to get to the end of the story. In movies, police interrogation is called tactics, as they lie constantly to bring to the truth.

Sometimes, the truth is that they prefer to be on their report and not the real thing.

I must be careful with the good and the bad cop interrogation as it is part of their tactics.

I wasn't an ordinary boy, and the recent transformations opened my mind to many things, not including my years of reading books, especially thrillers, crime stories, and comic books.

One of my favorite writers was Agatha Christie, as she was brilliant with her vivid imagination; she is the best.

In my mind, I planned to take Aunt Valeria into an everlasting labyrinth of lies, misleading, and fiction, only to give her what I wanted her to have and nothing more.

Mondo: It started in the morning while I was on the bus going to school.

I heard, but everyone on the bus heard the loud screaming from the street yelling at the bus driver (DÉTENTES) STOP, STOP.

That was Mrs.Blanca screaming out of her lungs for the driver to stop.

Otherwise, she would have been late if she had missed the bus.

The rumors in our neighborhood were about her old relationship with Mr. Alejandro, her boss.

He was always fascinated with her beauty and body when she chose Andreas instead as a husband. He never forgave her for that; his love turned to vengeance and hate whenever he gained the opportunity.

So, missing the bus and being late would make her day a nightmare.

It was the first time I had witnessed her extremity and anger.

She was so furious about something, but she was yelling at the bus driver to wait at the station until it was time to depart, and she was right about that part, as that driver never waited as he was supposed to wait, always in a rush.

Valeria: Is that something that happened more than once from the same driver on such a route?

Mondo: Yes, hmmm, well, I'm not sure exactly, but Mrs. Blanca wasn't in a good mood that morning.

Valeria: But why did you say she wasn't happy? Are you a close friend of Mrs. Blanca?

Mondo: I never said happy or sad, but I said not in a good mood, and again, I keep reminding you that I'm just a kid, and why do I have to be a close friend with our mature neighbor like Mrs. Blanca?

Mondo: Can I finish my story, as you're doing it again?

There was no reply from Valeria, so I said I usually sat in the back until my stop arrived, but the bus was much more occupied than usual on such a day(stop).

Valeria: Why did you stop, and why are you staring at me like that?

Mondo: I had to sit by the window in the middle of the bus; however, when she got on the bus, she was still mad at the driver, but she rushed and sat down in the seat in front of me by the window.

Mondo looked at Valeria and raised his hand for her to stop doing that, then he said to her: No, she did not say anything to me, and she didn't even notice me.

Is that answering your future question that spins in your present mind.....good.

Valeria looked at Mom and then back at me, yet she made that sign with her hand so I could continue.

Mondo: She always said good morning to me every morning with a smile, but on such a day, she didn't.

She held her son's picture, whispering to him as if he were sitting beside her.

Mondo: I must stop because of that look on your face, so here is your question.

Setting by the window gave me the advantage of seeing the reflections of everything she was doing and the movement of her lips.

Mondo: Oh, yes, I can read lips, Valeria; I'm gifted. Also, she whispered to him and constantly repeated the exact words. (Pedro, tonight you're not going to be alone.

Tonight, we'll be together once and for all.)

At that moment, she raised her hand and said: Wait, Mondo.

Let me make this part very clear. Try to relax and, most importantly, try to remember one word. Did she repeat the word TONIGHT?

Mondo: Yes, and yes, she repeated the word tonight more than four times.

Suppose you pay attention to my words and stop interrupting me.

The look on both of their faces was a clear sign of frustration and anger, but I let it be and continued with my best-selling fiction book.

Mondo: I got off the bus, but honestly, I wanted to wave goodbye.

She wasn't paying attention to anyone, so I put my hand down, watching her vanish with the bus smoke.

Mondo: I've always wondered about that.

Valeria: About what, Mondo?

Mondo: The pollution, and why no one cares about that; we will all die one day from the ignored pollution on this planet.

Valeria: Well, what happened after that?

Apparently, my small opinion and point of view regarding air pollution weren't irrelevant to the interrogation, and that was the reason Valeria asked me to continue the main story and not to get into any scientific things, so I switched to being the annoying child.

Mondo: Nothing

Valeria: What do you mean by nothing?

Mondo: Oh, I see.....Do you want to know what happened to me for the rest of the day?

Well, you see......hmm, I went to classes, then lunch and the food was terrible Ma, do you remember that I told you that the food at school was so bad, so I had to go to the bathroom and, Stop, stop....Valeria said.

Valeria: Listen, my dear Mondo.....hmmm, it is 0300 am, and I believe we are all tired here. I was hoping you could stop with the blathering and give me something good.

Maria: She's right, Mondo, tell her what you've said at home, tell her why and how you were soaked in water.....TELL HER.

The loud voice of Mom ordering me to tell the truth made me even more convinced that regardless of the consequences, I would defend Blanca's honor...No matter what.

Mondo: To answer your question, it is a big YES.

I went after her, but wait, I must tell you what I've witnessed on the way down the steps. Some of her trash bags were torn and opened, and there were traces of scattered trash down the steps. I didn't touch anything, so I focused on helping her immediately.

Maria: My poor Mondo, it was probably the cat shit as I smelled the nasty smell of her cat shit coming here.

Valeria: I believe you, and I do believe that the poor widow is a slave to that cat; she should get rid of that nasty beast. I know she was trying to keep her family's memories with that cat, but.....

Are the both of you finished with the cat.....Can I complete the story? Mondo said.

Valeria and Maria: Si, Si...Go on.

When I exited the building, I saw her turning by the corner of the Mr. Ortega bakery and(interrupted pause), Valeria: Oh, that old man is still very good...Maria, have you ever tried the honey-glazed Pestinos? Oh my dear god, it is so good.

Maria: OH, yes, you're right...but the other days he sprinkled some powdered sugar and cinnamon....oh, it was the best thing I had the entire day...you should try it.

Valeria: I will, oh Maria, you see what you did to me now. I am looking forward to tasting that one.

Mondo got up and was about to leave when Valeria shouted at him, saying: Mondo, where do you think you're going?

Mondo: I'm going home......Alone.

The two of you can chat about everything in life, as there is no room for a boy in the gossiping corner between two women....Food, fashion...she did, he did...I don't need that... I'm going home, or maybe if you're okay with it, I can break into Mr. Ortaga's bakery and get you all of his sweet stuff. You're probably going to arrest me, or maybe not. Do you know why?

Of course, not because I broke his glass and stole his good stuff, but in your case and your statement for a cover-up, you probably will state that we had to conceal the evidence in your belly. Mom and Valeria laughed at how I was mocking them; then they said: Mondo... you're such a fun kid, but....SET YOUR ASS DOWN AND FINISH THE DAMN STORY.

I was so frustrated with them, yet I had to finish my fiction story before I got distracted by their nonsense.

Mondo: After she turned on the corner of(pause)...hmm, The bakery store

Valeria: Hmmm, go on.

She heads straight toward Playa La Malagueta.

There was no one in the street, and truthfully, I wanted to turn around and go back home as I didn't feel safe, but on the other hand, I felt somehow very responsible or may be involved or obligated to help her....even though I'm just a kid.

She stood by the shore staring into the dark horizon for a long time, then suddenly and strangely, she was trying to take her shoes off, but her ring or something in her hand ended up ripping her skirt wide open from the center.

The wind got stronger and kept blowing her skirt, showing her legs, and her body was exposed until she lost her balance and fell on the sand. She was angry as her blouse was full of sticky sand and allergies. She was infuriated, wiping the sand off her blouse; yet again, she ripped off the button, and her breast was almost about to come out.

Valeria and Mom were looking at me astonishingly, only because I was describing her body with extreme details, and the secret of a good author is simply anticipating and expecting the aftermath of every detail.

My mind was thinking rapidly about my following line of words concerning the physical pieces of evidence. Suddenly, my mind wandered in different directions as I needed some crime experts in such a matter.

I had to wipe my eyes to ensure I wasn't hallucinating from what I saw behind Valeria.

There was a mysterious chalkboard with a moving poster on that beach with images of Mrs. Blanca and me. That wasn't the crazy part, but also the appearance of Sir Arther Conan Doyle, the leading creator of the great Sherlock Holmes, with notes on the board.

The crazy part was the woman standing next to him, Agatha Christie, and also, as I read most of her novels, that wasn't her real name as it was Dame Agatha, Mary Clarissa Christie.

She supported women's rights and roles in life, so she used pseudonyms or pen names for her novels. She was a Genius.

They appeared out of nowhere and were there for me with their unique analysis of everything I might need for my story. Sooner or later, Mrs. Blanca's body would float above the water unless a group of angry Piranhas that got lost in some Amazon river managed a miracle to survive in salt water and eat Mrs. Blanca's body.

The fact that her body will eventually float will go through an autopsy, and the part about her body and clothes must match any doubts from my fabricated fiction story. Now, with them being around, I had to ask them a scientific question.

Will any traces of DNA be erased and vanish with the seawater?

They smiled and looked at me, then said: Do you have any types of DNA on Blanca's body?

I looked at the picture on the chalkboard, pointed to them about what took place, and said: Si.

Agatha: Well, Mondo, from the pictures, we can see that you had your hand and body all over Blanca, Inside and outside, yet we have one question for you.

Sir Arther: Hmmmm, Did you go deep?

Mondo: Hell, no.

I was only stiff, excited, feeling her incredible body, as she was feeling me simultaneously, but No, as I had to abort my mission when I said STOP.

Agatha: I don't know, Mondo, but it doesn't look like the mission was aborted entirely.

Well, can you describe that significant thing in her mouth? What was that?

Mondo: Oh, that was my corpus spongiosum.

Holmes: Hmmm, you mean Penis?

Mondo: Yes, I was trying to be more scientific, but yes, that thing wasn't a lolly pop, it was my penis.

Agatha: Did she finish the lolly pop or just a few fast licks?

Mondo: No, she just tested it, and I had to pull it out and stop all that.

They smiled and said: Well, in this case, you don't have to worry about anything, as the salty sea water will take care of all that. Scientifically, saltwater exhibited the most significant DNA loss. Water immersion for over 72 hours in seawater will substantially affect the bones, skin, and everything else, especially DNA, and everything will vanish as if nothing ever happened.

I looked at them and whispered, "Thank you very much, guys, I owe you.

Mondo smiled, took a deep breath, and finally, he told Valeria and Maria: She rose off the sand and tossed the shoes to the sea with all her power.

Mondo: I didn't understand that part about her shoes, but maybe she didn't like them anymore and decided to get rid of them; I don't know.

Valeria: Mondo, please stop and clarify tinny things for me.

First, what exactly was she wearing?

In such a moment, I must act in a stupid, confusing way as an 11-year-old boy with no knowledge or experience with the female world.

Mondo: I told you before that she wore a black blouse and a skirt.

Valeria wrote down every word I said; then she said: Very good, now, and before you answer my next question, try to remember and be honest and not ashamed.

Mondo: Si.

Valeria: I recall you were saying that the wind blew up her skirt and exposed her body....hmm, what color was her underwear?

Maria: Valeria, are you crazy...what kind of a question was that? He's just a boy; how would he know about that stuff?

Valeria: Maria, please let me do my job. And it appears that your son knows more than you think he knows. So again, Mondo, what was the color of....

Enough, I can answer that. Mondo responds with anger.

Mondo covered his face with both hands, and when he took his hand off, he looked at Valeria and said: They were black satin with delicate, elegant lining, and yes, she had a great body as those panties were much older when she first bought them years ago, as they were a size smaller, and they were shoved more to her butt as some of her funny cheeks were popping out of her panties, as she probably gained weight from being lonely most of her time, yet I must say that she used to walk in regularly and that could explain how she was in good shape especially the lower part of her body, and the last thing to clarify the doubts off your wondering mind...hmmm yes, I'm not an infant...I know things you couldn't imagine, and again, her breast size was a B B.

Does that answer all your questions, or do you need more specific details?

Valeria and Mom were staring at me with their mouth open until Valeria decided to ask her a new question.

Valeria: I'm in shock; how old are you again?

Mondo: 10 or 11...whatever you want to put in your long report.

Valeria: How do you know all that stuff about women?

Mondo: You'll be surprised how much I know; look at my mom.

She is a B, and you're possibly DD; you need to work out, but that is not how I know.

I'm very observant, and I have a mother and an aunt; God bless her soul.

I've learned a lot about the anatomy of women's bodies. Shopping with them was always fun, and as you know, that department (lingerie) for all girls and especially women is the number one department to explore even if they are not going to buy anything. I know some of the women's fantasies, and one of them is that department store. Why?

Mondo: Do you want to know why?

But first, you can ask yourself that strange question about men and husbands.

Why do they wait outside until women finish with that department?

Women or female Do Not Like Sharing their secret fantasies with their husbands or men in general.

Valeria: You know the answer to that question, correct?

Mondo: Yes and NO.

Aunt Mar used to explain everything...... in detail about what women like to buy, especially in such a department. I've learned a great deal about fashion and know about your hidden secrets whenever that happens....if it does happen every month...Am I right?

The best of the best for comfort and protection for a non-stressful day demand unique stuff, and I know their names; if you want a list of the best in the market, I can write it down for you, but I understand you wouldn't dare to ask me such a question, now here is your final integration and wonder question...

Mondo, Have you ever done it with a female, or, more bluntly, did you ever have sex with any female?

Mondo: No....Of course not...and as you said, I'm just a kid.

So, without any more interruption, I would like to finish my damn story.

Please listen and keep writing your report; the next part will require your full attention.

So here it is.

I started walking towards Mrs. Blanca, but I was very cautious not to be caught by her or even scare her. Suddenly, while she was cursing her life and everything connected to it, her voice changed to crying, and then she turned around. We were frozen as we looked at each other in the dark until she screamed at my face: Who are you and what do you want from me...I will scream louder if you come any closer.

I wasn't afraid of her, so I took a few steps back until some street lights exposed my face to her.

Her scary face had changed to a beautiful, peaceful look, almost like an angel, when she recognized my face.

Now, as I said to the two of you....Listen and only listen to my story...officer Valeria, and by the way, Mom, try not to pretend you are a good listener, and please, don't act innocent, but just be patient and listen.

Blanca took a few steps toward me, held my face with one hand, and said: My dear Pedro, you are so beautiful, and I miss you so much.

I'm happy you came tonight; please come closer to my body, as I love to feel your warmth and scent, as it's been a long time since I had you in my arms.

I was speechless with my arms down to my side, almost like a marionette in her arms. She raised my face with both hands and looked into my eyes, then did the most crazy thing ever.

Valeria and Mom: What did she do to you?

Mondo: What did I say......shhhh and listen.

She kissed me intimately on my lips as if I were a lover, not just Pedro or Mondo.

Mom stood up with an angry face and then screamed: She did what?

In less than a minute, I heard every curse word from my mom's mouth in the Spanish slang dictionary.

Valeria: Maria, Por favor, calm down and let him finish.

Mondo resumes the story, saying: The second time she raised my face, she tilted her head to the left side, looked at me, and said: You're not Andreas; then she pushed me away and said: Who the hell are you?

I was about to state my following line of lies, yet another strange voice interrupted my story again.

Hola Mondo...What are you doing here at this time?

A female officer just passed by, interrupting the entire interrogation to say, hola.

Hola, officer Miranda, how is Blenda? Mondo said.

Miranda: She must be sleeping, but I will tell her you said, Hola.

Is there anything you want me to do for you? Do you enjoy a cold drink...Coca Cola?

Mondo: Si, si...thank you.

Miranda: Why don't you come this weekend and stay with Blenda by the pool?

I will also be off duty so we can all have fun.

Mondo: Yes, that should be fun...if I don't go to jail...

Miranda: Ha Ha Ha..... Who can touch our superstar Mondo?

You're always funny, but don't you worry. I will bail you out with my own money. Ha Ha ha, Jail, so amusing, Mondo.......Ciao.

Officer Valeria and my mother just sat there watching all that in silence; then, out of nowhere, Valeria looked at me and said: Is there any other woman or a girl that doesn't flirt with you....Do you wish to go hang out with Miranda and leave this mess for now, or do you want to finish this mess....Now.

Mondo: Fine, I'm so sorry.

Mondo: So I started screaming in her face, saying: Mondo, Mondo... I'm Mondo Mrs. Blanca...the kid from upstairs, Maria's son...I am Mondo, not Pedro, and not Andreas.

She raised her head, started covering everything, her face, her top, then went down to cover whatever was left of her ruined skirt; she was in complete disorder, confused, until I said: Mrs. Blanca, I'm here to help you....Are you in pain?

Do you want me to take you back home.... I'm here to assist you.

Blanca: No home, stay here with me for a little more before I go on my journey...Come, my dear, sit down with me by the shore and take your shoes off so they don't get wet...come, come.

Blanca: I have always liked you since the first time I saw you attending school, but I look at you now. You're grown up to be a young man, and I'm sure you have dreams for your future.

I can see you, in the end, being an engineer or a doctor, but no ....look how long your hair is, it's soft and adorable so that you can be a footballer, like Andreas, do you like football?

Mondo: I do, and I play for the Malaga youth club, and I'm good, but...

She interrupted me, saying: Si, Si, but I was saying I must go now, so please forgive me for that kiss as I wasn't myself. She stood up so fast and said: Please forgive Mondo.

I wish I could've known you longer, but I love you...

She stormed to the dark sea, dove, and vanished quickly.

The waves were pretty high, and the wind speed got stronger; then, it started thundering and raining out of nowhere. All that took place while I stood by the shore, frozen as a statue.

I was helpless, clueless, sad, and scared to death. What do I do?

I can't stand here like an idiot. I must save her; she is, after all, our neighbor.

I ran so fast and dove into the dark sea, trying to find her to rescue her.

I dove so many times under the water, up and down.

However, the waves kept slamming me like a toy, dragging me to the deep.

I couldn't feel the sand beneath me, and that was the moment that I knew she was gone and I'd lost her completely. Moreover, the thunder and lightning became so intense, and that was my moment of fear. I must return to the shore, but her spirit wanted me to join her in her underworld. I couldn't go there. It was too dark, and I wasn't ready to leave this life; maybe she wanted to end her life, but I was not. I start fighting the waves and whatever demons from the dark sea. I was screaming at the black sea, saying: you won't have my soul, never.

At last, I started to feel the sand beneath my feet, so I knew I was getting closer to the shore.

I was hysterically afraid, but that push helped me reach the shore's edge.

I stood up, gathering my breath, and then looked at the view in front of me, and it wasn't very comforting. The waves were very high, and the sky was so mad as if it denied her act, but I saw a glimpse of the moon for just a few seconds. The dark clouds covered it again, and the last thing I saw before I started running back home was when the lightning exploded in the sky, exposing the body of a Dragon.

They both said at the same time: A Dragon?

My lies had no end nor limits, and I was about to explode laughing, but I controlled my facial expression and shouted at them, saying: SHHHHHHHH!

I started running, not realizing that when I got out of the water, I was somewhere completely different from where I had dived, possibly because of the strong waves and the tide. I ended up far away. That dragon was a combination of so many things in my mind, and it was probably the unpredicted formation of the fast-moving clouds. Still, I was scared not of the dragon but because I lost my shoes, and my mom would punish me for that.

I ran so fast until I made it home, however, and sadly, I had to stop by her door, touch the wood, and whisper in tears....We will miss you, Mrs. Blanca.

The rest of the story ended with Mom bringing me here.

I looked at them and exploded crying; then I screamed: I couldn't save her, she's gone, and I couldn't rescue her....Why and Why?

Mom dragged me into her arms, but I couldn't stop crying, and that was the last lie to make my story much more dramatic and convincing to both of them.

There was a long period of silence.

Valeria: Mondo, come here and hug me; it will be all right. Calm down and finish your milk.

Mondo: I'm not a child and don't need any damn milk... I was so bad, and I had to explode again and cry.

Valeria: Don't say that as you're not bad, but on the contrary, you're an undiscovered..... HERO.

Mondo: I'm not a hero.

Valeria: Yes, you are; stay with your mother until I return.

She rushed to the other office to use the dispatch radio to call out everybody.

She was also gathering the other officers on duty and ran them straight to the beach, and in the meantime, she'd contacted the Guardacostas Epsilons.

The police station was fully activated at such an early hour.

Still, she didn't forget about us, as she came back and gave me a big hug and said: Mondo, my dear, I do believe that you had a very long day with such a terrifying experience, and I'm so sorry for all the things that you had to go thru, but I must say that you're a wonderful, brave young man, so, for now, I'm going to ask you to go home with your mother and try to get some sleep...I mean both of you.

Maria, if you want me to write a note or contact the hospital to give you the day off, you need some rest, and I don't think it will be a good idea to go to the hospital at all....Let me make some phone calls so you can sleep.

Go home, and I'll be in touch with more details if we have more questions for Mondo.

Valeria sent a police officer with a car to drive us back home, which was very thoughtful of her considering our status. The fact that I had a very rough, long day made my eyes close while we were in the car, as all I could remember was just the comfort and warmth of Mom's body holding me so dearly.

Mom didn't let the chance get away; she was entirely positive that I needed her more than anything. She put me to bed next to her with her arms covering my entire body, and at last, I was back in my dream world.

It was the first time I had remembered some of my dreams on such a night.

The only thing I could remember was my Queen's unclear face, yet her smile was the brightness of my dream. Her words were the comfort and the answers to most of my questions on such a frightening night.

She said: Mondo, you don't have to be a God to know the answers; I can help you whenever you have doubts. Remember to call me or say my name, and I will appear before your eyes to answer all your doubts. I asked her about her name, and her answer was another shocking one to my ears.

She said: I'm your Queen and your sister from another Universe, so my name is similar to yours.

You are Mondo, and I'm Mondona.

Mondo: I need to see you to believe you.

I can't identify your face; your lights are so bright, and I can't see your features.

Mondona: Be patient; when you're ready, I will be there one day.

You only need to know and believe that I am every woman and girl to you.

This is your first acknowledgment of your ability to be the savior and your first step for the Unstrung Lives.

CHAPTER XI

Football and Freedom 1970

I wonder about life and fate....Specially Fate.

It's been two weeks since the unfortunate event with our neighbor, and for some mental reasons, I prefer not to drag her name in my mind or my memory, so I prefer x-Vecina(x-neighbor)

After the funeral, my life started returning to normal, and the fact that we had a new tenant made my life less complicated. My mother mentioned that he is a journalist from Madrid.

No wife, no kids, just a single young man, but she never mentioned his name.

The school year end was approaching the same as the Football season.

My main concern was to win the last match, as it would elevate the team to a higher level of recognition and an excellent possibility for better endorsement for the club for next year.

My mind was programmed to practice hard after school, and the fact that we both had an agreement meant I could stay longer at the club until Mom finished her shift.

I can't deny that I'm dead serious about Tennis, but my main concern for the moment was one thing....FOOTBALL.

I had dreams like all the Spanish kids and wanted to be a football superstar.

It was a dream to be picked up by one of the most famous clubs in La Liga.

It was just a dream, but in reality, it is considered the most complicated dream a kid can achieve. Millions of young boys in Spain had a dream similar to mine.

It's never about the player, but it is about the system and how some people control it.

There are so many talented and gifted boys all over Spain, in Clubs, and more in the streets, but again, it is never a fair game, and simply it's not how talented you are...It's only who do you know to push you for the first step to fame and glory.

It is Friday, and the practice was arranged for 5 p.m.

We had to walk to the club, yet sometimes we even set up a goal to see who would win the race running to the club. Most of the boys accepted that there was no chance to win such a race since Flash always claims the glory of every race. Jose had a different point of view, as in his heart, he believed that he could be the first to arrive at the club's gate and win the race and once and for all beat the flash. Me.

He was so convinced that he could accomplish that. The strange odds for me to lose weren't that possible, except for one thing....

If Mondo is not in the race...That will be his only chance to win.

The race was all set in the street, and the joy of such a glorious race was the girls around such a neighborhood.

They had that spark in their hearts that one could steal my attention and win a good luck kiss from the great Mondo. I never pay attention to anything regarding a challenge, as I was built with an odd personality to beat myself to achieve my goal. I never say die, and I never lose.

My new transformation added more fire to my ability to accomplish things that I couldn't dream of performing, and with such a gift, my confidence became more of.... Arrogance.

My secret lucky charm was a girl, but I found her name today. She was beautiful in a strange way. She had light green eyes hidden behind her wide glasses, hair loose to her waist, and her body was more developed than the other girls for her age.

She had an unforgettable scent, like roses, but not from around Malaga.

She strolled towards the line and was touching, tapping on all the boy's shoulders as if she were about to choose the winner.

I was the first from the left, and Jose was the seventh from the right, and the ironic part was her plan. She wanted everybody to witness her ability and premonition, as she would pick and choose the winner, yet she started from the right, not the left.

She tapped one after one until she stopped by Jose, then tapped his shoulder twice, meaning he would be the winner. I didn't like that, and I angrily said: Hola, please leave the boys and stop with the distractions. She walked slowly to me, looked into my eyes, and said: The name is Jacinta...good luck, Mondo, then she went straight forward to my lips and said: Don't forget about La Rosa de el Hambra.

Her kiss stuck on my lips with a scent I will never forget. As we were about to start the race, I realized that I left my tacos(studs) in my school locker.

I had no choice in such a wrong moment but to turn around, jump in front of all of them, and say: Sorry, everyone, but you can go for the race on your own.

I have to go back to school, and I will see everyone on the field for practice.

The smirk on Jose's face was the winning status. I won so many times, so let him have that win...Vamos Jose.

I started running back to the school. However, I was just worried about running to the club alone, and it wasn't a short distance, so close to 15 Km long.

We usually take the long way from school to the club, then gradually start the race at the last 5 Km to the club's gates only as a group or a team.

Today was challenging, as we were the fastest two players on the team.

Jose is a great player, and together, we won so many matches because of his talent and skills. The main competition between us was always fierce, only to prove who was the best player in the team. I did lead the scoreboard with goals for this season, but he was the leader of the assist players.

I started drifting way back two years ago with the home match as it was against the defending champion. I was eight years old, yet I was on the bench the entire match because of my ankle injury. I was fully recovered and fit to play, yet the coach had a different idea.

Such a match was crucial, almost as a final. The division standing was close in points, and we were second behind Victoria Academy, 33 to 34 points.

Victoria Academy was one of the oldest schools in Malaga.

However, it wasn't just a typical school; it was more of an institution or a gathering for the rich. It is a British school for rich boys. They had the best athletic programs for various sports in the country. Moreover, it was a gathering of wealthy British and Spaniards.

They were the running champion for the last five years....Undefeated.

They beat us early in the season at Victoria Academy 3-2.

I managed to score both of our goals. The flashback of the last 10 minutes brought my memory back to the unfairness of the referee. It was evident that we had to lose because of him.

Every contact with the V players, the whistle goes on for a foul and another and another. Almost everyone in my team was issued a yellow card until the moment in which I was afraid to happen had arrived. I had to fall back to help the defense per coach Enrique's instructions.

Fred, their CF(center forward), cut through our defense line quickly, but my early anticipation of his intention allowed me to see the play. The invisible man came out of nowhere to block Fred's explosive shot on our goal.

I had to fly in the air, using my body as a shield to block his shot.

The fact that Fred was so frustrated with me blocking his 85% to score a vital goal for his school made him respond towards me as an animal.

When the ball bounced off my body to the right side, the follow-through from our defense cleared the danger for a comeback; however, in the meantime, I was still on the ground, watching my team clear up the dangerous area by the goal.

Fred looked at me with anger and, in spite, stepped on my foot with all his weight, followed by a harsh kick in my stomach, then spit on me and started running back to the center field.

I can't express if I was screaming or roaring at the intense pain he'd caused me, but the loud echo of my scream froze the entire place.

I remember that my scream was the deafening noise of the revolution bell.

Everyone at the bleachers was up on their feet, sheering about the cruelty and the violence towards me. The coach, the trainer, and the entire bench of my team rushed to the field to help me. The referee didn't blow his whistle to stop the match or even care about a kid screaming back on the defense line. The pain was intense, as if my foot was broken, but it wasn't.

I saw our goalkeeper telling our team members what took place, and it was the opposite of what he was not supposed to do or say. He jumped up and down angrily, calling Fred names, cursing him, and igniting the fuse for an absolute dynamite to explode. He told my team to forget about football and go after Victoria's team.

The entire team and the substitution were in a fistfight, taking them to the ground.

One of those days, the young Spaniard boys decided to say NO to the British control over Malaga, which was simply an interior war. The British had vast investments in Malaga for a long time, as they knew about the location of our Costa del Sol.

It is a gold mine if you have the money, and they certainly have the money and power.

Our coast is an undiscovered paradise on Earth.

The British knew that very well, buying and buying land after land everywhere. This was outside the football field. However, this is their school, part of their home.......We said NO, this is our land, our beloved Espana.

Those boys didn't care about who or what kind of power the British had; they only cared about one thing: Mondo, the humbled Spaniard Malaga boy....their brother.

Karate and the global superstar Bruce Lee's moves were all on the football field in real-life action fights. The gathering and the commotion of all the players pushing and fighting had put CF Fred out of the picture as if he was hiding from all that.

Our brave goalkeeper was a big kid, slipping away from the crowd and only looking for Fred. Jose checked on me, and when I mentioned what Fred did to me, he ran all over the field, looking for him.

He got to Fred before Manuel, our goalkeeper, and he just pushed him to the ground and was about to kill him, but Manuel managed to keep Jose from going any further and told him to go away. Manuel spread his arm to help Fred to get up with a fake smile.

The moment Fred got there, Manuel leaned back with his head, and at the speed of light, he rammed his head at his nose so hard that everyone heard Fred screaming from the intense pain. He broke his nose, and the blood covered his face with tears of pain and agony.

Unfortunately, the referee saw that and gave Manuel a red card.

The interaction virus spread so fast to the fans and parents all over the bleachers. Men were fighting, women dragging each other....Spaniards against the British.

There was something very unusual up on the high bleachers as two exotic women were taking down anybody coming their way...Men or women.

They were rushing down from the high bleachers as a storm headed down to the field until a group of fat, significant, and cruel British fans were about to stop them.

About 5 to 6 were more of those men and women surrounding them, ready for the spark to interact. I was still on the ground surrounded by the trainer, physician, coach Enrique, and the rest of my team, yet through their legs, I could watch the outcome of the two rebellious women.

I saw one of them jumping off the bleachers and rushing down as a storm.

Out of nowhere, she went down low, grabbed two big bottles of their famous stupid beer, jumped in the air, and landed in front of one of the big men.

She smashed both bottles on the sides of his face, and the big man crumbled down like a fly; then she kicked his body so hard that the big man started rolling off the bleachers as a bowling ball. The bowling ball took at least three pins down off the bleachers.

The pins were two women and another big man. All this was great fun for a kid in massive pain, but in such a moment, I was enjoying such a short movie from between the legs of everyone on the field.

The other pretty young woman was more relaxed and calm, hopping like a rabbit off the bleachers with nothing in her hands. The athletic medical spray Vikocoolant was like a shower on my foot, making me feel better, and the pain was way less intense than before.

I was more concerned about the second woman, so I tried to move their legs away from my site to be able to see her. She was cornered by two big men in front of her, and then behind her, there were two more sneaking down on her from the top bleachers. I was so worried that she was tiny and the gang would surely smash her, but she didn't move until they were so close.

Suddenly, something shiny and gleaming came out from behind her back.

The noise and the chaos were everywhere all over the stadium, on and off the field.

The only noise that attracted my attention even louder than all the chaos on the field was simply the clicking of her Balisong noise.

I started to push everybody away from me, pretending that I needed air, but in reality, I was more concerned about that butterfly knife that came out from nowhere.

She was flipping that Balisong through her finger like a soft piece of doe.

She was flicking the long blades all over her hand, left, right, and up and down, with absolute control with her tricks. The British were shocked to witness something like that and started to move away slowly, as they weren't expecting a beautiful young woman with a lethal weapon charging at them in such a manner.

The show got better as the other one, the more authoritarian woman, came quickly to back her up after finishing putting down a couple of women.

They were about to put on a bloody show with their flying Balisong.

The knives were flipping around their fingers like a YOYO.

No one dared to move until the silence was about to break.

The two women stood their ground, ready to slice the hell out of anyone who dared to come closer. They screamed at them simultaneously, so loudly saying: HA, HA.

The coast was evident as they were running like scared rats.

At last, no blood was spilled, allowing them to rush down to the field so fast that they hit the grass in no time. They ran towards me with empty hands as if those knives were an illusion. They pushed everyone off their ways until they held me in their arms, saying: Estås bien Mondo? Are you OK, Mondo?

Mondo: Si, Si.

The shift and the attention were altered in the field toward the three of us.

The whistling and the clapping were just questions of who these two gorgeous women hugged and kissed Mondo. The exotic beauty of my mom and Aunt Mar twisted their heads, and the chaos ended in our winning direction. They walked me to the sideline off the field, and then the doctor sprayed more ice painkillers on my foot, which was like magic.

It took a while until everything went back to normal and in order.

I was on the sideline, twisting and flexing my foot with the trainer, showing the side referee that I was ready to return to the field.

I was jumping up and down, waiting for the damn referee to acknowledge me and let me in the match again, but he just ignored the shit out of me. I was so frustrated, especially when I looked up at the score bug or the television screen, to realize that we were down 2-1, and it was 71 minutes on the clock.

At last, Jordi saw me and splashed the ball on the bleachers so the referee could let me in. When he allowed me back in the match, my Aunt Mar shouted out loud....Vamos Mondo.

Her voice was my spark of glory.

My determination to score was undeniable.

Torres passed the ball from the midfield to José by the sideline, and that was when his magic started to rise. He was in standing still motion when he received the ball, but the second his eyes caught the V player rushing at him to intercept the ball, he let the ball go under his leg, then he flicked it with his back heel so fast ahead of him, leaving that player in the dust.

He was flying on the field by the sideline, cutting through their defense line from the left side, and when he reached the outside edge of the left penalty area, he kicked the ball up in the air off the inside of his right foot, curving the ball to the penalty area.

That ball had a massive amount of spin as it moved slowly, passing one player after another as if heading off the field. The goalkeeper kept tracking the ball passing in front of his eyes, not noticing anyone by the goal.

He didn't have a chance to see the flying player going so high in the air, meeting the ball with a side bicycle kick to bring our team back to life.

I was up in the air, scorning one of my life's best goals to tie the game 2-2.

The atmosphere in the stadium was indescribable as the fans were going wild at such a goal; even the British couldn't deny such a beautiful goal as they were clapping their hand for such an incredible talent. The time was running out, and there were only 3 minutes left.

I was cutting through the players, dribbling my way to the left sideline, until a V player came from behind and pulled me down to the ground off my shirt, ripping it from the side.

I got up so fast, then rushed at him until we were nose to nose.

The pushing went far and beyond until the referee came rushing to stop us.

He turned around, and out of nowhere, he raised his right arm with a yellow card and pointed at me. I was the victim, and the ripped shirt was my proof, but he said in English: One more word, and you're out. I was on fire, but my teammates pushed me away to let it go.

One bad call after another until the ball was out for us. Carlos tried to sneak in between two players to get the ball from me, but the unfortunate happened.

They pulled him down to the ground right in front of the referee, yet he went the wrong way, and despite the clear foul on Carlos, he went crazy, warning Carlos to stop his aggressiveness; otherwise, he'd be sent off. The devil in my ears was whispering to do it...

Do it, and you'll be a hero. I was under a strange spell of rage, overpowered by such a devilish whispering.

The moment the referee came to me, rushing me to hurry and toss the ball, or it would be out-thru.

The strange thing about having an aunt as Maribella was simply the art.

She loved the idea of surrealism, and her greatest favorite painter was the great Salvador Dali. One day, she explained his ideas and mentioned the famous quote that she lived by.

She told me Dali's quote was: Learn the rules like a pro so you can break them like an artist.

It was whispering in my ears to break all the rules, yet not to be an artist, but to be a Hero.

I was so convinced that with my act, I would be completely breaking every rule in the book, as it was confirmed in my mind that the V team had an extra player on the field, and that was the man standing in front of me with a stupid whistle dangling off his mouth...the referee.

I took some steps backward off the sideline as if I was about to throw a long pass.

I rushed back to the sideline so fast, stopping right before the line and bending my back with the ball behind my head. I used a solid stance and bent back as a slingshot or a caterpillar.

I threw the ball directly at the referee's face as a cannonball with so much extreme, unmerciful power. That ball strikes his nose with a vengeance.

He was on the ground on his back, screaming at the intense pain of his bleeding nose.

He was flipping and turning all over the grass like an ugly worm.

The match was suspended for treatment, and my only hope was for him to be replaced permanently, but the bustard returned with a face mask as his nose was broken.

The only reason he came back on the field was to put his whistle in his mouth and blow every bit of oxygen out of his lungs. I knew what was coming my way, but I didn't care.

He was tall, mean, and ugly, yet with that stupid mask on his face, he was much more hideous than Jason from Friday the 13th. I couldn't hold my laugh until the unavoidable happened.

He pulled that red card out of his pocket so fast in my face as a sign to leave the field.

He was stumping the grass, saying in English: Get Out, out, out.

The clapping and the sheering drove him even more wild and stupid.

Despite this, I was dragging my feet, hugging every player in my team, yet his whistle kept on and on like a storm whistle alert. The referee had to wait for my exit, as he couldn't give two red cards. I had to stop before the line and raise my hand to the Spanish fans to add more spice to the fire. The referee was about to commit that greatest cardinal sin in the game when he came from behind me and was about to push me off the field with his hands.

He was fortunate that Coach Enrique came running and carried me out of the area before we ended up disqualified. He handed the V college an easy score of 3 points.

The game was almost over, and the score was a tie, 2-2. However, that son of a bitch couldn't let it go.

He said: Play On.

The right forward of the V school managed to get in the box, and he tripped over his feet out of nowhere. No one was near him, but the nightmare must go on.

The mad referee blew his whistle and pointed to the penalty spot.

There was more chaos, but this time, it was from our coach, Enrique.

He rushed to the field and pushed the referee to the ground, announcing that this man was a joke. The civil guard rushed to the field, escorting our coach out of the stadium with another red card. It was enviable that we had lost that match.

I lost track of time as I was still by my locker at the school, yet the memory of the home match dragged me back to that time.

Back to my present status for our home match, I sat on the bench, praying that Coach Enrique would let me play. I had to get close and whisper in his ears: Please put me in Por's favor.

When he turned his face, all he saw was my tears running down my face as a river.

He didn't hesitate and said the magic words: Mondo suit up.

Alberto couldn't replace me as the ball was in play, so I had to run to the sideline and yell at Jose to kick the ball out. When I got the sign from the referee, I went down to the grass with my hand and kissed it, then ran to my team and said with a firm voice: I need the ball.

The overconfidence of the V players, knowing that the game was about to be over, made them slack off, thinking that with such a score, they would win the division.

The crazy thing about football is that it never stops rolling, so they shouldn't underestimate my team's but my magic. The ball was switched from the center field to the right-wing Matias.

I raised my hand for him to look up and spot me, but he didn't.

He dribbled with the ball from the right side through players like a smooth knife through a birthday cake. Suddenly, he ends up inside the penalty box, but instead of passing the ball quickly, he decides to do something unusual.

He put his left foot on the top of the ball, then froze, doing nothing.

I could swear that everybody on the field was screaming at him to pass the ball, yet in his mind, he was sure of his next move. He knew very well that from the moment I stepped on the field, our team would be victorious on this day.

He also remembered that I told the entire team I needed the ball, so he froze.

He turned his head to the left, shook his head up and down, then slid the ball softly as if telling me: There it is, Mondo, go for it. I was rushing so fast from the left side to meet the ball, and everybody thought I would blast the ball into the goal with all of my power, but again, I did the unexpected.

Instead of kicking the ball straight, I'd decided to show off. I froze my run and decided to dribble my way more deeply into the heart of their penalty area.

I sledded the ball gently under the V defender's legs (nutmeg), then ran behind him and shot and curved the ball to the upper right side of the goal.

The ball spun in the air, heading to an impossible angle for any goalkeeper to reach.

The massive spin-off of my kick was taking the ball to the outside of the post.

Still, at the right moment and with some mysterious magic, I blow some invisible air off my mouth, diverting the spin from the outside to the inside, kissing the upper right post, and finally bouncing inside the goal.

The fact that I was on the field for less than 20 seconds made the impossible.....Possible.

I've turned the hand of time to a very dear victory. When the ball bounced inside the goal more than once, the referee's whistle and hand gesture pointing to the center spot confirmed it was a GOAL. The entire stadium erupted as an angry volcano.

The loud sheers never stopped until the referee whistled the final one, announcing the end of the match with a historical victory score of 3-2, and with that score, we also won the division.

It was the best day of my life.

I was looking at the shiny waxed floor in the school hallway, remembering that particular moment of my life touching the glass where that dear trophy was kept; then, I smiled and headed to my locker to get my boots.

I knew that I'd lost that race, but I was more worried about being late for the practice.

This is the last practice before tomorrow's big match. I was standing by the outside door of my school, with my head down, thinking of a possible way to beat the time to make it before practice started.

The shadow of a Red 959 Porsche convertible glazing in front of my eyes made me freeze and stare at the car going by me.

(What a car).....I said it loudly enough for someone to hear what I've just said.

The red rear light, the sound of a hard brake, and the smoke of the burning rubber were all signs that the driver had heard what I said. The red light turned white as the driver backed up, stopping before me. The scent was very familiar to me, yet my eyes had confirmed my assurance of such a person, and finally, the voice had erased any doubts.

She slid her sunglasses down, looked at me with blue eyes, and said: Hello, my little devil, we meet again. What is the matter with you?

Why are you all alone in the street? Is that your school?

Do you need a ride somewhere?

Mondo: Hello, Veronica. Yes, we meet again.

I paused with my following line for a few seconds, then said: In the name of all Gods, where the hell did you get this beast?

Veronica laughed so loud that I feared someone would witness our unexpected meeting.

Veronica: I would like you to meet my dear friend Betsy.

Do you want to say hello to her?

At such a moment, I couldn't say a word, as my devilish mind only thought of one thing: Which is more exotic, Betsy or Veronica?

The truth is that I wasn't only saying that in my mind, as it appeared that my thoughts were accompanied by the voice of Mondo as well. In such a moment of confusion, I heard Veronica saying: Well, you still the same way, a little devil, oh my dear Mondo. So, tell me where you are heading, or would you rather stay silent for the rest of the day?

I dragged my feet around the car, caressing Betsy's body so gently, then said: Ola, Betsy.

I'm Mondo, can we be friends?

Veronica laughed again, then said: Seriously, Mondo, get the hell in the car now.

I was still not able to control such a gift, and without any notice, my eyes started to glow again, which led to something that I wouldn't be able to maintain, so I closed my eyes fast, then squeezed my face to eliminate the evil thought and the beast in me.

I managed to switch myself to be the normal Mondo until I turned my head and witnessed her dress. The summer dress was very exotic, even more than Betsy's, exposing her seductive thighs.

Veronica had no shame, especially when I was around, so I had no choice but to close my eyes again, shake my head, and then say, That is some dress you're wearing, She stopped me, saying: Mondo, are you flirting with me now? I'm impressed; the little devil is growing up. Wow, I am amazed. However, I do appreciate the flirting compliment, but I want to be more serious now. So, where do you like to go?

And why are you wearing football clothes? Are you heading somewhere to play Football?

I just learned that you play Football. I thought you were interested in tennis, but what do I know.... you're a Spaniard...Devil...Haha

Mondo: Slow down, and let me explain things to you. First, we need to learn to know each other better. Secondly, I play Football not just because I'm a Spaniard, but because I like the sport and somehow I'm good at it.

Tennis is new to me, but I find it more fun because I have a good teacher who has made me believe in it.

Veronica: Oooh, I wonder who that might be?

Mondo: I thought you knew that already, that it was Anna who encouraged me to believe in tennis, and yes, she is an excellent teacher in that matter.

Veronica: Oh well, well, so it was Anna, Hmmm.

Mondo: What does that mean, Hmmmm?

Veronica: Anna loves tennis, but you're better off without her.

I do love Anna very much, and she's like a daughter to me; unfortunately, she can also be very moody and picky. I couldn't swallow what she said about Anna, but I kept my mouth shut with no comment to her statement until she said: I know you like her very much, who wouldn't? She is young, pretty, attractive, and comes from a good family.

I saw that in your eyes when we met at the Mercado, but I wasn't sure until now, but you have to be very careful as she is older than you and so I had to stop her quickly and say: If you don't mind, can we please change the subject?

Veronica: I understand, but you still haven't told me where to go.

I was so dazzled with the car, checking the unique gadgets of the 955, until my eyes caught the time, and it was 4:50 pm. I screamed at her, saying Is that the real-time 4:50 pm 4:50 pm?

Veronica: Yes, it is the correct time. Why are you in a rush? We could get to know each other better with ice cream and chat.

Mondo: Listen to me very carefully. First, I'm not a kid who falls for some ice cream and chats; secondly, and most importantly, I must beat the hands of time as all we have are 10 minutes.

I must be at the club at 0500 pm.

Veronica: Well, calm down; I wasn't aware of all that, so sit back and buckle your seat belt, and if you're the type of a scared person of speed, feel free to close your eyes, but before we take off, kiss Betsy for good luck. I kissed Betsy, and Veronica put her foot on the gas to go to the club before I finished my kiss. The streets were blurry because of the speed, but it was clear to my eyes how Veronica was an excellent driver, yet Loca.

I couldn't keep track of how fast she was shifting gears to accelerate in no time; however, with every shift and with more speed, Betsy was like a wild horse cutting through the air as if we were on a jet plane. The higher the gear, the faster Betsy flew, and with that, Victoria's dress was flying, exposing more of her legs and thighs, and it was pretty evident that she liked the blue color. The dress wasn't blue; it was rose with elegant, colorful green, red, and black roses scattered all over it. The blue was her underwear, and that was what my eyes were more concerned about. She was focused on driving to beat the time, but I couldn't miss her wicked, devilish smile when she noticed how I looked at her body while she was shifting gears.

It was 4:55 pm- 4:55 pm, and she found a great parking spot, but again, it was amazing how she managed to be at the club in five minutes. Mondo: I've got to run and will see you later. Thank you so much for the crazy ride, and thank you, Betsy; I love you for saving my life. I jumped out of the car, yet before I started to sprint away, I tossed a kiss to Veronica and then ran away. She grabbed my kiss, put it in her fantastic breast, and said: I will see you later, my little devil. As I was easing my way to the back gate, I noticed that she parked Betsy at the president's parking spot; however, in such a moment, I didn't even give a damn but to be on the field before 0500 pm.

Jose waved to me from the field to indicate his victory for the first time.

The practice was long yet productive, as we finished around 0730 pm.

The coach was very clear about his decision for the final lineup for tomorrow's match.

I'm not the favorite anymore, but Jose was the one. I was upset that I was not one of the starting players, as my place would be on the bench as a sub. I wanted to confirm my status, so I had to ask Coach Enrique why I was not in the starting lineup.

He looked at me dissatisfied and said: Well, Mondo, answer my question.

Mondo: Yes, coach.

Coach Enrique: You come late, and you think you're special, but above all that, who is the coach, you or me?

Mondo: You.

Coach Enrique: That is very clear, and I decide who and when a player is on my squad, so don't forget that hot shot. It was obvious that for a long time, I wasn't his favorite player, but Jose, however, the history book confirmed that I was the one with the winning goals, yet again it brought me back to that thought about joining Real Madrid one day. The fact that I'm no one special made such a dream impossible. Who Am I, and who is my mother?

Jose's father is the president of Banco de España, and his mother is the head of the Educational Aid in Malaga. They know so many people, and I can see his dream will reach FC Barcelona one day, but not me... ever.

It was dark, and most of my teammates left, and yet I was all alone in the dark, waiting for the bus and Mom.

My mother didn't show up as promised, and it was 0800 pm, so I had no choice but to walk it all the way home. If I pick up the pace, I should be home between 0900 and 0930 p.m.

I start drifting to a faraway place where my unknown future will take me.

My only dream was to be scouted or picked to play at the world's most fantastic club, Real Madrid. That was just a dream; then again, I doubted my goal would be faithful and wondered, what IF?

Football is the best sport in the world, and I'm so crazy about it, but again, I asked myself. Mondo, you know very well that it is a team sport, so what if anything terrible happens to you, such as an injury or even lousy luck or the worst thing in such a sport, Favoritism?

Where would I go from there?

Mom loves football and Real Madrid, but she's not me. She is more practical about life and very superstitious. She always fears that something wrong might happen and preaches that I should think of other options and a second and third plan for anything in life.

She also believes that with a good education, I can get a better job, which could lead to a successful life. My aunt, Mar, was more of the opposite. She was fun, dairy, wild, careless, selfish, complicated, mysterious, but most of all, living the moment without a single care of the next. She never cared about tomorrow, only now; that was her favorite quote about life.

I'm only 11, but since I've met the queen of the night, I feel incredibly different, older, and wiser, and I have other things that I'm still unfamiliar with and more to discover and control.

I know that my body and brain were in a race for fast development for an 11-year-old boy. The other scary thing injected in me, without notice or explanation, was the knowledge and the ability to understand languages. How the hell, yet how is it possible for me to understand languages so fast, not just English but more?

Such a transformation, or should I accept that they are multiple gifts that keep coming out daily, and I must endure them as they become part of the new Mondo. Maybe I should somehow follow my aunt Mar's quote: NO TOMORROW....ONLY NOW.

The long way home felt longer, and I needed a companion.

I remembered my magic tennis ball in my school bag. I started to feel the texture of such a fuzzy ball; then, I began to bounce the ball while I was walking my way home as my only companion. It was a street lamp, brighter than all the other posts on such a long sidewalk.

I had to stop as my tennis ball and, with such a strange light from a bizarre post, switched the color to semi-red. The ball was stained with red clay, and suddenly, the entire scene changed, and I was again in the middle of Philippe Chatrier's center court.

The place was cheering my name, and I jumped up and down for my great victory.

Well, well.....I guess you are going to need another ride.

I had to stop, close my eyes, take a deep breath, and think of nothing.

I wasn't winning anything; I was a stupid kid dreaming of the absolute rubbish as I was on the sidewalk, yet I may win a lift back home if I behaved well enough. Sometimes, when you think of nothing, it's just like an infant who has no clue of anything in life, yet with every open eye, life is such a new thing to the mind.

No worries; it is always a new surprise, Good or Bad. In the beginning, I prayed that her voice would vanish when I opened my eyes, yet I was wrong again. Victoria's voice said that made me freeze, as my mind was going in different, crazy ways, but this world.

The streets were empty and dark except for the dim light of the street posts. Honestly, I got scared until I recognized her voice.

Mondo: Are you stocking me?

Victoria: It's late and unsafe, so please get in the car and let me drive you home.

Mondo: Which is safer, the street or being around you?

I would have to say NO and walk the long way home.

Victoria: Hey, are you out of your fucking mind? Get in the fucking car, and I'm not asking this time. I can't believe you, Mondo; do you think I would let you walk in these dark, empty streets now? I can't do that.

When I got in the car, she threw herself on top of me, pretending she was helping me with the seat belt as it was dark. Her face and hair were rolling over my face as she was going back to her side slowly with no rush. She wasn't in a rush to get behind the wheel as her breast pressed on mine. Her exotic lips brushed mine slowly and softly, yet without a kiss, but her lips were on fire with a great desire to eat my lips, not just to kiss them. I saw her lips moving slowly, asking me: Is it too tight? Let's ease it a little bit or do whatever you wish me to do.

There was a scent of a different woman, not Victoria.

That scent was very familiar to my nose; it was the scent of wine. She wasn't sober, and that did not help the beast in me to stay in the dark. The color of my eyes and other things in my body gradually changed.

I said: I'm good, thank you.

Her scent was driving me wild, and that beast in me wanted to come out and rip her clothes apart and dive into her web of sins and passion.

Mondo: Can we go home, please, as it is getting late and I had a long, hard day(pause)?

I beg you, please.

Victoria: My dear God, how do you do that?

Mondo: What exactly are you referring your question to?

Victoria: I mean the way you say my name, the way you look at me as a woman, yet in a split second, you switch everything, and you become a child again, and it is driving me crazy that you can do that.

Mondo smiled and said: That is funny, but I am a child, and you're the mature one, but I believe, or probably I should say that somehow I do feel that you're the one acting like a child.

I could rephrase that differently if I say that maybe, in some mysterious ways, you want to be back in time and behave like a young teen girl.

Meanwhile, before you attempt to answer me in an attacking mode, I must clarify that I'm not implementing anything about age or being older than me.

The thing is, Victoria, and I must confess that I don't have the proper explanation of my status, but I do feel different when you're around me, and I don't feel that I'm eleven years old; on the contrary, I think as a man who genuinely see, admire and appreciate every little detail of you, regardless if it was covered or naked.

I want to point out one more detail, and I want you to understand what I am about to say: Patience.

Let's wait some years and see if what we feel towards each changes or gets much more tangled with intensity. Again, I like you very much, which is strange and against all odds due to the vast age differences.

The thing is ....I must be honest with you in such a delicate matter.

Since I was born, I have always been surrounded by beautiful women, and I grew up living and breathing with them as if we were the same sex. No barriers and no shame.

In some odd cases for boys, that strange way of raising a boy can be twisted, leading to two possibilities. Either the boy gets more deeply involved in feminine sexuality and gets confused about which side of the track he would be on. In most cases, the boy may end up being, hmmm, Gay.

The other case is the complete opposite. Being raised with fully developed females, blessed with beauty and natural exotic bodies, will lead to understanding what women need.

The physics or the anatomy of a woman's body exposure was gradually introduced to me as a daily routine. Still, again, it was never a forbidden thing in my eyes. I never had that crazy, wild hunger like other boys for the flesh of a woman.

Did I ever fantasize about a woman in my dreams? I would be a hypocrite liar if I said No, however, and if I do have a plan about a girl or even a woman, it must be something exceptional about a girl or a woman to make me go to bed thinking of her.

The exotic variety of female bodies can have a different impact on me.

However, I'm on the side of being much more sentimental and weak regarding lips. Again, it is only a tiny hint of what I wanted to say so you can gradually understand me better.

My dear Victoria, I will let you get to my secret world and confess that I'm not the typical kid you might see through your life. Not for a long time was I that child, but something did happen to me, and it did change so many things about me; however, as I promised not to tell, I must seize my secrets to this small portion so maybe you'll understand me someday in a different way, so, for now, please treat me as an adult, yet don't drift with your wild sick imaginations, and remember to be patient as long as you can.

On the other hand, I would be highly honored and appreciative if you could stand by my side.

I would say, and probably indirectly, as I'm faithful, I mean not to cause discomfort or complications. I need you to be my sponsor if I ever decide to pursue tennis as something serious in my future life. My mother is a very hard-working woman who can bleed for me to have what other boys have. The fact that she's the only source of income in our small family made tennis a much more complicated issue for me to handle. I do recall her saying that tennis is only for (pause), hmmm, only for rich people. On the other hand, I do feel that deep inside of me, there's a hissing voice telling me that I can change that statement, but again, I don't know the way or the road to lead on yet.

The silence was a thrill for both of us.

Her hair was flying all over her face, and that was only because of her speed, yet when I finished my long speech, I saw a very noticeable and significant change in Victoria's face.

With speed, something could've got in her eyes, but that wasn't the case.

A bizarre kind of tears were coming from her eyes, yet the moment they were out, they were gone with the wind. Her face was turning red, her cheeks were blushed, and the way she was eating her lips made me wonder about her new status.

Victoria: Mondo, can I stop the car somewhere, please?

She turned to a dark road, drove for a few minutes, then stopped and killed the engine.

The excellent Betsy was state of the art in the Automobile dictionary.

The roof was coming above my head, and then the Air Conditioning went on by itself, with the dim lights of all the gadgets in this beautiful car. From the outside, there was no street light, but the company of the secret moon exposed the true beauty of her face.

Victoria was a gorgeous woman; in such a moment, she was more stunning than ever and vulnerable. She struggled a little with her opening words.

Still, soon she managed to control her emotions, then said: Listen to me, Mondo, as I'm not going to tell you my life story at the moment, but what I'm about to speak to you is coming directly from my heart.

Before I say anything, I would like you to do me a favor and close your eyes so I can feel some control. The truth lies in your eyes, significantly when they change to that glowing color, for which I have no explanation, so please do that for me.

I beg you to keep your eyes closed until I finish.

Mondo: I promise I will.

Her lips were walking a very long road, almost without an end.

Such a road was not straight but filled with hills, valleys, and some mysterious rain moisture coming down from somewhere, but not the sky. The more her lips go, the more that road almost leads to infinity. Her tongue was the moisture in my mouth, and for the first time in my life, I felt the most fantastic sensation, pleasure, and seduction I'd never felt before.

The duration of such a kiss was the endless road to something unrevealed.

We were both lying back away from each other, trying to breeze, until she spoiled the air with her cigarette smoke.

The smoke was filling the inside of the car so fast that I had no choice but to open up the window to get this smoke away from me. At that moment, Victoria was still dragging one puff after another, and she reminded me of someone I used to know very well.

I used to watch her doing the same thing with her cigarette only when she used to get overexcited or having pleasure with something. I remember her telling me that the pleasure of smoking in such a moment relieves her anxiety and fills her with a joy that she can't describe for my young and innocent age.

That was my aunt Mar, but the tone was different, yet the words were the same when Victoria explained herself in such a moment. She flicked the cigarette far away from Betsy's window, took a deep breath, turned her head, and looked at me with a strange smile on her face, then said: Thank you, as I don't know how many years I'll be waiting for a similar moment, but now, after what I've encountered, I know very clearly that I will wait for you to repeat this moment with much more further details that I will not reveal for the moment.

My dear Mondo, I promise you that I will sponsor you directly and indirectly until the day I die. As I mentioned, it is not the right time to let you into my secret world, yet I'm married with no kids. It's not his fault. It's all mine, but I've learned to be strong and enjoy other things(pause) than children.

I'm very wealthy, yet not completely satisfied, so I feel strange whenever I look at you.

That you were very straight and clear, yet extremely honest with me, made me re-think that statement, Children. I wish I could adopt you, but you're more to me than a son.

Our secret connection is that we can't find the proper word for a relationship.

I do feel that sponsoring you is not the actual word for me; I think that maybe if you allow me to take you in as a(pause) secret member of my family, and again not as a son, nor a lover, as the word has not been written in any books yet.

Mondo: That is wonderful. Thank you in advance for a new friendship that only we will understand. I promise you that whatever secrets you might tell me, or the other way around, will only be between you and me. I'm overwhelmed by all these changes in my life, yet I would love for you to come and attend the championship match tomorrow. I would be honored to see you tomorrow, as it will be magical yet sad in a different way.

Victoria: I wouldn't miss it for the world, but why did you say...Sad.

Mondo: You'll be the first to know that after tomorrow, I will be a different person, only for tennis, which is why I said the word Sad. I made up my mind and decided to appreciate Football differently, only as a fan, not as a player.

Victoria: Don't you worry about anything from now on; I might get you a special surprise if you promise me to score at least a goal.

Mondo: It's a deal, but please drive me home now.

The drive home was silent, yet in her mind, she was thinking of one thing(I wish he could be a man tomorrow, as I don't think I can wait any longer, or maybe if I close my eyes and pretend that he's a grown-up man, I don't and I don't care anymore, I'm going to stop the car)

Mondo's mind was also wondering about crossing that dangerous liaison and committing a sinful mistake, yet he remembered the queen of lights' words and wisdom when she said to him:

Mondo, always remember what you're capable of and remember to control your gift, so be the savior.

I turned my face towards Victoria, and I saw the lust in her eyes, but also her lips were begging for another kiss, so I had to smile and say: Veronica, would you please turn your face and pay attention to the road and please erase those evil thoughts of your sick mind and act as a mature good friend, I know what's in your mind at this moment....Patience.

As Betsy cruised through the empty streets, our minds were speeding with Betsy for a new day.

I was standing in front of our building watching the vanishing of Betsy's red tail light when she turned left, and it was time for me to go upstairs and close my eyes for the Unknown.

CHAPTER XII

The Championship

Football is a very intense, crazy game.

The main attraction for such an incredible global sport is based on its simplicity and Freedom.

When the British came out with such a sport long ago, they intended to have it in a completely different perspective, rules, codes, class, color, sex, and race.

Nowadays, the entire planet sees the game with a completely different image, making football famous yet unique. The world has adopted football as a link for all sexes, races, and colors to enjoy the magic of fun and freedom.

The evolution in Football allowed some parts of the world, kids, boys and girls, Old and young, brothers and sisters....Gather somewhere and find a way to play in harmony anywhere and everywhere.

In the streets, alleys, parks, fields, beaches, or even on the sand of the vast desert.

There are no rules, special boots, unique clothes, or colors.

The magic behind Football can bring people together.

Football has no languages or borders. Football, in a straightforward definition, is....The true magic of Freedom.

I can speak to anyone and make them understand my words and message.

The football green field is my blank page; with my feet, I can write poetry that could turn heads around. Not only words, but I can bring music to their ears by chanting and cheering....Football, Football.

Today is my final day to write my last chapter in Football, and today is the Championship, so I must imprint my final signature on the field.

I've decided to pursue tennis instead of Football as a career.

The dream and the fantasy of playing for Real Madrid is not for me, as I'm only a poor, simple boy from Malaga who must live real life and the real world. I want to live in a world where I can make it happen and make a difference. My world will only exist by me, myself, and I. I will be the fate of my future.

I was drifting and wondering, full of chattered dreams and charades.

My mother interrupted me: Vamos, vamos, Mondo, We'll be late. It was time to head to the Malaga stadium(La Rosaleda) for the big moment, the Championship Final.

Are you excited? Well, I'm very happy for you. Mom said

Mondo: Si, si, si.

The sound of my tone was a sign of some doubt in Mom's ears.

Maria: Why aren't you excited? It's a big day, and the entire city will be there to witness your magic; with all that, you don't seem to be happy.

What is the matter with you...Are you sick or scared?

Mondo: Mama, I'm fine. However, I must be honest with you.

The thing is ...(pause), the coach, I mean coach Enrique, somehow is leaning towards Jose as a starter, so seriously, I can't tell you how long I will be on the bench or if he ever let me play.

I wanted to play from the start and, more likely, the entire match; however, it's not up to me, as he thinks I'm not fit for this match.

Maria: Entrenador de madre hijo de puta....mother fucker coach.

Mondo: Mama.....stop that.

Maria: How could he?

You're the best player on the team, and why will he not let you play?

I will talk to him and convince him.

Mama, Stop, no, and please don't get involved. The only thing that matters to me is to be there with all my teammates, whether I play or not, so let's forget that magic you're talking about.

Maria: That mother fucker,.....Stop it, Mom, please, and let's go.

My mother's background had Gypsy blood, and she was a very unique, special girl teamed with Aunt Mar. They both had their share of education and intended to attend a respected university to pursue the real thing. However, fate played his dirty game on them, and they settled for just regular street working class. Mama was calm and mature, yet sometimes, she could explode and transform into the old, rebellious Gypsy woman with no fear or regrets.

The medical field, the hospital, patients, doctors, and others made her tone up her vocabulary and knowledge as she was almost a tame lioness.

She can be very emotional, yet the word protective was written on her forehead.

Anything related to me, she can switch to such a lethal, protective wild female, regardless of the consequences. These days, I look at her and see how she can switch to be a real wild.

Her cursing and foul language were only her way to present her active role as my bodyguard.

The bus ride was damn long and silent as well. On the other hand, the bus was highly packed with parents and fans for my team, yet I was trying to hide or somehow be invisible, cuddling to mom's arm and body.

At last, when the stadium was in my sight, the fans went wild as they sang, cheered, and waived my club banners and flags.

No one was sitting down except us and some old mothers. I was trying to relax and zone myself out of all that, but unfortunately, that didn't last long.

Hey, everyone....look who's on the bus... It's Mondo, the magician... he's on the bus... Mira, Mira.....look, look.

Her voice was very familiar, yet with all the chaos she caused, I managed to look at her beautiful light hazel green eyes and whisper with my lips, saying: Gracias Blenda, shhhh, shhhh, be quiet.

She was jumping up and down, and the entire bus was on top of us, cheering me up, saying Mondo, Mondo...

Her mother wasn't on the bus as she was called in to be part of the security at the stadium. Miranda is Blanca's mother, and I haven't seen her since that night at the police station, but I'm sure she is more than enough to fill up her spot at the stadium and the cheering.

The stadium was familiar, but I saw a new site I'd never noticed when I got off the bus. People were rushing from every angle, heading to the gates, and it was impossible to reach the gate. I told Mama to follow me away from the crowds, as I knew the way back.

La Rosaleda stadium was white and blue, the club's primary colors.

Mama gave me a big kiss and said: If you ever get on the field, don't rush in, but stand up straight, look around you, and raise your arms to the crowd.

When you finish introducing yourself, get on your knees, touch the grass, and talk to it. Today you play with your team, so remember that.....Vamos Mondo.

The locker room became deafening the moment I stepped in.

They were so excited to see me as there was a roomer among them saying that Mondo would not show up. They had a bet that I would not show up, and the coach was part of it.

Coach Enrique: Where the hell have you been? Why you weren't at the school like all the other players?

You always think that you're so special, but you're not. I wasn't pleased with his anger and tone. I was shocked as no one had told me we were supposed to meet at the school in the morning. The last thing still ringing in my ears was his final words: Do Not Be Late.

He never told me we would meet at the school, but I must act calm and not show him my anger or disrespect. Otherwise, I would watch the game next to my mother on the top bleacher.

Enrique: Everybody gets ready for the final practice......Vamos, vamos.

Coming out of the tunnel to the field was something I'd never experienced until that moment. My heart was pounding differently, and for the first time in my life, I felt the magic of this sport....Football.

At such a moment, I had to close my eyes and dream, yet pretend I was old and entering the Santiago Bernabeu as a Real Madrid player.

Sometimes, for a child, reality can be very disappointing, and all dreams can chatter in a second, and that made me realize not only that I would never be a Real Madrid player but also that I would not be in this match.

All my teammates ran to the center field for practice, but the incredible sight of the stadium and the fans paralyzed me. They were cheering my team in a booming and crazy way.

I remember what Madre said to me.

I took a few steps inside the field, then stopped, looked up, and raised my arms for the fans to acknowledge me; then, I went on my knees, touched the grass, closed my eyes, and started whispering to the field of grass.

I felt a great relief doing that, yet when I stood up and looked up to the bleacher, I was shocked at what my eyes had witnessed. The top middle tier had a particular type of fans waiting for me to look up.

They let go of an enormous folded banner. It was dangling down with unusual writing saying;

VAMOS MONDO.

The stadium was on fire when they saw the banner coming down, and everyone stood up, cheering my name. My heart was pounding from such a crazy surprise, yet the rest of my team and the coach were also shocked.

I was spinning at 360º, witnessing something new to my eyes. At last, I managed to spot two familiar faces: Anna and the crazy Victoria. I can't believe what she did, but it was the beginning of her keeping the promise to be on my side and sponsor me.

Such a magical banner made everybody in the stadium chant Mondo, Mondo.

Another battle was about to start, and again, our opponent was the famous British school in Madrid, the Red Heart College vs. Malaga PS(public school).

When my team entered the field to start the match, the fans noticed I wasn't among the 11 boys, leading them to say BOOOO loudly.

I almost hid under the substitute's umbrella, not even wanting to watch the game.

The first half was terrible, but we held our ground with a clean sheet 0-0.

As we were coming out of the tunnel for the second half, I took fast steps towards the coach and said to him with anger: What is wrong with you?

Are you still mad at me because I was late? When are you going to let me in the match?

I was interrogating him, yet he ignored me and kept going, waving to the players to move forward. After 10 minutes of the second half, the coach stood up and looked at all the substitutions; then again, he looked me in the eyes, pointed at someone else, saying: Sergio started warming up on spite.

I couldn't believe I was on the bench most of this match.

The coach had one more substitution left; the time was running out with 12 minutes left, yet the score was still 0-0.

The sweat on my forehead wasn't because of the heat but because I was so worried, angry, and frustrated with the damn coach.

We had so many wasted chances, but the Red Heart had an excellent defense line, and with my team's talent, they couldn't convert any of those chances even to shake their net.

If the score remained tied, we would have to play extra time, and my chance to touch the grass could change the scoreboard.

Time is running away, and only 2 minutes left for the official time.

I storm close to the line and encourage my team to keep trying.

More substitute players came to my aid and were cheering the team to hold on to the ball for the remaining 2 minutes for a chance to play for the extra time.

The unfortunate thing did happen.

Their goalkeeper kicked the ball so high in the air that it went to our midfield.

Suarez had the ball in sight, but he missed calculating the spin on the ball as it bounced above his head and landed in front of The RH center forward.

Suddenly, he was inside our penalty area and one-on-one with Manuel, our goalkeeper.

He tried to block the shot, but it was too late, and he was on the grass looking at the ball bouncing inside the goal. That was a devastating moment for my team spirit and the entire Malaga. They worked hard, but somehow, it wasn't meant for us to win this match.

I had no choice but to head straight to the coach, screaming in his face, saying: What the fuck are you waiting for? Let me in.

The coach didn't care who played as he was defeated and just gave me the sign to get in the match. He didn't even look at me or say anything.

I was acting crazy, taking my jacket off, tossing it with an entire arm on the ground, and jumping up and down for a fast warm-up.

The moment I got on the field, I went down on my knees, kissed the grass, got up, looked at the crowd, and then, out of nowhere, I screamed out of my lungs, saying VAMOS.

That scream was a sign of the awakening of the sleeping lions.

The roar and the cheering from the fans chanting my name, Mondo, Mondo, was the point of no return. When my teammates saw me on the line for a substation, they jumped up and down, and everyone rushed towards me to be replaced.

They all wanted me to be the player number 11 on the field.

I gathered my team and told them what to do for one more chance.

Everyone, including the RED Heart players, expected me to fall in the front, but I planned to remain in the midfield.

My team passed the ball back and forth so fast and with absolute control that the final pass was made to Jose on the left wing. When he received the ball, he started dribbling, dancing with the ball, and dragging four RH players toward him.

He passed the ball outside the penalty box, not inside to Carlos.

I knew the tactic played very well; we practiced it many times without the coach.

I ran so fast from the midfield as I was wide open with no guard from RH players.

I managed to meet the ball; shockingly, the magic had just begun.

The ball came to the penalty arc from the left wing inside the box.

Everyone thought that I missed my run and the ball as well, yet I managed to flick the ball with my back heel; then, out of nowhere, the ball rolled over and flipped above the head of the defender, then dropped back in front of my left foot.

The magic moment was my first touch. Suddenly, everything froze, and it was a premonition.

I saw the entire scene before my eyes, but in the future.

A few seconds before, I saw the goalkeeper coming out to intercept me, and that was the moment for me to take the ball in the air before it bounced in front of him.

At such a moment, I knew what to do, as I kicked or placed it directly in the air to the right top corner of the goal.

I recall that I was down on my knees, covering my face, and suddenly, it was a complete silence. The frozen moment was gone, and my team was on top of me.

The sudden moment caused a hearing loss, and then I fell on my face, and it was all dark.

I've fainted, unconscious, almost dead for a few seconds. My mind went blank, and I was somewhere else. I was on the grass, but not on the grass of the Malaga stadium, but mysteriously, the grass of Wimbledon in England.

My eyes were closing, yet I could see the Tennis ball bouncing off the net, then dropping down onto the grass, winning the point and the championship of Wimbledon, yet that moment didn't last except for a second as the entire place went to darkness again.

Mondo, Mondo.....wake up, you scored.

Suddenly, I was back to reality as the loudness of the fans cheering and screaming GOALLLLLLLL.

The place was on fire as no one ever anticipated what I'd done.

My teammates helped me stand, yet I was still in shock, dragging my feet to the center field. When the referee blew his whistle, ending the official time, everyone was on the field, including coach Enrique. The match wasn't over yet, but Enrique went straight to me, unexpectedly collapsed on his knees, and said: I'm so sorry, Mondo, for my arrogance and stubbornness.

Would you please forgive me?

I fell on my knees, hugged him, and told him: Coach, if you believe you've seen enough, wait for the extra time.

Mom was just another Spaniard woman attending the match, just like any other average parent. We didn't have any credentials or privileges to be treated as VIPs.

She was sitting at the top cheapest tier in the stadium. I wanted her to feel what I felt on the field. I wanted her to get a better seat to see El Nino Magico....Mondo.

My entire day was filled with anger, fury, and frustration. I was like a hurricane, but again, I was just a kid trying to dream, yet the reality was always in my way in ruthless ways, telling me you have no right to even a dream.

The world was always denying my existence, rejecting my ability, and refusing to allow me to feel the happiness of anything. Such a cruel world ordered me not to dream, as if I had no right or chance. This was the time to say to the world and the sky above...Enough.

The entire lower tier was barely filled, only Anna, Veronica, and a few wealthy British fans, as if the match was taking place in the UK.

The sad part was the massive empty seat gap separating the British from the Spaniards.

Sitting on the bench constantly caused frustration that covered my face with unfairness. Not only that, I was on the field, but also the sad part of not allowing the Spaniards to purchase all these empty seats. The hurricane in me couldn't and wouldn't stay calm or quiet anymore.

I went to the coach and explained to him what I saw and my point of view regarding such a delicate matter.

He looked at me and said; Mondo, I know what you can do on the field, but it is entirely out of your reach. Please, let it go and focus on the match, and please try to remember the chaos you caused two years ago with your mother and aunt at Victoria College, so let it be .....por favor.

His lame answer was another smack and a complete disappointment on my face, but I couldn't let it go. We had a 5-minute break before the first extra half-time started, and I've got to do something. Winning this match must be something extraordinary, something historical for me and all the Spaniards.

Mondo, what are you going to do? Think, think.

I was standing in the field, not practicing with my team's practice, but only doing one thing....Staring at Veronica, laughing with Anna, possibly having a few drinks and having a good time. My teammates were calling me for the practice, but I ignored them entirely and focused only on Victoria's mind. I closed my eyes, and in my mind, I was trying to connect with her mind in a spiritual, Telepathic way, saying: Mirame, mirame, mirame...look at me, got damn it. My inner voice wasn't that calm nor entirely of any internal shit, as I wasn't relatively as silent as I thought.

Everybody was looking at me, wondering why I repeatedly screamed, saying, Mirame, and to whom?

My screaming got louder and louder; my eyes were glowing again with a new kind of radiation, something I never experienced before, much more potent in a terrifying way.

No one bothered to come near me as if some evil possessed me.

At last, Victoria looked at me, waiving, but that wasn't my intention.

I pointed with my finger at her face once; then the next pointing one was to get her ass down to the field. After several attempts to do the same things, she understood my signs, yet on the other hand, she was like a rebellion, pushing people off her way.

I ran to the tunnel to meet her. However, I couldn't see her clearly from the field, yet when she was close to me, she looked ravishing with a big smile. She was trying to rush towards me, but her fancy high heels were not helping her in such a matter.

The shadow of young Anna was right behind Victoria's shoulder.

Victoria didn't need an introduction. Moreover, she grabbed me by my shoulder and shook me, saying: What a goal! You're a fantastic human being.

I didn't care about all of her compliments, as my face was much more intense and filled with anger. Veronica acknowledged my anger so quickly, yet she looked to the ground while about to say something vital.

The fact that Veronica was somehow aware of the strange phenomena of my eyes made her very protective, not looking directly into my eyes and avoiding another collapsing in front of Anna.

Mondo: I thought you would sponsor me. I assumed that you'd stand by me, but I was wrong. All of you British are the same. All of your care only to take and take. You don't give a damn about me but only about manipulating my mind to your benefit. I bet you have a particular bet on my team to lose so you can make more profits out of this match and....STOP, Stop...Mondo. Veronica said.

I can't understand why you're so angry at me in the name of God.

What the hell did I do wrong....Look at the banners and the support we're providing; I'm only here for you and only you. Why are you accusing me of something only in your mind and heart?

Mondo: I'm not blind, and I'm not stupid, so come with me to the field so you can understand what I'm talking about, as you can only see and notice everything about you.

Your clothes, hair, exotic fancy dress, and forget about your shoes that you can't even walk with. Give me your hand, and please take your stupid shoes off and come with me to show you what I was talking about.

I took her hand, dragged her to the middle of the field, and asked her to look up and turn around to see the entire stadium.

Mira , mira....look and look....Do you see what I see...Do you?

Do you see all the empty seats separating your people from us?

This is Football in Spain, and it is all about having a good time together with absolute Freedom. Football in your country is only for the rich to please them and make them feel good and rich.

Here in Spain, Football is Freedom.

Do you see any goddamn freedom up there....NO, and NO.

The look on Anna's face was filled with tears, agreeing with my point of view, but she was silent yet in disbelief. Anna took her aunt's hand, and they started talking to each other until the talk turned into a very heated argument. It got loud as well.

Victoria said: Enough is enough.

Listen to me, Mondo; I did not come here for any of your bullshit accusations; I came here because of you; I'm here for you and only you, arrogant little bastard.

Do you want to see something better than your fantastic goal?

Do you want to see who the fuck is, Victoria?

As I told you before, you're just a kid, and you have no idea what I can or can not do, So....Just watch me and remember this for the rest of your life..... I'm going to do this just for you.

Her red face was about to explode in anger, but she kept walking up to the top bleachers, cursing, waving her hand in every direction as a witch until she stood up with my mother.

She took my mother's hand and asked her to follow her down.

My mother couldn't understand a thing, but she kept coming down with her to the VIP area until she sat down in the best spot in the stadium.

She flicks her finger for the young waitress to bring her drinks and anything she might desire.

The poor vendor girl was frozen until she yielded at her: Now.

My words somehow triggered Veronica, and she made it impossible to apologize to me.

She screamed to the fans from every corner, saying Vamos, vamos.

The Spanish fans started to creep down, slowly filling all these empty seats.

Some understood, and others didn't, until Veronica climbed on a chair and started waving to them to come down.

The waves of the fans rushing down caused the civil guard to get activated as things were about to get out of control. On the other hand, Veronica managed to bring it to the top, where the TV, the commentators, and the media sat in their special glass booth. She grabbed the microphone and announced to the civil guard that her company owned the empty seats and that she was allowing all the Spaniards to come down and use the empty seats. She also announced that the gates would be opened so that fans in the street could come in for free and fill up all the empty seats. The most critical part was when she said: Please do not harm the fans, let them be. Suddenly, she put the microphone down for a second, and that caused a significant distortion with a loud hissing, screaming sound.

She covered the microphone with her hand to stop that crazy annoying noise; then suddenly, she was about to give a speech.

Veronica: Please, listen to me. Some of you know me, and some don't; however, I'm not standing before you to talk about myself or my company. Someone in this magical, magnificent stadium on such a historical day said something to me. That person had taught me something very new to my ears and more to my heart.

I can't applaud his bravery and courage enough, but I can say that he has..... Her tone started to shake as her tears were coming down.

That young person moved me when he said: This is Espana and Football(stop).

Then she screamed out loud and said, He told me that in España, Football is Freedom.

He said: Esta es España, donde el Fútbol......Es Libertad.

Her scream and loudness moved everyone in the stadium as they roared, saying España, España.

Victoria smiled and said, " So I say again to that person, thank you.

Si, viva Fútbol and viva España.

That person is your son on that field, and that young person is my hero.

That young hero is wearing number 7 and his name (pause), then she explodes, saying he is Mondo....... Vamos Mondo.

That small speech erupted a sleeping lava, but when she was silent, the stadium was on fire, chanting my name, Mondo, Mondo.

The game was delayed because of me, more reasonably, because of the crazy, angry Victoria.

A few minutes later, the game was back in action with a packed stadium, and with the referee's whistle for the first extra time, it felt like it was the whistle of Freedom.

The daily practice, the additional hours of training, and the tactic play were always our team's core. It was our time to show everyone who we are.

They say that kids watch a football match on TV with their favorite team and enjoy being part of something that cheers them up for at least two hours as they become a family.

In practice, every kid brings the beauty of what they witnessed on TV to the field, shots, tactics, moves, and dribbling, but above all, they feel united as a family and free as birds.

Some kids can extend that on their own time, practice more, improvise, and improve their skills to reach the desired satisfaction goal. I wasn't the only one who did that; the 11 players on the field did it together without a coach.

Sometimes, kids feel older and responsible about something, even though it is just football practice. The fantastic thing about football is that people worldwide think about it in so many different ways. Some feel that with football, they can be leaders, protectors, defenders, and sometimes stars. With me, I can look back on the Moon, talk with my mind to Venus or Mars, and I can burn with the fire of millions of stars. In time and only time, we can all be forever stars.

I charged at my teammates on the field and encouraged them to shine and be stars; it was our time. The ball was attached to our feet, pass after pass, moving from the right to the left, back and forth all over the field, controlling the ball as if there were no other players but us.

We'd changed the game and only used half of the Red Heart's field.

They were all locked in defending, trying to get possession of the ball, but that was not the case. After 2 minutes of absolute control, the fans start chanting Oleay, Oleay with every pass we make. At last, the RH was confused, which caused their defense to break slightly for a gap. With one touch between Jose and me, he found himself all alone in front of the big goalkeeper. Three players rushed at him, but he was too fast to see what was coming toward him.

He put his foot on top of the ball, froze the move, then with his back heel passed it on to Sergio, yet Sergio didn't take the shot, but just faked his move and ran without the ball towards the goal, dragging the defense with him, leaving the ball behind him rolling along slowly.

The RH team ran to the wrong places, and their defense fell apart.

Pedro, on the other hand, was the lucky one as he gently kicked the ball, placing it on the top right of an empty net.

Oh, my God, Pedro scored, and he scored for the first time.

He scored only one goal for the year, which was magical. He was running all over the field, happy in disbelief. We managed to take him down, and before we knew it, the entire team was on top of him, congratulating him for a beautiful goal. The score is 2-1, and we are winning. My goal was the lifeline, but Pedro's goal made the fans move.

Enrique couldn't believe his eyes or control himself as he hugged everyone on the bench. Another whistle; however, the moment they gain the ball, the faster they lose it. We were like a monsoon, tackling them with every ball. Sometimes, when two players were on one to regain the ball, it was evident that the RH was suffocating more and more. Same play with the same control. Pass after pass, yet some of our players became more overconfident as they started to dance.

The dribbling, the skills, and the crazy moves that my teammates possessed all came out.

Faking movements, changing the pressure from left to right, and we did it better no matter what they were trying to do. The wild thing was that we were playing as professionals, not just a group of kids.

The game's maturity was on our feet, and we aimed to be all-stars.

Carlos looked at me, and through his eyes, I knew that he wanted to be part of the glory.

I started the play from the right, dragging two players to the corner post, yet when I saw Pedro coming to help, I realized I didn't need his help.

I was cornered, but not for a long time, as I pretended to be heading toward the goal. Suddenly, I froze and hopped above the ball, and in no time, the ball was in between my legs.

To the RH defender's eyes, I was stuck in such a position, yet the magic of my skills came out spontaneously. I used that skill in the street with a small rubber ball, playing with other kids.

I jumped up, flicking, squeezing the ball between my legs, then flicking it sideway with a twist of my hip, causing the ball to fly over my back, head, and shoulders, then land again in front of my feet. They were looking at the ball, lobbing them in slow motion.

When the ball touched the grass, the RH was behind me, and I quickly passed it to Pedro.

He was so fast cutting to the magic box, but suddenly he stopped the ball and ran without any ball, just dragging three players after him from such a fake move.

We were toying with them with absolute confidence and humiliation.

The ball was set dead on the penalty spot, just waiting for anyone to tap it inside the goal.

In such a moment, they recovered rapidly and built a wall before the goal.

On the other hand, the goalkeeper was blind, with so many players in front of him blocking his vision to see the ball. He couldn't tell who had the ball, but the fact that Carlos was the one with the ball made him the best man to score. He just lifted the ball in the air, placing it on the upper left side of the goal. The spinning ball was like a movie to all the players of the RH, including the goalkeeper. They were slowly watching the ball drop in the goal before their eyes. But that was not what had happened. To add more fire to that ball, the truth came out.

That ball did not go in, but it hit the inside of the left post, came out, dropped on the line, bounced like a YOYO, and then stopped. A ball on the goal line is waiting for a slight tap, and the tap came so severely.

One of the RH slides in a desperate attempt to block it out, but his slide made things worth it. He tapped the ball inside of his own goal.

The strange noise in the stadium was united as they all said OH, OH, then Ha, Ha, then finally GOAL.

That was some crazy goal, but Carlos still got the credit for the goal.

His reaction was wild, as he took his shirt off and started running like a wild animal toward the fans. They were touching him as a God until he managed to break loose, throw himself on the grass, and start sliding.

The team imitated his move, and everyone slid on the grass like boogie boards in the vast Mediterranean Sea. On the other hand, Coach Enrique forgot his position as coach and was jumping up and down with us, bypassing a crucial fact. He had an early yellow card in the first half, and with that, he earned his second, followed by a Red Card. As a united team, we believed in each other and were free.

The Billboard was flashing with a new score of 3-1 with 10 minutes left, and the final words of coach Enrique were to cool off and control the ball for the last 10 minutes.

With such a decorated Red card, we had no coach, and suddenly the game looked different.

Wayne Thomas, the center midfield of the RH, lobbed the ball inside our penalty area to Michael Dawn, the center forward. He completely controlled the ball while steering his way to our goal. The wild Pedro came up with a problematic, wicked play, as he had only one choice to make to stop Michael.

He couldn't steal the ball from him, but he stole his balance.

He cut him off the grass with a machete, causing us a penalty. We all rushed toward the referee, pushing him around and rejecting his unfair decision about the call.

We knew it was a penalty, but Pedro's red card was unfair.

All my teammates were angry; however, out of nowhere, Alberto came running, taking me under his arm, dragging me away from the scene. I had a yellow card already, and Alberto sensed the unfairness of the referee. And with my hot blood and temper, he felt I would be next on the Red card list if he didn't stop me.

He took me down to the ground and put his arms on my chest so I wouldn't get up, then said: Let it go, Mondo, we can't lose you...Tranquillo por favor.

Nigel was fixing the ball at the penalty spot, getting ready to change the course of the match.

I had a talent for reading people's minds, especially about Football and penalties.

The psychology behind the habits of human beings can play a significant role in manipulating their emotions. Nigel is a lefty, so I was, even though I was born righty.

I know how lefty can think, and with my experience of never missing a penalty, I can guess where he will kick the ball. I ran to our goalkeeper Manuel to cheer him up, but I went there specifically to tell him to dive to the left, not the right. I said to him that Nigel is a lefty, and with lefty, they prefer a safe angle to the left, not to the right, so be careful.

The referee was about to reach out for his pocket as I was delaying the penalty, but I ran away outside the penalty box and then apologized to the referee. He let me go and told everyone to stay behind the line until Nigel took the shot. The entire stadium was scary until a woman started whistling for a distraction. Her act awakened the whole stadium, as everyone was whistling as well. The loud noise was unbearable to our ears and, I guess, to Nigel's ears as well.

He moved slowly toward the ball, and then there was another moment of silence until the ball started to travel to Manuel's left angle.

It is hard to describe the few seconds when a player kicked the ball heading towards the goal in a penalty kick. Even the greatest commentator in the world can't put those dead few seconds in words. The dead silence of the ball traveling in the air towards the goal is one clip; if you travel a few seconds in the future, you can see through another clip that the goalkeeper had lifted off the grass and started flying against all odds of gravity. Our goalkeeper trusted me and did exactly what I said to him.

He went flying, throwing his stretched body to the left post, and miraculously, he touched the ball with the fingertips of his golden glove, blocking the penalty and pushing the ball away from the goal towards the left-out line.

I thought that Carlos's goal was the magical moment of the match, but with Manuel's save, the true definition of football changed.

The great disappointment and the sorrow of the RH players left them helpless with only 4 minutes to play.

Again, we may have the advantage with the score, but they have the benefit of more players and a coach as well. Our defense line blocked another attack from the RH, and Pico desperately tried to get control of the loose running ball. Ironically, he saw me cutting open towards the center field. He lobbed the ball with all his power to me for a counter-attack.

When I received the ball, I started running towards their goal, not realizing I was alone.

The fans were on their feet, and I swear I saw them all waiving the signal for me to keep going. Another moment of complete silence, as I could see everyone waiting for me to keep running forward, but there were no sounds as if I was deaf.

I pushed the ball ahead, put my head down towards the grass, and then the Flash came alive. The goalkeeper wanted to come out to intercept me, but when he saw my speed, he hesitated.

He rushed out of his box, but I was already inside the box.

I had no choice but to wave my body and move to the right, yet my calculation went wrong when I thought I was alone with the net. Suddenly, I was flying in the air with no ball.

The monster goalkeeper chopped my legs off the grass. I was lying down on the grass, flat on my face, yet the only loud noise I could hear was the referee's whistle.

He was pointing to the penalty spot, yet he had to make another tough decision regarding the goalkeeper. I was still on the grass, watching his finger reach for his pocket.

The FIFA rules state that if a player disallows another player from scoring a goal, the referee's decision should be a penalty and a Red card for the player who committed the foul in such a delicate area. The tip of the yellow card coming out of the upper shirt's pocket made me stand up and look straight at the referee's eyes, but again, the color of my eyes wasn't glowing, but it had the fire of the devil. I saw the drip of his fear sweat off his forehead and observed the movements of his eyes looking up toward the fans. The entire stadium had one word: Roja, Roja, Red, RED.

The yellow card was in a spiritual moment, and it refused to come out as if it were stuck.

The referee turned around and headed straight to the goalkeeper, almost nose to nose.

I took a few steps back in such a moment, and finally, the wonder card came out. It was RED.

The referee announced to the world that the goalkeeper deliberately disallowed the player from scoring and that he must leave the stadium immediately.

The match was filled with crazy, wild things, but the one that topped them all was the coach of the RH team. He pushed the second goalkeeper to the field as a substitution.

He was tall for his age, and I had doubts about fooling him.

Ramos was one of my teammates, yet he was the quiet one, but he was the most brilliant person I've ever met. He was a genius mathematician at the school, and he could memorize numbers as if they were part of his brain. He rushed to me at the penalty spot and whispered in my ears with some wonder words. He said that the RH has no more substitutions as the last one they used was at minute 121, and they have no right for the second goalkeeper to be on the field.

The referee was out of patience and asked Ramos to get out of the box, or he would get a yellow card. I started talking to the referee quietly and asked him to check his book to see if Ramos was right. He was angry but fair enough to get to his mini-book.

The impression on his face wasn't good; then he started running to the sideline officials to verify the facts. Ramos was correct with his calculations, and the referee didn't hesitate to have his magic red card flash to the RH coach to get out of the stadium, but that wasn't the end.

The red card also followed him to the second goalkeeper for their dishonesty.

The British fans were going wild for all the last minutes of chaos, but the civil guards were there to control the event. It was an unusual decision for the assistant coach to ask one of the players from the field to wear the goalkeeper shirt to replace the two goalkeepers, as they had no more substitutions.

The captain of the RH volunteered to be the goalkeeper and started strolling toward the goal line. We had no coach, so it was a unanimous decision from all of my team that our goalkeeper, the hero Manuel, was the one to take on the penalty kick.

He picked up the ball and started fixing it on the chalked spot.

He took 10 yards back, almost standing by the penalty box line.

The question was, which way he will go?

The sudden strange thing happened again, as he turned around to face the referee, explaining that he wouldn't take the penalty as he didn't feel good about his calf and requested to nominate another player instead.

The referee agreed, yet when he turned his head towards the fans and screamed my name.....Mondo, Mondo.

The crowd responded....Mondo Mondo, as if they wanted me to take the penalty.

My teammates were standing behind me with their hands in a fist pump, saying, Vamos Mondo. I strolled, picked up the ball, kissed it, then placed it gently on the penalty mark.

The stadium's silence was frightening, making me wonder about many things.

We won, and there was no more time left in the match. And this was my last match, so why not make Malaga proud?

I said to myself, looking at the ball, then at the fans, and whispered to the ball, I will let them remember my name forever. At such a moment, the thoughts of different minds were like a movie before my eyes.

Coach Enrique sneaks on the tunnel's edge to watch me taking on the penalty.

In his mind, he would say, Mondo, go left and blast the ball.

My mother would say...Mondo goes to the right, fast, and blasts it hard.

Anna...go left

Veronica...left

Jose....left

Manuel...right

Left, right.... What would it be, Mondo?

I looked into Wayne's eyes and realized I would take this penalty differently.

The anger on his face reflects some hate, arrogance, and disrespect, so I must do the opposite and humiliate him.

I started running baby steps, and just before I kicked the ball, I froze right in front of the ball and leaned my hip to the right as if I was going exactly to the right, yet I was still in that frozen mode. Wayne saw my upper body swing to the right, so he flew with his body to the right post, leaving an empty goal for me. I put my left hand on my left cheek as if I was saying to him...Oh, you fool, you guessed wrong.

Without even looking at the ball, I tap it as if I was taping the 9th ball to fall in the pocket so slowly. The ball was rolling so slowly towards the goal that it finally moved past the goal line and then precisely stopped in the middle of the goal.

I couldn't help myself but to say to Wayne to his face....Gloria Puto.

The final whistle confirmed the goal, yet the referee looked at me with a smile, shaking his head as if he was telling me.....That was very new, different, and the most funny yet unique penalty I've ever seen.

He turned around, pointing to the center field with another long whistle announcing the end of the match, yet telling us as the new Spanish School Champion for the first time.

The daylight had no place in the sky as the stars were about to sparkle through the night sky. The spotlight was on exposing the final score on the Billboard 4-1. It took almost an hour for the field to be ready after the indescribable rushing fans to the field with the last whistle. The unanimous decision was made for me to collect the trophy Cup. We were all on the wooden stage, banging with our feet until I raised the Cup in the air.

The fireworks shooting up to the sky was another way of celebrating our incredible victory, adding the most glorious day of my life as we were all free champions.

CHAPTER XIII

The Red Summer 1971

The sun's variations of colors were an encrypted definition of an expected hot summer.

Watching the old fan's blades spinning and spinning, blowing minor cool air over my sweaty face, was another invitation for another cold shower.

Today will be a new unwritten chapter of my unstrung life.

The early hour of the day was all about wondering, anticipation, and me and the fuzzy yellow ball. Today is my first day of summer and the first day I will move into the tennis world.

Mama kept her promise, yet she left me all alone for my choices to be mature and dependable for the next chapter of my life.

It's 0700 am, and my new job will start at 0800 am at the club. Mama left me a few things before heading out to the hospital. The table in the kitchen had a small vase with two roses, and they were both white.

I managed to clip them secretly from Marta's garden with the help of her little granddaughter, Amina. I remember when they first arrived from Morocco with nothing, but now Marta had a small beautiful garden, which is more of her living these days. There was a small brown bag made of canvas next to the roses, and it had a banana, an apple, two oranges, and a wrapped-up Bocadillo. There is a secret behind her Bocadillo, which is set to contain everything I like. First is the bread, which is similar to the French baguette but with more authentic Spanish flowers. The Bocadillo is soft yet crispy, and because it always has the heart and the effort of the old baker Ortega, it can be the best of the best.

I wish I had known how he made it, but that was the least of my concerns.

Mama use her special tomato sauce to add a spread layer in the heart of the bread, and then all of my favorites get spread layer after layer.

The Cabrales cheese is always the first layer, followed by the Aeceituna Alone olives de Malaga and then lettuce.

The next layer is a mix of the cecina and chorizo, then tomato slices, lettuce again, then a blend of Manchego and Tetra cheeses....There is more.

We live by the sea, and we love anything that comes from the sea, especially me.

The last layer is mostly anchovy, covered by more cheese and lettuce.

The bocadillo was always cut in 4 pieces, Mama's most famous sandwich on the planet. There is more in the bag, and that was a note...hmmm, it was more of a mini book.

Mama's book was simply instructions, and that made me very worried.

Her commands were particular as they were:

Be patient and listen. Be calm and observe. Be aware of the unknown before the known. Be brave, and never forget who you are.

Smile and be polite, respectable, generous, and flexible.

At last (I had to stop and read her final words aloud), be aware and careful with girls.

I smiled when I read her last line but was more concerned about her previous PS.

PS: I love you and wish you the best.

As I was gathering all my things, a small folded paper fell on the carpet on the kitchen floor.

I opened it, and it had money. I wonder if Mama ever forgets anything....she is the best woman and mother.

I was by my bedroom door, and I had no choice but to give her a quick look.

Her scent was still everywhere in my room, and her photo with me was on my night table beside my pillow. I wished she dared to stay with me longer, but deep in my heart, I knew she'd be watching me from above.

Early life in my hometown has always filled me with hope and life.

Everybody waved and smiled at me, sometimes free fruits, but my energy always came from random flying kisses from some girls in the streets or balconies.

Same people, same faces, some young who became older, and some wrinkles lines on others as a symbol of old age. On the other hand, some got taller and fatter, yet these new changes in me allowed me to see the differences in features and colors.

Boys will be boys, so their faces can remain the same, but somehow, the features of their bodies change to taller and fatter, or even change in their style of clothes.

On the opposite side of my dangerous road...girls can be drastically amazing as they change in different ways and forms.

The development of the girls in my neighborhood was astonishing.

My eyes were like a radar, spotting anything new, exploring those changes in girls as X-rays. My mother's wisdom made me walk like they didn't exist.

Walking that road again to the club brought back the lovely memories of how it all started. The primary and most important thing that changed was my confidence.

I don't have to be afraid of being curious, as those green vine gates surrounding the club were my gate to find...Home.

Hopping, singing, looking at the dangling bloomed oranges ready to fall on my feet, birds were my back coarse line singing, flirting with other birds, making those gates the entry to my paradise. I felt very much alive being in this place, with the magic key that Victoria gave me to get into the club from the small back gate.

I felt special, as if I belonged in this place until her voice ended all such confidence and ease.

Stop, right there, yes, you with the blue shirt, don't even move.

Who the hell are you, and where do you think you're going in the name of God?

The molecule of my sweat started a strange race over my forehead, and the fear that got in me made me forget anything and everything. I started mumbling in an unknown language, yet it was all the language of Fear.

I am....hmmmm, I'm ...

Well, speak up....or maybe not, as I'm very aware of your kind and for damn sure.... You look like them.

I couldn't understand anything she was saying, as if my gift of understanding languages had gone...Poooff.....disappear.

I raised my hand as if in the classroom, trying to explain myself.

Put your hand down....this is not your classroom, and I'm not your teacher, but I can be your worst nightmare if you don't explain yourself.

Mondo screamed in her face with a severe look and said in English: Enough. I'm Mondo, and I'm here to meet Anna.

In such a moment, I couldn't justify saying that in God's name, but I did.

She took a few steps back and snagged her sunglasses off her face, exposing her beauty; however, in some moments, beauty can be the most evil and ugly thing to my eyes, especially when it comes out with such anger and hate as that woman.

She did realize that she was wrong yelling at me or even talking to me with such a hush, rough tone. She looked down at her feet as if extremely embarrassed, trying to find a new statement of apology....But I was fucking wrong.

When she raised her head, her blue eyes turned to evil red, then screamed again in my face: Who the fuck is Anna, and besides, who the hell is Mondo?

Mondo again shouted at her in English: Anna is the one to show me the way.

What fucking way are you talking about....listen, young man, you will follow me until I figure out how the hell you managed to get into my club.

In such a moment, the entire street scene was the only clear thing in my mind.

What if I run out of here? She will never catch me. Yes, I must run out of this place.

As I was about to do that, my mother's words returned to me, especially when she said to be brave. I don't need to run; I need to be courageous and face that evil woman.

I followed her like a dog, with my head down to the ground, not knowing what would happen to me next. She stormed into a building, but my head wouldn't dare look around except follow her steps. She opened the door to an office, but it was more like a castle, and then she asked me to stop right there and not move an inch. She picked up the phone by the fancy huge desk, then started yelling and cursing at someone on the other side.

She clapped her finger rapidly and said: Hey, boy...what is your name again?

I couldn't answer her as I was afraid and, more likely, terrified of her.

Again, she clapped her finger twice and then said with a commanding tone: Did you hear what I said? What is your name?

Suddenly, my blood rushed so fast to my brain, and the only thing that came into my mind was my mother's words.

Be brave, and never forget who you are.

At such a moment, my eyes started glowing again, and when I raised my head, I was only looking straight at her eyes, and then I froze.

The fact that I was standing by her open office door made me listen to the whispering and mumbling of the workers in that building. I was pretty far away from her, yet strangely, my eyes were closing on her eyes. My eyes rushed towards her like a mystic ghost, even though I was still in the same spot.

It felt as if my body had left me there, and only my eyes were carrying my spirit away towards that woman, closer and closer, until my eyes were right in front of her blue eyes. Then, the silence was broken by me yelling in her face so loud, saying: YO, NO HABLO INGLES. (I don't speak English).

She left her desk and started heading slowly towards me, humming with an annoying tune, then she stopped, leaned down to my face level, bit her lips, then smiled and said: Are you fucking mocking me?

A few minutes ago, you were answering me in clear fucking English saying: I'm Mondo, and I have a date with a girl called Anna, so now you are telling me that(pause)...hmm, she bit her lower lip again, then exploded saying:

NO HABLA FUCKING ENGLISH.

Linda, Stop, and don't dare say another word to this young man.

I closed my eyes with great relief as I recognized the voice behind my back.

It wasn't just one female voice, as another voice cut through the conversation saying: Enough, I'm here now, so explain to me what the hell is going on here.

The voices were my savior from this beautiful, evil woman.

Victoria and Anna were the two savior voices.

Linda: This......greasy Spaniard boy snuck in the club saying that he is supposed to meet Anna, assuming that is you, yet he is claiming that he doesn't speak English.

Anna: Please allow me to explain everything. Will you please sit down...and I mean everyone in this room?

Anna looked at me with a lovely smile, took my hand, asked me to stand behind her, and warned me not to speak. I shook my head, acknowledging her instructions, and let her lead.

Anna: Linda....While back maybe two or three weeks ago, I recall very well that I informed you about a young Spaniard who will be offered a job and(pause)...hmmm, free practice in this club under my supervision.

However, he showed up one day earlier.

Victoria: I gave him the key....in case you ask!

Linda sat on her fancy leather chair, opened her bottom drawer, garbed a glass and a bottle of Scotch Whisky, and poured herself a nice portion, almost a full cup.

She was some magician, as that full glass of Whisky was buried in her stomach in a flash. She poured another one, took two sips, then looked at Anna and said: So, am I supposed to give him a job and allow him to practice tennis in my club, just because you said so....Well, I don't think so young Anna and...

Stop, stop right there: Veronica said.

Veronica: I'm so sorry, but I must put things in the correct perspective and correct what you just said.

You just said: In my club!!!

I don't think so, as I owned this place somehow, so without any further complications, please let the young man have a job...hmmm, and he will go with a unique training program with Manolo....so are we clear on that...Linda.

And one more important fact as a reminder to your brain....that this is my club, not yours.....DO YOU UNDERSTAND?

Linda: Yes, mam... Crystal understood. However, I wasn't aware of....

Victoria cut her off, saying: Anna, my dear, take Mondo with you and introduce him to Manolo and now back to you.... Linda, now you were saying that you aren't aware of what?

Linda: Nothing, mam.

Victoria became my hero at such a critical moment in my life. Not only that, but she was always beautiful, and I saw her power and control for the first time.

Leaving the office with Anna could have been a better introduction for me.

Yet, I couldn't miss all the smiles and the acknowledgment of the faces of all the girls and women in that building, and definitely when a young secretary said: Vamos Mondo....you're my hero. I smiled at her, yet faded away in Anna's shadow.

Meeting Manolo for the first time was something extremely new to me.

I wasn't expecting him to be that old (63), yet I wasn't expecting him to be young.

However, he looked inspirational to me. The echo of winning the championship made my face quite familiar in some places, including this place. I wasn't aware that Manolo was a football fan, and I was glad to be part of such a historic match.

I can't deny that the entire Malaga was there on that day. However, I wasn't well aware that we both shared common ground regarding football. Not only that, but he was a fan of our team. He was also an old fan of Real Madrid, as he was a Maridista.

He shook my hand firmly with a firm grip, then looked at Anna and said: Thank you, my dear; I'll take it from here so you can enjoy the rest of your day by the pool and have fun.

Anna: Thank you, coach, but I thought I was here to help.

Manolo looked at her, scratched his chin, shook his head, then said: Well, my dear, if you want to help, please take Mondo for a short tour and show him the grounds, the courts, and of course, don't forget to show him our excellent swimming pool.

I need to set up certain things for him, and please, guys, come back to me after an hour.

Anna: Thank you, Coach Manolo.

Walking in her shadow, made her stop, turned around, then looked at me and said: Mondo, why are you walking a mile behind me and not next to me...by my side?

Mondo: Thanks, but I prefer to keep my distance and observe everything.

Anna: You can do all that, but walk next to me...I thought we were friends...aren't we?

Mondo: I would love to be your friend, but it's better not to be....I mean, not so close to you...I mean...you know.

Anna: That is fine, and I understand your wisdom and perspective for such a delicate matter; however, feel free to catch up with me, as I'm fast. So...vamos vamos, let's explore this place.

In my mind, I had a whisper of a wish to be more than just a friend, much more than a friend.

Anna was a beautiful young teen. I was 11, and she was 17, and the fact that she was walking with me shoulder to shoulder made the staff wonder about such a lethal combination...Spaniards and British.

The beauty and the Greasy.

This is a very wealthy place, and they have a considerable staff.

And some of their faces were somehow familiar to me, as much as I was highly expected of them. I'm Malaga's youngest hero, and my face is quite familiar to most.

It's been a year, but who can forget the magic I brought into that match?

Anna: Look, did you see that mondo?

Mondo: See what?

Anna: Those staff girls from the kitchen were waving at you, and please don't tell me that you haven't seen the other girl kissing you in the air...Do you know them?

Mondo: NO.

Anna: Really?

Her voice wasn't as cheerful as before, and I felt a strange tone of jealousy telling me about the staff girls. I'm no one at her level, and too young for her to act like that, as I wasn't that deaf nor stupid. I was trying not to pass any comments, but I remember Victoria's words when she said: Anna is a lovely, sweet girl, but you can't underestimate her mind, so be very careful with her.

Here, I am trying to make sense of Victoria's words of wisdom.

Meanwhile, I wanted to understand Anna's way and everybody else rushing into my life.

This is a new life and phase, and I tried hard to understand every bit.

I can only control and trust myself, my instincts, and, above all, my emotions.

I can't deny or even ignore my secret attraction towards Anna, but again, I must keep my old promise to her.

This club is massive, like 20 tennis courts....all red clay.

There are two indoor and outdoor swimming pools, a dinner, and a social hall.

My favorite spot was the football field. It was excellent clean yet permanently vacant, as if the football field was just part of the club's structures.

This is a tennis club; most members aren't from Spain; they are more likely British.

There is some vast land that is still under development. However, I have yet to learn what will be there.

Mondo: Anna, what exactly are they building all the way there in that open land?

Anna: Honestly, I have no idea, but if you ask coach Manolo, he would probably know or have a good idea of what the constructions are all about. She looked at her expensive golden watch (Rolex) and said: The time has passed quickly, and we must go back to coach Manolo.

Mondo: Very well.

Anna: Are you OK, Mondo?

Mondo shook his head up and down, but again, she said: I've noticed that you've been very quiet lately. Is there anything that bothers you?

Mondo: I don't know how to describe my feelings about this place.

I'm not so sure anymore about this new thing you called Tennis.

Look at this place, the people, the members, Mrs. Linda, and I don't know who else.

I feel like a stranger, an outsider in this place. I do feel as if I'm in a different country.

Anna smiled, played with my hair, and said: My dear god, not only are you good-looking, but you're brilliant at seeing things. This is your first lesson about tennis.

Mondo: What lesson are you talking about?

Anna: Tennis, my dear, is a world of the unknown. Every day, you'll see new faces and people in many ways. You'll see colors, races, fashion, beauty, ugly, languages, and cultures.

Tennis is a sport that has no borders or nationality.

If they like you, you own them, but if they don't, it will be your nightmare, your first lesson will be called.... Intimidation.

When you're special, they will be intimidated by your presence, look, and game.

Your first lesson is never to let them intimidate you at any time, no matter what.

When you feel that cold breeze of intimidation, please close your eyes, take a deep breath, and find a way to reverse them.

You're the only one in control of that, so be the magician on the court, even better than you were on the football field. Let them fall in your magic, your brilliance, and your game.

Mondo: Intimidations.......I like that word. It is new to me, but everything here is new to me.

Anna: Move your feet faster; you don't want coach Manolo to get mad at you on your first day.

Mondo: Of course not....How about a race?

Anna laughed and said: I won't fall for that, as I can't race you.

I've seen you running after the ball, and I'm no fool; I have no chance.

Mondo: That is all good; now I do understand how you feel, as I know for sure that you're in so deep with such a thing, so-called intimidation with me, and you're worried about getting embarrassed in front of the members and the staff that a young boy beat and humiliate the beautiful Anna in a stupid small race, so please don't worry, it's all good.... maybe we stroll.

Anna: Is that how you see all that....let me tell you something hot shot, as you're getting on my nerves right now, but I promise you this.... I can beat your ass, so come on...bring it, and let's fucking race to court 9.

From where we were to Court 9, a long path was 300 to 400 meters.

Mondo: I believe it was all my mistake and my big mouth about such a race, so again, I apologize for that. Please walk and forget about the race.

Anna: Now, you are genuinely pissing me off, and if you don't honor me with the promised race.....Friendship is off...there.

Mondo: Well, how about giving you a heads up for the count of 5 or 10?

Anna: Fine, whatever.

I was standing there counting to 10, but that girl could run, as she was flying without even looking back. My count was over, but I hesitated to start the race.

Some sound came from nowhere, shouting from my left side: Vamos Mondo....GO., GO.

She was standing up somewhere, but the damn sun was very bright, and I couldn't see who that girl was. It was like a sparkling flame that could blind your vision, and all I could see was a bright, blinding star.

With her words saying Vamos Mondo, there was a strange electricity that got in me, and suddenly, I was bursting like a flame, blazing so fast through the 300-meter path.

My face was down to the ground, yet my target ball was Anna this time.

At one point, Anna just vanished behind me. Anna's hair flew off the wind because of my speed, overtaking her to the finish line.

When she saw me standing by Court 9, she gave up and started strolling until she was about to enter Court 9, yet she stopped as she was out of breath, leaning down, holding her knees, coughing, and almost vomiting her guts out.

Manolo saw that and rushed to me with a bottle of cold water to run back to her with the bottle. She snatched the bottle from my hand and drank the entire bottle in one shot.

She rushed at me, tossing the empty bottle away, then out of nowhere, she pined me to the green fence, shook me hard, and then said with anger: Don't you ever embarrass me like that again.

Mondo: Embarrass you... You're the one who doesn't know how to race.

I gave you an advantage of almost 100 meters, but you're the one who doesn't know how to pace herself. You don't blow out all your energy on one shot; you collapse right before the finish line because you can't pace yourself. The race is a mind game; you must train your brain to control your body and not the other way around as you did, but I do thank you for allowing me to compete with you, as it is my honor.

Anna: I'm so sorry; I don't know what is happening to me.

I'm so sorry, Mondo. Please forgive me; I didn't mean to do that to you.

I'm so stupid and rational; please forgive me. I know you're correct about pacing myself, but I just got upset or may be embarrassed when you burst next to me.

Honestly, I was choked by your speed, and yes, I was a lousy teacher as you intimidated me with such speed, so I'd lose all interest in such a race.

Mondo smiled at Anna and said: There is nothing to forgive; on the other hand, I'm the one who must apologize to you, as I never meant to embarrass you, so again, would you please forgive me?

Anna: Enough; let's not forgive what is not meant to be ignored, as forgiveness is an unforgiven act to all our foolish mistakes. I couldn't respond to all that and said: You're right, forget all about it.

Deep in my mind, I was unconvinced about a simple fact: Why are the British always apologizing....sorry this and pardon that? Why can't they be more straightforward and less complicated....We Spaniards say it as it is.

Manolo: Are you kids all right?

Yes, sir..coach...We both replied at the exact moment.

Manolo: Well, vamos Mondo, that was an excellent fast race, and I'm astonished by your speed, but we'll talk about that later.

Anna felt like she was left in the dust in so many ways, and to avoid less embarrassment, she said: I have to go right now but remember Mondo what I said, and please listen to coach Manolo.

Mondo: Am I going to see you again?

Anna: Absolutely. You'll see me again, but now I need another race to the bathroom.

Mondo: I understand, but if you need me to accompany you, ensure you're all right.   Anna: I will be more than fine going to the bathroom....Alone..hmmm, but thank you anyway.

Her decorated yet coated words drifted my mind away back when we first met. Asking her, or even hinting in such a stupid way, made me wonder if her answer had anything to do with our forbidden kiss in the bathroom.

I should be much more careful with my words, especially with Anna.

On a mutual subject, yet through a different mind, Anna's mind went to that day as well, yet when she turned her head and gave me such a look, she confirmed that I wasn't the only one thinking about that.

Anna: My new transformation from a young teen to a mature woman occurred in that bathroom. That day had everything to do with me, not Mondo as I was six years older than him and still am, but I can't deny that strange glow off his eyes that made me fall profoundly and quickly under his spell; I mean he's a great looking kid, but here am I again mumbling in my mind about a kid....Is he an ordinary boy or even an average human?

His magic is something that I must learn. I must build a wall to protect myself from his spell. In the future, I might find a way to climb that wall; for now, I must keep my space from him.

Mondo whispers: Anna is a girl, a woman I must learn to understand.

My desire for her is something that I must control, as she is the fire that will burn and ashes my heart to dust. I'm learning to adapt to be the new Mondo, not that greasy kid anymore.

With such power comes a great responsibility.... Wait, that is not my line; it was Voltaire, but what the hell?

With my ability, I must endure and cease my pain and only focus on my path...Two minds shattered and wondering about one thing: What If?

Manolo: Come closer, Mondo; we need to have a conversation.

Mondo: Yes, sir.

First, you must learn how to break the barrier between us, and for a starter, you can't call me sir for more than one reason. First, I'm not British, and I'm not that kind of a man.

I wouldn't say I like fake, superficial things such as...sir and other titles as they won't suit me, but the coach is an excellent name to address me with until we get to know each other better. The first thing you need to understand is your place in this club.

This place is not part of Spain or Malaga, and it will require a magnificent effort on your behalf to understand that very well.

On the other hand, you are here for two reasons, so listen carefully.

The first and most important one is that you're here to work on and off the court.

The off-the-court is for your benefit to earn money; you must work to make money.

We're all here for the same purpose.

Do you know what that purpose is...Mondo?

NO sir....I mean, Coach...

The primary purpose is to make everything friendly, pleasant, comfortable, easy, safe, entertaining hmmmm, fun, and above all, respectful to this club's members. Ahem, they pay the bill. The reputation of this club is settled in our hands; we make it happen.

This club is a getaway place for all the members, old and young, including Anna, but I'll come to that part later.

The second thing is ...YOU.

Mondo, you're here to learn how to be someone special and to know everything about Tennis. So, let me simplify it for you.

Your day will start with us ...the staff at 0600 am.

Mondo: What, 0600 am ...that is very early.

Manolo: Mondo, sit down on the bench and listen to me. This will be the first and last time you'll interrupt me while I speak. Your first lesson for today is to listen.

This is not a democracy, nor argument, nor interruption...Do you understand?

Yes, coach.

From 0600am to 1000 am(4 hours) of tennis practice step by step...From the very beginning. I will explain later what work means from 1200- 1500(3 hours).

After 1500, you will have the advantage of choosing either to go home or stay for overtime...and the overtime will also be explained later. The job is from Monday to

Friday. Now, the weekend you're off, you're free to come and practice on your own...I mean without me.

We are early working people to set up everything perfectly for the members.

The courts will be open for them at 1000 a.m. Our gift here in Malaga is our climate, not only during summertime but also all year around. As you know, the summer can be hot, so most older members prefer to play tennis late past 1700.

Here comes the part where you can stay two extra hours or go home.

The members of this club are not ordinary people but simply rich people.

They like the attention and can be very generous with their tip.

Mondo: What is the tip?

Manolo: You'll never see professional players here, as we call the members something else...They are all recreational tennis players.

The rules of tennis somehow don't apply that much to.... wealthy recreational tennis players. They are here to have fun, show off, and meet. Others can use tennis as a runaway place for business meetings. So if you decide to stay, you will make money if they like you, which is the tip. It is an appreciation of what you do for people.

For example, when you eat at a restaurant, you leave some extra money on the bill as a sign of good service. Here in this place, the tip is different, and in some cases, it could be money, such as pesetas or any other foreign currency. Sometimes, it could be a hat, a cap, a shirt, or just a gift. Remember that you never wait for the tip and never ask for it, as it comes by itself; remember that...Never ask for a tip!

The members always leave a tip one way or another, sometimes the next day or the next week, and that is why I said," Don't expect it; just let it come to you.

The first part of the day will be for your practice, and that part will be for you and me ...Alone.

In the second part of the day, you'll be with the other boys and girls but under the supervision of the groundkeeper master. He is in charge of all the courts.

He oversees such preparations with the courts, lines, and nets.

The master groundkeeper will teach you the foundations of tennis.

His name is Costa, so be nice to him. Now, take your shirt off.

Mondo: What?

Manolo: I need to see what is missing from your body.

The coach was examining my body as a doctor.

Manolo: Well, not bad, but we must do massive modifications to your skinny body; now, put your shirt back on. You have a gift, and I'll give you that, as I witness it more than once.

I've seen you on the football field, and you were a pretty fast player.

I've noticed you racing Anna, but that was between a boy and a girl, so don't flatter yourself with that race. We must work on our muscles, especially the upper part of our body—arms, shoulders, back, hips, and stomach. We must build a solid core to endure a long time on the court. In this club, we have a great gym equipped. In such a place, it will be your temple, and we will use the GYM to reform your muscles and fitness.

Now, it is your turn to ask me anything.

Mondo: Well, I wanted to thank you for such a great opportunity, and I promise that I will be the best student that you've ever seen, Coach.

Also, I wanted to know about the pay. Well, my mother wanted to learn more than I did.

She liked to understand how much I would get paid and when exactly.

Manolo: Your mother is a very wise lady. However, I'm here for you as a coach, not a payroll. The one who can answer that is Mrs. Linda, but be careful as she can be lethal if you say or pass the wrong comments. Linda is the Boss of this magnificent place, but you know that already.... Don't you?

On the other hand, to my knowledge, you, out of all the people....working people in this place, don't have to worry about that part...The Money. You are new here.

However, you're coming with a force that backs you up....I don't know how to describe it, but you're like(pause) a prince, and your queen seems to like you very much.

Mondo: Prince and Queen, now you're talking in riddles.

Manolo: The queen, my boy, is the owner...Mrs. Victoria.

I saw what she did for you at the championship match; not only that, but I also have direct instructions from her mouth to make sure that you will eat and drink tennis.

Her direct words to me were: Manolo, take care of Mondo, and don't fuck it up.

We laughed as the barrier between us slightly faded, or that's what I thought until he said: Listen, I'm going to tell a short story. We are human, and we invented tools for everything to help us. One of the common ones is called Money.

We use the money to buy other tools. The truth is that Money has no value, and it is not that important. The day that money becomes an essential tool to control our lives, the evil part will rule our lives. The more you ask for more money, the faster that evil will consume your life and conquer your soul. To be possessed of Money can turn your life upside down, and misery will get in your blood.

Now here is my valuable advice and again it is just my advice to you, so it's all up to you. Ignore Money; it will pour over your head from everywhere as we draw the lines.

Please let me ask you about something significant.

Mondo: Yes, coach.

Well, when I asked you to go with Anna. What did you see?

Mondo: Anna showed me the entire club, and I counted 20 courts, and they were all Red.

Manolo: Stop.....Did you say 20 tennis courts? That is impressive, Mondo, but what I wanted to know from you is how many were occupied with players.

Have you noticed if they were old or young men and if there were any old or young females? What they wore, how they hit the ball, their movements, and most importantly, their agility and fitness on the courts. Well, Mondo, tell me what you see, and please advise me.

Mondo: I was more overwhelmed with the club; Anna showed me things her way.

Manolo: Anna...Anna again and again...hmmmm.

You see.... Mondo, you've got to draw another line, and that line is well-known as a distraction. I know and am very much aware that you'll see and meet more than

Anna....meaning other girls and boys. Some will also be good, harmful, mean, jealous, cruel, and competitive. You'll meet seduction, admiration, friendship, and many other distractions.

In your early stage, you need to focus on Observation, an essential tool in Tennis.

It would be best to learn to channel your mind to your work, whether practice or your job as a Ball Boy....No Distractions and no reasons. Manolo...Mirame.....Look at me!

Why do you have a sad, upset face?

Mondo: Nothing... It's just too much to learn and observe, but I promise I'll change and earn respect, so please be patient with me if I ask so many questions.

Manolo smiled and said: I like your spirit and promise to teach you everything about Tennis, inside and outside. So today, you learn your first lesson, but before we do anything, come with me to the locker room to meet everyone.

The building was near the courts, yet I first noticed the significant climate change from the outside to the inside. The fresh, cold air went through my nose and filled my lungs with cold, crisp air. The entire place was fully equipped with central air conditioning.

Our school only had open windows and gigantic ceiling fans, but this place was completely different. The building was split into separate sections....The ball boy and girl sections had the same thing for the members; they were far from our area.

There were many lockers, an extensive shower room, an equipment room, a washroom, and a dry clothes room. The cafeteria was also significant, yet everything was painted white and Navy blue. This place was mind-relaxing, as everything was well organized, clean, and inspiring. Manolo asked me to follow him to his office, but again, it was smaller than Linda's.

His office was filled with picture frames of tennis players, old and new, male and female.

Some of his private frames with a girl about eight years old in white with a tennis racket, so my first assumption was that she was one of his students, but I was wrong.

I wanted to ask him about the girl in the frame, yet I felt if I did that, I would be noisy, so I better keep my mouth shut and observe, listen, and learn. My eyes were like a radar sweeping everything until they locked on something strange yet familiar.

The beautiful white banner was right above his desk....

The Real Madrid banner in which it was double the size of what I have in my room. Manolo cut my line of imagination when he said: Mondo, here is your new working uniform and two sets of practice outfits; the bathroom is over there on your right, so change, but wait...Take this bag and put your regular clothes in it, so you can change again when you finish your day.

His bathroom was more like a clinic. The bathroom was overcrowded with medical supplies, first aid, bandages, etc. I tried very hard to change my clothes in this tight room with all that stuff until I heard the knock on the door telling me that my time was up to come out.

Manolo: Mondo, please give me that bag and follow me.

We headed back to the boy's locker room, and he stopped at locker number 7 and said: This is your locker so that you can use it for your stuff. My mind was wandering about Manolo, as he treated me in a lovely way, but the most strange thing was for him to offer me locker number 7. I know he loves football, and he admitted to watching me playing in the final and, more strangely, wearing number 7, but with all that going and swirling in my head, the word thank you had to come out of my lips.

Mondo: Gracias, coach.

Manolo: Vamos, we have so many things to cover, but before we go or do anything, take this folder. This folder is unique, and I prepare it just for you.

At your Home, please read it very carefully. I want you to memorize every single detail. Cover to cover. It has everything you need to know about this place and, more importantly....your training program. Also, do you remember what I said to you about Observation?

Your particular homework is to fill up one page about your daily observations in this club...anything and everything, even if it is personal. We need to build a solid foundation bond between us. We need honesty, as I'm here for you, not because I was paid to do so, but(pause...with a sniffle); I must be honest with you, Mondo, and you can take that as a compliment.

How you've handled everything made me believe I've finally found El Nino Magico.

Mondo: What did you call me?

Manolo: You have something strange, something incredibly new and unique, a quality I've never seen before. I know you're a gifted footballer, but now we will need all your magic to come out, polish, and skill to become a magical tennis player.

There is one more thing that I need to understand, but you're free not to answer my question.

Manolo: I must admit you're an excellent footballer, but what has changed your mind about Tennis, and why soon?

Mondo: I'm confident I can answer your question. However, I must admit that you weren't the first to wonder about my choices, especially with Tennis. I may be young, but I'm wise enough to know the difference between a team sport and an individual one such as Tennis. The thing with football is that I must work hard to achieve my goal, yet I must work harder as it is a team sport. I can't be just good, but we must show everyone that we are a good team, which is complex and involves many changeable factors. Some can be in my control, yet so many are out of my control. As you know, football is the number one sport in Spain, and every kid plays football. However, only some kids will get the chance to be recognized, even if they are good and better than the ones in big clubs. It is a complicated sport, not to play, but to get involved with the details to reach your dreams played in a club such as Real Madrid.

I'm just a poor kid living with my mother and no one else: no father, no brother, nor a sister.

I have a minimally small family, and my limitations with football are slim to none.

Another important fact.....Injuries.

If I get injured, I can't play, and if I can't play....hmmm, No Money.

Now, with tennis, I'm all alone. If I work hard, it's for myself.

If I Win games, it's for myself. If I get the endorsement, it's for myself.

It is an individual sport, and it is for myself.

It is my loss or my glory.

I can take a break, educate myself, and attend college, but football is complicated, as I said before. So I chose Tennis, even though my heart will always lean toward football.

Did I answer your wondering question...Coach?

Manolo: More than just an answer, but a book.

How old are you, Mondo...Again?

Mondo: I'm 11 years old.

Manolo: I think I've learned something new today and from an 11-year-old, so thank you, Mondo, and I can promise you this.....The more you work and practice, the more I will show you the world. I have one more question; your answer must be cautious.

Manolo: What is the main thing that made you love football?

Mondo: The passion for the sport.

Manolo: Passion, outstanding. So, can you have the same passion for tennis, or are you still determining?

I was deeply thinking about the correct answer; then I realized that to answer that, I must tell him the theory behind my passion for football or any other sport in general.

Mondo: The thing with playing any sport is understanding how to discover the hidden fun in any sport, which comes with knowing how to read.

Manolo: Reading?

Mondo: Any kid hates school when it comes to using the brain in learning, reading, and writing. However, once they learn the basics, the reading will be challenging, and the fun will begin to capture their minds, which is uncontrollable because they have no choice but to learn.

Sports, on the other hand, require less effort using the brain as they play, and again, it is controllable because the passion for the sport gets into their blood, so they practice more and sweat more to achieve the most significant discovery of the game(Pause) The hidden fun.

Without passion, the sport will become homework and boring, the fun of playing will vanish, and kids will quit the sport. The Passion is like the most beautiful rose on Earth; everyone is trying to grab it, yet so many people are afraid of her thrones and prefer not to bleed for just a flower. The more dedicated players are the ones who bleed for the passion of such a flower because it is the best thing in life to bleed for passion.

So, passion has always been my drive to be better and unique.

Manolo: Well, I got the point, and my advice is to keep searching for such a passion and stay humble. Today, I will introduce you to every court, and you will practice with me alone.

One-on-one, so let's go.

Everything in this place dazzled my eyes, as so many new and unusual things were everywhere. In one court, I observed young girls all wearing white skirts and blouses, hitting the ball around, and having a wonderful time.

Another court also has an older young female flirting with the balls and boys.

A court with men running all over the court to win a point, breaking a sweat with every move to win a match.

Money, money, money, is always funny in the rich man's world.

This place is a gold mine for me. The ball boys and girls were earning tips after tips to keep the Fun going for the people in this place.

The ball boys and girls were running like Bees, hustling, picking up balls, and offering drinks and towels to keep the members happy with their services and dedication.

Other groups of men were rushing to brush up the lines; others were hosing the courts with water, coaming the court surfaces with the long, wide net brooms.

Every court was better than the other; every court was fully stacked and equipped with needs for the members to keep them happy and satisfied.

Tennis balls, ice boxes filled with icy water, Pepsi, and other refreshing soft drinks.

On the other hand, the Tennis shop was another place to make more fluid Money.

Some members are never ready to play Tennis, and some guests are similar.

Flourishing and wealthy people from Spain or other countries always need more time to prepare for a tennis match, which is the value of the tennis shop.

That place is like our Saturday flea market. The Martiricos Flea Market is the place to find anything and everything, yet here in the tennis shop, you can find anything and everything that has to do with Tennis and sometimes not to do with tennis.

Tennis balls, rackets, sportswear, sneakers, souvenirs, magazines, newspaper posters of famous tennis players...old and new.... Cigars, and more.

I never understood the idea of that stupid thick sausage they put in their mouth to smoke.

My Aunt explained that some men like to show off by smoking cigars.

The idea is to show off and not to inhale it in your lungs. It is heavy and dangerous for your health, but it smells unique. I'm not too fond of its smell at all.

Money is everywhere, and with the members' money, this place is blooming daily, but only if they enjoy their time here. The cafe, the restaurant, and the massage room were attached to a sauna. Indoor courts are exceptionally fascinating. I can always remember the swimming pools everywhere in this club. The tour with coach Manolo was much more convenient than with Anna's. At last, we were back on the court, yet something caught my attention, and so quickly I said: Coach, who's that?

Her voice has a remarkable harmony, a tone that filled my heart with joy, the voice of an angel. The moment our eyes crossed and tangled together, floating to a different world...not this world.

A world of purity and beauty. Her eyes were different and yet unusual.

One was light Hazel green, and the other was solid green. I had never seen eyes like that before, yet there was also a strange kind of glow, more of radiation that filled my heart with love, warmth, and joy. Her face was a face of a little girl. However, her body said otherwise. Her body was toned firm, and the sun rays flirting with her face with a unique rainbow over her profile side made me so eager to take two steps forward with my eyes fixed on hers, stretching my arm with an open hand as a gesture for a handshake. I couldn't wait for Manolo to introduce us as I told her: I'm Mondo; how are you doing?

She put her hand in mine, shook it very gently, smiled, exposing her bright white teeth, then said, almost whispering: So, you're the one....El Nino magico...Mondo.

When she said that, her hand grip changed to a robust and firm handshake.

She squeezed my hand as if she wanted to be melted with hers, never to let go.

When my eye's colors changed to a slight glow, her grip returned to soft.

Suddenly, she leaned down, looking straight into my eyes, and said: It's my life's honor to meet El Nino Magico finally, but above all, it will be my even more incredible honor and joy for you to remember me when you get older and become famous, even though you are recognized to me, but I mean in the future to maybe remember me....Eve.

Yes, my dear...my name is Eve.

I was speechless, and my hand never let go of hers as she switched again and held my hand dearly, this time with both hands as if she wanted to tell me that she approved that and for our relationship to remain forever.

My heart was about to explode from the rapid and fast beat, and I had to do something before I fainted in her hands. I had to respond quickly to what she said, yet the first stupid thing that came out of my mouth was a foolish joke.

I smiled and said: My actual name isn't Mondo.... It's Adam.

Manolo: Mondo, you're such a funny boy.

Adam and Eve... hahaha.

At last, she let go of my hand covering her face and then laughed at my joke.

I started laughing as they were hysterically laughing for quite some time until I managed to stop and said to her while I was still giggling: So it's Eve...that is a name that I will never forget as long as I live, but in the meantime, I'm still wondering...What is Eve doing here on this court while she is supposed to be up in the eternal Paradise...unattended?

Eve: Manolo, this kid is magical with his words, but do you think he can be enchanted on the court?

Let's see what he can do on the court right now. My face started to change as she was serious about her intentions.

Mondo: What court...please coach, she can't be serious.

Manolo: Well, I wasn't expecting that, but your training will start ahead of the schedule and my plans. You must know that Eve is a charming young girl, but be careful as she can also be very deceiving.

How old do you think she is?

Mondo: I'm sure she's a little bit older than me, by a few years, so I would say 14 years old....Am I right?

Eve: I'm so sorry to disappoint you. You were way wrong about my age.

I'm 20, but I'm small and short. However, I've been around for quite some time in the tennis field, and perhaps to add more spices and excitement to your daily work to be able to see me every day, as I'm the coach for the girls in this club....and sometimes for the boys as well.

I'm only here for the summer, but again, it is my good luck to be here to meet you.

However, please don't get excited, as it's still being determined.

Not long ago, there were rumors about a special guest in our club, and I heard someone exceptional would join us this summer. And with that, I was trying to convince Coach Manolo to be his assistant and coach you as well.

My dear god...Two coaches are too much to handle; I'm lucky. Mondo said.

Eve: Well, not only is this young man funny, but for sure, he's humble as well; I'm so impressed, but for now, let's go to court 7.

Again, with the number 7.

Manolo: Go ahead before me, as I need to get some equipment.

I'll meet you there shortly. She was slightly taller than me, so she put her hand above my shoulder and then pulled me closer to her body as if she were my unique girlfriend.

Soon later, she said: Mondo, we're home.

Those words were magical to my ears, so I told her....I think you're right... I'm Home.

It was the first time in my life that I felt that way. The red clay, the net, the lines, and everything around me felt that, at last, I found my natural true Home.

I couldn't grasp the idea, but that dream made sense, and then I started to believe.

Eve: Mondo... here's your first lesson. How fast are you?

Mondo: I think I'm fast enough.

Eve: Well, don't think, but believe in your heart that you're the fastest, do you understand?

Mondo: I do.

Eve: Well, show me your speed. I will race you, and if you beat me, you'll get a special prize from me.

What is it with girls Today.....Everyone wants to race me, and it always ends up with their disappointing faces.

If she wants a race...she will get my speed.

Mondo: In which way the race will be....Is it five laps around the court, or will your race differ?

Eve: You're still funny, yet charming, but also naive.

No, Mondo, the race will start from the baseline to the net and back to the baseline.

Mondo: That will be the most straightforward, easy race I've ever had.

Eve: Don't rush, and don't be. Hmm, what is the word for that?

Oh, over-ambitious, yuppie, hot shot, or more likely over-achiever person.

Listen, as I wasn't finished with the race rules yet, we ran from the baseline to the net....without touching the net, then sprinted back to the baseline....simple.

Oh, and it's twenty-time laps.

Mondo: What, twenty laps... I wasn't expecting that kind of a race, but I know I can still beat you.

Eve: Stop saying that....Believe it, don't say...only believe you can.

So are you ready, Mondo? Then she blows her loud whistle for the race to commence.

I ran so fast, beating her to the net, but I couldn't stop. I was almost about to hug and hit the net, but I remembered her rules not to touch the net.

I only realized her technique once I saw her sliding on the clay.

I had never seen anything like that before, but with the way she was sliding, she could stop right before the net, shuffle, twist her body back, and sprint to the baseline repeatedly. I had to stop by the baseline to observe her sliding technique as a ballerina performing Swan Lake with extreme elegance and flexibility.

The blood rushed to my brain, yet my eyes memorized her moves.

She goes low with her body as if her knee is about to scrap the clay; her head is low, and her legs are stretched forward as if sliding on ice. She used her back foot to control her sliding, as a brake to help her dead Stop in such a moment.

Also, it was notable that she was right, putting her body weight on the right and sliding.

I started to do her technique, but she yelled at me, saying: Don't go in the future with your body, don't lean forward with your head, stay low and float on the clay, control your balance with your hands.....The front is front, and the back is back.

One leg is forward with the hand, and the other is sliding from back to front with the balance of the other hand; your butt has to remain low, and don't let the speed interfere with the gravity...slide and float, slide and float.

My gift of adaptation started to be mature enough to duplicate her technique, yet with my confidence, my sliding became much faster and better than hers.

My improvement became a weapon, as a dagger in her heart.

I started gaining laps over her until the final lap, and then she said Stop, stop.

We stopped at the baseline; she looked at me with her face dripping crazy sweat, breathing heavily, trying to find saliva in her throat to swallow.

Then she managed to say: Listen, you're a beast. However, this is the last lap, so let's see if you can beat me.

My expertise in football taught me a valuable lesson: never to stop moving your feet, especially if you're about to burst in speed. You must beat gravity and keep moving your feet up and down, even if it is just rapid baby steps. Keep your feet moving like a stick on the drum.

She wasn't aware of that, holding a solid standing still pose with her feet glued to the baseline. Mine were beating the drum so fast and so loud, never stopping.

Go...she said.

Before she finished the Go, I was halfway to the net. I started sliding way ahead of time from the Deuce court (the service box) with my entire body floating on the Red clay so smoothly towards the net, stopping a few millimeters by the net, then switching my whole body bursting back to the baseline, then again from the edge of the service box starts to slide again until my foot touched the baseline finishing and winning the race.

As I turned my head to my left, thinking she would be next to me, I realized she wasn't by the baseline. I hopped off the baseline and looked back at the court.

I saw Eve running slowly to the baseline, and when her foot touched the baseline, she bent down, holding her stomach of exhausters. Gradually, she could control her breathing; she looked at me and said: Very well done, Mondo...and again, you're not an average person.... you're a beast in a kid's body. You're the first to beat me on such a drill, as I never lost before, yet by far, you proved me wrong, and now I'm petrified of what you're capable of achieving after.

I just wanted to know one thing...How did you beat me?

Have you ever practiced this drill with somebody else before?

Who taught you to keep your feet moving like that?

How did you manage to adapt the slide that fast....How and how?

Eve: Who are you... indeed?

Mondo: First, you owe me a prize. Secondly, you're an outstanding teacher, and I did listen to what you said, adapted, improved, and created, but above all, I believed.

So thank you very much.... you're terrific.

The interruption of our conversation was loud enough for us to turn around.

The fast and loud clapping of coach Manolo was the reason.

Manolo: That was incredible, and I'm astonished at what you guys did with that tough drill. I'm very impressed, as I've never seen anyone execute that drill so fast, with such speed on his first attempt. Eve was so tired, but she managed to control her defeat, and with her eyebrows raised to the sky, she was pointing at me, trying to find her words until she'd finally said: Coach, you clapping your hands and saying things that you haven't seen, but this kid...(pause), I mean, Mondo is not a normal kid.

Have you noticed how he slides on the clay? Have you witnessed his speed...this is an incredible phenomenon. I'm speechless.

Manolo: Calm down, my girl...I did see what he did; again, this will be a complex task.

I will say this to confirm what I said a while back.

Mondo is.... El Nino Magico, and (pause), and you will help me coach him....there you go, I said it.

But for now, let's all have some ice water.

Mondo: Can I have a Coke instead...por favor.

Manolo and Eve screamed at his face at the same time, saying: NO.

Only Agua, and there is a reason behind that, is just ice water.

Mondo: Si, Agua...por favor.

As I was sipping my ice water, the sun blocked my vision again, and all I could see was her shadow for the second time as a ghost. I jumped off the bench, jumping up and down hysterically, pointing my finger in the air, as I screamed at them: Look, look....Up there.... Who's that girl?

They both stood up and looked up, covering their face with their hand to block the sun, then they both turned around and said: What girl?

Mondo: Look up there; she is standing by...

Where did she go...I swear that girl was there and...I saw her before when I was racing Anna, and she waved to me and said, Vamos Mondo....I believe she was the reason I won the race, but where and who is she?

Eve rushed towards me, placed her hand on my head, and said: Your head is hot, and that happens with this kind of heat; maybe you're just hyperventilation from the sun; come with me. She placed a cold towel around my neck and asked me to sit down for a few minutes to cool off. On the other hand, Manolo wasn't happy, and he was so anxious to get back for practice when he said: Enough, forget about that ghost, and let's get back to training.

Well, now we both know that you're fast, but for how long, or more importantly...how about the focus and concentration?

Eve will demonstrate the drill; you observe and learn.

He was standing by the net, and next to him was a massive box on wheels with an open top. The box was filled with tennis balls, possibly over 300 balls.

Manolo: The drill is straightforward, as I will toss one ball at a time to her forehand, and she will receive it and place it in a different place on the other side of the court without hitting the net. It's simple. Every time he tossed the ball, she would get ready using her non-dominant hand(left) to aim at the ball's direction coming at her after it bounced once off the clay.

She waited for the ball to bounce, then hit it with her racket, yet her follow-up motion never stopped. She completed her proper arm rotation with a swing towards her left shoulder as she was a righty. The impact of her hit bounced the ball of the strings from down to up with a spin to curve the ball clearly above the net to the left side corner by the baseline of the open court, then bounced up again, hitting the fence. It was beautiful, and I enjoyed her technique very much.

Her technique and flawless body rotation with her hips, legs, and shoulders...Vamos Eve...I started clapping my hand until Manolo said...Mondo...shhhhh, watch and learn only...again.

Eve bent her knee and bowed as a ballerina, thanking me...but again, the party crasher said....Eve...come on...get ready.

Coach Manolo had so many tricks in his bag that even the great Eve couldn't tell when one would arise. Every time he tossed the ball to Eve, he changed the direction of his toss, yet she was always ready for every angle, and she didn't miss a ball. She managed to hit a perfect 16 balls.

Manolo's first trick was with the tricky balls. He had some flat balls, old and bold, but Eve had no idea that the Old wizard hid them in his pocket and then slipped one at a time into the box. Ball number 17 was the first one.

Everything was the same, same toss, same angle, but the fact that Eve had no idea what was coming made the drill very interesting. When that oddball bounced off the clay, it bounced low, so Eve had to scramble, sliding, trying to reach for the ball, but it was too late as the ball bounced twice, and she missed it. Eve's face changed, and she asked him: What the hell was that?

Manolo: If you focus and stop flirting with Mondo, maybe if you move faster away from the baseline, you'll get to even a dead ball. Eve wasn't happy with his dirty trick, but I understood his philosophy. Another dead ball, and again, she fell for it.

The last and final ball wasn't sure of Eve's expectations, as she was somehow angry and may be intimidated by the coach's tricks. She took this ball so hard and flat with extreme power, and then when the ball hit clay, it bounced so high and got stuck between the fence's wires.

That was fun to me, and again, I lost it, and I was clapping so hard that my hand felt numb for a little bit. I was having a good time in the presence of that young Eve.

Manolo: Perfect, Eve, now it's your turn, clapper boy; go to the baseline and pick a racket.

I was so confused as there were so many of them; some were heavier than others, so I was trying to decide which one to pick. One racket was lying down on the clay away from the others, very old and beat up, yet the strings looked as new as they could be. They were substantial, as if a magician strung them.

I strolled to the baseline, but Eve came running and said: Mondo, get rid of that racket.

She grabbed a new one with a Wilson logo and said: Use this one better.

Manolo was looking at both of us, waiting for my final choice.

I said: Eve, thank you, but I feel comfortable with this racket.

Manolo smiled and said: Wise choice, young man, now get ready.

I never knew that was his daughter's first racket, but again, I just learned about him Today.

He left it there for me to choose, and I felt some glow in his eyes when I decided on that racket.

Are you ready? Coach said.

Mondo: Si.

I was holding the racket so hard with both hands, yet in my mind, I was whispering to the noise or asking the racket to be my friend and help me complete the drill successfully.

The first ball bounced so high, almost like a body ball, and I was so confused about making slight contact with it that I missed it completely.

Vamos, vamos...Mondo...again.

I was so angry for missing the ball, but Eve said: It's OK, focus on the next one and forget about the past...concentrate.

I had to close my eyes and breeze in and out; then I re-visualized every move that beautiful Eve made. Anna's words fell between all that when she said I must choose which hand to use....right or left.

She also advised me to use my left instead of my right, even though I'm naturally right.

If I become a lefty, it will add more guessing and confusion to my opponents.

I slowly let go of my right hand of the racket and chose to be a lefty tennis player.

I started to listen to the sound of the ball departing Manolo's hand coming my way; then, suddenly, the world had stopped when I opened my eyes.

The ball was coming very slowly, as if the air had disappeared, and so was the gravity.

The slow motion of me letting go of my two-hand posture off the racket slightly bounced to only my left hand.....

I shuffled my feet, estimating the ball bounce direction, calculating the wind speed and the spin on the ball as if I were a professional tennis player. When the ball was in my perfect reach, the moment of truth came to reality and said to the racket; Here we go....I have to give you a name..hmm, what would it be?

Gaby.

Come on, Gaby, don't let me down.

Gaby's strings came alive, and they hugged it briefly when they met the ball.

Then, they all decided to spin the ball at the fastest speed and then let go.

The ball left the string with an extraordinary spin that made it fly over and above the net so clearly with an explosive speed that when the ball hit the clay scraping the corner left baseline, it exploded with a bounce that ended up being stuck next to Eve's ball on the fence.

I always remembered the same follow-up body rotation as Eve's technique, which gave me more racket speed than I expected. Instead of hitting my shoulder with the racket, I managed to lower my head, almost duck, allowing the racket's head to flow above my head to complete the full rotation.

Eve: Wow, Mondo, what was that? Where did you learn to hit the ball like that? Are you lefty? Did the racket hit your head, as it was so close? Are you OK?

Mondo: Si. I'm also a righty, not a lefty.

Eve: That is impossible; please do it again.

Again, I hit the ball the same way, but this time with a good clearance from my head.

Manolo: What was that? Could you do it again?

This was the first time I learned how to control my new gift with tennis.

I adapted and converted something I've seen or learned into my invention.

I've invented a new technique that only works for me. A ball after another, and it was evident and apparent that the more I hit, the more my accuracy became more effective, positive, and precise. Manolo forgot what he was planning to teach me, as he was going crazy tossing faster balls, one after another, and I still haven't missed a single one.

The maturity of my brain, the extreme focus, and my concentration made me read him to where he would toss the next ball until he started with his dirty tricks. Ironically, I was also aware of that, and I've learned from Eve's mistakes that those balls were dead and had no weights.

They need to bounce the proper way.

The first ball dragged for a second bounce, yet I had to slide from the baseline to the service box and barely clipped it with the racket. It still passed the net, but almost as if it was a drop shot. The last ball was even worse, as he tossed the ball more to the Add court by the service box; moreover, when I saw the ball leaving his hand, I started running, then slid so fast to get to the ball. However, my speed was too much for being at the right spot, and I was ahead of the ball. I couldn't do anything but lay the face of the racket in between my legs, with its head slightly touching the clay. The ball hit the strings, bounced above the net several times, then landed right down, brushing the net from opposite my court.

Her shadow was there, and I was very optimistic that she was watching all of that, but again, why she doesn't reveal herself to me, at least to know her name?

A voice screamed from nowhere, saying: You know my name, as I'm all yours and in your hands.

Coach Eve.... don't tell me you haven't heard her....I know you did.

Manolo: I've never seen that in my coaching career, have you, Eve?

Eve: No, coach, what we've witnessed is something not natural or normal.

However, I'm so excited to see more, so how about a new drill?

Mondo: I'm not doing any other drills until one of you tells me you've heard that girl talking to me.

Manolo and Eve: We don't know what you are talking about, but whatever is in your mind, it has to stop, as the next drill is essential, and this is how it will go.

Eve will receive your hit and return them to your court; you, on the other hand, must return her balls back and again. That is called a rally in Tennis.

The longer it will be, the better for you to understand how slow or fast you have to react to reach and return the ball in a different spot, which is complicated, awkward, and difficult for her to get to. I will demonstrate with a few balls, and then you follow. Manolo is like an old fox that can lure you so close until you are sure you got him; then, with a trick, you'll fall to his spell and lose. He started very slow with his rally, almost playing and toying with her.

If you come from the outside, you will say he is an old recreational tennis player.

His returns were way above the net, Tennis's safety dance. He keeps dancing with you slowly; the speed gets faster, the angles get tighter and more complex, and the more the rally continues, the more he makes you run and scramble all over the court, side to side, front to back.

The first rally was almost 20 balls, and it was obvious that poor Eve had to be all over the place with his returns. The old man hardly moved from his spot, yet he forced her to return every ball to his feet.

Come on, Eve; you can do better than that; move your feet. Manolo said.

The next rally started with something new to me, and that was with a serve.

Eve served at Manolo, and it was my first time witnessing something new called serving. Such a new thing helped her place the ball in a difficult spot for Manolo to return, and with that, I must learn how to do that in so many ways and with different techniques. I stood by the bench in the middle of the court, watching them. Meanwhile, I was trying to observe how she held the racket, and so was Manolo.

They were holding the racket differently from the way I had my racket.

They were righty, and I was lefty.

Coach Manolo wasn't a mover, but he was more of a baseline hugger.

He controlled all the returns from the baseline while Eve was all over the place.

At last, Manolo smiled at Eve and said: Let's take a small break.

I wasn't concerned about his generous offer, as I was more curious about the service than anything else.

Mondo: Can I try a few things while you both rest?

They agreed, so I gathered some balls and went to the service box to imitate Eve's service.

I tossed the ball low and didn't bend my knees; as a matter of fact, I didn't do anything right, and when I hit the first ball, it flew above the fence and disappeared completely.

I saw Manolo sipping on his cold, icy water bottle, giving me the sign to keep repeating that.

I tossed the ball repeatedly, with all my balls way above the fence.

I was so angry with myself, but I couldn't let those balls get lost, so I said: I'll bring them. They were in a different world, talking among themselves, and ignored me.

I ran out of the court, and I was sure they kept saying: Forget about the balls, but I was somehow stubborn and kept looking for the crazy balls. The crazy balls flew to the back wood, which has a trail for the members to use to get away from Tennis sometimes.

I didn't realize how far I had to go deep in the woods, but fortunately, I saw one of the balls sitting by a big tree. When I picked up the ball, her voice returned as a whispering ghost.

I was terrified and about to run back, but her soft voice said: Don't be afraid of me.

I'm here for a particular reason, and that is you...Mondo.

Who are you, where are you, and how do you know my name?

I'm extraordinary, but you can't see me, as I'm a ghost...not a scary one, but I promised that I shouldn't interfere with your past life or, in your case, your present. I'm someone from the future, and again, I can't reveal myself to you nor allow you to see me.

Mondo: I don't understand what you're saying, so either you show yourself up, or I'm gone.

Listen, Mondo...When I told you those words at the court, I meant them dearly, so please try to understand them again. You know my name; I'm all yours and in your hands.

Think Mondo and try to figure it out, yet for now, focus on the training and listen to both of them as they will take you to a new world that only you can string with all the lives wrapped around you. You're the key to so many Unstrung Lives.

If you don't understand that, so many lives, including you, Mondo, will vanish.

Suddenly, it was dead silent, as if all the lives were gone but me. I looked at the ball and said: We meet again my fuzzy yellow ball.

Mondo: Hola, hello, are you still there?

The silence was a confirmation of her vanishing. I ran and ran until I was back on the court, but the looks weren't pleasant towards me.

Manolo: Well, you must listen to me when I call you, as I said to forget about the damn ball, yet you ignored me and ran nowhere.

Mondo: I'm so sorry, coach; it won't happen again.

The drill wasn't easy, and Eve had me like a YO-YO all over the court.

I was exhausted but couldn't stop; neither could I say die. I ran back to the baseline and had a small sip of water. I strode to the baseline, closed my eyes, and inhaled a very long, deep breath. The sun was in my face, and suddenly, I did something unusual. I opened my arms as if stretched on the cross, transferring the sun's magic into my body and just breeze and breeze.

I stood there for at least a minute but became different when I opened my eyes.

I became el Nino magico.

I'm ready. I said.

The astonishing looks on their faces were an exclamation mark to what I'd just done.

With every ball she hit toward me, my return was better and faster, with unreturned angles all over the court. The sun energized my body, and tennis transformed my mind like such a sport possessed me. My sliding, shuffling side to side, and reaching for every ball made it difficult for Eve to win a point.

The technique of hitting the ball starts to make sense to me, and in sports, they say: There is only fun in any sport once you learn and adapt the actual technique.

Otherwise, the sport will be boring and will not improve, which is why many people, especially young ones, quit the sport. The image of players hitting the balls, including Anna, Manolo, and the great Eve, was just a rewinding machine in my head.

It was like a perfect song you'd heard only once, yet because of the words and the musical notes, it became a constant echo in your ears, and you kept singing it repeatedly.

The posture, the preparations, and the movements all came to me as if I had been playing tennis for the last ten years. I still have to learn to serve, but for the moment, I must do well with this drill. She played Manolo's method with a sneaking drop shot to bring me to the net. However, she underestimated my speed.

I was sliding to the net, and just before the ball bounced twice, I managed to get to the ball, but instead of just taping the ball above the net anywhere in a desperate attempt, the beast in me came alive. I slammed the ball so hard that she had to duck down to avoid getting hit in the face.

Enough, take a break, Mondo. Manolo said.

Eve was furious, and she rushed to Manolo and started whispering, yet her whispering was loud enough for me to hear.

Eve: Do you believe this kid? He is lying to you and me.

Eve: Mondo, will you come here, please?

She put her hand over my shoulder as if trying to hold me still and not move.

I raised my head, and when I looked into her eyes, she let go of her hand from her shoulder, took one step backward, and then said: First, I'm sorry to grab you like that... I'm so sorry.

I want you to tell me the truth, and please don't lie to me...por favor.

I shook my head up and down in acknowledgment of not lying.

How long have you been playing Tennis..... Oh, no, no...forget that.

How many times have you been on a tennis court?

I've seen you playing football, and you were terrific, but you must be honest with me so I can help you.

So I will ask you again: How many times have you been on any tennis court?

Mondo raised his left hand with five fingers.

Eve: Are you trying to tell me that you were on any tennis court in your life only five times?

Again, I shook my head up and down, telling her...YES.

Coach, this kid is lying, saying that he has no experience with

Tennis and has been on the tennis courts only three times...FIVE TIMES ONLY.

This kid was killing me on the court; how is that possible?

Manolo: I said it before, and I will repeat it...He is magic, and we are both very fortunate to witness the miracle of a newborn Star. Their argument became more whispering, yet I could hear some of their words.

Manolo: Listen, Eve, you know me very well, as I have trained you since you were a kid, and you know that I coached so many people before you and after you, but with that kid standing there. I can only tell you that he will be a fast learner, but I will be the one to learn from him.

I need help explaining why he is here

and how his brain functions. I can't justify his ability or capability in Tennis, but I'm very optimistic that he will write a new chapter in tennis history.

Now, Mondo, are you tired, or do you want to rerun the drill with Eve?

I looked at Eve and said: I will do the drill one more if you stop getting angry at me, and bear in mind that you lied to me as well. Also, you don't keep your promises....but I'll be a good boy and forgive you. Didn't you promise to give me a special prize if I won, or did you forget about that too?

Eve: NO and NO.

First, I'm not angry at you; on the contrary, I'm confused about your capabilities and skills. Secondly, I keep my promises, so please forgive me, and I promise you if you do the drill again, I will double the prize.....Hmm, are you satisfied now?

Mondo: I'll be the judge after the drill.

A moment before we started, Manolo walked fast toward me, leaned to my ears, and then said: Mondo, I want you to do the drill differently. I want you to hit every line, not the middle, but the lines only. Can you do that?

I want you to be fast, precise, and accurate in every shot, clear your mind, and know where exactly your return will be. It is more promising if you build a plan for more than one ball in case she returns any of them.

Visualize your lines, and don't believe that you may be...I can, but only think that I CAN AND WILL.

Vamos, Mondo...Go.

His words were astonishing to my ears, yet I started to feel something strange crawling through my veins, something growing in me, and that was the power of belief.

I had so much confidence in my ability and genuine faith that I must let it all out.

I had to close my eyes again and visualize the lines, but nothing else came out.

This new gift and abilities were developing incredibly fast as if I were an older professional tennis player, not from this era, but from a future one.

I must control my grip and use my unique technic to hit the lines.

My shots' speed, accuracy, and precision did not disappoint Coach Manolo.

There are 20 balls on the lines and no returns from Eva's side.

The fast clapping and the scream of the coach saying: Vamos my boy, vamos Mondo.

Manolo: You didn't disappoint me once, and now we must conclude our practice for the day. Manolo asked me to return to the locker room and change as my first practice ended.

I put back the old racket (Gaby) leaning by the back fence nicely, then took a step back and bowed to the racket, saying: Gracias.

Everything happened so fast.

As I was leaving, I had a final quick look at Eve's face, and all I saw in her was anger and frustrations that led to another new thing to witness. She smashed her racket on the bench into a million pieces.

Manolo: Eve, stop that you're not a little girl anymore, so grow up and learn to be a role model for that kid.

Mondo: I had to hide and listen to Coach coaching Eve.

Manolo: Let me explain something to you about Mondo.

That is a Natural kid... Hmmm, forget that. He isn't natural, as he is a new phenomenon to me.

A natural athlete has something unique, and it is not passed on ability to become a natural. The scary part about Mondo is his brain. It is the mastermind of his speedy learning.

He has the best hand-eye coordination, the fastest ever quick twitch muscles, hyper-focus, and confidence I've ever seen. He is extra competitive with intelligence and leadership, also don't forget an essential factor....Motivation and passion.

He loves the game and will do anything to be the best quickly.

He is built with an explosive drive that can crush and wipe out any competitor his way.

He is the first to me and will be the last for me.

I know exactly what I have to do with him, as Mondo doesn't need a coach or a teacher; he needs someone to stand by, guide, advise, and support him, even when he is wrong. At last, if you wish to be part of his team..., encourage him, no matter what.

Eve: I understand now, but just one more question.

Manolo: Ask.

Eve: Well, if you're right about all that, would it lead to becoming blind and madly in love with him?

Manolo: Yes, yet you must be careful, as he will know faster than you can imagine if such a love was only for a purpose or it was a pure love.

He is that majestic kid who can read your mind, so be careful with your emotions towards him, as he is impossible to read. I put my head down to the ground, ignoring what I'd witnessed from Eve's reaction, and rushed to the locker room. I washed up, changed my clothes, and started heading to the court again until I heard a loud voice saying: Stop.

When I turned around, I faced a tall, big boy older than me, and he had a very sharp, mean face.

He said: Who are you, and what are you doing here? You're not supposed to be in here.

In such a moment, I realized that in this life... Looks definitely can be deceiving.

We are a simple family, and in the real world, we fall into the poor category when describing a class of people.

My mother is a very hard-working woman, and every peseta she earned is for me not to feel that way...Poor.

My clothes were always clean, but I was never the first owner.

Many donation places were for clothes, shoes, and even house stuff.

My mother could only get what she could afford, yet she used her talent to enhance and clean them as if they were new.

Sometimes, at Christmas, she used to put a fake tag with a price just to let me feel that I had new clothes, but I never complained or even let her know that I knew that.

How my clothes looked to that big boy proved my point, and the judgment wasn't fair to me.

Before I answered him, I was surrounded by at least ten other boys staring at me as if I were a scum. My hair was long, covering my face, yet it dripped cold water after washing up.

A strange man's voice came to my rescue saying: You must be the new kid.... Mondo, I'm Costa. The name rang a bell, but it was more like a life ring to save me from drowning in the middle of the sea as easy bait for sharks and predators. On the other hand, I was gathering strength and building up the momentum to defend myself.

A long time ago, I had a great fight master who trained me well.

I do not deny that I had so many bleeding noses, but I managed to make a reputation at school and other places that I wasn't a pushover, as I stood up and fought.

My Aunt Mar was my fighting master. She taught me how to box and drop people on the ground like flies(Judo). As much as she was wild and crazy, she was wise, confident, and never a pushover. She was my hero, but importantly, my Don Quixote.

I do recall her words when she said: Mondo, in your life you'll come to Stops, Alleys, Corners, Rules and Regulations. We live in a cynical, misanthropic, distrusting world based on fake words, descriptions, and judgment from people who always feel superior.

The real world is still the same, yet in some strange ways, it may get covered or dressed up with new things called Civilization. Live your life without fear, and let others live as well.

Don't ever be greedy; be kind, as greed only comes from evil.

It is a poisonous whisper in human ears to lean to evil acts, yet on the other hand, there is always the beauty of Paradise, where you can enjoy the gift of life without greed, jealousy, hate, and killing as they all lead to great evil.

God may protect us in mysterious ways, but again, if god is busy shopping or fishing, then in that case, you've got to learn to stand up and be a God.

Look at your aunt. I'm a goddess, and Mondo is a god. If we are gods, no one will ever touch us. Why is that Mondo?

It is a straightforward cause. We stand up and fight back until we feel it is right and fair.

We stand our ground and bleed, fighting for our pride and dignity.

She also said: If you ever get into a fight, remember to clear your mind and focus on the sudden air movement. Just try to pretend that the air is visible smoke.

Every move will cut through the smoke like a knife, and you can only see it in such a way with a clear mind. The anticipation of any sudden move prepares you for a fast counterattack, the same as football.

She knocked me down to the ground thousands of times, training me to be strong.

Be small for the big guys and be a giant for the short ones. Hit low to bring them down to your height, then attack. Go to the weak, undefended parts of their bodies.

Legs and the weak parts below the belt. It's always effective.

Hit high, not in the face, but hit their ears to break down their stability, and again, when they come down low, hit the noise, not the mouth, as you need to blind them.

Nose Tears = Blindness.

Since she disappeared from my life, I've learned to defend myself.

My mother wasn't happy with her ways, especially if I came home with dark colors on my face because of a fight at school. She used to tell me to be wise and use better methods using words than fists. Mama can be right sometimes, compelling but convincing. I would say that Aunt Mar was much more believable than Mama.

Costa's appearance at the right time saved my day from getting into a fight on my first day.

To get involved in a battle on my first day won't be a good thing, as it will always all round it up with how other boys may look at me or even say words just because of how I look or dress. I'm not an intruder, a thief, and more likely not a tramp.

When Costa touched my shoulder and accompanied me to the lounge, everybody followed.

The whispering, the mumbling, and the flirtation were all coming from different angles across the lounge. The rumors of the new ball boy traveled quickly, but only to the girl's locker room. They were coming from everywhere to witness the new boy. The lounge was getting crowded, with almost everyone in the club as workers, including Eve and Manolo. Some older women recognized me from the school, and others from the historic match.

There were so many new faces as coaches, trainers, and the physical staff.

That led me to wonder, as I wasn't aware that they had a staff meeting, yet it appeared from the gathering that filled the lounge that something important was about to happen.

Costa: Hello everyone. I want to start this meeting by asking you a simple question.

Why do we come back the next day to this place...anyone?

There were scattered flying answers from all directions and with different tones.

Some said work, security, stability, Money, boys, girls, ambitions, power, and future.

Costa: Well, that was very good...anyone else?

Fun and friendship.

Costa: Who said that? Will you please stand up?

When Mondo stood up, there was complete silence, as if he were standing like a giant to their eyes. That silence was intense until someone broke it with a hand clapping.

Everyone turned around to see who she was until she started walking from the back to the front, joining the rest of the staff. She was walking as a queen, still clapping her hand until she stood next to Costa in the front.

Her clapping wasn't special regardless of who said that statement; it was more of a star-casting clap. I was still standing as I was told to do so; meanwhile, in my mind, I was trying to understand the purpose behind her clapping. Was it harsh sarcasm or acknowledgment and appreciation?

Linda: First of all, I want to thank everyone for being here... hmm, so fast as the attendance is very overwhelming in front of me, however, I would like to mention that it is pretty ironic that no one ever told me that we would have a staff meeting in .... Today, Now.

I'm still baffled by the sudden disappearance of the staff in every department, which was somehow astonishing to me. Yet, when the words reached my office, I became more curious about who was running this place.....Is it me or all of you?

I came here to see the sudden purpose of the unexpected meeting.

I have to admit that I'm not that happy about that. However, I must confess again that my day didn't start as well as some of you had.

Linda: Costa, would you please have a seat? I need to take over and be in charge of this unannounced meeting as I should be.

So...Fun and friendship.... hmmmm, heavy meaningful words, but again I shouldn't be surprised as it came from the mouth of our newest member in this club...The one and only... Mr....Mondo.

I wonder about your last name. Do you have one, or maybe you don't have any?

Oh, it's shocking to see you somehow follow orders, as you are still standing, but you can sit down now. I didn't follow her orders as I remained standing pretending that I didn't understand a word she said, yet Costa gave the sign with his hand to sit down. Meanwhile, the evil radiations from my eyes staring at Linda was about to burn her until she said; So, I see....you only sat down when Costa asked you to do so, but not me, and that makes me wonder again: Do you understand any English, or is it just my words that you don't want to understand?

The echo of my name was like a new statement to their ears.

My name was very familiar in Malaga because of the excellent championship victory. However, people forget through their daily lives, and again, it was the fact that I was only a kid. The fact and mystery were only the name Mondo, not the look or face.

No one knows me in this place, yet the character was much more popular to many to remember me again.

Linda: In our lives, there are facts, theories, and myths. The facts of our lives may be expected in the shape of work and making Money, yet theories and myths can be limited to particular and only specific minds. Now, in which part do we believe in?

Facts, which can be work and money, are what everyone should believe in.

Some of us can be dreamers, and those will end up with Nothing...hmmm, Nothing at all. Work is power, Money is much more power, yet dreams leave you with an empty pocket.

Linda: Why are we really here?

We are here for Money and power, not some fun and friendship....Crap.

Wooo, Ahhhh...Those were the loud noses that everybody was making after what she said, yet with her sharp eyes, they were enough to silence them again.

Linda: Everyone, staff...Please meet, yet let me introduce you to the new member...Mondo....with no last name.

The sound of the hand clapping was very weak, as only a few hands dared to clap. Linda, Eve, Manolo and Costa.

It was a slow motion of clapping, maybe a fear, yet soon enough, the clapping started to get louder and louder as many others got the courage to join the wave. In less than a minute, the place was almost rocking as if it was a concert for the Beatles... or maybe someone better and more famous.

The scary part wasn't because I was a new member of the staff or the new ball boy, but because of my name and being able to see Mondo for the first time in the flesh and blood.

It was inspiring and overwhelming for me to be acknowledged in such a way. Linda: Please, please...be quiet...shh..shh.

Mondo is here in this club for so many reasons, some of which I can't reveal, and some of them have no answers or explanations on my behalf.

The main reason to me is because I was told that he has to be here and another thing(pause) him, that he is....Magical.

He is magical in an exceptional way, and he will put this club in a different category of a tennis resort.

I don't believe in magic crab, yet I'm obligated to accept such a thing.

So please welcome him as a Friend and have Fun in his company.

The way she'd singled me out with my own words made me smile, but I made her eyes browse the roof when I unexpectedly stood up and bowed slightly out of my respect as if she was the Queen of Spain.

She only shook her head once. However, that bow threw a lot of questions and wonders among the staff members. Many staff patted off my head and shoulder and shook my hand to acknowledge being a new club member.

It was a warm welcome until one person made it hotter with what she did.

The prettiest girl in the room made her way through people and laid a friendly kiss on my right cheek. Many people noticed that, including the queen...Linda.

At that moment, the atmosphere changed as Linda clapped her hands for attention and said, All right, everyone, the party is over. We have a very promising summer this year, so I expect everyone to return to their working stations...Right Now....she screamed.

Now, it was loud and clear for the staff to vanish away like flies from the lounge and return to work. I looked around and noticed that almost everyone except Linda, Eve, and Manolo was gone.

Linda: Mondo...please come closer.

The moment I got closer to her, she screamed in my face, saying: What the hell are you waiting for? Go, go with the others... don't you have a job to do?

As I was about to turn around, I just gave her a look, and it wasn't a nice look at all.

Mondo, Stop, turn around and come here. Linda said.

Listen to me carefully, you little shit, as I will say this once and for all.....Are we going to have any conflict with each other?

Are we going to have any problems with each other because, with that look, I doubt you might have a long future in my club?

Manolo: Easy, Miss Linda, he didn't do anything wrong at all, and he is young for this kind of treatment on your behalf.

Linda: Stop right there and don't say another word.....Mr. Perez

First of all, he needs to go to work with all the other court's caretakers.

Costa and the other boys will teach him the ropes, so don't worry about him.

Secondly, and please don't you ever forget your place in this club... you're just a coach...may be the head coach, but again, you're not his father, nor his guardian, so remember your place in this club, and don't you dare to cross me again are we clear...Coach?

The older man was down and hurt, but he saved the day and said: Yes, mam....all crystal. She was an unstoppable demon as she mumbled transparently to Manolo, saying: Mr. Perez, don't forget why you are still in this place; it is all out of respect for your daughter.

Her words were like a dagger to his heart, yet they made me wonder about that old picture in his office and ask myself if she does exist in this world.

Why is this great man by himself? No wife, no daughter, not even a house.

He lives in a small shack by the woods, but all that is not my concern to worry about, at least on the first day.

I left the room hurriedly, but at such a delicate moment, I knew for sure who the boss was in this place, and it was only...Linda.

The remainder of the day was much more tiring as I've learned so much from Costa, the boys, and the girls. The courts are our holy ground and must be perfect for the members. After a short break, Costa asked me if I wanted to stay longer for extra overtime. I was very tempted as he explained how I could make the extra money.

The older wealthy member will come alive as the sun rests for the day.

The courts were equipped with lights, which would be fantastic to play on.

The money comes from them and their tips. They are all wealthy recreational players with other things on their minds, so a tennis court is a relaxing special place where they get treated as kings and queens. That is the job of all the ball boys and girls.

There are many preferences in choosing the crew, some based on their experience and knowledge of the members, others about the comfort of having pretty faces servicing them during their tennis matches. He also mentioned that if I changed my mind and decided to stay, as he was short of a ball boy, it would be a good experience for me to handle the VIP. I was tired, but I wanted to maintain his confidence in me, and I also wanted to take advantage of an excellent opportunity to learn how to service VIPs.

I was about to agree, but a voice in my head kept telling me to go home; that voice was much more of a hunted voice in my head; it was her voice again, my ghost girl.

I looked at Costa and said: Maybe another day, as I started my day so early and I need to rest for tomorrow, so please understand my condition, and again thank you for the offer.....hmmm, it is, after all, my first day.

Costa: You're right. Go home and get some rest, and I will see you tomorrow.

The long way home was much better for me, even though I was exhausted.

I wanted to be alone to figure out what I had seen and encountered all day.

I must remember Manolo's words to stay focused and have no mind, and those hunted crazy voices in my head must stop. The street lights guided me to find my way home, and I was finally back in my room, wondering about the new Mondo. I was about to close my eyes, but her strange words haunted me again, so I jumped off the bed as if a snake had bitten me.

I remember what she said, and it started to make some sense.

She said: You know my name...as you chose it. I'm all yours, as you're mine.

I'm in your hands, as I'm your fate.

What is your name? That should be my first question, and her voice only came to me today, so, Mondo, who else did you see today?

Anna, Victoria, the evil Linda, Eve, and the mystery girl who kissed me, which I couldn't even get to ask her about her name, but again, who else?

What names did I choose today?

A strong wind blew up the window, which scared me, so I had to jump off the bed to close the angry window before the glass would be shattered into pieces.

The moment I closed the window, everything became quiet and silent.

I had to stop before bed, as I swore someone was standing in the dark by the bakery.

I turned around so fast, opened the window again, and looked at the same spot, but there was no one there, so I had to close my eyes, bit my lower lip, and said to myself: Mondo, you need to forget about her and sleep.

The first step heading towards my bed, the voice came back to me saying: You chose me.

The only thing I could select the entire day was that old racket....Oh my god, is that's it the old racket....

I gave the racket a name; what was the name...damn it, I can't remember the name I chose.

I had to lie on the bed, close my eyes, trying hard to remember the name, but it never crossed my memory again.

The dreams muse was so much more powerful than my mind, as she managed to control my inner mind and drag me to her world of dreams. I had to close my eyes and let my mind and soul be at her mercy as she took me back to my world of dreams and fantasy.

CHAPTER XIV

2 B OR NOT 2 B 1975

My life was like a cyclone; every day was a discovery.

The calendar on my wall said that today is June 6, 1975, my birthday... hmm, I'm 15 years old; what a shocker.

With birthdays, I prefer a different time or day. I'm not a child anymore, and I have to work...and train.

My life has changed immensely in the past years, yet I'm still the same Mondo as I recall in the summer of 1971.

It's as if I was dreaming, yet here I am again, with the memories of my first summer at Club Athena. Today is also the final for the junior championship in Spain, but that was the least of my worries. My main concern was a wish to hear her voice once more.

It's been a long time since she whispered in my ears; it was a relief, yet sometimes I miss her and her mystery.

A terrifying and strange connection was about to be engaged with my life, yet she was gone for quite some time. I know she was a ghost, but to me, she was all real...

The ghost without a face. Her words are still in my head, yet it's been four years since I've heard her voice, the mystery ghost girl.

I wish she could be honest and appear for the match of my life.

The club was busy with fans from all over Spain and other countries.

The preparations were terrific, and the place looked like a grand slam.

The staff was filling up more seats than anyone else, as I'm the magical boy to them.

This was the first time a boy from this club made it to the final, and also, it was the first time the club hosted the final of such an important tournament.

All the previous champions were from England, France, and Sweden; this year, it could be from Spain or a first for the USA.

Meanwhile, it was unique when Club Athena hosted the Championship of Spain here in Malaga.

The famous Court 12 was all set for the big moment.

The moment we entered the court, the cheering was terrific, more leaning toward me than the Americans. We've met before, but that was four years ago; however, he wasn't an opponent, but it was a meeting filled with anger and hate.

There were so many faces; some were familiar, and many were all new to me.

I was surprised when I saw the young sister grow up to be a beautiful teen and sit on my side with mom, Anna, Victoria, Linda, Eve, and coach Manolo.

I can't forget the great company of the staff all over the court.

It was a beautiful, hot day with a soft, cool breeze from the far Mediterranean Sea.

There were more surprises for me than I had expected, including the attendance of some big names in the tennis world. He received a standing ovation when he entered the court as everyone stomped like a hurricane drum.

Manuel Orantes was our Spanish hero in Tennis, and his name was well-known all over the world. My tears were about to fall, as this was the best birthday present I will ever have.

He came to me and shook my hands, but my tears couldn't wait any longer when he said to me: Happy birthday, Campion.

Pictures were taken, and a few speeches were said. The empire finally tossed the coin to choose, serve, or receive. Losing the toss was more of an advantage to me, as it was an excellent advantage to push myself to try to break his serve from the beginning.

I stood far back, almost beside the baseline umpire, preparing to receive the first serve.

The unbelievable, unexpected thing did happen.

I saw a horrifying black cloud moving closer and closer until it was above the court.

The place almost turned dark, but that wasn't the scary part. A gusty, strong wind filled the court as the wind swirled like a cyclone.

Everyone was trying to take cover, but it was everywhere. I had to protect my eyes, as the clay shaped like a monster heading straight at my face. I had no choice but to go down on my knees and cover my face.

Such a phenomenon didn't last for a long time, as suddenly the loud noise of the storm was gone, and only some noises of people talking to me as it sounded from a faraway distance saying: Is he OK?

The voices got louder and more apparent until the final voice was booming and clear, saying: Mondo, are you OK?

I managed to uncover my face, as I wasn't afraid anymore.

However, my fear switched to extreme fright, and when I opened my eyes, it appeared that I was back in 1971 on Court 12.

That was the same day I met my present opponent; that was when everything became clear to my mind that I would rule Tennis.

This is unbelievable to me, and it can't be real.

I was standing in disbelief, watching all the boys and girls before me preparing for that VIP match on June 17, 1971.

Louisa, Ramon, Andreas, Lucas, Lucia, Pedro, Alonso, Isabella and the lovely Maya.

They were the best of the best in the club, Athena.

Costa: Vamos, everyone, get alive. This is a big match, and I want you to be super fast for those VIPs.

This club had so many visitors from all over the world. Regardless of the misunderstanding between Mrs. Linda and me, I MUST ADMIT THAT SHE WAS THE BEST OF THE BEST.

She was always knowledgeable and connected as she used to reserve many events with wealthy and famous people to be in the Athena's Club.

Such an event may not have been significant, but it was crucial to many people, including Victoria.

Maya was always my favorite girl in the club; not only was she gorgeous, but also a good player as well.

She was 14 years old, yet she looked like a boy hiding her beauty behind a strange cap.

Such a style in America is well known as ...Tom Girl.

Her dark black hair and hazel green eyes make her very noticeable as a famous model.

She was the one who came running, leaving her line to check on me, as that serve was almost about to take my face off. It is odd to be in two different places at the same time....future and past.

Again, this club had many visitors worldwide, which might explain her strange cap.

It's an American cap for a club or a league in America. That cap was a gift from an American businessman, one of the VIPs playing on this court. 12.

During the match, I couldn't tell from her eyes about the mixed signals hints and, above all, the confused signals. I knew she was following me with her eyes during my walk with Costa, and I felt very comfortable that somehow she'd accepted me as a new club member.

Ironically, Ramon was not the same case, and he was jealous of me, as Maya used to be his girlfriend a few months ago. He was a tall boy, the oldest member of the ball boys as he was 16 years old, and that type of young-looking boy made me drift even further away to another day on the past calendar.

I had a long conversation with Aunt Mar about understanding the different types of males and females.

She quoted: If you can describe with your eyes a male, young or old in a superficial way, it means physiologically not being judged by the color or the race, then suddenly in your mind you get to feel different.

In such a moment, and then when you start to ignore their presence by looking in a different direction....hmmm.

That is for boys and men; it is typical to see it that way.

However, the effect from the male side perspective can be confusing.

In plain, simple language, it will be described as if you don't care, which is OK with men because sexually, they are the same gender. However, you must be completely careful if you act the same way towards the other sex...Female, the results can be scary.

If you ever do that to a young or old female and get caught with your eye's suggestions, you will....Wait, I have an idea... let's play a game.

Mondo: I'm excited, but what's the name of the game?

Mar: The game we will play is called" Truth or Dare."

Mondo: What does that mean?

Mar: This game is scary and....dirty.

Mondo: I don't want to play a scary or a dirty game.

Mar: Be patient; you will learn a precious lesson after the game.

Mar: We are the female, lone survivors, the most dangerous species on this planet.

We can play that game with men...almost forever until they bend down and change their minds.

Sometimes, the game can turn out to be dirty, cruel, and mean until the male loses the battle with a broken heart. We can tease, manipulate, twist words, lie, and more.

Women are beautiful, dangerous creatures, so you must be very careful and prepared with all types of women.

Mondo: You're telling me girls are evil and dangerous...That is terrible.

Mar laughed and said: Well, it is a Yes and a NO.

You can turn a witch into an angel, and only you can turn a woman into a real horrible demon that will haunt you even in your dreams; it's all up to you, my Love, to see through our kind.

Mar: Mondo my dear, you're a different type.... you're sweet, gentle....I can't even reasonably describe you... you're just(pause) Nino Magico.

That was the first time in my life that someone called me by that name.

Nino Magico.

Mar: To describe a female, you must be ... a woman, and even with that, you still can't be just fair with our kindness or cruelty. You have to see through her persona, her efforts, and her control of her looks. Never look at a woman through her color, culture, shape, or appearance and try to see her through her objectification. Women are not to be compared to the meat as body; that is the first thing men see and compare.

Men might see us, female, as an easy piece of meat, so easy to rip apart and swallow to fulfill their wild hunger. The experience with females will come with time, so take chances to learn new things, but never get tangled in their webs.

Don't be afraid to be bold with your words describing a woman's sexuality; sometimes, we like to be graphics, as it will again give us the edge.

If you, as a male, looked at me in a dirty way, a sexy look, as if I'm a Madonna or a whore...we will know and will take such a look to our advantage as you are in such a moment so weak because you've exposed your desire and interest. Enough describing women, but before we change to men, I need to add one more thing.....Even if you don't like it.... Find a way to feel sorry for yourself and sympathize with us.

Only then can you turn into a God.

We adore and appreciate Love, endurance, and sympathy as we like to be touched from the inside before the outside.

In the court of men, you can use respect, idol, appreciation, or flirting to describe them.

Be careful with the flirting because you may cross a dangerous railroad track, knowing that the train will definitely come and run you over.

Mondo: I don't understand how flirting can lead to all these riddles.

Mar: Well, you're very young, but again, you're gifted, and somehow, someone proficient with your beauty can walk safely parallel to the railroad track.

You will come across different types of men and women in your life.

Again, it is what we call life...regardless if it is right or wrong.

We're human, not Gods to judge, but we learn to adapt, observe, and ignore. After all, we must keep living, trying new things, and moving on. One day, you may encounter that road of flirtation with the male side.

For example, a male can be interested in another male for whatever reason, so flirting can be a reason to start a friendship.

Mondo: Wait, friends... it's a good thing, but what did you mean about the coming train?

Mar: Well... hmm, I can't really explain that part with much more detail, but that type will be...somehow, or always be the one to get hit by the train.

Mondo: Where the hell is that train coming from?

Mar laughed so loud and said: Oh, Mondo, Mondo...the train is just a metaphor, not a real thing, but what the hell... I'll explain it, and it's up to you to understand it or even grasp it. Remember that I'm your loving aunt, and you can't judge me no matter what I say...are we clear, and do you agree?

Mondo: Si.

Mar: If the flirtation between two males became intimate with body and everything that preserves the rights for the body of a woman, then in this case, I must admit that it isn't normal, nor natural, and breaks all the rules that God set up for all humanity, so again and as I explained to you before...stay away from that type(pause), Or...Mondo interrupted her and said: Or the train will kill me... hahaha.

My aunt laughed at my comment and couldn't stop until she had me in her arms; then she whispered in my ears, saying: Yes, you're right, yet you're a Monogamy.

Mondo: Monogamy...I like that new word, but what does it mean?

Mar: It has Greek origins; you know where Greece is, right?

Mondo: I know it from the map from school, but we haven't studied any of their history yet. Mrs. Olga mentioned that she will be in our Greek history next year.

Mar: I'm happy that you are learning about Greek history, and you'll love it.

The original Greek word was divided into pieces, one called Monos and the other called Gamos.

Monos is a single person, and Gamos is a married person.

They combined them into monogamia, meaning married or tamed to one side, male or female, and then the French twisted it into monogamy.

So what I was trying to explain to you is that you're a Monogamy, meaning that you're an old-fashioned male, as you prefer one girl to be your, for example, lover or girlfriend and not a lover with so many girls at the same time.

Mar: Now, if you ever describe a female with precise details....in our book, we call that Interested.

To be interested in a female is not a bad thing. However, you must be careful about your interest in such a female. The thing with a female is that we're never...hmmm, delighted, as we always look for more. It comes in pieces, only some at a time.

We want you to be interested for a long time, prolonging your admiration, which can lead to two different roads. The first is the usual, as we get bored until we get struck by lightning.

The second way is when that lightning gets through our veins; we feel the spell, charm....in your world is much easier and very familiar by one name, Amor or Love.

So, interest can lead to Love. In your case, you only have to let your heart be like a sponge.

The more you absorb, the faster it will expand.

If your heart is filled with interest, admiration, flirting, siren, teasing, seduction, and peace, then it may turn everything into that one thing called Love or falling in Love.

All we need is Love.

Mondo: That is very sweet of you; I like that ...All we need is Love.

Mar: Stop being silly; that is a song.

Mondo: A song by who?

Mar: It's a British boy band.

Mondo: And what is the name of that band?

The Beatles.

Mondo: Wow, that is a hideous name...Beetles...like the bugs...uhhh.

Mar laughed and said: Not Beetles, but Beatles.

Mondo: I still need to understand why they name themselves bugs.

Mar: Listen, wise boy, and stop being an obnoxious kid. It's a fucking British band, and they are famous for so many good songs that I happen to like them, so forget about the goddamn name and tell me if you want to listen to their music or fucking not.

Mondo: HMMMM, I understand how I can get under a woman's skin.

Mar: Oh really, and how is that?

Mondo: You see, how you were very annoyed because I was persistent and precise of knowing something or knowledge out of you, and more importantly, how you were cornered because you can't tell the whole story behind their names, but the fact that you liked the idea of being dominated and stubborn made you loose your confident cool when you got angry.

Mar: I'm very impressed with how you can read all that from my facial impression or the change in my tone of voice, but I do like how you're growing up with choices and thoughts, so let's listen to the song.

Mar: I have the record, and we can listen to it later, you'll like them very much.

So again, it's all up to your heart and imagination how you would describe a specific person to another person.

Mondo: There is one thing that I would like to understand.

Mar: Of course, go ahead.

Mondo: If it comes to a girl or a female, how can I be sure it is Love?

Mar: This is a delicate subject, but it has so many doors and alleys....hmmm, almost a Labyrinth.

Mar: First, you must understand that age can change the type of love, meaning if you're as young as your age, you can fall in love with a female because of her look, how she speaks, or if she is someone famous...

Mondo: Like Audrey?

Mar: Yes, like Audrey Hepburn; however, with someone like her, you may feel that you love her because of the way she acts, dress and talk.

Meanwhile, that is a fantasy of love, especially with your age.

That is the part of love and age; on the other hand, you may fall in love with a girl that you feel that she is the one. In such a delicate matter, you must give your heart enough time to see and feel that person in many shapes and moods.

Sometimes, she can be a smiley face; other times, she can be in tears, sad, or mysteriously complicated with hidden secrets. So you need time to understand if this is the love of your life or just an infatuation. There is a dangerous kind of love, and I'm not sure you will be able to understand it entirely at your age.

Mondo: What is that kind of love?

Mar: Hmmm, it is the love of the flesh.

Mondo: Now, you're back with riddles.

Mar: Do you have any idea what sex is?

Mondo: I wouldn't say yes, but to be honest with you.....It's a NO.

Mar: Well, that is the dangerous love, as it is always accompanied by the blend of flesh(SEX). Sometimes, you will come across falling in love because that female gave you pleasure and lust, but that doesn't mean that it is the love you're looking for, as I must go back again to the age of love. Boys or young men tend to fall in love with the first female they had sex with(for example- a paid whore), so that is not love; it is strictly sex.

Mar: The most valuable lesson you'll ever know is to love and be loved in return.

Mar: So, after that long lesson....will you be able to describe me?

Mondo: Well, nothing of what you've told me.

Mar: How come, or what do you mean about nothing I've told you?

I explained so many things briefly, so tell me why you can't describe me.

Mondo: The words written on the walls and caves, or even in books or movies, need to include what I have in descriptions of terms.

You are my only example; you are the real thing.

If my heart never finds you in another girl, you're a Goddess who can't be duplicated or replaced. I know that I'm young, yet sometimes I feel that I'm not normal, as my mind can understand things beyond my age, and in my dreams, I don't dream as any other boy, as I have nightmares that come and go.

I agree with my age; I still lack real-life experience.

The things to describe you are that every time I look at you, awake or asleep, somehow I see myself in you, yet differently in a unique way.

I see you as a blossoming rare rose, standing all alone in a dry, dead land, but when the sun dazzles your cheeks, you cry, and with your dropping tears, the life and hope come alive, and the green fills the Earth with your magic.

I see you when the sun smiles with its first light above the sea horizon, filling the water with different colors of life, hope, and Love.

I see you when it's dark, yet the shadow of the full moon lights reflecting on your eyes alters the world of darkness to some amazing bright stars that fill the hearts with electricity.

I see you standing in the gathering of all the goddesses, and with your beauty, they turn to ashes, leaving you as the only goddess. I know by now that there isn't any horror in any female as I see you changing, altering all their sorrow and sadness to beauty, hope, life, and happiness.

Even when you close your eyes, I see you in my dreams as your scent is simply a breeze of heaven, so sweet that the more I smell it, the stronger my desire for more.

You were born with a blessing, a touch, and a laugh on your face that I see and feel in my dreams. I will always be by your side, never going away, and if your lights fade away as if you're sending me out, I will still find you here and everywhere and within my dreams.

I know that I must stay, holding to your string to my life, and no matter how hard you'll push me away, my Love.... I will still want to stay.

My darling, my hope and internal beauty telling you in a secret language with an alphabet known just for you and me that this is what love is.

So you see, I can't describe you as you will always be the great mist of me.

You are the love of my life.

Mondo...are you still here? Ramon said.

I was drifting to faraway places, and when he yelled at me, I realized that I must stay away from the railroad track, as I still had so many things to accomplish with my life and not be crushed by any trains.

Ramon: So let go of my hand, and don't you ever stare at me like that again... you're a strange and weird boy.

Mondo: I'm so sorry; I didn't mean anything, so sorry for that.

Maya: Mondo, stop and come with me.

She sat me on the bench, went down on her knees, held my face with both hands, and said softly: Mondo, look at my eyes and only my eyes alone; don't turn your head, dive deep into my eyes.

Looking into her eyes, I felt like I was swimming alone in a deep ocean.

The glimpse of an unknown shore made me see you; your voice called me to swim hard and join her. Maya's eyes and face changed as if I were looking at my aunt Mar.

Mondo, listen to me carefully; I'm here for you, so it's only the damn sun, but don't worry, I will help you, and you must trust me as I'm not who you think I am.

It is me, and as I told you when we first met, I'll come back to you whenever you need me....in any shape or look.

Mondo: I need clarification...I saw your face changing from Maya to Aunt Mar, then to a new face....So, who are you?

Maya: Mondo, I'm your Queen of Lights and your sister.

Mondo: Oh, my God, Am I still dreaming? Is this a real thing?

Maya: Mondo.. shush, and be quiet, as I will explain to you later, but for now, you need to focus on this coming event and follow everything I do.

I need you to shine, to be recognized, and to be the number one in this place, so forget the rest of the world and stay with me. I was hypnotized by her glowing eyes, as her gift to me in such a phase was altered back to her, and I'm the one with no control whatsoever, yet I was dazed just staring at her eyes and said: Yes, my Queen.

From another angle on the court, there were new faces of two men and two women, a boy and a girl, who wore white. One man had a mix of silver, gray, and white hair.

He was tall with a mustache on his face and a very noticeable belly.

His face was covered with strange sunglasses I'd never seen before.

When he got on the court, he went directly to Costa and shook his hand for the excellent preparation and everything he did. Being fully aware of everything made me observe the money handshake between Costa and that man.

He slipped some green bills in his hand, and Costa's eyes were so wide open from the excellent surprise...The US dollars.

The man with the gray hair turned around and waved to us, then said: Hello, girls and boys. We all waved back but never moved from the left sideline by the net.

I noticed his accent, and it wasn't Spanish or British, but it was something new to my ears.

He appeared to be a decent businessman, respectable and friendly.

The other man was also tall, with short blonde hair. He wasn't smiling; he just had a straight, serious face as if he were so special. On the other hand, his wife was a pretty woman, almost the complete opposite of him.

She was of moderate height and brunette with very bright blue eyes.

She had a wonderful smile, and she was pleased being here as it seemed.

Her outfit was exquisite, possibly made especially for her only.

Her white dress was very different from the women I've seen in other courts as it was a sleeveless white dress with fine green lines off the border. It had a V-shaped open top with buttons, yet it was more exposed than it should be.

I wonder if she was missing some buttons or if it was a defective dress, but again, I'm here to serve, and please, not to judge. The bottom part of her dress was pleaded elegantly with a slight opening from the center, and with a dress like that, most girls and women wear it with a pair of shorts under their tennis dress, but that lady wasn't. She had a green windbreaker jacket around her neck. However, it was boiling for any coat on such a day, but what surprised me the most was when she took it off, her body was much more exposed, as if she was heading to the beach, not to a tennis court. Andreas, Louisa, and Ramon looked at me and said at the same time, whispering....Wow, she's on fire.

I smiled at their comment, but I kept my silent composure until she turned her back to us, and then she made an unnecessary move that blew off my composure completely. She bent over to place her stuff on the bench, yet I couldn't move my face anywhere but to look at her white satin underwear and her erratic legs in such a pose.

The irruption of the volcano in my throat made me say: Malediction....Damn.

I couldn't look anymore, as it got worse with her bending like that. Meanwhile, the back of her dress was open with green straps, adding more fire to my eyes and cold sweat on my forehead.

I said to the gang: Who are these people?

The show must go on when a young teen boy ends up hopping, jumping up and down, full of energy, entering the court to join the VIP. He was so active, as if he was about to get in a boxing ring for a match.

It was undeniable that he was the dear son of that big man as they looked alike.

He was 14 but overconfident and an arrogant son of a bitch. He kissed that lovely lady, then tossed his racket and stuff on the same bench, yet he turned around and started repeatedly snapping his fingers in the air to catch our attention towards him.

The sad part was when he opened his mouth and said: Hey boy, yes, you with the long greasy hair... fetch me some ice water and hurry up.

Ramon also had long hair, but I had the most extended, shiny, and greasy hair, so I wondered if he was addressing Ramon or me. It didn't take long to clear up the confusion as he said to me, pointing to my face, "Hey, are you bloody deaf?

Maya pushed me hard to move, yet she was almost about to knock me off my feet with her shoulder push. I ran to the cooler, got a cold bottle of Evian water, then ran back to him.

He snatched the bottle from my hand, then snapped his finger for me to go away.

I turned around so fast, trying to avoid any unnecessary confrontation, yet with my hot Spaniard blood, I felt that my blood was shooting straight to my face, and I was almost like a hot red Jalapeno.

A voice came from nowhere saying: Hola, hola, please stop, por favor.

When I turned back towards the voice, I realized away that the mother had come rushing my way, patted my shoulder, and said in broken Spanish: Please forgive him. Sometimes, he can be foolish and immature, but you look young and handsome with a new face. I've never seen you here before; you must be very unique...wow, what is your name?

I was speechless as she was talking so fast, but I managed to smile and said in English: My name is (pause)...Mondo.

Oh, my dear God...You speak English, which is impressive. What a name is, and I'm so terrible with names.

I'm so sorry. What did you say your name was?

Is it Ondo?

No, it's Mondo, my lady.

Oh, mine. My lady.... And he is a gentleman as well...I like that very much, and she turned around talking to her husband, saying: Honey, have you met this wonderful new ball boy...His name is Mond....O. Her sentence was cut short as

the man didn't pay any attention to a word she said as he was talking to the other man, pretending to be stretching out for the match.

Well, Mondo..... Here's something for you. She said.

She stretched her hand with some money, but it was green money, not our normal Peseta.

My hands were behind my back, and I had to turn my head to the girls as if I were asking them how I would respond to that. They shook their heads to tell me to accept the money and smile. I was flipping and checking the green bill in my hand, and then I realized from the numerals and the alphabet that it was a 20-dollar bill, American money....I'm impressed.

The lady noticed her mistake and said: Oh honey, I'm so sorry about that.

It's a bad habit not to remember which currency I must use, but you know...Why don't you keep this one as a souvenir? To correct my mistake, here is a tip with a familiar currency: Please forgive my boy's temper.

I didn't know the value of the $20 bill, but I was sure about the value of "La Fuensanta."

I wanted to scream, but I kept my cool to myself. Cine Peseta...one hundred Peseta, oh my God. I wondered about that lady as she is one of the two things. Either she is very stupid or wealthy and generous. However, I prefer the second option very much.

I don't think she knew what a Cine Peseta meant to me, as it was my first time holding that much money.

My poor mother will be dancing when I show her that bill.

Mondo: Thank you very much, my lady, and if you ever needed anything(pause)...anything at all... I'm your man.

Oh, my dear, you're so sweet, but I will remember that indeed, so Ta, Ta, for now, she said.

I was very excited to show the girls what she gave me, but again, I was halfway there, and then I heard her voice calling me again: Oh, Mondo.

I froze, thinking that she was probably returning to her senses after giving me all that money...damn, nothing lasts for a long time.

I shove my hand quickly in my pocket, holding the money all crumbled like a ball to return them all to her. I was dragging my feet, strolling until I stood silently before her.

Mondo, my dear, I'm so sorry, and actually, I'm so ashamed of myself for being so rude like that, forgetting the very first rule of ethics.

I'm unforgiven for not introducing myself, so please forgive me.

She extended her slim arm as a sign to shake my hand, then said:

My name is Ellen Traverse III, and the lovely girl sitting on the other bench is my daughter Emma, and that hansom boy is TT, Trevor Traverse III, and that man over there is my loving husband, Bill.

Then she laughed hysterically with a fake stupid laugh.

I don't know what possessed my sick brain, but during her entire conversation, my mind and, more likely, my eyes were elsewhere.

She was talking to me so nicely, yet she had to lean down to my height so I could hear her clearly, and with doing that, her entire breast was almost about to be in my mouth, but I couldn't look anywhere else only to dive in her beautiful blossom breast.

Stop it, Mondo, what a sick boy...I hate the new Mondo.

I was speechless, and the few words that came out of my mouth were: Thank you, my lady. It's my pleasure and honor, my lady.

I turned around but flew like the wind back to the line, standing like a statue without a single word. The second I was back on the line next to Maya, she gave me a rough elbow with a crazy smirk on her face, and then she whispered in my ears: She's pretty, right?

Mondo: What is wrong with you? She is almost my mother's age.

Maya: No, you idiot, I was talking about that young girl, wasn't she?

Oh, Mondo...look, look, she turned her head for one more look at you.... oooh, she's interested...lover boy.

Also, I almost forgot to add something I've witnessed, but you must be careful.

Mondo: What do you mean about being careful?

Maya: Listen, kid, I know all your pages, as I've read your book more than once, so stop being brilliant with me as I see how you looked at that woman, Ellen, and that is something that you must be careful, as you might expose your gift of knowing too much for your age, I understand very well that she is a beautiful woman, may be more attractive to fall for your magical secret eyes, so be careful what your twisted mind wish for.

Mondo: Shhhh, be quiet.

If she only knew what was in my sick mind... It's not Emma, it was Ellen.

The unfortunate Emma was sitting on the bench looking at all of them having fun, yet she was carrying a sad face as if she were just another silly, ignored girl sitting on the bench doing nothing but reading a book.

I felt terrible for her, but I'm here for the service, am I?

I am supposed to be the savior, but for now, I'd rather be the server, not the savior. There was some confusion as they talked to the older man with gray hair. That man's wife was supposed to attend this match as his partner, but he was all alone.

Bill, for some crazy reasons, wanted to start the match, whether she was there or not, so he suggested that he lend him his wife Ellen as a partner, and TT would be his partner...Powerhouse, what a scum bag.

Bill and his son were killing the other couples, but our job was to get the ball back to the court fast and serve them drinks, towels, and anything they needed.

I was observing TT hitting the ball at his mother with no mercy.

He was terrific, with skills and good technique as well. Bill was just there laughing as they were winning all the way. On the other side of the court, the older man wasn't bad at all, as I noticed, even with his age and shape, that he was a good player once, but for now, he was trying to keep up with the score, so they don't lose badly.

Ellen also tries hard to get to the balls, but TT has no mercy for his mother.

She raised her hand so I could bring her a clean towel and cold water.

She was trying to stay in a cool area by the baseline, but when I gave her the towel, she said: I'm so exhausted, as this boy has no mercy for me.

Have you seen how he slammed the ball in my face? Luckily, I managed to duck down, not worrying about losing another point, better than my face; then again, she came out with another crazy laugh. What do I have to do?

I hesitated to say anything; it was a one-way conversation, yet I'm a server.

I felt it was my time to be a savior, so I whispered into her left ear.

Mondo: Will you accept some advice from a boy like me?

Ellen: Advice, I will take anything from you to win a point, so tell me, tell me, what do you want me to do?

When TT is about to get ready to serve you, do this.

Ellen: What?

Mondo: Wait for him to bounce the ball twice, then move fast inside the court, stop right before the service box line, then wait. If he still managed to serve hard, you have the advantage of raising your racket and letting the ball bounce with his power back to their court, and he will not recover from that sneaky attack.

Another way to intimidate him is to shuffle sideways inside the baseline like a goalkeeper bouncing on the line before a penalty kick.

Also, you can hug the net and whatever comes your way, bump any balls back in their faces, and try to take them off their game rhythm. Sometimes, you can raise your hand and say that you need a towel to delay the service and irritate them.

The last thing is to argue with the empire about every ball close to any lines, let them come to the net, and keep delaying the match, making them frustrated with you.

Ellen: Oh, mine. Are you a coach, and would anything you said work?

Mondo: Trust me, the plan will work.

Ellen: If I win the next game, you will get a lovely prize from me.

In a short time, she was executing the plan. Everything worked her way, and she did win the game and broke her son TT's serve.

She was so happy jumping up and down as a little girl, and that made Emma
She left her book and started cheering for her mother as well.

On the other side of the net, the atmosphere was different, as that boy was so mad, slamming the racket and cursing with lousy sportsmanship.

On the other hand, that game made her partner, the old man, gain some confidence, so he raised his game and won another easy service game.

They still lost the first set 3-6 to Bill and TT.

The empire spoke loudly, informing them about the break time between the sets.

This is not a real game; the break could be an hour until they return to the court. Further, we all needed that brake as we ran all over the court, providing them our service on such a hot day.

The older man suggests returning to the lounge for refreshments and cool air.

Ellen was following them, yet unexpectedly she called me and thanked me for the tips, and she said: I don't forget as I always keep my promises, so don't worry about your prize....Ta Ta.

Costa dismissed all of us to get a break as well. Meanwhile, all the ground keepers were doing their job so fast, working like bees before their return.

Costa and the others were done with the lines, court, and all the other stuff.

As he was about to leave, he saw me sitting on the clay by the baseline in the shades with a bottle of water in my hand.

He came to me and asked me: Why are you not taking a break with the others inside?

Those rich people can be in the lounge for more than an hour, and they had a long day, so either you get a break or, if you wish, you can go home.

Mondo: I appreciate the concern, but I'd rather wait here in case they come back unexpectedly so I can be prepared for them.

Costa: Well, if you want to stay, you can, but I need a break, so see you later, Campion.

I was overwhelmed to be called with such a title, even though I'm new to Costa, so for him to say that will motivate me to excel with everything in this club. I forgot about young Emma, but I was so intrigued by the empty court that I grabbed a racket and some balls and started hitting some shots I'd learned from Eve and coach Manolo.

Shot after shot, line after line, as my shots were getting very precipice on the lines everywhere.

The secret was my unique key to the back gate. Victoria's key helped me come early daily and practice alone in a very far deserted, almost abandoned court.

Observation, adaptation, determination, and precise execution were all my homework in the past months. My technique was improving, and my secret was the ball machine.

There were so many ball machines; some were old, and some were very advanced.

Apparently, Victoria didn't realize what key she had given me.

She showed me a master key, not only for the back gate but to open every cabinet in the club. One of the cabinets had some old ball machines, and they probably didn't want to spend more maintenance money to fix them. The first time I saw the machine, a strange idea clicked into my brain about how to resolve it.

I had no experience with a machine like that, but I drew a sketch and showed it to Miguel Vida, the janitor at my school. He was a rich man with a business in Cuba long ago.

He had to escape after the revolution, as it wasn't safe there. He lost everything as he left his fortune behind in Cuba for his life.

He wasn't that old but alone with no wife or kids.

When I showed him my sketch, he knew the machine and promised to fix it.

He used to date my Aunt Mar and was a big brother to me. I snuck him into the club early in the morning, and he fixed the ball machine with his magic hand.

There was nothing wrong with it except a small belt, but Miguel replaced it, and it was my hidden tool to practice alone.

It was a Playmate with a capacity of 200 balls, and with the machine, I managed to enhance my ground stroke from the baseline, the volley, and the drop shots.

Miguel warned me that speed on such a machine is very delicate.

I didn't listen as I was so eager to push my learning to the highest level in no time.

In six months, my skills and the gift of adaptation made me a trained player, almost professional with all the tennis skills.

I burned the motor, as the machine's speed couldn't match my speed, and the faster the ball was shooting, the quicker my returns. At last, after six months, I had to hide it back in that unique cabinet, as I burned the motor and couldn't afford to buy a new one, but Magda was a good coach for six months.

I named the machine Magda in honor of a young ball girl who died two years ago from Leukemia.

I never met the young tennis player, but the boys in the locker room said she was lovely and talented.

Magda helped me immensely with many things like she was alive tossing the ball for my practice. Besides the noise of my strings, her voice came from nowhere, saying: Wow, you're awesome...The way you slide and hit the ball so smoothly is new to my eyes, and you're better than TT.

I forgot that Emma was still sitting quietly on the bench; that bastard left the poor girl...what a fucked up family.

Mondo: I'm so sorry, miss; please, don't tell anyone I used the court, their rackets and balls...I beg you.

She was hysterically laughing at me and the way I was begging her.

Emma: You're so funny but also good at Tennis and English. I bet you know everything about this beautiful sport, but I will keep my promise not to say anything under one condition.

Mondo: I agree, so please go on and state your condition.

Emma: Here is my only condition: you'll be my secret coach and teach me how to play Tennis.

What is your name again?

My name is Mondo, and you're Emma?

Emma: So, you do remember my name? That is very nice of you, while everybody else was not pleasant to me or even remember my name.

Emma: You see, Mondo, I love tennis. I know all the players worldwide; I even have their posters in my room. I watch matches and all the grand slams, but I always do that alone.

The thing with Tennis is that it is all about TT, and that's it.

Emma is just another ghost; no one bothers to allow me to play.

In Texas, at our big house, we have two tennis courts, but again, I'm not allowed as TT has to practice; TT must get better; TT is this, and TT is that...Sometimes I hate them all.

Mondo: I'm just amazed that your mother doesn't pay attention to you regarding something you like, such as Tennis. However, why does she not allow you to take tennis lessons or admit you to a summer tennis camp?

It's summertime, and you should have fun playing and enjoying anything you love.

It's not a common idea that girls like you will be interested in sports as it's expected to be much more interested in books, music, and fashion, but sports are always a far option.

Emma: I envy your sister with a brother like you, who is caring, helpful, and willing to teach her anything.

Mondo: I hate to disappoint you, but unfortunately, I don't have any sisters or brothers.

On the other hand, I will gladly teach you tennis anytime you want; however, as you called me earlier," A secret coach."

Emma: Well, thank you very much, but I need to explain my point of view clearly.

Here in Spain, it is different for girls, who have much more freedom with sports.

I saw girls in this club playing soccer in the backfield and some other girls playing basketball and Tennis. Back home in the US, we have many tennis academies, including the Green Bird Academy, where my brother TT gets training in Texas.

Boys have much more advantages, and you were correct about the interest.

However, I wanted to play tennis so seriously, and believe me, if I say that money is never an issue in my family, time is the issue.

Mondo smiled and replied: Well, I'm delighted that your eyes can wander in such freedom, observing all our girls participating in all different types of sports, however, and if you don't mind me correcting you about one sport in particular.

Emma: No, absolutely, please do correct me.

Mondo: You said girls were playing....Soccer in the backfield. Well, here in Espana, we call it Football, yet that other name, soccer, is also familiar to our ears, but we don't like that word at all.

Mondo: What do you call Tomato in America?

Emma smiled and said: Tomato..the same.

Mondo: This one could be tricky, so what do you call potato in America?

Emma: Potato.

Mondo: Excellent, so you see, originality sounds nice, but when people changed names to their liking or connivance, that doesn't sound nice at all.

It is all about respect; we play football with our feet, and in America, they play the same sport with their hands, so it isn't proper to call it a hand-weird ball.

Emma laughed so hard that her tears came out of her eyes because of how I described American Football.

Mondo: Am I right?

First, the ball has a weird shape as it's not round; second, the player never touches the ball with their feet, so where does the foot fit in that description?

Why steal the name of the most famous sport on the planet and give it to a completely different sport that does not even have 2% of the number of fans and players on our planet who play real football?

I happened to be one of those players, but now I have switched to Tennis, and I hope I did the right thing.

Emma: I'm so sorry for the confusion, but once again, you're correct.

Why did you stop playing soccer...Sorry, I meant Football.

Mondo: Don't worry about that part, and let's play Tennis.

But before we get deep, please promise me that you'll honor your promise and keep it our secret. I just started here in this club, and it is a good job, and it also allows me to practice tennis for free, so please feel free to come and find me, and I will teach you how to play tennis.

I'm here from 0600 am till 0500 pm every day of the week for the entire summer vacation, so again, I can teach you how to play and even lead you to be a professional player.

Emma: I'm so excited that finally, someone will do that for me, and I promise you that if we accomplish that before the end of the summer vacation, I will owe you my life.

Mondo: Please, you don't have to owe me anything now or never; I want to spread Tennis through my life with people I care about or will care about in the future.

We hit some balls, yet I noticed that Emma was holding the racket off the grip the wrong way, so I had to ask her to come closer to correct her grip.

Mondo: The racket is your friend and the extension of your arm, so let's be friends with the racket. Before that, I want you to shake my hand.

Emma: Shake your hand?

Mondo: Yes, please.

Mondo: OK, that's good from a girl to another girl using the tip of your hand like in the movies. Stop that; firmly shake my hand as if you don't want to let go.

You see, that's better, as you can feel the bones of my knuckles as if you can feel the skin of my hand, and as if your hand is blending and melting with mine.

Remember that feeling. Now, I want you to close your eyes and shake the racket's grip precisely as if you were shaking my hand.

Emma started jumping up and down as she felt the connection between her hand and the racket's grip.

Mondo: Now swing the racket in any direction; let your arm blend with everything.

Emma: Wow, I never felt that way before. You're terrific, and it's fascinating how easy that lesson was. Wow.

The next thing is to shadow me with my move as I hit the ball.

Mondo: That's wonderful, you see, you're doing it.

A ball after a ball, and she was floating on the court, hitting every ball I tossed her way until I realized the great danger of what I'd done.

Mondo: Emma, please stop.

Emma: Why do we have to stop?

Well, come with me to the baseline. Now look at the court and tell me what you see.

Emma: A lot of red clay...ha, ha, ha.

Mondo: I'm not joking right now, but do you see all the marks of our movements on the clay.... That's the danger I was talking about.

The tennis court, especially the clay court, is like a memory machine.

It will record and remember every step and slide. This court was brushed to perfection, and all the lines were clear, but now, the court is a mess, and if they come back, I will not have a job in this club.

So, please, you sit down and let me fix that mess.

Emma: I will help.

Mondo: Get the broom from that closet and brush all the lines until you see the white line clearly; I will take care of the court.

I grabbed the net broom and started going back and forth until the court came back to life and to the perfection that Costa left.

Apparently, we needed more time, but the noises of different people were getting closer and closer, so we had to do things faster and then put all the stuff away.

She ran to the bench and sat down as if nothing ever happened.

The undeniable fact was her face. She was red as a tomato from the heat and her fast movement trying to keep up with me, so sooner or later, her face would tell her parents that she was in some physical activity, and I would be in deep trouble.

I waved to her as a sign to run to the bathroom and wash her face.

The same thing happened to me, but the only difference was my shirt.

It was stained with my sweat, so I had no choice but to pour an entire bottle of water on top of my head as If I were trying to cool off.

When Costa entered the court, he told me: I told you to get inside and stay away from the heat, so now you must go inside and change your shirt and return quickly.

I looked at Emma, winked, and flew to the locker room.

When I came back and entered the court, I noticed so many changes, noticeably the fans.

The second thing was the new edition for the old players.

The boss, Linda, was there, and with her being on the court, she must have company, and that kind of company was the entire staff in the club.

They were filling up the seats so fast, not just because they were instructed by Linda, but only because of the two new females following her.

They started waving to me, which was excellent but shocking to me and everybody else.

My Anna and Aunt Victoria were the two new players.

The Empire: Ladies and gentlemen...the game must go on, but the teams have changed.

TT and his father Bill as a team against the old man and Victoria.

I couldn't understand anything....I started asking myself: If Victoria is the female owner, is that man her husband?

Maya explained everything to me briefly right before they started the second set.

The old man is a very wealthy businessman, and this place is one of the things that he owns. He was Greek, which explained the club's white and blue.

Things started to emerge in the clear, but again, I was just another tiny pawn to do my job; the rest was none of my business.

My surprise was Victoria. She was a good player, not just fancy heels and expensive dresses. She wore a simple white tennis outfit, but I could've sworn that she had a fire in her eyes and was ready to make the second set exciting. Now, I know how Anna got to Tennis....Victoria.

After shaking hands, Victoria waved to me to attend to her needs.

Mondo, go to my bag on the bench and get my red bandana.

I ran to her bag, wondering why me, and why she didn't wear it before getting to the court....but again, everything Victoria does has something twisted behind it.

I hold the red bandana as if I'm representing her with a trophy.

The moment she put it on.... The fans, or I should say the entire staff, went wild.

I couldn't understand the secret behind that, but Maya also told the story behind it.

Victoria used to play Tennis a lot and was a real-time winner, but only in a small circuit of tennis players. Most staff saw her playing, but she became a different beast when she started wearing that red bandana. It was a gift from someone, yet it changed her look completely.

During the warm-up, I noticed something different about her technique as she used two-hand backhands, which was new to me. As the second half resumed, I observed her technique very closely, as she had so many winners with the drive backhand on the line, almost as if it was her best-winning shot. Again, that was very new to me, yet impressive.

As a ballboy, I was supposed to be more neutral and not take sides with players, but again, I was new and somehow emotional. I used to jump up and down when Victoria won a point or cheer, clapping my hands. However, that didn't go well, as TT noticed that.

He even asked to dismiss me from the court. However, he wasn't aware that he would start a losing battle regarding me. Everyone on the court denied his request, including his mother, Ellen.

On the other hand, the father wasn't even better, as he was too much of a drama player, complaining about anything and everything, especially when they lost points.

The atmosphere on the court became very uncomfortable to some, yet for others, Victoria's fantastic job was the key to changing the match upside down.

The transformations they'd accomplished, winning the 2nd set in a tiebreak 7-5, led the third set to be a new kind of war.

The same day, they ignited a personal battle between two people, Mondo and TT.

Costa asked me to stay on Victoria's side to avoid further unwanted confrontations with the TT team or his family. Another surprise for me was the money.

As Manolo said earlier, money can be a foolish tool, easily altered to evil.

They weren't playing for the game's fun, but as rich people do, they always have a purpose: to make more money from nothing. That match wasn't just a regular one, as there was a very high bet before the game.

For that class of people, money always comes first before anything else.

One person in that court cared less about the money: the beautiful Victoria.

Winning that match for her was a must at any cost.

The final set's complete switch turned the game's balance entirely.

The old man stepped out, allowing Anna to be his new partner.

Initially, it was deceiving but very satisfying to the TT team.

They believe that the odds are better for their team....Two men against two women.

Such an advantage, odd to TT, made another change in the game, but that time was a completely different tactic. Linda decides to suspend the club activities and allow the entire staff to rush in and fill up the court for free.

As the third set was getting heated with shots from both sides, the fans had their way of appreciating team Victoria. The noise, the roar, and the crazy comments made that match wild and crazy. The part that I couldn't understand was the fans.

They weren't only the staff members, but for some unexplainable reason, some fans were outsiders, even though it's a private club, yet it was the act of the staff getting the words around for people to pour in the club cheering from outside of the fences.

It was us against the Americans.

Anna could have been more focused in the first three games.

There were no returns, so many double faults with her serve, and so many unforced errors, but the most challenging loss was her confidence in herself.

On the other hand, Victoria was very frustrated but furious, losing 0-3 in the final set.

They call in for a short break, and again, that wasn't legal in the real world of tennis, but all the rich people can make their own rules.

Not only was that short break the turning moment of the match, but it was also the beginning of my belief in the old British saying" To Be or Not To Be."

I carried some cold, wet towels and water and headed straight to their corner.

Anna: Thank you, Mondo, for all this, but honestly, between you and me, I don't know what else I can do. They relentlessly beat us, perhaps because they are better than us...I can't win.

Mondo: Stop. Can I give you a few pieces of advice?

Anna's sweet, lovely face changed to a new face for me.

Her personality wasn't stable, and she became that rich, spoiled girl.

Her star-casting laughs, looking at me like I was that greasy poor Spaniard, was a mistake. The sudden change in her behavior made me remember Victoria's words and advice about Anna. She was covering her face laughing at me, then she said: An advice from you; this is not your world yet; this is all new to you, and I believe that you have no experience to qualify you to give any advice on the other hand, I'm the one who is supposed to be an example to inspire you, but right now I've got nothing, and you got nothing as well, so please spare me your advise and go away.

Mondo: I'm sorry for what I said, and you're right, my lady...I have no experience and no rights, so please forgive me.

I walked with my head down to the clay, and my tears were dripping from my poor disappointment and shame. I stood beside Louisa, so silent as a statue, until the break ended.

I closed my eyes as if I was sleeping, standing like a horse.

My mind was going too far to places I'd never seen or even been to before; I was in areas with professional tennis players hitting balls in many different techniques.

Shots were terrific, and the game's tactics were much more advanced than the present types of the current tennis games. Their game is much faster in pace and every other move.

I couldn't figure out how those visions were coming into my head, but suddenly, I said to myself: I think I got it.

It was as if I had a vision from the future about how tennis could be played entirely differently, and I said: I got it; it.

I was talking to myself, yet I meant, for some wild and mysterious ways, I was programmed with knowledge beyond my grasp, and I could see the fundamentals and principles of the core of tennis.

The two ladies I care about(hmmm, one lady for the moment) were playing an old game and seeing the game in a slow-motion way, and I do have the answers to fix all that.

Louisa looked at me and said: Mondo, are you talking to yourself, and what exactly did you get? I smiled at her and said: Sorry for that, it's nothing.

I couldn't believe my inner voice was loud enough to come from my fantasy world, cross the timeline, and land in my reality moment. The loud noise from the fan indicated Anna's poor serving game, as she lost her second serve, and the score was not helping her.

She was down 0-30, yet her red face and glowing blue eyes were a pure indication of low self-esteem. Her unexpected move opened my eyes, indicating that I must interfere in that game regardless of the outcome.

Suddenly, she raised her hand so I could bring a towel. I sprinted fast from the spot beneath the empire, and then I realized that my speed was somehow over quickly for such a short distance from the empire to her place, so I had to slide on the clay to break down my pace.

That slide was also more than what everyone anticipated.

The line behind me was almost five meters of sliding; then I was in front of her eyes on the dime with the towel in my hand for her. The cheering went wild for what I did, as that slide made everyone look my way, saying ....Ole, Ole, Ole.

Anna: Listen, Mondo, what you did was terrific, but I need more than just a show-off slide to save this game. But also, how did you manage to slide like that?

I'm not going to even ask about how you are doing in practice, as for the moment, I need to do one thing to make it right.

So, first of all, I want you to accept my apologies and(pause) ask for your help. What do you suggest?

Victoria came to us and said: What's going on in here? Come on, Anna, get your shit together; Mondo doesn't know shit about tennis yet, so swallow all your fear and focus on your serve.

Anna: Well, right now, I have to listen to whatever shit he has to give me, so back off and let him say some shit so we can beat those American bastards.

I was laughing as the two women that I care about were on fire with their mouths.

Mondo: Victoria...Anna, please trust me; I can see and predict their moves before they happen, so listen to me carefully, and please forget about me and about that kid, Mondo; he is not here, so for god sake, listen to my damn words and advice.

I do agree with the fact that I've been practicing and working here for only six months. However, I did excel in my practice and my game.

I'm not going to Bragg and say that I can beat those two bastards across the net all alone; however, I'm good with seeing something new in tennis.

I have a new game for both of you and don't bother asking any shit about how, so would you please listen to my advice...God damn it.

Victoria and Anna were shocked at how confident I was with my tennis knowledge, but they just waved their hands for me to lead with the new tactics.

If you serve to TT, spin your serve wide; there is almost no power, just a spin or slice to have the ball fly nicely to the edge of the deuce box. You need to take him completely out of the court and win the point; however, if he manages to return the serve, it would be a desperate, weak return, and that is when the other girl rushes fast to the net and slams it back at his feet....Victoria, I was talking to you; yes, you are the one who must finish the point.

I will change my position and stand right behind you for your next move.

Mondo: Hey, Louisa, switch with me. I will serve Anna, and you will serve Victoria.

There is some strange battle music playing as if this match has been televised, and the director is adding some background sound effects to add more excitement to the game, but again, it's only me and my imagination.

Anna did everything I advised her to do, and luckily, he was too lazy to move for that spinning wide serve, and she won the point. Anna looked down while she bounced the ball and said: Now what?

It was as if I was in the classroom during the year's final test, and Blenda was not far from me asking for help, saying the same thing: Now what?

I gave her the correct answer, and she earned an A for that, and she promised me a surprise. The fact that she never did anything as a surprise prize and I hardly ever see her after school ends.

Anna is different, at least to me, and I must encourage her to win this match.

Mondo: Repeat the same serve, as the father is much slower, and he wouldn't expect you to serve the same serve twice. Aim and slice the serve.

The score improved to 30-30, and the fans went wild. My words were an order dictating her action, and finally, she was a marionette in my hand.

Mondo: Now serve to the T.

Mondo: Serve wide again.

Every word I said was a winner, and they pulled the first surprise, and the score became 1-3.

TT was furious and slammed his racket on the clay, breaking it into hundreds of pieces.

His red face was about to explode, but with his luck, they had to feed new balls.

Mondo: Hey, Victoria...it's distraction time. Please do it.

That boy, TT, had no mercy if he started bouncing the ball for his bomb serve, so be ready with any distractions.

The moment he looked up to aim for the spot, Victoria raised her hand and smiled for him to wait and hold on with his serve, then she waved rapidly for me to come closer and tell her what to do. I wrapped the cold towel over her neck and whispered in her ears, saying: Now it's teasing time.... He's not a patient person and is also arrogant.

Trust me; it's legal that when he tosses the ball in the air for his powerful serve, you rush fast inside the service box and start shuffling left and right.

His eyes will catch that sudden tactic, which will confuse him.

Now listen to the possibility of his outcome:

1- He may miss the ball and fault the serve.

2- He may hit the serve slow and short in the service box, then, in this case, you take the ball on the rise and slam it back at his feet to paralyze him entirely.

Victoria: That is new, yet I wonder all the time about what's in the mind of the little devil. For now, I will fucking do as you said.

TT got confused and served poorly to her mighty backhand. Her return was a textbook of what I said, and she won the point. The unexpected roar from the fans scared the shit out of Ellen and Emma as they bounced off their seats.

The Opponent was arguing with the chair umpire about her sudden move to the box, but he waived his hands to indicate that it was good and no fault.

Mondo: It's time to distract them with your sexy beauty.

Victoria: Come again, what the hell does that mean?

Mondo: All you have to do is show him your butt while he is about to serve, pretend that you're tying your shoes, face the fence with Ass exposing your thighs, and ... Ass in his face.

Victoria: Are you out of your fucking mind? I can't do that before all these people; shame on you.

Mondo: Listen, Victoria, do you want to win this match or not?

Victoria: Absolutely.

Mondo: So, stop acting like a Nun; I know you're a woman of no shame, so do what it takes to win the match.

Victoria: I got it, so you're saying to moon him...right?

Mondo: I don't know what the hell is mooning him means, but show him your Ass...Simple.

The trick worked, and his face was red as Victoria's butt was a treat to him and everyone else at Court 12.

I must admit in such a moment that Victoria had one of the best bodies and a lusted Ass.

That itself made everyone live a wet dream, just watching Victoria's ass.

Anna did her share, and the poor TT lost one point after another, and it shows that he was about to have an orgasm during the match.

The match looked different, as if it were a show with Eva Leon, Maria Canted, and the great Barbara Rey.

The look was different between Victoria and Anna compared to those famous showgirls, yet how my girls showed their bodies made them get closer to winning this match, legally or not.

From Anna to Victoria, with the teasing, aggressiveness, and fast anticipation, they managed to break TT's serve, and the score climbed to 2-3. The father, Bill, was unhappy with the new team, so he asked the chair umpire to substitute and bring back the old man instead of Anna; otherwise, they would forfeit the match.

It was overruled when he said: The game must continue with the present players, no more changing players. It was time for Victoria's service, but instead of getting ready to serve, she adapted my ways and made it charming. She strolled to the net and called TT with her two fingers to approach it.

She told him: Honey, I have a message to your father, so please open your ears to what I'm about to say to you.

First, if he plays that game of forfeit, he will lose $10,000; however, if he decides to continue, which he will, then in that case, tell him that I will wipe his sorrow ass in the next game...go, go. The boy delivered the message, but the father's response could have been better.

His face was red like he had some Piri-Piri for lunch—the famous Portuguese malagueta pepper.

He screamed at her and said: Oh, yeah....Bring it on.

Victoria had no mercy, and with her service, she was perfect for an excellent game, bringing the score dead even...3-3.

There were different concerns in the TT stands as she was in doubt, confused, and disbelief that two women were humiliating her husband and son out of nowhere; that was Ellen staring at them, clapping her hand as an encouragement sign to move on and beat those two bitches.

On the other hand, Victoria, yelling at me....Come on, Mondo, my little devil, tell me more.

Mondo: Well, you haven't called me by that neck name for quite some time, but I'm here to serve you, my lady, so listen up carefully, as now the little devil will tell you how you will win this match.

This is your chance, now or never...You must break TT's serve again; if you do that, you'll win the match.

Victoria: Ha, Ha, that is so easy to say when you are in the shades, not on this court.

Victoria said in a star-casting way. You must be blind; don't you remember how fast his serve was?

Mondo: Listen, and stop mocking me...You stay far behind the baseline this time, so he will have two options to guess. He's arrogant and pissed off simultaneously, so he will think you're afraid when he sees you far back away from the baseline.

He will serve a challenging, fast serve at you; if he misses, you win, but if you catch the return, it must be a slice.

Use his powerful service speed with your slice, convert his action to reaction, and keep it low, barely above the net. If you must slice the return, you must, and I will repeat that, you must maintain a low posture with your slice...   Head down, body down, and slice with spin as much as you can.

The return will be weak, and the ball will drop short by the net, forcing him to run to the net, and Anna....Hey, stop looking at me and focus on my words.... You will get in the picture frame as well.

When you see him running to the net, you run faster, rush to the net, and turn yourself into a goalkeeper.

Mondo: Being a goalkeeper at the net, you must stand your ground and block anything to pass the net, and that will be your job, as you must block his return to the open court behind him or even to the confused, lazy father.

 Don't let him have a clean shot, not a return; make it difficult and awkward.

Anna looked at me and was in disbelief at how much I knew about all those new tactics until I yelled at her: Pay attention; if you block the net, keep your racket face up so the ball will bounce above the net.

Don't block with the racket face side way or low; it will hit the net; remember that very well....Face up.

After all my bits of advice and tips, the idiot TT doubled fault twice and saved my long advice for what may come later.

The psychological state of mind is the one thing I didn't mention to them.

At that moment, Bill started to yell at his son for missing two servings and ordered him to focus on his serving. The father told him to serve wide, and with a hand signal, I realized the play, so I ran to Victoria with the towel, then said: Get out of the baseline.

 He's going to serve wide to your backhand.

Victoria: Are you sure? How the hell do you know that?

Mondo: Trust me and stay away from the baseline.

She couldn't grasp that, yet it felt to me that I was maturing during this match.

 I started to believe in my gift of adaptation, and in such a short time on the court, I could read TT's moves, his serve, and even his bluff.

He was an open book to me, but only me, not Victoria or Anna.

He aced her, and she froze on the baseline as she didn't believe me or even listen to a word I said. Anna wasn't any different, and she didn't listen as well, and again, he aced her with another great serve.

The score was very vital.... 3-3 and 30-30.

I looked at them with a smirk and an open palm gesture to the sky as a signal to let them know: I told you so. Anna started to believe in me, and her return was short and weak.

TT, in such a moment, believed that he could win the point, so he sliced the ball back to Victoria's backhand, which was his biggest match mistake.

Victoria's experience and good observation of their position hugging the net made her look at me to see where she would return that slice. She leaned down with her body, putting all her power and precision into her shot. She took the ball on the rise with her backhand straight to the open court, passing the ball to Bill blind right side straight on the line, leaving both of them watching the ball drop, scraping the white chalk, bouncing all the way, hitting the backboard with a clear winner. The fans were increasingly engaging with the match and were on their feet, cheering like crazy as that match became incredibly intense.

The father, Bill, was never a good coach but a lousy business partner.

His hand gestures were all over the place, pointing to his son that he should've covered that part of the court. Faraway, the young Emma had an evil smirk when they lost the point, which made me wonder about the relationship between her father and brother.

From our short conversation before the start of the second set, she wasn't happy about how they treated her as only a lovely face, with no consideration of her feelings or her love for the game.

Does she wish for their loss? I wonder!

TT was losing confidence, and he missed his first serve. At that point, he was afraid to gamble with the second serve, so he chose to serve for safety.

His service was so weak that Victoria became a lioness hungry for more blood.

She pounded that soft second serve with her backhand to his right side on the sideline, leaving him a flat foot or more paralyzed. We all could experience something familiar or similar watching a car race.

When the track is empty, yet everyone is anticipating the hazy shadow of the car's approach, the eyes of the spectators become wide open for that moment, and in their minds, they all say. Here they come.

In a flashy moment, the first car flies by, followed by the rest of the vehicles, making everyone move their heads in a flash, following the vanishing cars in thin air.

That was when everyone did when Victoria's backhand hit the back of the far baseline, as the spectators had that same reaction. The extreme silence on the court was deadly but not long.

When that ball hit the clay and bounced up in the air, traveling outside the court, it was the Bomb. The loud noise of that ball bouncing and hitting the back wooden board fence was the most audible noise the father and son had ever heard.

Winning and breaking TT serve for the second time was the short dead silence.

The place was on fire after winning that incredible game. The fact that it was a tennis match linked to the game's rules had changed to something different.

The standard thing in tennis is silence so the player can focus.

Breaking TT's serve changed the rules; the fans cheered like a football match.

Some crazy fans(Of course, they were outsiders) had a drum, and some others had something strange. The cook and kitchen staff had something unique yet boisterous.

They all had glass jars filled with dry beans and rice, and they started shaking them repeatedly, creating a Samba beat. The drummer was pounding his hand drum, blending with the kitchen staff, and the fiesta had just begun. People were dancing on the bleachers, waving their hands, and the atmosphere became a nightmare for the Traverse family.

That was the moment of no return to encourage Anna to serve for the set.

Her eyes were not focused on the court but only on me and my hinting moves to guide her to where to serve. My finger goes right, she serves wide, and my finger brushes my palm.

It means I'm shaping a T, and that is where she needs to serve.

She was winning until the score was 30-0.

Bill was angry and still yelling at TT for missing the returns until fate had to change the game. The father wasn't ready to lose the big money but couldn't control his destiny.

As he returned to the baseline to receive the serve, a strange loose ball rolled out of nowhere to the court and landed, stopping right behind his left foot.

The ironic fate was when he turned around and stepped on such a mysterious ball, twisted his ankle, and, in no time, dropped on the clay like a dead elephant.

The impact of his body hitting the clay was very painful, and his roar of agony and the pain were excruciating. That ankle was the size of a watermelon, my favorite fruit during the summer heat. I do remember that man from up North used to come to our neighborhood as an Arabber with a small horse-drawn cart filled with fruits, but mainly Watermelon.

He had the best watermelons ever; they were red as blood but sweet, and my mother used to run down to get at least two watermelons.

Life had changed, and I never saw him again, and we never had any good luck with the same kind of big, sweet watermelon.

The father had his ankle almost the same size as one of that sweet watermelon, and the last thing he said to TT before the ambulance carried him away to the hospital was: Do not forfeit the match; have your mother by your side; she's good, so use her to your advantage.

The lovely Ellen is on the court. The game took another unpredictable turn as Anna ended up losing her service game only because of Ellen's bravery and her excellent anticipation of Anna's serve. Emma was so pleased for her mother, and she was barely one of the few yelling: Come on, Mom, come on.

It's a tiebreak as the score turns to be 5-5

At this point, I lost faith in the chair umpire's judgment. This wasn't a professional match; it was just recreational, and I know it was based on money.

They were all gathered by the net, discussing how to finish this damn match.

They changed the rules again and decided to do it the American way...Best of 10.

I had to alternate my side to serve everyone fairly. I ended up on the TT side.

Ellen was always friendly, thanking me after a towel or water bottle, but TT wasn't happy seeing me behind his back. My girls were doing very well in such a strange tie break, the so-called American tie break, leading 5-2.

The Traverse team was falling apart, losing stupid, lazy points.

Anna was trying hard to recover, sliding all over the court to get to whatever ball she could to enhance the score somehow. Fate had to interfere again, yet it was deliberate on my behalf this time.

I collected two balls, as I was supposed to, and prepared for the players 'call.

TT was about to serve, but my eyes were elsewhere as I focused more on his drink, the cold bottle of lemonade.

He liked adding more sugar to get him any extra energy, so it was more like honey lemonade, as thick as it can be a sticky drink. He called for two balls, but again, I was floating with my mind in that place of doubt.

I ran clumsily, knocking his sticky drink, and not by accident, but deliberately.

I submerged one of the balls with that sticky drink, then pretended I had the wrong balls.

He was angry and started yelling...Boy, I need a ball now.

I had two balls in my hands; one was the sticky one, and the other hand was a dry, clean ball. The devil in me couldn't decide which hand to present to him.

Do I have to be fair, honest, and neutral as a ballboy, or should I be the devil himself? I said no to the evil side and decided to do the right thing.

That decision lasted for a short time. The moment he looked at me with such a mean, arrogant, and cruel approach, I had to switch and change my mind...the hell with him.

Hey, boy, is he fucking deaf...I said, I need a fucking ball, you stupid Spaniard-greased monkey idiot.

Ellen rushed to intervene to save the moment, but it was too late.

My decision was speedy as I said: Sorry sir, here it is.

I hand him the wet, slimy, sticky ball off my left palm.

His reaction wasn't what I expected when he held the ball in his hand.

It was the irrupt of the Las palmas volcano. The dirty ball was so sticky, and he was disgusted with such a ball, cursing every curse in the dictionary curse book.

He slammed the ball hard back in my face, but he also pushed me violently with his two hands, which was violent enough for me to collapse backward on the red clay.

There were many things that I gained from playing football. The most important one is knowing how to fall without injuring yourself. However, any professional football player with vast experience knows exactly how to fake an injury, a hit, or even a foul.

I was very well trained from the street and playing with the Malaga club to fake an injury.

I was excellent, and nothing happened from such a push, but if you want to play dirty, I can be the devil itself.

The moment I hit the ground, I was rolling all over the clay as if a Cobra bit me.

I was holding my chest, pretending I couldn't breathe; I was covered with red clay all over my face, making people believe I was bleeding.

I've made a masterpiece act. It would be best to have music, sound effects, and background scenery to make a play watchable. Well, my scream was a combination of the exact sound effect and the drama behind my fake tears, making the scenery and the music something I hadn't planned. It was an improvisation lyric written by the fans from all over the court.

Oh, Ah, OOOh, Wow, that's not right, what a fucking ass hole, you should be disqualified, Puto, shame on you, are you crazy.....and of course, someone had to add a soprano singing...You can't be serious.

TT was terrified, not because of my act, but because he was in a foreign land.

The fans wanted to eat him alive, and men with broken teeth came from their caves with swords and broken wine bottles and wanted a piece of his white meat.

The women were like vampires who tried to suck his blood dry, but definitely, after they made love to him vigorously, taring his white clothes off.

There was another wave of angry orphans that managed to escape from the terrifying convent; as the nuns were witches dressed in nuns' clothes, they were rushing at him with angry small knives eager to stab him a million times and.....Stop, Stop, that wasn't the story nor that movie...Stop Mondo.

Get back to the court and focus on what took place. That was my inner voice, reminding me to get real.

Well, that was phase one.....Attention.

Phase two was the response and the consequences.

The final phase was...Action and Reaction, or as the French say, cause et cosset.

The physical trainer was one of the spectators; however, with that great act, he jumped off his seat and rushed to the court to attend to my case.

Please, everyone.....I need some space, please. Max said.

There was a tiny red spot on my chest, but nothing major. However, Max wanted to be sure there were no broken ribs or any unknown internal bleeding; besides, he wanted to be sure I could breeze.

He exposed his strange flashlight in my eyes, testing certain things, then after all of his examinations, he said: Mondo, can you see me? Can you hear me? Do you know where you are? How many fingers do you see....Mondo.

I open my eyes, then whisper a few words in Max's ear.

He smiled, helped me get back on my feet, and gave me a cold bottle of water, but instead of drinking the water, I poured it on top of my head and let the water drip all over me and the court. He held my hand to help me walk, turned around, facing the spectators, and shouted: Mondo is fine.

I couldn't be any happier standing on my feet watching everyone with their hand on their hearts, as if they were telling me," We feel you, Mondo...Vamos"

My mind wasn't quite satisfied entirely, but I wished everything was filmed then so I could replay all the clips.

So here are my favorite clips from when I was on the ground with Max.

One clip was: The tough TT was hiding under his Mama's arm for protection, terrified of the coming monster, as Victoria was held and pushed back with more than one man blocking her from getting closer to TT, disallowing her from eating him alive.

Clip two: Anna was too dramatic and poetic at the same time.

She rehearsed every nasty curse word in her unknown dictionary at TT's face and finished her lines with a nasty spit on his face...not literally, as he was still hiding under Mama's arm.

Clip three: All the ball boys and girls were furious about what he did, but they just gestured without curses or foul words.

Clip four: The old man, the wealthy owner with gray hair, told him that his father should be ashamed of him as his actions were entirely out of line.

Clip after clip exposes the chaos that I've created.

The only clip that satisfied me the most was when Maya smiled, yet her head moved from left to right as if saying: What a little devil you've become...Mondo!

My response was simple: I smiled with my hand open, showing her my palms, twisting and dangling my lips as if I were saying: What can I do?

The match must find an end, but how? I couldn't guess that part.

The Chair Empire was the one with the final answer, and that was to forfeit the match for insubordination and bad sportsmanship; however, after a lengthy consultation, as it was just a recreational match between rich people, they settled down with just an apology.

I couldn't tell at that moment if TT's face was red, of being ashamed of his act, or just pissed off that he had to shake my hand.

Boo, Boo, that was the noise accompanying his handshake to me.

To add more spice, I extended my hand pretending to shake his hand, but at the last second, I pulled my hand back so fast that I combed my wet hair instead, then walked back to my favorite team...Victoria and Anna.

The place was so ignited with loud laughs for such a dirty trick, but I had no choice but to prove my point. I ran around the court waving to the crowds, saying vamos, vamos, igniting more fire to the court and the match.

At last, the crowd calmed down, but more chaos was yet to come as I advised my team on what to do next. The British Empire had a familiar ugly face, as he was one of the doctors at Mama's hospital. Still, he didn't know me, and I was even optimistic that he never acknowledged my mother, even though she was the head nurse of the pediatric department.

He said: Excuse me, ladies, what is that boy doing...is he coaching you...There is no coaching period.

Victoria walked towards him, placed her hand on the chair, looked at him, then said: Do you know who I am?

Yes, of course I do, Miss.

Well, if you know that, please do me a great favor. Victoria said with a nasty smirk.

The Empire: Absolutely, please tell me, what favor will it be?

Victoria: Go back up on that chair and shut the fuck up.... He's just a kid; what fucking coaching are you fucking talking about? He's just a kid, you moron.

The doctor couldn't take such an insult in front of all the spectators, so he decided to leave with a final statement: This is an outrage; this is obscured rubbish.

They were booing him for leaving the court, yet someone had to be the chair umpire for the remainder of that crazy match. Victoria made a spin, trying to find a quick replacement, until she pointed to a girl from the bleachers.

Hey, you...Do you want to be an empire... I'll pay you.

The old husband got involved and waved to Victoria to calm down as he would negotiate that part. The lights went on, and the spotlights were popping like champagne one after another until the court was almost as daylight.

She said: Yes, I'll be the Empire, but for how much?

The old man said: I'll give $100.

The girl responded to him saying: How about $500?

Victoria looked at her and said: Fine, I'll pay you $500, so get on the fucking chair.

My name is Gaby, and I will accept your offer for $600...The $100 extra is for your bad attitude and filthy lips....so are we good?

Victoria: I'm sorry. So, please do your job and wrap up this match. Please.

Gaby was on the chair yelling: Please, ladies and gentlemen, be quiet while the players are in motion...hmm and please... Behave.

She tried to hide her laugh, but the microphone didn't help. The score is one set all, and the tiebreak is 5-3 for the Traverse team. Mr. TT, please serve.

Victoria was back at her corner but silent, as she was mumbling, saying: Who is the fuck that bitch?

Now I know who that girl was; she is the same one whose face was blocked by the sun; she's the same girl whispering to me in the woods. That can't be right; I must be dreaming.

I understood when she said: You named me, and I'm in your hands.

But again, who is that girl?

TT was a different player as he was lost, shaking with all the chaos and the mess he'd created. He served poorly to Victoria's backhand, and with her return, he lost the point.

On the next serve, he tried to slice it wide, but again, she followed my advice and pounded him with an unreturned-winning end.

The score is 5-5, change serves.

It was Anna's time to rise, and I was looking at her with my fist on my heart, gesturing to have compassion and believe. Her serve was wicked, as it's known as body serve.

Ellen had no answer for that serve, yet the ball bounced and slammed her perky breast, and then they lost another point.

Later, Anna lost her first serve and had to serve safely to TT, which was more than ready to attack her second weak serve. The rally lasted longer, back and forth, until Anna and Victoria were stuck by the net, and with that, TT took advantage of loving them with an open court. That lob was terrible and retrievable, so I screamed at Anna to return to the baseline to get to the ball. Anna's response was fascinating; she got to the ball and then reversed the lob with a better one with a massive spin.

TT tried hard to run back to get to her lob, yet the spin on the ball was too much for him to handle, and he tripped on his feet and fell on his face with red clay covering his face.

The ball touched the ground, then spun fast to the sideline, giving Anna the advantage for the first time in the match to 6-5.

The intensity of the tiebreak was incredible; the rallies got longer, the fans got wilder, and the winning was near Anna's team. The score is 5-9 to Victoria's team until the Empire starts yelling: Please be quiet....Match point...Silence, please.

The desperation of the Traverse's team wasn't recoverable as Ellen was about to serve to survive match point.

TT: Mom, you must win your serve; please focus and aim.

He was in tears, begging her as a little boy.

Ellen: Honey, I'll try. I will.

Distraction was part of my vision to win that match, and I felt that Ellen was more sympathetic to my condition, being on the clay screaming at the pain her son caused.

Maya and I composed part of the plan.

Ellen asked for a ball, but Maya showed her hands. And she had no balls left, yet she waved to me to get two balls. I ran to the baseline with two balls, and the moment I was in front of her eyes....my eye's colors changed, glowing off the beast in me once more.

Mondo said: Is this a good time for my prize, mam? You've promised, or shall I wait for you in the locker room in private?

I said those words, then ran to the other side, still staring at her eyes, even though from that distance across the net. Ellen was shaking, confused, and lost with my words and seductive eyes. She was under my spell for a few minutes, but that didn't help her save the match.

In such a vital moment, I advised my team to double up by the net when the ball landed on the service box, as she would serve a very weak serve.

The distraction caused her to serve a terrible, weak serve, putting Victoria and Anna in a strange race to the net. The winner was Anna, and the moment that serves bounced off the Add service box, she was on top of the ball like a hawk. She hit the ball with extreme power, so flat, no spin, just passion.

That ball passed by Ellen and TT's feet, exploding on the red clay, then bounced for a clear winner. The roar was unbelievable inside Court 12, and the atmosphere under the light was all new to me. It was as if the players were in black and white, yet when the lights brightened the bleachers, everything changed to living colors.

On the other hand, the joy and glory on Victoria's face were more, as they call it, in Hollywood, America, Technicolor.

The process of making a Technicolor movie was defined as an artificial color scene(Lab shit); moreover, what was in front of my eyes was way better than that, as everything was alive.

Every color blended with her face, the sweat dripping off her red face, the messed up hair, the dirty white outfit that was stained with the red clay as if she was bleeding on the court, but again, she was bleeding, yet emotions, motivations, dedications, stubbornness, anger, frustrations, losses, tears, smiles and beauty.

She earned her victory, as she was simply the Victorious Victoria.

In such a precious moment, she was like a little girl, so happy in tears of one the best moments of her life. At that moment, money didn't mean anything at all, and then I realized the wisdom of Coach Manolo in its true colors.

Money is just a tool, yet it is evil and poisoned to the Traverse.

Victoria's victory was all about the beauty of this game, blended with prosperity and sacrifice.

They may have won money, but my prize was more valuable and prosperous.

I got two kisses, one from Anna and a lovable kiss from Victoria.

That kiss changed our relationship to something much more warmer.

The feeling became more caring than just being poisoned with affection and seduction.

I started to feel that Victoria was more of an aunt or even a second mother.

Her kiss wasn't on my cheeks like Anna's, but it was a mouth kiss.

It was the same kind of kiss I used to get from Aunt Mar or my mom.

No one noticed, and that was only because of her quick follow-up as she pulled me to her sweaty, warm body with a firm, strong hug. It was a dear hug that made me feel safe and loved. The three of us were hugging each other, and we were jumping up and down, singing strange songs in English that I'd never heard before, not even paying attention to the chair empire girl saying: The final score is 10-5 to Mrs. Victoria's team.

The celebration was going wild, yet I had to go to Maya and say: I hope you enjoyed that fantastic, crazy match as much as I did, but we need to talk about serious things.

Maya looked at me strangely with a scary look, then said: You and I....Talk...what is wrong with you, boy?

Her tone, face, and, seriously, everything had changed entirely with her, as if she were a different person. In such a moment, I realized my queen was gone and no longer in Maya's body.

I was upset because of her sudden departure, yet again, I was interrupted by my inner thoughts when Maya said, Hey, boy...did you hear me?

Mondo: I'm so sorry for my behavior. I'm somehow drained.

The other crazy part was the mysterious girl....Gaby

I looked for her, but she vanished as a mist, and when I asked the other ball boys and girls about the Empire girl, they thought I was crazy as they all assured me that the new Empire was an old member woman.

My head was about to explode as if I was dreaming or imagining things in my mind, but again, I was only sure about one thing, and that was to run home.

I ran to the locker room, changed, got all my stuff, and started running the long way home.

I ran and ran so fast, yet I could hear the loud noise from the club. Moreover, that didn't stop me from running.

The change of scenery made me feel more relieved and content as I was looking at my mom with a wonder smile on her face, asking me: Well, my dear, how was your day?

Mom, I love you, but I'm so tired and need to sleep, so can we talk about the details of my day later?

Maria: Yes, but you must be hungry as I made you....

Mondo: No, Mom, I'm only hungry for sleep.

After a long cold shower, I couldn't wait for my soft pillow as, at last, all alone, lying in my bed, thinking and rewinding my entire day, had made my eyes weak to resist going to another new journey, a journey to my fantasy dream world.

Opening my eyes was expected, yet it wasn't normal for my eyes to experience my present status, as I was back in 1975 in court 12, looking at everyone cleaning their face and clothes from the past flying red clay storm.

It was a strange phenomenon that hit the court as a sandstorm, but I wasn't sure if It was just me who managed to travel back and forth in time.

After asking permission from the chair empire, I had to run to the locker room. I must forget everything that happened in the last half hour and focus on the championship match....and win.

I washed my face, and then when I put my hand in my shirt pocket, something soft touched my fingertips, something strange yet highly unique. It was a headbandana.

Someone had put that thing in my pocket, and I knew it wasn't my mother.

The colors were also extraordinary: red, yellow, and red. It was almost like the Spanish flag but with no royal armor; it was plain. My question was, why is it in my pocket?

The moment I stepped out of the locker room, carrying that thing in my hand, strolling, and staring at the bandana, I lost my surrounding site and bumped into Eve.

I was almost about to knock her down to the ground, but I managed to hold her close to my body. Her eyes strangely looked at me, yet the color of her eyes suddenly changed as if they were glowing. Then she said: Mondo, why are you here? You are supposed to be ready for the match, and what is that in your hand...The Spanish flag?

Mondo: Well, I was, I mean, I don't know....

Eve: Well, that looks like a lovely bandana before the match. Please give it to me and let me help you. She folded it as a triangle; then she rolled it until it became like a line of red, yellow, and red, then she wrapped it up on my forehead, then tied it hard with double knots on the back of my head, then said: Wow, Mondo that is a magical one, you look like a champion with it, and it will help to absorb the sweat from dripping on your eyes....Vamos, Mondo.

I felt very different like that bandana was the key to my transformation into a new person. When I went to the net to shake hands with my Opponent, his eyes only looked at that bandana until the Empire said: Cara O Cruz. Head or tail?

I chose heads, and he chose tails. I won the toss and everything else.

The fans were on my side as I played at home for the Spanish junior title.

The glory of that day was the beginning of my unstrung life, and from that day on, my life was never the same....Ever.

Chapter XV

MADRID

The news of being famous in Malaga encouraged my confidence, and I excelled rapidly, as my eyes were like a special scanner from the future; the more I saw, the more I believed in my gift of adaptation.
 It was a Sunday morning in the first week of summer 1974.
My old gang from the Malaga team was planning to play in a friendly match against Real Madrid in Madrid under the Cadet Level (14-15 years old).
It all happened after I won my Berlin open part of the ITF tournaments.
The media started to pay more attention to my success outside of Spain, and it was in some of the local newspapers with my picture and a few words about the new rising teen, Mondo.
 Later in the same week, Manuella, the CEO of Bank Santander, called my mother at the hospital to verify the news about my tennis success. To her surprise, I wasn't part of the old Malaga Football team but something else as a teen tennis player. The fact that her son was part of the team as well, yet after he was injured, he decided to be more into books and study and move on from the football sport.
Ferran was a left-back, a powerful player, and he was still in good relations with the old gangs with their news, victories, and defeats.
He asked his mother to join his old team for such a trip to Madrid, as he had never been there before and he would love to be in the company of the old team as well, even though he wasn't a player anymore.
 I was more of the hero of Malaga after winning the championship for the first time, and my performance left an imprint on everybody's mind, including Manuella.
I must admit that she used to come in every practice to chat with me about how I play and dribble and other stuff that might help her son reach my level.
 I can't forget that she invited the entire team so many times for ice cream, pizza, and tapas to have more time with me.
She was a single mother with two young kids, Ferran and Alicia.
Ferran was my friend, yet Alicia was more of a secret girlfriend.
Manuella was half French, half Spaniard, a very successful banker from Santander, yet because of her husband, they had to move to Malaga, as he was also a banker, and with his promotion, they had to move from the North to the South and reside in Malaga.
I must say that they were pretty rich, and their house wasn't far from La Malagueta, yet I used to love being in their house because of the magnificent swimming pool.
Manuella's life started to take a different, unexpected turn after the birth of Alicia, as her father was never home, late, or traveling for some meetings with the bank.
I do remember when I was nine years old, I had to sleep over at their house, and unexpectedly, in the middle of the night, we all heard them fighting and yelling at each other as Manuella discovered that he had an affair with someone.
The only reason that we all ran to the living room was when we heard Manuella crying after he beat her up so badly with his belt, and her left eye was in terrible shape.
The husband left the house, and she stood with us until we fell asleep.

The fact that I was worried about her terrible condition made me sneak out of the room and search for her in such a big house.

Again, drinking with her tears made me approach her silently until I was behind her back, and I whispered in her ears, saying: Are you alright?

The moment she turned her head to acknowledge me, she smiled and said: Mondo, I thought you were sleeping, but you're here now, so sit next to me as I do need your company.

Mondo: Is there anything that I can do to help?

Manuella: You're such an angel, but no, you can't do anything; it is all my fault.

Mondo: I know how to fix your eye, so please let me help you.

Manuella: You can fix my eyes; I wish that you could fix my life, not just my eyes; yet again, I wonder about you and what you're capable of.

I can't forget that day of the championship and the joy you generated when you stepped foot on the grass in the last few minutes of the match.

I still can see how you managed to change everything, but I don't believe you can change my face or even my eyes.

How will you do that?

Mondo: Well, I will need your help with specific materials, so vamos.

Manuella: Tell me what you need, doctor Mondo.

I laughed and said: I need sunflower oil, rice oil, grape seed oil, any oil with vitamin E, coconut oil, peppermint oil, clove, fennel seeds, orange peeled skin, and, of course, a big bowl.

The amazing part about Manuella was her money and influence, yet it was late, and she didn't have everything from my remedies, so she asked to put my clothes on while she was changing to go to the pharmacy to cover everything.

Because I was so concerned about her face, I was ready fast and had to head out to the living room until she got dressed.

To my surprise, as I was heading to the living room, she had her bedroom door open, and my eyes caught her naked body unintentionally.

 I froze as her body was extremely toned in a very athletic shape.

I felt the tingling in my young body, and I was very much enjoying every bit of her naked body until I heard her saying: Mondo, what are you doing?

I had to run to the living room and sit down, looking at the floor, wishing for such a moment to be home.

Soon, later she was all dressed up with dark sunglasses over her face, then she smiled and said: we have to be very quiet so they don't wake up, Vamos.

The car was something different to me as it was a Seat sport model known as 124.

Manuella: Do you know which pharmacy that might have all your stuff?

Mondo: I never said a pharmacy; I meant the old Chinese market, as they never sleep, and I know that we will find everything and maybe more.

Manuella: How do you do all this stuff?

Mondo: Are you forgetting that my mother is a nurse?

Manuella: Of course not, but we are going to the Chinese Market.

Mondo: Mom, buy all our remedies and medical stuff from them, as they are much more advanced in the treatment of the old Chinese ways, and they are always somehow accurate with their remedies, so can we please go before Ferran wakes up?

Because the market was too narrow for her fancy car, she had to park in the street, and we walked to the old Chen Chao.

When he saw me, he said with his terrible Spanish accent: Mondo-sun, it is too late for you to be here, and who is the lovely woman next to you?
Mondo: I'm here to get some oils.
Chen: Ahh, what oil do you need?
I wrote the list at her house and handed it to him, yet he looked at me and said: Why do you need all that? Your face looks very healthy, so why do you need all that?
Mondo approached the old Chen and whispered in his ear: It is not for me. It is for the lovely lady next to me.
Chen: Hola, can you take your glasses off your face, por favor?
Manuella was hesitant, yet she had no choice, and the moment he saw her eyes, he said: Mondo-sun, did you do that to her face?
Mondo: Absolutely not; it was her husband.
Chen: I was joking, but I have something special for the lady.
He went inside and came back with a small piece of paper, then said: Lady, what is your name?
Mondo looked at her and told her that he was a secret keeper.
She said I'm Manuella.
Chen: Manuella Wang, this is your medicine; use it.
When she looked at the piece of paper, she said to me in a strange tone: Mondo, look what he wrote. Look.
The paper said: Policia, is he crazy?
Mondo: He is correct in a way, as you should report your husband to the police, but I will talk to Chen. Don't worry.
Mondo whispered to the old Chen, and he finished; the old man said: Follow me inside.
The back of the room was filled with jars and brown canvas bags with herbs from all over the world, and in less than 5 minutes, he had my list ready, yet he said if I needed fast results, I must use one of his special remedies.
He gave me some special clothes and special oil, yet the smell was unbearable, and he said: It will take long to mix all your list, but for the moment use what I gave you and you will thank me later.
He didn't charge us any money as he was an old friend of my mother.
When we returned to her living room, I asked her to lie down on the couch and keep her face up. She was gagging as the smell of such a remedy was very strong, but after I covered her face with canvas clothes, she almost fell asleep, but she said to me: Mondo, please stay next to me on the couch, as I need your company so bad.
In a few hours, she was asleep, and I had to sneak back to Ferran's room and pretend that I was asleep all that time.
The morning was filled with many good surprises as Manuella's face transformed into something new. The incredible remedies worked magic on her face, and she had no traces of bruises or blue eyes like she had yesterday.
It was Sunday, and because of what I did, she took us all to the Retiro Park, and we had a magnificent day.
She never forgot that day, and with that, she organized a plan for me to be with the old team for their Madrid visit.
I was surprised when I learned about her plan as I had never been to Madrid or the Santiago Bernabeu before.
The screams and the loud noise in the locker room were very emotional to me and Ferran. The moment we entered the locker room, the team ran to us, overwhelmed with

the surprise as they hadn't seen me for at least 3 years, and coach Enrique was thrilled to see me again.

The stadium was magical to me, and I was blessed to have a seat with my old team.

The strange thing was the match, as Manuella, with Bank Santander support, managed to gather fans from all over Spain to fill up the stadium.

The fact that there were so many promising teens in the Real Madrid team made the place look like another Classico.

I was enjoying my old team, with their talent on the field, yet the score wasn't encouraging, losing to Real Madrid 2-1.

Again, it was just a friendly match, and the score didn't mean much to either team, yet in the last 5 minutes of the match, I heard a thunderous voice saying: Mondo, suit up, you're playing.

The statement made all the players inside the substitution bench look at Coach Enrique, wondering about his request.

I stood up and approached Enrique and said: Coach, I'm no longer a player in the team, and I'm just a guest, so I can't just change and play.

Enrique: Mondo, it's a friendly match, and no one will know that you're not part of the team. Change and get in quickly.

My old team was whispering, mumbling about what he said until Mado one of the new players in the team, approached the coach and said: Coach, are you drunk? Mondo can't play; he's not part....(pause)

I'm the coach, Mondo get in, hurry, vamos vamos.

I had no choice but to speed to the locker room to change, yet on my way, I was lost looking at the wall with the pictures and paintings of the incredible players from Real Madrid's history until my eyes froze looking at Di Stefano's painting.

My god, he was a legend, but I can also be a legend; I'm here at my favorite spot in the world, the Santiago Bernabeu; what can go wrong?

The amazing part was the jersey number 7.

It was there as no one had ever worn that number after my unexpected sudden departure from my team. I had to kiss it, and quickly, I was transformed one more time into El Niño Magico.

The light of the Santiago Bernabeu coming out from the tunnel made me feel invincible again. I ran to the line, waiting for the referee to let me in, yet the assistant referee called coach Enrique to do the right thing with the name and the number of the substation player, which in my case was Mondo, number 7.

He spoke a few words to the assistant referee and allowed me to enter the field.

The amazing part of such a friendly game made the entire Malaga be at the Santiago Bernabeu to support their kids and maybe the promising stars of Malaga.

The moment I entered the field, the place was silent until I made my famous introduction trademark entrance.

I went on my knees, kissed the grass, and I stood up. I looked at the fans and screamed out of my lungs, VAMOS.

The players came running to me, hugging me, patting my back, and the old images of the Championship match were almost duplicated.

On the other hand, when the fans from back home, including Manuella, stoop up, the roar is unstoppable, sheering Mondo, Mondo, Mondo.

The other strange thing was the astonishment of the Real Madrid players, as they had no idea who Mondo was at all, yet with the incredible overwhelming sheer, they were confused about who this teen was.

The Real Madrid coach walked to the edge of the field, staring at me from a distance; then he looked at Coach Enrique with his hand gesture as if he was asking him, who the hell is that player?

The unfortunate confusion was in the VIP bleachers as some people recognized me not as a football player with the Malaga team but as the new Spanish rising star in tennis.

Same old play, pass after pass, controlling the ball, pressing the Real Madrid team to fall back in a defensive way, yet it didn't take long until I passed the ball to Jose(the superstar) on the sideline, and he did the same trick and broke inside their defense line, and with one look he saw where Mondo was.

The ball was crossing from the right to the edge of the penalty arc without any interception, and when it was closer to Alonso, he ran towards the goal, dragging two players with him as a bluff, leaving the ball rolling to me.

My fitness with tennis made me move faster than when I was a kid playing with my old team, yet I never forgot the magic that I've left behind.

At such a moment, I rolled the ball a few inches ahead of me and bent it to the far left corner, scoring another magical goal.

The sheering was nothing, but the most noticeable thing was coach Enrique.

He forgot his position and started running in the field like a kid until he took me down to the grass and hammered me with kisses as if he were another player on the field.

Such an unexpected reaction caused him a yell card, but the moment was glorious for everyone. The score became 2-2 with almost nothing left in the match time.

The Real Madrid players were still confused about number 7, yet the moment of glory came the second they kicked off after my goal. After the kickoff, I was fortunate to intercept the ball unexpectedly from Raul, the CF.

I started running, but when I raised my head, I saw the goalkeeper way off his goal, almost outside the penalty box.

I knew the referee was about to whistle soon, but I saw the play and couldn't wait for his whistle.

I shot the ball with all my power from the center field high in the air towards their goal, catching the goalkeeper with a surprise shot(Lob).

The ball was traveling in the air, rejecting all the laws of gravity, until it hit the upper post from the inside, bounced down by the goal line, until finally, I had to pretend to be Superman and blow air for a kiss to push the ball inside of the goal.

The second the ball crossed the goal line, the entire Bernabeu were on their feet, witnessing something historical and magical.

The fact the scoreboard was flipping to 2-3 for our historical win had a different impact on everybody. The Bernabeu field was filled with massive fans running after me to lift me up in the air, and the place was out of this world.

The crazy part was that Coach Enrique had never changed the team member since I left the team, as he used to register me every year as if I was still a part of the team; his only cover-up was that I was injured.

I was injured for three years and today was my debut at the Santiago Bernabeu for the first time. The crazy part was that he had to use that as an excuse, as Real Madrid was rejecting the fact that I shouldn't play and that it should be a fortify.

The president of Real Madrid was on the field with some medals and a small trophy for the winner of such a friendly match, yet when he shook my hand, he said: How do you feel about wearing number 7, but with a white jersey for Real Madrid, and I'm talking about the first team, not the one under 15 years?

Mondo: I must say that this moment was just a dream since I was a kid, but right now and after what you said, I must apologize and announce my retirement from football, as I prefer to continue with my journey with tennis.

The amazing part was the presence of the great Santana, the Spanish tennis legend, as he looked at me and said: Retired after what you have accomplished, that is insane, but now I can say that your face will never be forgotten, whether in football nor tennis, so good luck. The trip back to Malaga was incredible and historical. With just their eyes looking at me and saying goodbye, there were so many scattered emotions inside everyone, including me, yet the best day of my life had come to an end with that trophy on my desk and a smile on my face for a new undiscovered dream world.

CHAPTER XVI

Adiós Malaga

Life can be very exhausting, yet unpredictable somehow.

The doubtful question of my life was always the key to losing my insanity.

Do I know my fate?

Will I be able to change my destiny?

Is it true that our fate is written up with the stars from the day we were born?

So many questions will always be in my mind, yet sometimes, just thinking about them drags me to an empty, deserted world, alone, lost in a vast desert of uncertainty and confusion.

I can understand the magnitude of my path to glory, which will always be a solitary road, just me alone and always alone. I'm surrounded by people who like and love me, yet it will always be me when I get to any court.

Today is the day of my Unknown. My life could hopefully be different today, and only today will I say Adiós Malaga. My mother always says to me: Mondo, knowledge is everything.

Today is the day for me to reach out and seek the reality of life.

Meanwhile, today is the day to leave on a ride for doubtful, unknown knowledge and education. My calendar says that the new edition of Mondo does not come with a racket or the fuzzy yellow ball but with a book and a pen.

Being accepted at the great Universitat de Barcelona gave me a new perspective on transformation. The reality was always the book and football, sometimes just books.

I'm always fascinated by knowledge, history, math, space, and science.

My identity was split in half, as I was the child who loved to play, yet I was also the child of knowledge. The curiosity to know and understand were the main things that drove my life to the uncertainty of my tomorrow.

Do writers, or can authors affect my life?

I would say.....Si.

I recall a quote from Einstein: Anyone who has never made a mistake has never tried anything new."

I wanted to try new things and be a new person, and that was when I had to leave Malaga for a new world.

My suitcase was still open, and I couldn't decide what to take from this life to my new life. The room was a total mess, but in an excellent way. The fact that I'm an only child revolved around my mother.

She's the most annoying, superstitious, organized freak I've ever known.

Mom never sat down and watched TV or read the newspaper...never.

She's constantly cleaning, dusting, decorating, cooking, and washing clothes, but most of all, her constant guardianship takes care of me. She barely has any time to take care of herself, and with that, she is still the most beautiful woman I've ever known.

She's always on the move, working extra hours at the hospital to save a peseta here and there. The one thing I couldn't understand was her relationship with men.

She was never on a date, always the caring mother, no matter what.

I never asked her if she had any male friends, as it didn't concern me; maybe I would call that selfishness.

I'm 15 and very energetic, yet I've always felt that a female must be in my life, close to me, care about me, or even love me. That feeling was always hunting me, as I can't be alone.....I wonder.

My interaction with the male side is only attached to competitions.

The other boys found other interests in doing things together, but on my behalf, it always led to being better and competing with them, no matter what they were interested in. If it comes to school, I have or must be the Alpha student; if it is football, I must be the center of attraction, simply because I've always been ahead of them with the work. I practice more, I run more, I adapt faster, and above all, I score more.

The thing is, tennis was all about me and just me.

When I set foot on the court, I became an animal. No regrets, no sympathy, no fear, no minds, no free points, and never say die. Every ball is a must-be winning point, no matter how much running, stretching, or sliding...I must get to that ball.

I never settle down for fatigue or weakness.

My most significant improvement wasn't about how to play the game, but it was all about my body. I've become possessed by that strange GYM that I discovered a few years back; even though the club has much more modern equipment, I felt much more appreciated or possibly...I belong to that GYM.

She introduced me to that place; she pushed me to get better, more vital, and more significant with my muscles.

I was somehow misdirected or misled into such an area.

It was an extraordinary day two years ago.

I was over-tired, and that match came from nowhere. It had no points for ranking, no significant gain from it, except...Money.

The underworld in tennis can be risky, especially for a young player like me.

I wanted to have money fast for many reasons, which was my biggest mistake.

The rapid rise of my name in tennis echoed in so many places and with so many dangerous people. The bad part here in Spain is that fame only sometimes leads to a paved road; not only that but yet again, the importance of money can affect and divert the absolute path of the youth.

I was fortunate to be chosen, as I recall dire misfortunes to other kids my age, boys or girls.

I heard in the school and saw it on TV that boys and girls died because of the wrong path that they chose. Some roads were deliberately selected for them, and that led to the dark world of death. I have no control over that except my path; however, sometimes, and in my case, the deception, the seduction, and the evil thoughts lead me to take the wrong path, which was always the money path.

I was dragged to that world briefly, as my underground agent Munez got me that match and other previous matches. He was not my agent, as it started as a good friendship, and with his help, I used to get so many things for free under the terminology of sponsorship.

In one of the ITF tournaments I won, we met in Brussels, Belgium.

The approach was great, and I fell for his fancy words and promises.

I must admit that he showed me a new world of riches and fame.

Because I was 13 years old, I had no experience with such a life, but Munez led me and dragged me into this life. My coach wasn't happy with that at all, and actually, he did warn me of the consequences, but I was fascinated with the luxury, cars, hotels, VIPs, and the women. It was my weakness at such a time, as I wanted fast money, lost my way, and forgot about Manolo's wisdom.

Money was falling off my hand as Munez was organizing the underground matches.

I was hooked on so many matches for money. Every sport had a black market for underground cash games.

I was young and inexperienced with many things, and even with my secret abilities, I was still unaware of such a dark alley. Money and winning were the only things that I was able to see.

The color of money was the wrong choice, and I fell for it.

It was my first time playing on a hard court....Green.

The place was well protected with private guards, close to Rhonda, almost nowhere.

The place was extensive, and the court was virtually hidden below the owner's villa.

We had to take a strange elevator down to the court.

The wagers, or the bets, were somehow big, but I was aware of that later.

My share was 5000 peseta, but the price was even more than I anticipated.

It was the most significant prize money I had ever been offered.

The money was a step to becoming much more in control to help my mother with her constant struggle with life and our financial status.

My earnings from the club as a ball boy weren't enough for my gear, especially when Victoria and Anna weren't around. That special treatment was missed, and I was alone, with work, training late hours, and more and more.

I had that fire in me to get better fast, as I had no patience with the long training program with coach Manolo and Eve. The underground matches helped us recover some of our late bills and expenses. I wasn't happy because I had to lie to my mother about the extra money.

Sometimes, I used to tell her that I had to work extra hours at the club as a ball boy; some other times, it was just selling stuff to some people to make extra money.

Still, they were all lies, as I couldn't tell her about my sick secret underground matches.

Munez was a snake; after winning, he came to me and asked me if I had an agent to represent me, and my answer was a NO. He took advantage of being naive about tennis's hidden secrets and offered me his help. He also offered me money and a new line of athletic clothes.

He was booking matches for me, and I was somehow under his spell, or I should say....The Money.

Match after match, I became greedy and obsessed with the fast, easy money.

I played matches with young and older players; even when I played against women, I accepted everything as long as I had money. The lack of sleep made me more distant from everyone who cared about me, including Manolo and Eve.

The only advantage I gained from the underground games was my playing level.

The rules were leaner, and with that, I managed to bring my game to a professional level, but I also had to show off some spectacular shots and crazy tricks to win all my matches.

I was undefeated, and somehow, I became famous in such an unbelievable, dark world.

The fact that I was winning made Munez more greedy, as I was the golden boy for his pocket.

The match was with an Italian...older than me.

I was on the edge of being 14, and he was 20 years old, yet in such a world, the only thing that matters is the money. The match was going very well and fast...My way.

The first set went so easily, 6-2.

I was 4-0 in the second set, and I was on fire. The first two games I lost in the first set were much more difficult, not because he was a better player, but because of the court.

He was up 2-0; finally, I understood the court and the surface.

It was more prevalent in certain parts of the world, such as Australia and America(USA).

I can't do what I used to do on the clay or slide on such a strange, hard court.

The other part of being discomfort was the spectators....

I wouldn't say fans, but the rich people on the bleachers were more cheering for the Italian Fransisco.

I would be a liar if I said fans, as they were only there for the money, not the tennis.

I wasn't aware of the magnitude of that match, but from how the women and the men were dressed....Fancy, it felt like I was playing in a nightclub for other entertainment.

It was almost as if they were for a boxing match, not a tennis match.

The exotic girl was serving drinks, tapas....But that day, I realized new names for the typical Spanish food. They don't call it tapas; they call it Hors d'oeuvres....French for sophisticating rich people because they can't be expected and, say, Tapas.

Another thing that I noticed was the faces of the people in suits.

The lights were insignificant except on the court, yet one girl was older than me.

Her look wasn't just an everyday one as she carried a heavy secret message for me.

Her smile gave me some support and encouragement, as she was the only one who cared about Mondo. The name was Esperanza, probably 22 years old.

The majority of the fans were Italian. However, some faces looked different as they were Japanese, but there were some Spanish faces for either simply prosperous or bad-deal people.

I focused on my game and killing Italian side-to-side, drop shots, and tricky services.

It was the unofficial match to bring out all the fantastic tricks I learned from the old man Manolo. Tricky, frustrating serves, magic by the net, and explosives forehand and backhand in every point. The scary looks on the fan's faces weren't encouraging to me, as they were all mad. The smoke of their filthy cigars was filling up that indoor hard court.

It was almost like a thick, heavy cloud of smoke above my head, and that was my main concern: the polluted atmosphere for my game.

The score was 0-4 in the second set, and I wanted that match to find an express end, to get out of that place. Munez came to me during the exchange, leaned down to my ears with a scary smile, and said the strangest thing ever. He spoke with an evil smile: I see you are winning this one so quickly, which is not good here. I like your play, but I want you to take it easy.

Mondo: I thought you were on my side, so what do you mean about ....Take it easy?

Munez: Look, kid, all the people in this court are..... betting against you, so you see the dilemma of my sensitive position here. It's not about you winning, it's about you.....Loosing.

Mondo: Are you Loco....Do you want me to lose this match?

Munez: Si, Mondo....The bets were all in favor of the Italians, so you had to lose.

It was my first time feeling that way, as I had never had that in me. I never lose a battle unless I die, so I'm not losing.

Munez: Kid, Did you understand what I said?

Mondo: Si, Si.

It was also my first time seeing evil right before my eyes; it wasn't safe and, above all, unprotected. The scary looks on their faces sent death messages to my mind, so I had to change my game somehow.

Every time I won a point, I had to lose the next, as the look on their faces was intense and scary. I had to pretend that I twisted my ankle on one of my crazy slides on the hard court, and I also asked for a time-out when the score was 4-2. Munez came to me and said: Vamos, kid... You're doing great; keep doing that...Keep loosing.

He never even bothered to check on me to see if I was in pain, as all he cared about was for me to lose and lose.

I asked for some water, and to my surprise, Esperanza came to my rescue.

I was breezing heavy until she looked at me, opened the cold water bottle, and said: I know you.... you're the magic kid....The hero of the Championship match, the match against the Red Heart Academy team, don't you remember, it was the best football match I have ever seen. I witnessed your magic, and I was sure you'd always be my hero no matter what you did.

I never guessed I would see you on a tennis court, yet what are you doing here on this scary tennis court?

I am standing up for all those bastards and proving that Spain still has some heroes.

Your presence, power, and dedication to the game inspired me.

I'm not here to judge you or even ask what has become of that footballer, yet to my astonishment, seeing you here in this dangerous place playing a different sport...Tennis.

I'm also impressed to witness your magic again in a completely different type of game, but my dear god, you're incredible on the court, but be careful as you're killing that man on the opposite side...Vamos Mondo.

Gracias...I said.

After I emptied that cold bottle in my stomach, I felt so much energy as my eyes were glowing again for something wrong yet to come. She kissed my right cheek and said softly: Win.....win Mondo.

It was the first support I got since arriving in this doomed place.

The match turned into something different, but tennis, as the dull and loud noise from those strange spectators affected my game until I started losing stupid points, giving the Italians a little hope to turn the match around. Munez never stopped bothering me as he was only interested in the running match and kept reminding me to lose and LOSE.

The score was 5-6 to the Italian, and I had to serve to keep this match leaning to my side, yet with Munez being so close to the baseline, he whispered to me that my cut had been increased to 25000 pesetas.

That number played in my head so badly, and I had to ask for time off.

The chair umpire didn't like that, so she asked me to be quick with the sudden break in the bathroom. It was my first time to have a woman umpire, but she was mean and ugly.

The thing was with those types of underground matches...Flexibility.

The official tennis rules don't control that type of tennis, so I can prolong my break and consider the new offer. The offer can change our lives to something better.

My mother and I can move to another place, Madrid or even Barcelona, to escape Malaga.

My desire was based on money and nothing else, and finally, I was optimistic about the consequences. I will accept that deal; no one here knows me, and it won't affect me in tennis.

I played so poorly, losing my serve with repeated double faults, and then a few minutes later, we were tied in sets...6-2, 5-7.

The atmosphere had changed as the spectators were pleased with the sudden changes and with the loud noise and the laughs I realized the fact...I lose...

They win massive money. The shadow of Esperanza passing by wasn't even encouraging me anymore. Being in this place, she had a job to do, yet I couldn't comprehend her actual status at such a moment.

I was alone in the locker room, sweating like crazy, almost like Victoria waterfall in Zimbabwe. A familiar voice told me: You must shower to cool off and wear this outfit.

In her voice, there was confidence, yet it was more for an order than a request.

When I looked at Esperanza's eyes, I knew exactly what I needed to do.

She didn't move, and the shower curtain was missing as well. She was dead focused and locked on my body, with the cold water falling on my hot, warm body, causing artificial steam, adding a more exotic atmosphere to the locker room.

She turned around and went straight to the door, then blocked it with a double layer of the two benches in that locker room, making it very difficult to open.

Get out of the shower and dry yourself. She said.

Esperanza: Mondo, put this T-shirt on and the dry clean shorts.

Listen to me carefully as the game must change.

I'm very optimistic that the criminal Munez offered you money to lose, but my question is....How much?

Mondo: Hmm...25000 peseta.

Oh my dear god....I do like you very much, Mondo, and I don't want to see you getting hurt.

I won't ask you how you end up with that evil Munez or even this dirty atmosphere unique with....Hmmm, Tennis.

I won't ask you what you will do with that much money, yet I will ask you one thing.

Mondo: Si

Do you want to get out of this place alive or dead?

Mondo: Alive.

Esperanza: Excellent, as the people that run this place and these types of illegal sports are considered the most dangerous criminal in Espana, yet under a different look.

For them, money is everything, so if you don't lose and try to win this match, your punishment could be the simple thing: to break your legs or arms....Do you have any brothers or sisters?

Mondo: No

You're fortunate, as they will also go after them.

One more thing...How about your family, your parents?

Mondo: It's only me and Mama.

Listen to me carefully, as I can protect you, but you must listen carefully to my plan.

Do you want to be a champion or a loser?

Mondo: Champion.

ZA: Very good...then you know what to do, and I will protect you.

So here is my plan. At match point, I will signal you, yet the moment you see me running, you drop everything and follow me....Understood Mondo.

You have to run; you must run for your life and never look back....Do you understand me?

Si...Mondo said. I have one question.

Za: Ask me anything, Mondo.

Mondo: Well, what's after...what will you do with Munez?

Za: Don't worry about him; we'll cover all that later.

The final set was short and fast, as I managed to play every dirty play in the game to win the last set until the moment of match point came before my eyes.

Munez rushed to the baseline and said it with an angry tone and a scary face.

Boy, if you don't lose... You're DEAD, and so is every member of your loved ones.

I can double what I'd offered you...I can even give you(pause)...hmm 500.000 half a million peseta, which has never been on any table for tennis or any other game, so think about it and think about it fast.

The money or your life, I don't want to deal with the Camorra, nor do you.

Mondo: The Camorra?

Nunez: Si, what do you think? I was playing with you.

Mondo smiled and said: Will you let me go in peace if I say yes, or will they hunt me forever?

Munez: I will keep my promise and leave you in peace.....Promise.

Mondo: How about them with the golden chains on the third row and the guns under their fancy coats? Will you be able to convince them....I don't think so, so my answer is NO, and I will bet on my chances...now get the fuck off the court.

Za's sign was earlier than I had anticipated, and she told me to leave now and forget about serving. I nodded, agreeing; however, my ego wouldn't allow me to be a coward and run. I was stubborn and naive. I decided to go for it and serve for the match and my life.

So many scattered scenes were before my eyes, and none looked good.

The echo of the ball bouncing off my hand, my sweat dripping on the service line, the spectators screaming, the Camorra pointing at me with anger, and finally, Munez screaming at me to lose as he was on his knees begging me to lose.

Everything went into a mode of dead silence. The look on the Italian player's face, wondering about his coming defeat, Za was jumping up and down for me to run, yet Nothing would stop me. Not even that gun that glows in the dark from the big man on the third row will stop me from winning that match. Tennis for life.

I served to the T with extreme power for an Ace. The second the ball touched the line, the slow-motion movie began.

I drop the racket on the ground and start running. I didn't even turn back to see if I won the point; I just became the Flash for my life one more time.

My eyes were wandering, looking everywhere for Za, but I couldn't find her.

It was dark, and the lights outside this place were not helping me until her voice said: Mondo...here, run and jump in behind me...Vamos.

The Widow Maker, or the Kawasaki H2, was roaring by my feet, and I had no chance to survive this place except to ride with her on that H2.

The place was fading away quickly, as she was exploding so fast on the road with the Widow Maker. My eyes were tearing, but not of sadness, but from the gusty wind cutting through my eyelid.

The speed of that Bike was terrific. I've heard about it, but I never guessed that it existed here in Malaga, yet above all that... I'm on it, flying to nowhere with the mysterious Za.

The streets started changing to flying on dirt roads until she decided to do something unexpected. The spot was almost dead, with no souls but trees and scattered red dirt everywhere.

Ten minutes later, she jumped on the brake so hard that my body went forward, smashing into her back so badly.

Za said: Mondo, I need you to get off the Bike quickly and wear these clothes.

Please hurry up and change quickly; we are still unclear from the danger...Hurry.

A black leather full-body overall jumper and a goggle. She converted me to Robin, as she was Batman, but in her case, it was The Bat Woman.

The speed was almost the speed of light, and I was in no more tears, but I felt invincible, holding her warm body. She was flying, trying to get to the highway, yet she stopped and said: We have to take a different road; we must get on A-366 instead of A-367.

That road was so dark as it was an inside road. The darkness and the road weren't scary, but she was driving at high speed on a dangerous road.

It was her choice in case they ever tried to follow us; they would use the safe highway A-367, yet her choice was the question of life or death.

It felt like we were on the dark road for a long time, but with her speed, she said: We're almost there. I had never been in that neighborhood before, but I'd heard about it, and it was the real gangland.....Hampa.

It was an old Compra or a junkyard. However, it wasn't the accumulation of the crushed cars that bothered me, but the darkness and the smell.

She slowly went between the steel piles until she turned to a high steel gate that was almost to the sky. She stopped in front of the access control monitor, then punched the codes, and suddenly, the noise of that gate was squeaking as if she had opened the hell gate.

There were at least ten armed guys with masks and a vest similar to Za's vest, yet with a different color.

She said one word, and then she flew inside.

She said: Amica.

I've learned some Latin, and she told them Friend-Amica, and they let us go.

The place was like a fortress, with men and women everywhere watching Za getting off her bike with a stranger, even though I was wearing one of their outfits.

My outfit and helmet made me look like one of them.

A big, bold man was heading slowly toward us. Meanwhile, he was wearing a black T-shirt that was the completely wrong size.

His muscles burst out from every part of his body, and that T-shirt made his muscles even more enormous. He had a goat beer and a very mean look on his face, and with the lights and my goggles still on, I felt as if I was invincible in such a scary place.

He started walking, yet before he reached me, Za had to intercept him; then she grabbed his arm and started whispering in his ears, pointing at me. At that point, I wasn't sure of anything left in my miserable life, and I hated myself passionately.

I knew I had made a wrong choice to agree with a low life like Munez, as I fell into the poverty trap and greed.

On the other hand, being in this place, I was so positive that I had made another big wrong decision and was also sure that definitely, my life would end in one of those crushed cars.

The dim lights around that place didn't prevent me from having a quick peek at that gun tucked in his pants on his left side. One hand was touching that gun and the other was waving in the air, repeatedly waving and pointing at me while the conversation with Za was getting loud and hostile. When they started moving, closing the gap towards me, I began thinking about running, but only briefly, as so many surrounded the place and me.

I knew I managed to run away from death back in such a place, but now I'm so positive that I'm surrounded by death and must fight to stay alive. I jumped off the bike and held a fighting position, and finally, I opened my mouth, shouting at them.

Mondo: Listen, you mother fucker, I got nothing to lose anymore, but if I have to go down, I will take as much as I can down with me, so let's GO.

I grabbed a long pipe from the ground and was ready to enter the dragon.

Mondo, what the hell is wrong with you?

That is another bad movie; Bruce Lee is not going to save your ass, so wake up and think.

In such a moment, the entire attention was completely altered towards me.

Some guys were adjusting their heavy machine guns, aiming at me, yet others were creeping on me slowly. I was standing there sweating from the inside of my helmet, frightened and scared of what may come my way in the next few seconds.

Knowing that you'll die no matter what makes you wonder about accepting death with style....Why the fuck not?

Bruce Lee's influence on me was highly electrifying as I used to practice his moves from the movies whenever I got the chance. However, any young kid in Spain was doing the same thing as me, practicing Lee's moves, which was more of a global phenomenon, imitating Lee's movements anywhere and everywhere.

In such a moment, it wasn't just a movie or anything related to some fun between friends; it was all-natural, and all I had to do was to decorate my..... Coffin.

The dark black helmet, the dark leather biker outfit, and my sweat from the inside made me start preparing myself with some Kata; then, with the same move as Bruce Lee used to do in The Green Hornet, I was waving with my two fingers pointing to the first bastard to come and fight me.

The bold man turned around and looked at me; then he looked all over the place from all angles, then shouted to them to stand down, there will be no fight...Stand Down all of you, and that includes you, Mondo.

Mondo: Who are you, and how the hell do you know my name?

Mondo: I'm not afraid of you; I will fight you...come on, come on.

The man looked at me with a severe face, then said: Take that fucking helmet off.

Mondo refused to take his helmet off as he believed it might come out handy with a punch here and there, so he looked at the big man and said NO, then again got in position for the fight.

The man looked at Mondo, then exploded laughing, followed by everyone in the warehouse.

He said: Mondo, please put your hand down and relax. You're among friends, and there is no need to fight me or anyone in such a matter; on the other hand, you know very well that your chance to win such a fight is slim to none, so please follow me....Por favor.

I had no choice but to follow them to that huge building, but I was still holding the long pipe in case anything might change.

The word deceiving was far from how this place was.

The place was filthy with broken furniture, broken stoves, and empty pallets, and the outside of that building was like a fractured shitty wear house. Rotten water and the smelly path lead to a green steel door. The big man pressed a secret button.

Suddenly, that steel door opened wide. We all took a freight elevator to a lower level, but when the door opened, I was shocked.

It was a completely different place, spotless and very well decorated.

The place inside was huge. The air was cool and crisp, and that shitty scent from the outside was gone.

I wondered if that warehouse was a hang-out place or a miniature version of a unique GYM.

Fitness machines, such as weights and benches, were everywhere; they even had a basketball mini-court.

I had chances to witness different GYM during my matches abroad, and they were entirely modern, but this place is almost like Batman cave with the latest technology equipment, some amazing machines with an explosive setup for the entire area; I mean real Football club doesn't have all these newest fitness machines as this place does.

Suddenly, I heard a calm voice knocking off the top of my head, saying: Take your helmet off; I want to see your face. I took a few steps back away from him and ultimately transformed into a crazy different person and said: I know that I'm not getting out of this place in one piece, but I will take you all down before anyone touches me.

With my helmet on, I assembled the Karate defending position again, which I'd learned from Aunt Mar long ago. They all exploded, laughing again at what I said until Za came to me and said: Mondo, you don't have to be afraid; the dangerous part is gone, and you're among friends here. However, I do understand your fears about the middle of this place, but again, I assure you that nothing will happen to you..... We're all here to help and protect you, so please remove your helmet and get out of that suit....por favor.

The moment my identity was exposed, the young girls in the gang screamed, saying: Oh, my god... It's Mondo.... guys.

Apparently, my face was very well known across Spain, and between football and tennis, and of course, underground tennis, my name was more popular than my face.

The big man took a few steps, but in the meantime, his face changed as he was smiling, and without any more doubts, he spread his arm to shake my hand and said: Ola, Campion Mondo... I'm Alvaro.

The atmosphere switched to be more pleasant, especially when he said: Listen, Mondo, I know you've met Za, and she was right when she said that you're in safe company, and to make you feel more relaxed about this place and especially me, I must tell you a small secret.

We're not related, but I used to know your aunt. God bless her soul...Maribella.

My eyes started to glow when he mentioned her name, and I was shocked to hear that from a man like him. So you see, I'm here as a big brother if you allow me, and Za asked me to help you, but above all, and to my surprise, I find out that the person she was talking about is you.... Mondo, so again, you're safe here with me.

Mondo: First of all, I need to know exactly about this place, and secondly, who are you people? Are you a criminal?

Mondo: Also, How did you know my aunt?

Alvaro was laughing, but when he stopped and looked at me, he said: I'd instead leave the past in peace and focus on the future, so are you good with that?

Mondo: Si.

The next thing that you must understand is that we are not criminals.

This is our home, an extraordinary place for all of us. Do you understand Mondo?

Mondo: Si.

Alvaro: Very good, now let me walk with you and show you my place.

Mondo: Yes, what is this place? Alvaro: This is our home or our fitness place.

 It can be unclear to your mind with us, so I'm giving you an idea of who we are.

 In Spain, there are some varieties.... types of people.

Wealthy and poor, educated and illiterate, good and evil, and finally, weak and strong.

We call it a little strong Espana, meaning we are all I've mentioned, except that we're all strong and don't accept the word Weak...at all.

We're brothers and sisters, and we all help each other.

I'm a businessman; some guys here are doctors, lawyers, engineers, artists, dancers, builders, and many other jobs. Our small community is dedicated to helping others surpass their daily obstacles and fears.

Mondo: First, I've noticed something from your words and sentences, which were limited to high and low, no middle.

Wealthy and poor, educated and illiterate, good and evil, weak and strong, nothing in between at all, so what is the wisdom in that?

Mondo: What about that gun you carry?

Mondo: What about all the men and women outside with heavy machine guns? Is this part of your statement?

The gun is just for protection....You see, we're not criminals, and we're not violent, but again, as I said before, we are strong, and it will be our excellent task to make you strong.

Mondo: What do you mean....make me strong, I'm strong.

Alvaro: I do agree, but I need you to be Stronger.

Tennis is like anything in our lives; only the strongest will survive in any battle.

I give you a simple example, and that is related to tennis.

How many balls can you hit or return in a 20-minute rally?

Mondo: I've never tried to count, but I suggest a 15 to 20-ball rally.

Alvaro: That is quite impressive; however, if you continue having long rallies in one single match, your accuracy and precision will fade away through the game, and then your unforced errors will rise, pilling up to a level that will lead you to lose the match of physical fatigues.

Mondo: Maybe. How do you know all that about tennis? What is your point?

Alvaro: The new ways in any sport are based on how strong you are and how much endurance you can face for an extended period during your physical activity in whatever sport you play. Our unique programs will help you get stronger, or we will transform you into a stronger athlete, so are you ready and up for the challenge? Remember to mention the combination of two programs in one.

One is to get you fit and strong, and the other one is to increase your self-confidence about yourself.

Mondo: I understood the purpose of the first program but need clarification on self-confidence.

Alvaro: We will train you to defend yourself...martial arts, Judo, and Thai Kwon-do.

Mondo: Wow, you'll train me for Karate; that should be fun.

Alvaro: Before we do anything, I want to introduce you to my team.

You've met Za, and she will be your dancing instructor.

This is Leena or Lee Na, and she will be your martial arts instructor.

That big man Adria will be your physical trainer and fitness as well.

Also, you have so many other people here to help you directly and indirectly; please let me introduce you to someone exceptional.

Before that, we weren't a small group; we were everywhere worldwide.

Our organization can be reformed in different shapes, but we are all under the same umbrella for the same purpose.

Mondo: What is that purpose?

Alvaro: Power, and I will explain that later.

Finally, I would like you to meet your great challenger, Clara.

I wasn't moving; my eyes were dead, frozen, and more confused than ever.

I couldn't find any hints about how to describe her, even to myself.

I have never seen a fearless goddess except now. She didn't belong to this place but to paradise, as she was the most beautiful thing I've ever witnessed.

Her eyes glow whenever I look at her, as if I was always under an unbreakable spell.

Mondo...did you hear what I said? This is Clara, your tennis instructor, and as I stated, your ultimate challenger, so say hello or shake her hand or anything. Alvaro said.

Za: Mondo, are you here with us? What is the matter with you? Do you know Clara? Have you ever seen her before? Why you're not responding?

Clara: Let me break the ice, Alvaro; I will introduce myself.

Clara: Hello, Mondo....I've heard so many stories about you, but I wondered if you're that good or if it was all just some bull shit hogwash lies.

I want you to understand me very clearly, as I will make you sweat, I will make you cry, and if you don't keep up, I will be your nightmare demon through your miserable sleep; I'm not just a pretty face, but I'm the devil's cursed daughter, so how are you, Mondo?

The place went in a terrifying quiet mode, as no one was expecting that at all, until Za came to me and took me under her arm and said: Back off bitch....Mondo is mine, so watch out.

Mondo: I thank you all for what you're offering me, but I don't need protection; I don't need anything at all.

I'm very comfortable with how I am and would like to remain free without commitment to anyone. So, I must deny your offer and ask you to let me go.

I promise I won't say anything about this place to anyone...EVER.

Clara: I knew you were just a street bum, and whatever victory you've won was just a scam.

Alvaro, let him go; He's not one of us, and he will never be one...EVER.

The place was silent, including me, but not for long.

Mondo: Can I ask you for a small favor, Alvaro?

Alvaro: And what would that be, Mondo?

I need some time alone with Clara.

Alvaro: No problem, she's all yours.

Mondo: No, I think you misunderstood me, as what I meant was alone on a tennis court....Her against Me.

Clara was 21, but her body was older than just 21. The assembly of her muscles was unreal....Not a single piece of fat in her, besides her face, as I mentioned before....a goddess.

Alvaro: Are you sure about that? You just finished a long, terrifying match a few hours ago, and you may need a shower, a good meal, and some sleep.

Mondo: I'm fine and ready.

Alvaro: How about you, princess? Are you ok with that?

Clara only shook her head, a sign of Whatever.

Alvaro: Follow me to our secret tennis court.

We all got in a giant elevator, and everybody passed comments and jokes; others were silent, and some were excited about such a strange challenge.

The peculiar thing about that place was its secrets.

As I looked around my shoulders, I caught all the gang collecting money and whispering about me and Clara.

The surprise was the big man, Alvaro, as he turned around as if he was serious about the bitting and suddenly he took money out of his pocket and slammed it in the collector's hand, saying: I'm in.

In my mind, I was wondering about my shitty life and how I ended up in a different world of tennis, betting, money, guns, and extreme danger.

First, it was a vast warehouse, very well built and equipped, but it was clear to me that it was only one level, so I wondered what the story was with the elevator.

The fact that we're going down, not up, made me freak out more about this place.

It was a long ride down under as the air started to get colder, yet the moment the elevator hit bottom and the door was opened, the ventilation kicked in as if it was 27°C.

I was in a different world as they led me to the most incredible tennis court ever.

The magic of the red clay almost changed the color of my eyes to red.

The lights were unreal; it felt as if it was daylight.

The special court was decorated with an artificial background as if I was entering the famous court" of PHILIPPE CHATRIER."

Is it possible that it is the same red clay, or is it just my imagination?

The court hypnotized me, but it felt as if one of my dreams was coming alive to reality.

Clara: You got your wish, but I assure you it will be your worst nightmare...so change your clothes, for the biggest humiliation of your life...Mondo.

Hey, Mondo, before you come back to the court, make sure that you take a shower... You're stink like a dead fat rat.

I wasn't happy with the way she was talking to me with no respect at all.

I was wondering if she knew me from somewhere, but her beauty turned out to be my great disappointment of her kind. I was sure that Clara was not herself, or maybe beauty wasn't everything after all. It was a cold and fast shower.

Before returning to such a court, I had unique clothes and gear.

The bathroom was huge, and from the sign on the outside door, it had both genders (Male and female). There were also lockers with names, stickers, and posters of their owners.

I looked at the mirror, and my mind drifted to a strange place....Germany-Landesberg.

It was a different locker room, but not in Spain. It was a small village, not far away from the big Frankfurt, and in such a place, I was one of the players competing in a small ITF tournament. There, and in such a place, I saw Clara for the first time. Meanwhile, I was just 12 years old, and she was one of the tournament organizers.

She was younger, but her beauty wouldn't disappear from my memories.

I never got the chance to talk to her, but she was an earnest person and a famous player on the women's tour. I couldn't let my opportunities slip away, and I managed to ask and dig deep about her ranking.

They informed me that she was among the top 20 players in the world and that she is currently the champion of the Frankfurt Open. I wanted to have her autograph.

However, I was much busier with the training and the matches.

Winning in tennis can miraculously open the secret door to other things, such as popularity, fame, and sometimes companies and sponsorships.

After winning the tournament, I was so close to talking to her, yet the excitement and the ceremony made her disappear from my reach. I followed her progress when I returned to Spain, but again, I was dragged to the real world of working, practicing, and, of course, my involvement with tournaments and matches....Legally and illegally.

The place was bright and filled with almost all the gang members except the one out for security. The atmosphere inspired me, but only some luck was going my way.

My first question was to Alvaro about the red clay of such a court.

He smiled and yelled to a young man to come and meet me.

Alvaro: Allow me to introduce you to Gerard; he is a gifted French architect, yet he had a passion for tennis, and his gift to me was to build this special tennis court with the same build as Philippe Chatrier with the same type of red clay.

Gerard: How are you, Mondo?

I've heard many good stories about you, but I always wondered about your name, Mondo...what is your last name? Are you Italian?

Mondo: It is my pleasure to meet Gerard; this place is a fantastic work of art. Wow.

Now, it's only Mondo.....hmmm, I have no father and am not Italian.

My confirmation was entirely of a statement to everyone except Clara.

Clara: No, papa, what a poor boy; I'm still going to wipe that smile off your face once you're on the court.

Alvaro: Clara, Enough, is enough; what the fuck is wrong with you? Get on the court and get ready.

In the first 20 minutes of that match, she came very true, and she was toying with me all over the court. The only thing she or anyone around that court did not know was my gift and ability to adapt. I've accepted my easy defeat for a specific reason: to explore her technique, movements, and skills.

I had to pretend that she had beaten me fair and square. In the past few months, I played many matches between tournaments and others under the Munez circuit.

I played matches with so many women and girls for the money.

With that, I gained so much confidence and experience, but not one of the games I won made me feel that way. The new, unique technique I invented made it impossible to lose a match, so for Clara and everybody, I'm just a new kid on the block.

The first set was done in 20 minutes, and she won it 6-0.

I was somehow ashamed, maybe more embarrassed about my performance, so I was just about to leave for another shower when she stopped me.

Clara: Mondo, my dear, come closer by the net. Don't be shy; get closer, please. What is the score?

Mondo: 6-0

What did you say? I couldn't hear you speak louder.

Mondo started to get annoyed with her arrogance, yet he had to be humble and answer her again, saying 6-0.

Can you repeat it so everyone can hear you? What is the score, Mondo?

Mondo: 6-0

Clara: No, in tennis, we call it a bagel...Zero, Nada, Zip.

So I was right about you.... You are just a joke, zero, nada, and a waste of my time.

Mondo: Yes, you're right, and I'm so sorry about that. Thank you for the chance to play with the great Clara, the undefeated Frankfurt champion so far; I wish I could have your autograph.

Clara: First, how do you know about such a tournament?

Mondo: I won that tournament a few years back and desperately wanted to meet you, but I had no luck.

Clara: You were there....hmmm, and you won that tournament, impressive, I didn't recognize you at all, as you look different, oh, yes you look like (A looser).

There was a deadly silence on the court, yet more humming outside of the court.

I was heading to the baseline to get off the court, yet I stopped in the middle of the court, looked at the red clay, and did something that surprised everyone.

I went down on my knees and grabbed some clay in my hand, brushing it all over my arms until I was covered with clay; then I turned around and called Clara, saying: Can we play another set, por favor?

Clara: Boss, this kid isn't worth it; why do I have to waste my time and deal with that?

Alvaro: No problem, but he is right somehow; give him another chance and play another set for me, Please.

Clara: Boss, why are you doing this to me? You know me, and I can't do that again, especially with this, Mondo; the answer is NO.

The look on Alvaro was more than enough for her to play another set, as it wasn't a request anymore.

Za rushed to my side and gave me the same bandana Eve gave me a while back, before the Spanish junior championship match, then said: Vamos Mondo, put it on.

The moment I wrapped up that bandana, I was a different player.

Mondo: If we play another set, you may change your mind about who Mondo is.

Alvaro: One more set, come on. The collector was grabbing more money from everyone for a new bid, yet one of the girls, who I believe was Lee-Nah, yelled: The bid is 25000 pesetas ....wow.

Mondo: Wow, that is a lot of money; what is my cut?

Lee-Nah: It's up to the boss, not me.

Alvaro rushed to the collector, slammed another 10,000 pesetas, and said in a loud voice: The winner will get 25% of the money.

The second set had a different spirit, and definitely, the money had to do something with the outcome of the set.

I had a different point of view, and I didn't care about the money but the victory over that snub girl, Clara.

All of her moves were just like a flashback in my mind. The gift starts to re-adjust every reaction to answer her moves and technique. Her skills, movement, Power, and experiences have transformed my mind.

I watched every move she made and every step she took during the first set.

The fascinating part about my gift was the fast adaptation, as it was the first time I could see her future moves in the past.

Her technique and speed were all in the past, and I was ready to show her something new that she had never seen before. The second set started with a big smile on her face, yet that didn't last for a long time.

All of her serves were lost points, as I had answers to all of them.

Breaking her serve time after time made her angry, and at last, she lost control over her game.

I learned so many tricks from the old man, my great coach Manolo, and the most lethal ones were drop shots, serve, and volley. Clara's fitness was way better than mine but with certain limitations. My game was a frustrating one for her. Kick serve that bounced to her body and chest, serve and volley, drop shots one after another, lobbing her the moment she rushed to the net. She couldn't have a long rally, as I wasn't allowing her to win any points, or I would say easy points, no let go, and never say die on the clay.

The fantastic factor that she needed to understand was my unique sliding technique on the clay. It was a new experience for everyone to witness something they had never seen before, and that was simply the way I slid and danced on the clay.

I had some mercy and let her play for 30 minutes to lose the second set 0-6.

She broke four rackets, shattered them into a million pieces, cursing and screaming over every easily lost point, but what made her wild was my smile and statement after winning the second set, saying to her: I'm so sorry, Clara, but what is the score?

She did an unexpected act that drove everyone to rush to the court.

She tossed her racket with all of her Power across the court, ran so fast, jumped over the net, and rushed to my body, knocking me down on my back; then she was sitting on top of me, screaming in my face, saying: What did you tell the score....boy?

Everyone ran to the court, but Alvaro was there first. He lifted her off me like a baby in his arms. She was kicking and screaming, saying: Let me go, let me down, I'm going to kill him.

On the other hand, the rest of the gang was helping me get back on my feet, yet Za was about to bring into a fistfight with Clara until the Boss shouted to all of us, saying: I want everyone to calm the fuck down....I mean it...Everyone.

Mondo looked at Za and said: I must leave now, but can anyone tell me the truth about a straightforward thing?

Because I need to know something vital right fucking now.

Za: Mondo, I will drive you home, but what exactly do you need to know, and why are you so angry?

Mondo's eyes were glowing at all of them, and that made them all move a few steps back until Alvaro raised his hand for me to calm down as a sign to speak.

Mondo: Clara, I asked you a simple fucking question: What is the fucking score?

Alvaro: You're right about going home, but you're also more right about knowing the score, which was 6-0.

Mondo: No, you're fucking wrong, that is called in tennis a fucking bagel, fucking Zero, fucking Nada and fucking Zip, are we all fucking square here, and Clara....please don't get upset, because you still the most beautiful women I've ever seen, and I was so excited to lo learn from you as you're one hell of a tennis player, but in the future don't ever judge the book by its cover, just be patient enough to flip thru the pages, and you'll be surprised what wonders you may learn from each page. Remember me as one day you may say to yourself that I was able to take a set from the great Mondo, not the other way around.

Mondo: I'm not angry at you, but please find the fact in your dark, twisted heart about who the fuck you're dealing with, as I'm not your everyday average beat-up kid that you think you can humiliate any time you fucking feel like it.

I am Fucking Mondo...beautiful Clara.

Mondo: I must tell you the truth about my trip to that place in East Germany.

I was so overwhelmed and excited after my victory. Yet, I was more excited knowing that I would get the chance to earn your autograph back in your hometown in Landensberg because you motivated me greatly, but look at you now, just a beat-up player from a no-one.

Mondo yelled as he was leaving the place, saying: Wow. Wow...a bagel; let's get the fuck out of here, Za.

Everybody was shocked at what I said and done on the court, inside and outside. Meanwhile, Alvaro shouted my name, and when I went to answer him, he handed me 8500 pesetas and then said: That is your winning money; I wish we could've afforded a third set, but after what had happened, both of you should calm down until your next meeting, you are coming back for your training aren't you?

Mondo: Absolutely, as I like this excellent court and the place, I might feel safer once I get to know everyone, so the answer is YES.

The night went by so fast after that as I managed to enter my dream world and close my eyes for another new day. The development of that place and El Hampa, or as they call it, NYX.

I never cared about the origin of names, including mine.

However, I discovered that NYX was an old Greek Goddess (The goddess of the night).

The NYX reshaped my body and ability to be solid and fit.

The resistance band, TRX, and the reaction ball were my favorites, and the competition with the reaction balls was the real challenge for me and Clara.

The reaction balls had odd shapes, yet their bounce was always strange, so they called them reaction balls. I used to challenge Clara on how many to catch per exercise session.

I must admit that in the beginning, she used to win, but with more practice and hours with those balls, my reaction was off the chart, and I began to understand the idea of that ball.

On the tennis court, the ball bounces differently, however, in some strange ways, and due to the surface, the ball can bounce in crazy, unexpected ways, and with the fast reaction and extreme fitness, I've reached the level of not missing any of those strange balls. Sometimes, the ball can clip the top of the net and bounce in unexpected ways, and because of the rubber reaction balls, my body became flexible, as if my response could have a few seconds of reaction delays.

That allowed me to wait and see the final reaction of the ball and react fast enough to recover a drop shot or even a ball that bounced on the chalk by the baseline, in which the ball bounced off the slick part of the white line, not the clay.

Other drills using the suspension strap, the agility belt, or even the core ball(medicine ball) were more challenging, but in time, I became a master in all of them, and I must admit that they helped in tennis.

The only drill that used to be fun for everyone to watch was the ability to move my feet in a very tight and short space. My dear Clara used to proceed to the side and enjoy watching me in such a drill.

It was a handball court, but only one-half of the court was used, with a smaller goal.

The handball is smaller than a football, so the control must be precise and accurate.

The court is split into square boxes and spread cones everywhere.

The drill was to maneuver my way with the ball going in and out without touching the cones, going from one box to the next until I was in front of the goal, and then scoring.

The tricky part is not reaching the goal but scoring the goal.

There were three cones in such a small goal, and the goal only counts if I place the ball without touching any cones. The drill was always fun, as I invented it, yet it was only possible for Clara and all the other NYX members to finish without any mistakes.

The only one who was so close to finishing the drill was the Boss, Alvaro.

He used to be a good footballer, but he saw a football career the same way I saw it: not easy and may be impossible for ordinary people like him and me.

He passed all the cone obstacles until he was in front of the goal.

Yet, his hip couldn't support him as the previous drill in which going in and out from one square to another, killed his balance, and he couldn't win the drill, but I must say, when he kicked the ball towards the goal, he took out all three cones, and it was fun to watch all that.

The NYX was a fun place to be, and I can't forget the efforts of all the other members, including Lee Na.

Her way of defending yourself was unique, as if she was training me to be a girl, not a boy. Her self-defense technique was based on reaching specific targets in the human body that don't require real power yet are very effective in defending female perspectives.

Most of her techniques are to hurt the male before even getting to the position of being in control. I must say that she used to kick my ass until one time I managed to take her down, and it wasn't that I was better, but the secret that she didn't know was my gift and the ability to adapt, yet also the preparation for the sudden attack. I had to use the chess tactics and the art of deceiving and misdirection.

Her ways were more of Karate tactics, but the way I beat her was the Judo technique that I've adapted from Aunt Mar. It was fast, and when she was one the rubber Matt, everyone was screaming, as I was the first to put her down.

The excitement and the fun in such a place were more delightful than winning matches and tournaments. The flexibility I earned from NYX made it almost impossible to get hurt as their protection for me exceeded the limit. In such a short time, yet with extreme practice, I transformed into an absolute beast with so many detailed muscles that helped me go on a streak of winning matches and tournaments, local and some outside of Spain.

I became much more famous outside of Spain than domestically.

My relationship with Clara turned in a different direction, as she was able to teach me so many things about tennis and other things as well. The strange thing she said to me after she won the Barcelona Open was: Mondo, you made me a better player, yet between you and I, the transformation led to change me into a better person, and I will miss you, but I will never forget you. However, the simplicity of the communication between us in her language made her becoming a very dear friend to me. German was the language that drove her crazy, and until the day she left the NYX for New York, she couldn't find out how I could speak her language so fluently at such a young age.

She was a big girl, and between her new job and tennis, I was confident she would do very well in America.

Clara's last words were like a charm in my ears to never forget her or her help.

She told me: Mondo, if you ever come to New York, please call me, or at least find me, as I will always remember the name Mondo and the face.

Her voice and words were like a mist to my ears. There was another strange voice with a far echo, yet I couldn't tell if she was angry or happy. The voice started to change to yelling.

Maria: Vamos Mondo, we're going to be late...Hurry up.

My room has no privacy, as mom is always in and out. She's wiping off the dust, fixing the bed, organizing my books, collecting trash and my dirty clothes.

Our biggest arguments were always about her ways with everything.

Maria: Mondo, I don't understand why can't you be like me.

Why aren't you an organized person? Why and million why?

The perfection measurement in mom's eyes can never find the limitation length as it's simply.... Infinity.

Her famous quotes were: Mondo my dear son, unless you're a God, you'll never be perfect; however if you are willing to seek perfection, you must pretend to be a god.

To be perfect, you will come to deal with sacrifices, yet no regrets, as you must aim to the sky and never settle for less.....Believe in yourself as you have a purpose, and trust your goal.

I constantly clean my room, yet with Mom, more is needed to clean.

The mess in my room is consolidated in the definition of space. I have no space in my room as it was filled with trophies from all the tournaments I've won in the past 3 to four years.

I must thank so many people for getting me into the shape, stage, and skills to win all those trophies and for allowing me to join the ITF(International Tennis Federation).

The name that made all that happen was my coach, Manolo, and NYX.

That was simply the mess I had in my room that made it congested, stuffed, or even jammed with so many things that could've been put away, but I was more obsessed with looking at them every day as a reminder of my achievements.

I must choose carefully what I will need to put in my suitcase, no trophies...check

Pictures frames of me winning those trophies....No, check

The frame on my night table with Aunt Maribella, Yes...check.

It symbolizes the sacred. M.

Gaudi invented Sagrada Familia and so as Mondo.

My Sagrada Familia is Maria, Maribella, and Mondo.

It is the only bloodline that I care about in this life, and that frame means the world to me and must be next to my head when I sleep.

The fear of the running river made me shake and tremble so intensely that I couldn't find a shelter to hide from such a brutal, angry river. That was the river of tears over my face just looking at her distant eyes.

They talk to me in silence, but only in a one-way conversation.

I stuffed the picture quickly in my bag, then rushed to the bathroom to wash my face and continue to get ready. It has always been my greatest weakness since the day I lost one of the M. I took an oath to protect the legend of the M, and I swear that I will honor, fight, and save my Sagrada Familia(M) until I die.

Dios mio, Dios mio....come on, Mondo, we'll miss the train... aura, aura.

Mondo: Mom, stop screaming. I'm ready.

Maria: Come on, my dear, I got all the essential documents with me, HMMMM, I can't trust you, especially at the last minute before we leave.

I stood by the door, looking and staring at our humble small castle filled with memories, wondering when I would ever see it again.

The train's speed made everything move along so fast, yet my eyes were still captivated somewhere else.

Looking at the blue sky through the train's glass window made me drift and drift so far away from the past year's memories.

1977 was the best year of my life, yet being considered a later starter in tennis made me even more special for what I'd accomplished in such a short time.

The typical and practical special quote of coach Manolo was that I was too old to start a tennis career as a player. He also quoted me through my first year with tennis, saying that I'm too skinny and that there will be too much physical work to reshape me to be strong and fit for a tennis player.

The odd thing about coach Manolo was that during my last visit before heading to Barcelona, he told me: I've never trained anyone who can prove me wrong.

I do recall my statement when we first met, but now, and perhaps with the fact that I wasn't aware that one day I would get the honor to train a legend,

Mondo, everything I said to you in the beginning, you've changed to something that I've never seen in my entire life with tennis.

Be careful, my son, as you are on the very step to be remembered, and that isn't an easy transformation in the tennis world.

Players come and go, and most of the time, you get to say: Do you remember that player? Oh dear God, what was his name????

And just like that, the name vanished through time, but your name is simply a name to remember forever, so god be with you, and please come and visit if you ever come back to Malaga. In the past five years, I managed to rebuild my entire body, and the NYX had too much to do, as they did a phenomenal job with my secret training. I made many mistakes, made wrong decisions, and suffered losses in matches and tournaments.

I was broken, defeated, and hurt in so many ways. The fact that I lost so many things in the past five years made me realize that you'll never know the real pain unless you bleed.

I was bleeding inside more than from the outside.

I was bleeding from losing my aunt and watching my mother work like an animal for long hours to make enough money to support my dream, sacrificing everything: her youth, her health, and herself.

I owe my life to Mom, and I will never cover my debts to her, but I can only make her proud of me, and that is to her worth millions of trophies.

My coach, Manolo, isn't just a great magician coach but also a great man, at least to me. Respect was his big Billboard label. I recall him advising and lecturing me at the beginning of our time together as he was very concerned for me to fully understand the meaning and definition of the word (RESPECT).

Mondo, remember my words: Respect people, and they will respect you back.

Please respect the rules; with time, you'll find ways to bend them to your satisfaction.

Respect the fans, and they will give you back a glorious victory.

Be humble and stay hungry. A man with a full stomach will turn to be slow, lazy, and comfortable to fall and collapse, so stay hungry for more victories and glory.

Respect the elder; the younger will love you more.

Respect yourself, and you'll be a victorious legend.

Respect your gears and court, as it will be your temple.

Never forget who you are, nor where you came from, and at last, remember it's all about having fun as you're....just playing.

Being on the road for the last five years, competing through the ITF, made my face somehow familiar or popular, especially being on the cover of some European sports magazines with so many given names...The rising Spanish teen, the new tennis sensation, the wild, the monster, the sweetheart, the gentle teen, so many names and titles. However, I couldn't remember which magazine gave me the title" El Chico Magico."

Setting right here on this train and looking at the sky also made me confident about our joint decision that tennis is not enough, as knowledge and education are more essential in life.

Today is the beginning of my new, daring journey.

Today is January 7th, 1976, and it is cold as hell, but it is worth it to seek knowledge.

As Mom said, the long trip to Barcelona will require a good time for rest and sleep.

The look on Mom's face, leaning on the cold glass of the train's window with her eyes closed, made me ask myself a severe question. Maria, my hero....my mom is simply a woman who can move people, not only because of her beauty but also because of her personality and strong character, which will lead me to my question...

Will I be able to go on with my journey without her close to me?

The whispering scary voices in my head were saying: Barcelona, Barcelona.

My answer was: I am Mondo, and I will be your humble guest for my new future days and years, so be gentle with me and allow me to be a citizen of your temples; I'm coming..... Barcelona.

Acknowledgments

Unstrung Lives is a journey to the undiscovered worlds.

Two parallel universes struggle to blend together in one universe: reality and dreams.

For so many years, this book was always kept in the dark, yet one day, I believed it was impossible to finish it. In some mysterious I didn't want to finish the story.

It is very unrealistic to describe my true feelings about each character as they became my friends, lovers, and, most of all, my new family as I was sucked into the rabbit hole to be Alice in Wonderland. I became one of them, breathing and living throughout their lives with such impossible, Unstrung Lives.

Some nights, I used to dream, yet I always found my way, traveling secretly to their universe and enjoying being with them as if I were one of the characters.

The wonderful universe of Unstrung Lives always makes me doubt whether I wake up for my reality or never come back and die in my sleep, diving into such a fantasy world.

I must acknowledge and admit that I wouldn't have accomplished this journey without the help of my best and only friend, my wife, Carmen. Her belief in me made me a better person, as she encouraged me to keep dreaming and writing.

In the story, I questioned my daughter Gaby about the journey and how long I should keep writing to find an end, yet she always said: Why stop? The story can last forever, as every life needs a savior, and the savior must be the one to string all these lives, so don't stop believing. Hold on to such a wonderful dream as one day, maybe in your sleep, your wish will come true.

Remember her words when she said: My world is bright and made of light, while yours is dark and full of doubts. When my nights melt away all your fears and doubts, there and only there, I can be found.

Even though I may not say it out loud, I know for a fact that they were always my secret beacons to my journey. My beautiful four daughters thank you for their direct and indirect support for Brandi-Lee, Corinne, Heaven, and Julieanne.

I can't forget my Gaby, as she was and still is enriching me with her undisputed love and inspiration.

Sometimes, it is said that magic may need some special tuning, and this book brought the magnifying magic through the incredible, amazing book cover.

The magic of the amazing Alexander Von Ness and his creation of my book put the book on the ledge of perfection, and I am in his debt forever.

The Amazon group, Kindle, and everyone who helped publish this book was the real magic behind the curtains of greatness, so I thank you for all your support and assistance.

The greatest musicians describe the magical notes that were written over their musical sheets as floating notes, as they used to see the inspiring notes before even using their ink on their musical sheets.

They adapt and create magic with their music.

I come to feel the same way, yet with words floating above my head inspiring me to adapt from great authors, actresses, and famous historical people.

Even the great Salvador Dali said: Those who do not want to imitate and adapt anything produce Nothing. I adapt and use words to reshape my story in such a way. I thank the minds of all the people who helped me use some of their words.

Sport has been my driving force through life because no matter how old I am, I'm still that same kid who loves to play.

Tennis and Football were my tears and laughs.

I must take a small pause as I do remember someone expressing the idea of how long or short an acknowledgment should be.

I may only write one book, and if I write a case, then I should take all the time and space that I may need to thank everyone sincerely.

I can't re-thank the people I left out because of some " Rules."

Wow, that felt great expressing all that.

Some may say tennis is very clear, but what did he mean about football?

Football is the only name or word representing the sport, as I will never call it soccer until I die.

It is Football, and it will always remain like that, regardless of the renaming or changing the origin of the sport....it's FOOTBALL.

Tennis made me laugh and cry with the performance of the players.

Do I have to skip mentioning iconic names in tennis that brought great happiness into my life? Hmmmm, No.

Rafael Nadal, Santana, Bruguera, David Ferrer, Carlos Moya, Joan Ferrero, Manuel Orantes, Alcaraz, Roger Federer, Novak Djokovic, Borg, Edberg, Wilander, Agassi, Courrier, Sampras, McEnroe, Lendl, Andy Murray, Andy Roddick, Arther Ash, Blake, Becker, Yanick Noah, Sinner, Fognini, Seppi, Safin, Medvedev and more that I can't recall, yet I can't forget the female side that also, made my eyes tears for their victory and defeat as well.

The Williams Sisters, Serena and Venus, Graf, Seles, Hinges, Davenport, Evert, Navratilova, Dementieva, Schiavone, Penetta, Arantxa, and the magical Gabriela Sabatini, and the list can go on for another book.

All of the tennis players that I've mentioned and forgot to mention inspired me to find all the unstrung lives, and I'm so grateful for what they had and still offer the world.

I must say or use a special quote to my heart as the magnificent Audrey Hepburn said:

Impossible is nothing, as nothing in this life is impossible as the word itself says: I'm possible.

And finally, I have to ask a question that was asked before by someone:

What is your favorite book?

A favorite book is the one that was written for only one reader, and that is you.

So thank you all, readers, for being that special reader.

Impressum